The Basics of
American Politics

The Basics of American Politics

FIFTEENTH EDITION

Gary Wasserman
Georgetown University

PEARSON

Boston   Columbus   Indianapolis   New York   San Francisco   Upper Saddle River
Amsterdam   Cape Town   Dubai   London   Madrid   Milan   Munich   Paris   Montréal   Toronto
Delhi   Mexico City   São Paulo   Sydney   Hong Kong   Seoul   Singapore   Taipei   Tokyo

Dedicated To: My Students

Editor-in-Chief: Dickson Musslewhite
Acquisitions Editor: Jeff Marshall
Program Manager: Beverly Fong
Editorial Assistant: Isabel Schwab
Marketing Manager: Wendy Gordon
Project Manager: Carol O'Rourke
Full Service Vendor: PreMediaGlobal
Art Director Cover: Maria Lange
Cover Photo: Fotolia
Manufacturing Manager: Mary Fischer
Operations Specialist: Mary Anne Gloriande
Printer and Binder: Courier Corporation/Westford
Cover Printer: Courier Corporation/Westford

Credits and acknowledgments borrowed from other sources and reproduced, with permission, in this textbook appear on the appropriate page within text.

Library of Congress Cataloging-in-Publication Data
Wasserman, Gary
    The basics of American politics / Gary Wasserman, Georgetown University. — Fifteenth edition.
        pages cm
    Includes bibliographical references and index.
    ISBN 978-0-13-381543-6 — ISBN 0-13-381543-9   1. United States—Politics and government.
I. Title.
JK276.W36 2015
320.473—dc23   2014012091

10 9 8 7 6 5 4 3 2 1

ISBN 10:   0-13-381543-9
ISBN 13: 978-0-13-381543-6

CONTENTS

Preface   **xi**

Chapter 1   **What Is Politics?**   **1**
    The First Day of Class   2
    Politics and Power   3
        Elites   4
        Authority: Legitimate Power   4
    The Need for Government   6
        What Is Government?   8
        Making and Supporting Decisions   9
    The Study of Politics   9
        Political Science and Microsoft   10
        Why Give a Damn about Politics?   11
    What Is This Book About?   13
    Thought Questions   14
    Suggested Readings   15

Chapter 2   **The Constitution: Rules of the Game**   **17**
    The Second Day of Class   18
    Background to the Constitution   19
        The Articles of Confederation
            (1781–1789)   20
        The Constitutional Convention   21
        The Framers   22
        Motives behind the Constitution   23
        Federalists versus Anti-Federalists   25
        Ratification and the Bill of Rights   26
    Four Major Constitutional Principles   27
        Separation of Powers and Checks and
            Balances   28
        Federalism   30
        The Debate over Modern Federalism   32
        Limited Government   36
        Judicial Review   36

How Is the Constitution Changed? 37
Amendments 37
Judicial Interpretation 39
Legislation 39
Custom 39
Why Has the Constitution Survived? 40
CASE STUDY   Federalism Caught in a Storm:
The Katrina Disaster 41
Wrap-Up 44
Thought Questions 46
Suggested Readings 46

Chapter 3   **The Executive Branch: The Presidency**
and Bureaucracy   **47**
The President and the Constitution 50
The Electoral College 51
Vice President 52
History of the Presidency 53
Types of Presidents 56
Buchanan Presidents 56
Lincoln Presidents 57
Eisenhower Presidents 57
Modern Presidents 58
The Obama Presidency 61
A President's Power Hats 62
Chief of State 63
Chief Executive 63
Chief Diplomat 64
Commander in Chief 65
Chief Legislator 66
Party Leader 68
The Public Presidency 68
The Federal Bureaucracy 71
Executive Office of the President 71
The Cabinet Departments 76
The Executive Agencies 78
The Regulatory Commissions 78
Problems of Bureaucracy 79
Rise of the Civil Service 82
Bureaucrats as Policymakers 82
The President and the Bureaucracy 83

CASE STUDY   9/11: A President's Trial by Fire   85
Wrap-Up   88
Thought Questions   89
Suggested Readings   89

Chapter 4   **The Legislative Branch: Congress**   **91**
Makeup of the Senate and House   93
Role of the Legislator   93
Who Are the Legislators?   94
Organization of the House of
Representatives   100
Organization of the Senate   102
How Congress Works   103
The Committee System   105
How Committees Work   105
Committee Chairmen and the Seniority
System   107
Specialization and Reciprocity   108
Major Committees in the House   109
Major Committees in the Senate   111
On the Floor and Beyond   112
Filibuster   115
Presidential Veto   116
The Budget Process   117
Budget Deadlocks and Sequesters   119
Other Powers of Congress   120
CASE STUDY   The Limits of Limiting Global
Warming   122
Wrap-Up   127
Thought Questions   128
Suggested Readings   128

Chapter 5   **The Judicial Branch: The Supreme
Court and the Federal Court System**   **131**
Federal Court System   132
U.S. District Courts   132
Courts of Appeals   133
Special Federal Courts   133
The Judges   134
Jurisdiction   137

U.S. Supreme Court   137
The Final Authority?   138
Early Years of the Court   139
Judicial Review and National
Supremacy   139
The Court after the Civil War   141
Mid-Twentieth-Century Courts   142
The Rehnquist Court (1986–2005)   143
The Roberts Court (2005–)   145
"The Least Dangerous Branch of
Government"?   147
Internal Limits on the Court   147
External Limits on the Court   150
Strengths of the Court   150
The Court as a Political Player   153
Judicial Activism versus Judicial
Restraint   153
CASE STUDY   Separate but Equal?   155
Wrap-Up   160
Thought Questions   161
Suggested Readings   161

Chapter 6   **Civil Rights and Liberties: Protecting
the Players**   **163**
What Are Civil Liberties and Rights?   164
Expanding the Bill of Rights   166
Civil Liberties: Protecting People
from Government   167
Freedom of Speech   169
Freedom of Religion   171
Right of Privacy   173
Due Process Rights   174
Civil Rights: Protecting People from People   176
Which People Need Protection? Suspect
Classifications   177
Race as a Suspect Classification   178
Is Sex Suspect?   180
Actors in Civil Liberties and Rights   181
Judges   182
The Justice Department   182
"Private Attorneys General"   183

Legal Strategies   184
Obeying the Courts   184
Public Opinion and Civil Liberties   186
CASE STUDY   Fighting Terror, Guarding
Liberties   188
Wrap-Up   192
Thought Questions   193
Suggested Readings   193

Chapter 7   **Voters and Political Parties**   **195**
Voters   196
Who Votes?   196
Political Socialization   198
Class and Voting   199
Who Doesn't Vote?   201
Explanations   205
Political Parties   208
Party Functions   208
The Rise of Today's Parties   210
Maintaining, Deviating, and Realigning
Elections   211
The Elections of 2000–04 and 2008–12:
Whose Realignment?   213
Polarizing the Parties: The Growth of
Partisans   215
View from the Inside: Party Organizations   217
Machines—Old and New   217
American Party Structure   219
National Party Organization   220
Fundraising   221
The National Convention   223
View from the Outside: The Two-Party
System   225
Causes of the Two-Party System   226
But Do the Two Parties Have a
Future?   227
CASE STUDY   The 2012 Reelection—Obama's
Online Operation   229
Wrap-Up   233
Thought Questions   233
Suggested Readings   234

Chapter 8   Interest Groups and the Media   235

Interest Groups   236
Types of Interest Groups   237
Lobbying   238
Campaign Contributions   243
Citizens United and Its Aftermath   245
Do Groups Interests Overwhelm the Public
Interest?   247
Media   250
What Are the Media?   251
What Do the Media Do?   255
Media and the Marketplace of Ideas   258
Media and Government   261
Media and the Public   263
CASE STUDY   Google: The Rise and Rise of a
Washington Lobby   264
Wrap-Up   268
Thought Questions   269
Suggested Readings   269

**Chapter 9   Who Wins, Who Loses: Pluralism versus
Elitism   271**

Pluralism   272
Examples of Pluralism   273
Criticisms of Pluralist Theory   274
Elite   276
Elite Examples   276
Criticisms of the Elite View   277
The Debate   279
Newer Views   280
Wrap-Up   282
Thought Questions   283
Suggested Readings   283

Appendix   285

The Declaration of Independence   285
The Constitution of the United States   288

Glossary   303
Index   311

PREFACE

Teaching American politics outside of America raises questions in class not heard at home. Foreign students will ask where the Constitution gives individual freedoms to its citizens, only to be reminded that the First Amendment doesn't grant rights. It *stops* government from limiting freedoms that people already have—"Congress shall make no law...." Or, students ask, why is it that Americans rate Congress lower in popularity than North Korea and yet reelect their own congressmen time after time? Or how can voters and media turn out administrations in Washington so easily while other countries spend lifetimes, and lives, trying to remove thugs with a death grip on power?

Americans are hardly alone in lacking perspective on their own government. Nor should textbooks be about celebrating a political system that frequently elevates partisan greed to a religious calling. Both appreciating and improving U.S. politics is part of the inheritance this text aims to pass on to students.

It is a book filled with reminders that democracy is both a route and a destination still some distance away. An introduction to American government should help us stay on the road, headed in the right direction.

This edition follows the same brief, current, readable goals of previous *Basics*.

It also reflects recent changes in American politics.

President Obama in his second term remained at the uncomfortable center of the political game. He shaped the office as chief diplomat from threatening Syria to negotiating with Iran to trying to close Guantanamo. He expanded the use of wiretaps and prosecuted security leaks, but he refused to use the veto and pursued a "lite-news" press strategy to avoid policy debates. He had views on federalism, on educational reforms, and on managing the White House. And he joins other presidents in complaining about the limits of the presidency.

Congress added to his problems. With government shutdowns, budget deadlocks, and partisan bickering, Congress's popularity plummeted. In the House, Speaker Boehner had difficulties with the Tea Party, the Senate was tied up by a tidal wave of filibusters, and the president decided that issuing executive orders was better than waiting for a paralyzed legislature—a point underlined in the case study of his failure to pass a bill, "The Limits of Limiting Global Warming."

Politics and elections played their role. New discussions include: Voting Rights under Attack; the Vanishing Young Voter; Polarized Parties and the Question of Partisan Realignment; Explaining Voter Turnout; and Obama's Online Operation for Reelection. John Roberts's Supreme Court surfaced in its decisions that ended campaign finance reform, as well as rulings on free speech, same-sex marriage, and Obamacare. In the media chapter, reporting and newspapers kept declining, while blogs, Twitter, and social media kept ascending.

New boxes, stories, and cases illustrate these changes. A case study on "The Rise and Rise of a Washington Lobby" traces the political growth of Google. "Fighting Terror, Guarding Liberties" looks at citizens' rights trying to survive the war on terrorism. Critical discussions include the following: Congress as a Ladder to Lobbying Riches; Privacy under Internet Attacks; The Undemocratic Ways We Choose Vice Presidents; How Redistricting Protects Incumbents; America's Increasing Inequality; Obama and Whistleblowers; Campaign Fundraising on Steroids; Hollywood and Presidents.

ABOUT THE AUTHOR

Gary Wasserman has shaped a career in teaching, public service, political consulting, and writing. Currently he is a professor of Government at Georgetown University's School of Foreign Service in Doha, Qatar.

ACKNOWLEDGMENTS

Thanks go to Professor Elliott Fullmer who provided excellent research and drafts for much that's new in this edition. Writing was supported by a grant from the faculty of Georgetown's School of Foreign Service in Qatar. I appreciate the sage advice of Jan Constantine of the Authors Guild, Joel Koblentz and John Rea. And I'd like to thank my colleagues at our innovative campus, especially Kai-Henrik Barth, Mehran Kamrava, Patrick Laude, Josh Mitchell, Robert Wirsing, Mohamed Zayani and Dean Gerd Nonneman who supplied wise insights.

Production was overseen by Carol O'Rourke, Beverly Fong, and Jeff Marshall from Pearson, as well as Saraswathi Muralidhar who supported the project with competence and cheer. My family, Daniel and Adrienne and Will, Laura and Priyesh, wife Ann, and brother Ed, helped by holding me in the light. And my students taught me at least as much as I taught them. Any mistakes that follow are still mine.

CHAPTER 1

What Is Politics?

The First Day of Class

This class is unbelievable. The first day of my intro to American government the professor comes in and asks us to sit in alphabetical order. Inconceivable. Of course all the freshman sheep shuffle off to their seats. But since I am sitting next to an attractive lady, I don't want to move. So I ask him whether he might want us to wear Purple Barney *t-shirts to his next class. A bit too cute, perhaps, because he asks me if I think politics goes on in the classroom.*

I reply, "No, we study politics, but very few of us actually indulge."

"Incorrect," he responds, and would I mind leaving the class?

"Well, yes, I would mind," I say, "considering the costs of my first seven years at college."

"Will you please *leave?" he says.*

OK, so I start to go. He then stops me and asks why I am departing. I remind him that while he may have missed it, he has just asked me to remove myself. But he persists and asks why I'm doing what he asked. Maybe I have missed something. I respond that he is the kahuna *here. I am just a sometimes-paying student.*

"In other words," he says, "my position as the teacher influenced you to do something you didn't want to do. In fact, it influenced everyone to sit in alphabetical order. So we just saw a process of influence in this classroom that affected a group of people. That's politics."

"Oh, by the way, do you have a cigarette?"

"Hey, you can't smoke in here."

"You mean my power as a teacher is limited, in this case by your right to have a nonsmoking classroom. And of course all of you have other rights that limit any teacher's power. If this gentleman here didn't have such a good sense of humor he might bring me before some university committee for harassment. That too is politics."

This story reveals a process of influence between the teacher and the students. Their relationship is not only educational but political as well. It is political in the sense of political scientist Harold Lasswell's famous definition of *politics as the process of who gets what, when, and how*.[1] The teacher (who) gets the student to leave the class (what) immediately (when) by using his authority to persuade and threaten him (how). This indeed is politics.

Our definition of politics centers on actions among a number of people involving influence. How do people get others to do what they wish? How does our society or any group (like that classroom) distribute its valued things, such as wealth, prestige, and security? Who gets these *values*, and how? The dialogue hints at an answer in the concepts of *power* and *authority*.

Politics and Power

Note that the teacher influenced the student to do something he didn't want to do (leave the class). The teacher demonstrated his power over the student, though limited by the student's rights. *Power* is simply the *ability to influence another's behavior*. Power is getting people to do something they wouldn't otherwise do. Power may involve force (often called *coercion*), persuasion, or rewards. But its essence is the ability to change another's actions. The more power one has over another, the greater the change, or the easier the change is to accomplish. Having more power also could mean influencing more people to change.

Power involves a relationship between people and groups. When someone says that a person has a lot of power, one should ask: Power to influence whom to do what? What is the power relationship being discussed? Take the statement "The United States is the most powerful nation in the world today." If this means that because the United States spends more on its military than the next 13 countries' defense budgets *combined*, it can influence any other country however it wishes, the statement is wrong. These resources (including the world's largest economy and educated population) can give only a *capacity* for power. Whether this capacity is converted into effective influence will depend

[1]Harold Lasswell, *Politics: Who Gets What, When, How* (New York: World, 1958), 13.

on the relationship in which it is applied. Certainly the United States has far greater military capabilities than its enemies in Afghanistan. Yet attempts to stabilize the country under a friendly democratic government seemed by the 2014 draw-down of troops to be beyond America's power. These limits were shown by the costs—casualties and resources—as well as the uncertain results from using American forces to influence Afghan behavior.

People generally do not seek power for its own sake. They want it for other values it can bring them—for fame or wealth or even affection. Power, like money, is a means to other ends. Most people seek money for what it can buy—whether food, clothing or shelter. Just as some people go after money more intently than others, so too do some people seek power more than others. Of course power, like money, does not come to everyone who seeks it.

Elites

Those who do gain power are called a political elite. *Elites* are those who get more than others of the values society has available (such as wealth and respect). We could answer the "who" part of the question "who gets what, when, and how?" by saying the elites are those who get the most.

There may be different elites depending on what value is being considered. In a small town, the owner of the largest business may be getting most of the wealth in the community, whereas the poor but honest mayor may have most of the respect. In most cases, however, the values overlap. The wealthy businessman will get plenty of respect, and the mayor will use people's respect for her to make income-producing contacts and investments.

To see the difference between an elite and the rest of us, we can look at one value (wealth) in one society (the United States). Clearly, wealth is not distributed equally among the population; some (the elite) get more than others. The top 1 percent of the American population now owns 40 percent of the nation's wealth, while the bottom 80 percent owns 7 percent. Further, inequality seems to be growing. Between 1979 and 2007 the average income of the bottom 99 percent of U.S. taxpayers grew by almost 19 percent. At the same time, the average income of the top 1 percent grew over 10 times as much—by over 200 percent. (See "The Growth of U.S. Income Inequality.")

Authority: Legitimate Power

Elites often reinforce their position by gaining authority. *Authority* is legitimate power. By *legitimate* we mean even more than "legal": The word implies something *accepted as right*. This correctness or *legitimacy* is connected in people's minds to both the position and the wishes of the authority. People may think an authority is legitimate if it was chosen using an agreed-upon procedure, such as an election. People recognize certain others as having the right to influence them in certain ways (say by leaving the class) and not in other ways (by giving them a cigarette to smoke in class). Most people feel that students *should* listen to teachers, children *should* obey their parents, and vice presidents *should* follow the wishes of presidents. People have many reasons for obeying authorities including habit, the authority figure's personal appeal, desire to be accepted by the group, and self-interest. But although they may not always follow it, people widely recognize authority as deserving obedience and that is what gives it legitimacy.

Therefore, authority is an efficient form of power. If people feel they *should* follow the wishes of an authority, then there is no need to force or even to persuade them to do so. The cost of influence is lowered for the authority. If, however, people do not respect the authority's legitimacy, its power can disappear quickly. A glance at a newspaper's front page will provide examples of authorities somewhere in the world having their legitimacy challenged. The civil war in Syria makes it clear that a large part of the population no longer consider the regime in Damascus to be legitimate. By attempting to violently suppress peaceful demonstrations, the government lost popular support. Because the government had lost its authority in the eyes of many Syrians, the cost to the police and military of influencing behavior went up. Armed men in uniform could still force people off the street—and an element of force lies behind most authority. But anyone can clear a street with a gun. Only an accepted authority can do it with just a word.

PRIORITIES MENU
Afghanistan War as of 10/13
$660 billion OR
all three of the following
for 1 year:
a. Funded Head Start
for 30 million kids.
b. Given 30 million
college scholarships.
c. Funded 2.7 million Police
or Sheriff's patrol officers.
Source: www.nationalpriorities
.org

▌ The Growth of U.S. Income Inequality

The richest 1 percent of Americans are taking more of the nation's income than anytime since 1928. According to University of California–Berkeley professor Emmanuel Saez, inequality has been increasing steadily for the last three decades. In 1982 the highest-earning 1 percent of families received 10.8 percent of all pretax income, while the bottom 90 percent received 64.7 percent. By 2012 the top 1 percent received 22.5 percent, while the bottom 90 percent share had fallen to just under 50 percent.

The United States is more unequal than most other developed countries. America ranked 10th out of 31 developed countries in income inequality based on incomes before government tax and income transfer programs (like Social Security and unemployment insurance) were considered. However, after including taxes and transfers, the United States got worse, with the world's second-highest level of inequality, after Chile.

Americans in the upper fifth of income earn 16.7 times as much as those in the lowest fifth, the widest such gap among the 10 most advanced countries. Perhaps it is not surprising that 54 percent of low-income Americans called the rich–poor gap a "very big" problem, whereas only 36 percent of high-income people agreed.

Source: Based on Data from the Pew Research Center, Drew Desilver, "U.S. Income Inequality, on Rise for Decades, Is Now Highest since 1928," December 5, 2013; and "5 Facts about Economic Inequality," January 7, 2014.

Power and authority, then, are central to politics. They are also central to many other aspects of life—almost all human relationships involve people trying to influence others. In a political science course, we could study the politics of a school, a hospital, or a family—who influences, who is influenced, and what are the process and limits of that influence. But most students of politics are interested in a bigger question: How does our whole society decide who gets what, when, and how? To find out, we need to study the most important organization that decides who gets the values of our society—government.

The Need for Government

Government is one of humanity's oldest and most universal institutions. History records very few societies that have existed without government. *Anarchy* (a society without government) may be an interesting theory, but it seldom has been applied for long. Instead, people have lived under forms of government that vary from the tribal council of a Native American village to the complex party dictatorship of communist China. Why is government so common?

One answer is that government is as common in society as is *political conflict*—the struggle over distribution of a group's valued things. These values (such as wealth) are limited, but people's demands for them are pretty unlimited. This imbalance means conflict. Whenever people have lived together, they have needed a way to regulate their disagreements. The question is not *whether* there will be conflict, but *how* the conflict will be handled. Who will decide on the rules that determine who wins and who loses? How does one get the loser to accept the decision? The usual way to channel political conflict and thus preserve society is to have some form of government.

Today most governments in the world claim to be democratic. A *democracy* is a form of government in which most people can effectively participate. Because it is generally impractical for all the people to take part in their government directly, their participation is usually through representatives chosen in free elections. (What many countries call "free elections"—without competing political parties, freedom of speech, and an independent press—would not impress many Americans.) Hence, the people rule themselves indirectly through their representatives, in a form of government often called a *representative democracy*.

An essential part of democracy is a tolerance of different opinions and interests. Unlike ideologies such as militant Islam or communism, democratic politics doesn't assume that some groups, like Christians or capitalists, are wrong and shouldn't participate in politics. Politics in a democracy acts like a marketplace, continually reacting to demands by different groups and reaching compromises among them. Politicians in a democracy practice an ancient and respected craft—to reconcile conflicting interests and beliefs in society in order to preserve the community. As British political scientist Bernard Crick wrote, "democratic politics . . . chooses conciliation rather than violence . . . as a way to maintain order and adapt to change." Reaching decisions this way means that democratic politics is likely to be messy, with few clear-cut victories by anyone. It also accepts that groups must be free to stand up for their own interests and that none has a monopoly on the truth.

Yet establishing governments, even democratic ones, does allow a few people great power over many others. This power includes the ability to coerce others more effectively than if government didn't exist. As illustrated by the genocide of Jews by Nazi Germany and the starvation of millions of Chinese under Mao Tse-tung, control of government may even mean the power to kill massive numbers of your own citizens.

As we will see in Chapter 2, the skeptical politicians who wrote the Constitution understood the problem of power. The journalist Robert D. Kaplan described our founders as "constructive pessimists" who "worried constantly about what might go wrong in human relations." James Madison's famous quote in *The Federalist Papers* No. 51—"If men were angels, no government would be necessary"—justified the elaborate hardwiring of checks and balances and the divisions of power and civil liberties designed to limit the future leaders of the United States. Yet as the Supreme Court decision following the 2000 conflicted presidential vote in Florida reminded us, the control of powerful judicial and political offices can allow those in authority to determine the outcome of even the most honored ritual in a democracy—a free election.

What Is Government?

Government is a political organization that does two things:

1. It makes rules determining who will get society's values.
2. It alone regulates the use of legitimate force in society.

The first part of the definition deals with how society distributes the values it has available—wealth, respect, safety, resources, money, and so on. The second part deals with how these decisions are enforced. Government, then, has the final word over who gets what and has the ultimate say over how it will be done.

The government does not always *directly* determine who will get the valued things in a society. The United States is a capitalist system, based on the private ownership of the economy. This means that the government doesn't directly decide on what jobs people will do, what products they will make, or who will get the income from the sale of the products. In theory, the U.S. government only protects the private distribution of society's values, with minimal interference. At the same time, the government places higher taxes on those with higher incomes and gives welfare to people who are getting the least of society's wealth. Both taxes and welfare illustrate the government's authority limiting the private distribution of the value of wealth.

This is not to say that somehow the economy is outside the reach of America's government. Following the 2008 financial meltdown, the Obama administration rescued the nation's largest banks and automobile companies by buying their stock. But even in more normal times the so-called free market depends on a framework of public laws and administrative regulations. The American economy is joined at the hip with a complex network of government agencies that makes sure that we find comfort in our hotels, meat in our Big Macs, and a return on our investments. The trust behind countless economic exchanges in society rests on political and legal rules and expectations. When these break down, as many suspected happened during the lax government regulations that led to the recession of 2008–2009, then peoples' confidence in banks and businesses declines as well. Those who proclaim that the strength of the economy lies in maintaining mythical barriers to political "interference" are talking ideology, not analysis. The successful American economy rests not in the detachment of the market from government but in their functioning relationships.

Making and Supporting Decisions

The government may also intervene directly in disputes among its citizens. Folks in a town near a river may not be able to swim there because a paper mill dumps sewage into it. The town residents or the owners of the mill may ask the government to settle the dispute. The appropriate part of the government may respond by passing a law, by a ruling of an administrative agency such as the Environmental Protection Agency, or by a court decision on whether the town or the paper mill will get the use of the river ("the value").

How the government supports its decision brings us to the second aspect of government—its exclusive regulation of legitimate force. In enforcing its decisions, the government may employ, allow, or prevent the use of force. Either the paper mill or the town's swimmers may be ordered not to use the river and may be fined or arrested if they do so. The government is the ultimate authority in regulating what kind of force is used.

The government is not the only one in society that can legitimately use force. Parents may discipline their children to keep them from swimming, or the paper mill may employ guards to keep people off their property. But only the government can set limits on this force. Most governments permit parents to spank their kids yet outlaw physical abuse of children. The paper mill's guards may be forbidden to use guns to keep swimmers out. Government does not *monopolize* the use of legitimate force, but it alone *regulates* its use.

The Study of Politics

What is the study of politics? One thing to notice about political science is that it's a lot like other *social sciences* such as history, economics, sociology, and psychology. Each studies aspects of the relations among people. In any large group of people, many social interactions are going on. Each of these disciplines may look at the same group and ask different questions about the relationships that are occurring. This division of labor is partly traditional and partly a way of separating complicated human relations into more easily understood parts. Political science fits in by studying one type of interaction between people—that involving power and authority. The following example will make the approaches of the other disciplines clearer and distinguish them from political science.

Political Science and Microsoft

What questions would an economist, a psychologist, and a historian ask about the operations of a "society" like the giant computer software company Microsoft? An *economist* might ask questions about the production and distribution of the various Microsoft operating systems and other programs. In designing its Microsoft Network, how did the company attract subscribers and content providers? How were buyers of the Windows program discouraged from using rival Web browsers? A *psychologist* might concentrate on the motives and goals of Bill Gates, the founder of Microsoft and the richest man in America. What is the psychological makeup of this successful entrepreneur? How did he deal with subordinates and competitors? A *historian* might look at the origins and development of Microsoft. What factors within the industry explain why at one point its operating systems ran more than four-fifths of the world's computers? Why did it become a multibillion dollar corporation while competitors fell by the wayside?

These different fields of study overlap. Members of one discipline often are interested in the findings of another. Economists may find answers to their questions about how focused and innovative the company is in a psychological study of Bill Gates. The historian might ask the economist about Microsoft's mergers with potential competitors to determine the strategy behind its expansion. Certainly the economist and the psychologist would want to know about the history of the corporation before studying their particular parts of it.

A political scientist, although interested in the other disciplines' findings, would most likely focus on this central question: *Who is getting what, when, and how?* How do Bill Gates's successors run Microsoft; how do these executives reach decisions and implement them? How does the government influence their decisions through regulations, taxes, and, on occasion, lawsuits? How did Microsoft try to dominate its industry, and how do its leaders keep themselves on top? Political science focuses on the study of power and authority—on the powerful, the ways in which they exercise their authority, and the consequences for the rest of us.

As Lasswell wrote, "The study of politics is the study of influence and the influential." That is the core of what a political scientist would want to find out about Microsoft.

Why Give a Damn about Politics?

After looking at what politics is and what government and political scientists do, you could still be asking one basic question: Who cares? Some students conclude, "Politics is just ego. I don't want to have anything to do with it." Why *should* any of us give a damn about politics?

There is a problem: We are already involved. Apathy is as much a political position as is activism. Either position will influence who gets what in our society. Safe streets, good schools, and clean food are political decisions influenced by who participates in making them, who is prevented from participating, and who chooses not to participate.

Our lives are webs of politics. Think of what you have done today and how politics has influenced you. What you had (or didn't have) for breakfast was probably influenced by the price and availability of the food. The quality of the food you ate was regulated by a government agency that made sure those Grade A eggs were Grade A and that the milk was indeed pasteurized. The cost of that milk or those eggs was affected by the decisions of government to aid farmers, as well as the ability of agricultural groups to influence the government by lobbying and campaign contributions. The news you saw on your favorite website about what the government was doing for the economy was conditioned by what officials felt they should tell the public and what reporters or bloggers could uncover from official and unofficial sources. The college you attend, the tuition you pay, and the student loans you may or may not receive are all the results of someone's choices in the political game. (See "Who Needs Government?")

Sometimes the influence of politics is subtle. Many of the ways we expect to be treated in our daily lives reflect recent changes in the laws. Identity politics, "Who Is What" as well as "Who Gets What," has risen in public attention as groups have made demands based on their shared identities. A few examples would include the rights of lesbians and gays not to be harassed, or of elderly workers to not be fired because of their age, or the right of nonsmokers to learn in a smoke-free class. These rights have evolved because of the support given to them by people joining demonstrations, going to court, and voting. We are rights-bearing citizens, often without thinking that these too are the result of political choices.

The truth is that most of us don't participate in the government decisions that affect our lives. Let's take a personal example. Studies of American government have pointed out that federal regulatory commissions have often not effectively regulated the businesses they oversee. These commissions have tended to be closely tied to the powerful economic interests they supervise. This lesson was brought home when I was in graduate school.

Some years ago the cargo door blew off an American Airlines DC-10 flying over Windsor, Canada, causing violent decompression. The pilot managed to land the empty jumbo jet safely. The government's independent National Transportation Safety Board investigated the near disaster. Their recommendations went to the Federal Aviation Administration (FAA), the government regulatory commission in charge of airline safety. The Safety Board recommended that the FAA order that all cargo doors have modified locking devices and that McDonnell Douglas, the plane's builder, be required to strengthen the cabin floor.

The FAA, headed by a political appointee, was operating under a policy of "gentlemen's agreements" with the industries it was regulating. After discussions with the plane's manufacturers (who were large contributors to President Nixon's reelection campaign), they allowed McDonnell Douglas to modify the door on its own instead of under FAA supervision and simply to issue advisory service bulletins for the 130 or so DC-10s already in operation. McDonnell Douglas was allowed to reject as "impractical" the idea of strengthening the floor.

Somehow the changes were not made on the door of a DC-10 flown by Turkish Airlines. The plane, flying from Paris to London in March 1974, crashed, killing all 346 people aboard. At the time it was the world's worst air disaster. The cargo door had blown off. This loss produced explosive decompression, collapse of the cabin floor, and loss of control. Passengers still strapped in their seats were sucked from the plane. A subcommittee of the House of Representatives, in a report on the crash, attacked the FAA for its "indifference to public safety" and for attempting to "balance dollars against lives."

A teacher and friend of mine, Professor Wayne Wilcox of Columbia University, was on the plane. With him were his wife and two children.

We have no choice over *whether* to be involved in the political game. But we can choose *how* to be involved. We can choose whether to be a *subject* in the political game or an *object* of that game. The question is not whether politics affects us—it does and will. The question is whether we will affect politics. The first step in this decision is choosing how aware we wish to be of the game. This text may, with luck, help that awareness.

Who Needs Government?

Americans' conflicting emotions toward government programs are legendary and unresolved. On one hand they have been increasingly dependent on government spending. Veterans returning from past wars went to college on the GI bill, bought their house with an FHA loan, had kids in a VA hospital, started a business with an SBA loan, and got electricity from TVA. Their kids participated in the school lunch program and attended college through government-guaranteed student loans. Their parents' lives were saved by drugs developed by NIH, and their families' finances were protected from bankruptcy by Medicare. (While no program is more popular than Medicare, a worker's average wages only contribute $1 in taxes for every $3 in benefits he or she receives.)

Yet the citizens who depend the most on government spending give the greatest support to candidates who promise to reduce these benefits. Support for Republican candidates who want to cut government spending has increased since 1980 in states where government spends more than it collects. In states that pay more in taxes than they receive in benefits, voters tend to support Democrats. Some analysts explain this anti-government vote from concerns about social issues, like abortion. But currently these are not as important as voters' worries about taxes and spending.

Source: Based on quote from Jonathan Yates, "Reality on Capitol Hill," *Newsweek,* November 28, 1988, p. 12.

What Is This Book About?

In a way this is a scorecard covering the major players in the game of national politics. This first chapter introduces some of the terms and dynamics of politics—the means (power and authority) and goals (values) of the game. Chapters 2 and 6 cover the formal constitutional rules and the civil liberties and rights under which the competition proceeds. Chapters 3, 4, and 5 deal with the governmental players—the president and bureaucracy, Congress, and the Supreme Court—their history and organization, their strengths and weaknesses. Chapters 7 and 8 are about four important nongovernmental players—voters, political parties, interest groups, and media. Though they are not official parts of the government, they influence the outcome of political conflicts. Finally, Chapter 9 goes into different theories of who wins and loses, who plays and doesn't play the game of American politics.

Let's be clear about this "game"; it is not "Monday Night Football." It is important, complex, ever changing, and never ending; it includes questions of life and death. Actually, many games are going on at the same time with overlapping players and objectives. They are games in which the participants often disagree, even on the goals. The goals (unlike the touchdown in football) vary with the objectives of the players. A business group may seek higher profits from its involvement in a political issue, a consumer organization may want a lower-priced product, and a labor union may demand higher wages for its workers. They may all compete over the same issue but "winning" may be different for each of them. They all seek to use power to obtain the values they consider important. We can analyze objectively how they play the game, but which side we root for depends on our own interests and ideals.

Another problem is that the players we've grouped together may not see themselves as being on the same team. Each participant, whether the bureaucracy, Congress, or the media, is hardly one player seeking a shared goal. They are not only players but also *arenas* in which competition goes on. We may read of Congress opposing the president on an issue, but a closer look will find the president's congressional supporters and opponents fighting it out in the committees of Congress. Some of the media may oppose a certain interest group, while allowing or limiting the use of television news and online opinion sites as platforms for the group's views.

Finally, in a brief introductory text all the political players are not discussed. State and city governments are certainly important in national politics. Ethnic groups and foreign governments may have a role in the outcome of the competition. Someone even more basic is missing. As one student asked, "Whatever happened to the majority of Americans in this game? Where are the people?"

Alas, politics today is a spectator sport. The audience is mostly on the sidelines. To be sure, people do influence the players. The president and Congress are selected by election, interest groups depend on their members' dues, and media need to please an audience to stay in business. But the making of foreign policies, the negotiations over legislation, and the discussions of what news the media should cover all get done behind closed doors. Though it is played for the crowd—who certainly pay for the game—the competition on the field generally doesn't include them. Whether it will depends on the players, the rules of the game, and the people watching.

■ THOUGHT QUESTIONS

1. In the opening dialogue of this chapter, we discovered politics in a place that may seem unlikely—a classroom. Describe some other everyday situations where politics takes place.
2. How do authorities gain legitimacy? How do they lose it? Do elections and demonstrations, here and abroad, provide examples of both?
3. People sometimes justify their apathy by the way politicians behave. Do you think this attitude is justified?

4. When you shop in the supermarket, do you notice the role of the government in your choice of what to buy? Do you see it on labels or do you just expect regulations to set minimal standards?
5. Have any decisions in your life been affected by government action? Did you have anything to say about those actions? If you didn't, do you know who did?

SUGGESTED READINGS

Crick, Bernard. *Democracy: A Very Short Introduction*. New York: Oxford University Press, 2002. Pb.
   A historical discussion of the definitions, conditions, and development of modern democracy.

Golding, William G. *Lord of the Flies*. New York: Capricorn Books, 1959. Pb.
   A pessimistic novel on what happens to British children on a deserted island without adults or government (way before the TV series *Survivor*).

Hacker, Jacob S. and Paul Pierson. *Winner-Take-All Politics*. New York: Simon & Schuster, 2010. Pb.
   Two political scientists dissect the political choices that led to the wealthy getting wealthier in modern America.

Loeb, Paul Rogat. *Soul of a Citizen*. Revised Edition. New York: St. Martin's Griffin. 2010. Pb.
   An inspiring argument for getting involved in grassroots politics.

Orwell, George. *Animal Farm*. New York: Alfred A. Knopf, 1993.
   The classic political fable of the communist barnyard where all the animals are equal but some are more equal than others.

Wasserman, Gary. *Politics in Action: Cases from the Frontlines of American Government*. New York: Pearson, 2012. Pb.
   Fifteen brief histories of how presidents and lobbyists, journalists and judges, students and bureaucrats engage in modern politicking.

CHAPTER 2

The Constitution:
Rules of the Game

The Second Day of Class

The second class was as bad as the first. This time the prof announces that we're going to be a focus group to test public opinion. We'll be interviewed to see what a small group of citizens thinks about American government. He starts by asking us, what words come to mind when you hear "politician"?

Well, I happen to know the answer to this.

"How about 'Slime balls'?"

Fist bumps all around.

Then he says, "What about 'government'?"

Not too hard—"Corrupt," "Games," "Boring."

So then he says, "What about when I say 'Founding Fathers'?"

"Patriots," "Freedom," "George Washington."

"How about 'The Constitution'?" he asks.

"Liberty," "Equality," "Bill of Rights"

Some of us are beginning to catch on.

Then he lets us have it. "Didn't the framers of the Constitution run for election and make promises to win people's votes? And not all of them were perfect in their personal lives. Didn't they meet in secret and wheel and deal in putting together the government in their Constitution and getting it accepted? Many people at the time, perhaps most, were unhappy with the results. And with their leaders. Just like now.

Sounds to me like our Founding Fathers were a bunch of politicians."

The Constitution did not fall from the sky. It was created by political leaders trying to form a government, resolve immediate problems and conflicting interests, and hold to the political ideas of their age. The Constitution has lasted because the politicians into whose care it was given proved flexible enough to adapt it to different times and because it commanded loyalty as a symbol of a nation's traditions and ideals. But the Constitution has never been "above politics." Its words cannot be understood apart from the politics in which they were written then, and applied now.

So far we have discussed the game of politics, what winning means, and why one plays. This chapter deals with the principles and organization of the competition. First, the chapter discusses the politicians who wrote the Constitution, their debates, the regional interests they represented, and the compromises they reached. The Constitution contains the official rules of the American political game; it also establishes three major players and their powers—the president, Congress, and the Supreme Court. Further, it places limits on the game, providing civil liberties protections for both players and people. By creating a central government that shares power with state governments, the Constitution establishes the playing field of federalism.

What led to the adoption of the Constitution, its meaning, how it has changed, and its political influence today are what this chapter is about.

Background to the Constitution

On July 4, 1776, the Declaration of Independence proclaimed the American colonies "Free and Independent States." This symbolized the beginning not only of a bitter fight for independence from Great Britain but also of a struggle to unify the separate and often conflicting interests, regions, and states of America. Only after a decade of trial and error was the Constitution written and accepted as the legal foundation for the new United States of America.

The politicians who gathered in Philadelphia in May 1787 to write the Constitution were not starting from scratch. They were able to draw on (1) an English political heritage, (2) American models of colonial and state governments, and (3) their experience with the Articles of Confederation.

The framers were inheritors of an English legal heritage that included the *Magna Carta*, which, in 1215, declared that the power of the king was not absolute. It also included the idea of natural rights, expressed by English philosophers, most notably John Locke, who wrote that people were "born free" and formed society to protect their rights. Many colonists felt that they were fighting a revolution to secure their traditional rights as Englishmen, which had been denied them by an abusive colonial government.

Their 150 years as colonies had taught the states much about self-government, which they used in the Constitution. Even the earliest settlers had been determined to live under written rules of law resting on the consent of the community: The *Mayflower Compact* was signed by the Pilgrims shortly before they landed at Plymouth in 1620. Similar documents had been written in other colonies, most of which had their own constitutions. Other aspects of colonial (and English) governments, such as two-house legislatures, were later to appear in the Constitution. After the American Revolution, in reaction to the authority of the royal governor, the colonists established the legislature as the most important branch in their state governments.

Most of the colonies had a governor, a legislature, and a judiciary—a pattern that would evolve into the constitutional separation of powers. Most had regular elections, though generally only property-owning white males could vote. There was even an uneasy basis for the federal system of local and national governments in the sharing of powers between the American colonies and a central government in England. Perhaps most important was the idea of limited government and individual rights written into the state constitutions after the Revolution.

However, unity among the colonies was slow in coming. Attempts to tighten their ties during the Revolution were a limited success. Most political theorists of the time thought democracy could only exist in small states. This idea added to the reluctance of many leaders to give up their states' powers to a presumably less democratic national government. The First Continental Congress in September 1774 had established regular lines of communication among the colonies and focused anti-British sentiment. The Second Continental Congress, beginning in Philadelphia in May 1775, created the Declaration of Independence. At the same time, a plan for confederation—a loose union among the states—was proposed. The Articles of Confederation were ratified by the states by March 1781 and went into effect even before the formal end of the American Revolution in February 1783.

The Articles of Confederation (1781–1789)

Looking back, the shortcomings of the Articles of Confederation are pretty apparent. No real national government was set up in the articles. Rather, they established a "league of friendship" among the states, which didn't have much more authority than the United Nations does today. The center of the federation was a *unicameral* (one-house) legislature, called the *Confederation Congress*. Each state had one vote, regardless of its size. Most serious actions required approval by nine states. Amendments to the articles needed unanimous approval by all 13 states.

The confederation had no executive branch and no national system of courts. Perhaps most important, the Congress had no ability to impose taxes; it could only *request* funds from the states. Each state retained its "sovereignty, freedom, and independence." Nor did the Congress have any direct authority over citizens who were subject only to the government of their states. In short, the Congress had no ability to enforce its will on either states or citizens.

The confederation did have some muscle. Unlike the United Nations, it had the power to declare war, conduct foreign policy, coin money, manage a postal system, and oversee an army made up of the state militias. The Articles of Confederation were also anti-elite in requiring compulsory rotation in office, what we would today call *term limits*—no member of the Congress could serve more than three years in any six. Finally, real achievements were made under the articles, such as the start of a national bureaucracy and the passing of the *Northwest Ordinance*, which established the procedure for admitting new states into the Union.

But by 1787, the weakness of the articles was more apparent than their strength. Too little power had been granted to the central authority. Many people worried that Britain, France, or Spain would attack America because of its feeble central government. The confederation was in deep financial difficulty: Not enough funds were coming from the states, the currency was being devalued, and the states were locked in trade wars, putting up tariff barriers against each other. In late 1786 Shays's Rebellion, an angry protest by Massachusetts farmers unable to pay their debts and taxes, reinforced the fears of many among the property-owning elite that a strong central government was needed to avoid "mob rule," economic decline, and foreign invasion.

The Constitutional Convention

Against this background, the convention met in Philadelphia from May 25 to September 17, 1787. The weather was hot and muggy, making tempers short. All the meetings were held in private—with the windows shut and the press excluded. This was because Congress had reluctantly called the convention together "for the sole purpose of revising the Articles of Confederation." Yet within five days of organizing, the convention had adopted a Virginia delegate's resolution "that a national government ought to be established consisting of a *supreme* legislative, executive, and judiciary." In other words, the convention violated the authority under which it had been established and proceeded to write a completely new U.S. Constitution in a single summer.

The Constitution was a product of a series of compromises. The most important compromise, because it was the most divisive issue, was the question of how the states would be represented in the national legislature. The large states proposed a legislature with representation based either on the taxes paid or on the number of people in each state—both of which gave them more power. The small states wanted one vote for each state no matter what its size—giving them more influence. After a long deadlock, an agreement called the *Great Compromise* established the present structure of Congress—representation based on population in the lower house (House of Representatives) and equal representation for all states in the upper house (Senate).

Other compromises came more easily. Southern delegates feared the national government would impose an export tax on their agricultural goods and interfere with slavery. A compromise was reached that gave Congress the power to regulate commerce but not to tax exports. In addition, the slave trade could not be banned before 1808. The slave issue also was central in the strangest agreement—the Three-Fifths Compromise. Here the debate was over whether slaves should be counted as people for purposes of representation and taxation. The South, which did not want to treat slaves as people, did, however, want to count them that way. It was finally agreed that a slave should be counted as three-fifths of a person for both. (This provision was later removed by the Thirteenth and Fourteenth Amendments.) Another key issue, the right of a state to withdraw or *secede* from the Union, was simply avoided. The questions of secession and slavery had to wait for a later generation to resolve in a bloody civil war.

The Framers

It is a bit surprising how quickly and relatively painlessly the Constitution was drafted. No doubt the writing went so smoothly partly because of the qualities of the leaders in Philadelphia. The universally respected General Washington chaired the meetings, bringing with him the pragmatism of a successful landowner and the commitment of a nationalist. Alexander Hamilton, the self-assured financial genius, frequently dominated the debates, whereas the shy but equally brilliant James Madison often secured a consensus at discussion's end. Benjamin Franklin, at 82 years old, added the moderation and wisdom of age.

The delegates possessed a blend of experience and learning. (See "Colonial Drinking and Voting.") Of the 55 delegates, 42 had served in the Continental Congress. More than half were college educated and had studied political philosophy. As a relatively young group—averaging 40 years old—they may have reflected a generation gap of their own time. Having politically matured during the revolutionary period, they were less tied to state loyalties than were older men whose outlook was formed before the war. They were nationalists building a nation, not merely defending the interests of their states.

But there was more to the consensus than this. The framers were not exactly representative of the population of America at the time.

They were wealthy planters, merchants, and lawyers. Fifteen of them were slaveholders; 14 were land speculators. The small farmers and workers of the country, many of whom were suffering from an economic downturn, were not represented in Philadelphia. Nor did leaders who spoke for this poorer, more radical majority, such as Thomas Jefferson (who was in Paris as ambassador and disliked the face-to-face arguments in political meetings) or Patrick Henry (who stayed away because he "smelt a rat") attend the convention. Only six of the 56 men who signed the revolutionary Declaration of Independence were at the convention. The delegates were a conservative, propertied elite, worried that continuing the weak confederation would only encourage more and larger Shays's Rebellions. Thus, the debates at the convention were not between the "haves" and the "have-nots," but between the "haves" and the "haves" over their regional interests.

Motives behind the Constitution

Much scholarly debate has gone on about the motives of the framers since Charles Beard published his book *An Economic Interpretation of the Constitution of the United States* in 1913. Beard argued that the convention was a counterrevolution engineered by the delegates to protect and improve their own property holdings by transferring

▌Politics and Alcohol in America

The popular politics of the framers' day were at least as rough and tumble as what we are used to today. In some ways campaigns were even looser.

One practice that was widely accepted was for candidates to buy drinks—for voters. It was practically considered an obligation for every candidate who expected to gain the public's support. Rum punch was the preference, sometimes supplemented by ginger cake and other delicacies. In 1758 George Washington, not yet the father of his country, had to cough up some 160 gallons of liquor for less than 400 voters, which added up to over one and a half quarts of booze per voter. He did win.

Not so lucky was the arguably more idealistic James Madison. While running for reelection to the Virginia House of Delegates in 1777, he decided to make a stand against bribing voters with alcohol. He may have had a point; however, his refusal to compromise with the popular politics of the time proved costly to his hopes to continue in elected office.

That year James Madison lost to a tavernkeeper, a gentleman who presumably offered voters fewer principles but more drinks.

Source: Fred Barbash, *The Founding.* New York: Simon & Schuster, 1987, p. 131.

power from the states to an unrepresentative central government. Certainly the 40 delegates who held nearly worthless confederation bonds stood to profit from a new government committed to honoring these debts. Certainly their interests as creditors and property holders would be better protected by a strong central government. Nor did the delegates particularly favor democracy. Most thought that liberty had to be protected *from* democracy (which they thought of as "mob rule") and agreed with Madison's statement in *The Federalist Papers* No. 10 that "those who hold and those who are without property have ever formed distinct interests in society."

Critics of Beard's theory argue that the framers' motives were more varied. They conclude that the delegates wanted to build a new nation, to reduce the country's numerous political disputes, and to promote economic development that would benefit all. They point out that having a central government able to raise an army to protect the states from foreign attack appeared to be the most important reason that George Washington, among others, backed the Constitution.

But the arguments of the two sides don't necessarily cancel out each other. The framers' *public* interest of building a strong nation and their *private* interest of protecting their property could work together. Like most people, they believed that what was good for themselves

Is the Constitution Antidemocratic?

There is an argument that the Constitution was an antidemocratic attempt to limit popular participation in government. Many of the framers saw liberty and democracy as very separate, with people's liberties needing constitutional protections from democratic pressures. Certainly presidents, senators, and Supreme Court justices were not selected by a direct popular vote and were viewed as restraints on democracy. Critics often quote an antidemocratic framer like Roger Sherman of Connecticut, who wrote that the people "should have as little to do as may be about the government. They . . . are constantly liable to be misled."

The late Thurgood Marshall, the Supreme Court's first black justice, pointed out that the Constitution's preamble that begins "We the people" did not include the majority of citizens—women and minorities. He called the Constitution "defective from the start" because it required tremendous social upheaval "to attain the system of constitutional government, and its respect for the individual freedoms and human rights, we hold as fundamental today." He warned against a complacent belief in the original vision of the founders. Instead, Marshall praised those who, through the Civil War, created virtually a new constitution using the Fourteenth Amendment to ensure the rights of all Americans.

was good for society. It was not surprising by standards of the day that most of the population (workers, the poor, blacks, women) was not represented at Philadelphia. Nor should it be surprising that the delegates' ideas for a government did not work against their own economic interests and, in many cases, aided them. (See "Is the Constitution Antidemocratic?")

Federalists versus Anti-Federalists

The framers were divided. Many of the debates during the writing and ratification of the Constitution separated the elite into two camps: the Federalists and the Anti-Federalists.

The *Federalists* generally favored a strong federal (national) government, with protection of private property rights and limits on popular participation in government. (Alexander Hamilton, a leader of the Federalists, described the people as "a great beast.") In the debates over the Constitution, the Federalists pushed for high property qualifications for voting, an indirectly elected Senate modeled after the English aristocratic House of Lords, a lofty indirectly elected president, and a strong nonelected judiciary. The Federalists, being more pessimistic about human nature (including the nature of the rulers), wanted these "cooling-off" devices in the government to filter down the popular will and create guardians of the people's real interests.

The *Anti-Federalists* were more optimistic about human nature though just as suspicious about the nature of those in power. Led by men like Patrick Henry and George Mason, they favored strong state governments because they felt the states would be closer to the public than a strong central government. They wanted fewer limits on popular  participation and pushed for the legislative branch to have more power than the executive and judicial branches. Believing that the majority was responsible, though agreeing that it needed cooling off, the Anti-Federalists wanted government to be accountable to officials elected by the people.

The Constitution is a compromise between these two positions. It was designed to prevent tyranny from the bottom—the people (whom the Federalists feared)—and from the top—the rulers (whom the Anti-Federalists feared). Neither side could foresee a federal government of the size and complexity that exists today. Both generally agreed that the government is best that governs least.

Ratification and the Bill of Rights

The struggle for ratification of the Constitution focused the debate between the Federalists and Anti-Federalists. Conventions in nine states had to approve the Constitution before it could go into effect. Because a majority of the people were against the Constitution, the fight for ratification wasn't easy. The Anti-Federalists wanted a more rigid system of separation of power and more effective checks and balances. Fearing that the president and Senate would act together as an aristocratic clique, they proposed compulsory rotation in office (as under the Articles of Confederation).

The Federalists' difficulty came from supporting a strong central government that could tax and endanger people's liberties—the very arguments that they had *opposed* during the Revolution against the British. They criticized the Anti-Federalists for their lack of faith in popular elections and for ignoring the advantages of a national union. Their propaganda campaign in the newspapers pointed out the failures of the confederation, reassured people that the proposed president would be more like a governor than a king, and dismissed charges that the judiciary would be a threat to individual liberties. A series of these essays in a New York newspaper written by Madison, Hamilton, and John Jay was later republished as *The Federalist Papers*. The book stands today as the most famous commentary of the framers' thinking about their Constitution.

The debate over whether to include the *Bill of Rights*, the first 10 amendments in the Constitution, became a key issue in the struggle over ratification. The Philadelphia convention, dominated by Federalists, had failed to include a bill of rights in the original document, not so much because of opposition to the goals of the bill but from a feeling that such a statement was irrelevant. (A proposed bill of rights was voted down unanimously near the end of the convention, partly because everyone was tired and wanted to go home.) The Federalists, from their conservative viewpoint, believed that liberty was best protected by the *procedures*, such as federalism, and checks and balances, established by their constitutional government. No matter what ideals were written down, such as freedoms of speech, press, and religion, the Federalists argued that support for them would depend on the "tolerance of the age" and the balance of forces established by the Constitution.

For the Anti-Federalists, the Bill of Rights was a proclamation of fundamental truths—natural rights due to all people. No matter whether other generations might ignore them, these rights were sacred. Any government resting on the consent of its people must honor them in its constitution. Although the Anti-Federalists had lost the battle in Philadelphia over the Bill of Rights, they eventually won the war. Massachusetts and Virginia agreed to accept the Constitution with the recommendation that such a proclamation be the first order of business of the new Congress. It was, and the Bill of Rights became the first 10 amendments to the Constitution on December 15, 1791.

Four Major Constitutional Principles

The U.S. Constitution did three things in creating a government. First, it *established the structure* of government. In setting up three branches of government within a federal system, it gave the country a political framework that has existed to the present time. Second, the Constitution *distributed certain powers* to this government. Article I gave legislative powers, such as the power to raise and spend money, to Congress. Article II gave executive powers to the president, including command over the armed forces and wide authority over foreign policy. Article III gave judicial power, the right to judge disputes arising under the Constitution, to the U.S. Supreme Court. Third, the Constitution *restrained the government* in exercising these powers. Government was limited, by the Bill of Rights for example, so that certain individual rights would be preserved.

The Constitution, then, both *grants* and *limits* governmental power. This can be shown by looking closely at four major constitutional principles: separation of powers and checks and balances, federalism, limited government, and judicial review.

Separation of Powers and Checks and Balances

The first major constitutional principle is actually two: separation of powers and checks and balances. However, the two principles cannot be understood apart from each other, and they work together.

Separation of powers is the principle that the powers of government should be divided and put in the care of different parts of the government. Although never exactly stated in the Constitution, this principle was in practice in the governments of the colonies. The idea that power was needed to balance other power was a key concept of the French political theorist Baron de Montesquieu, who was often quoted in Philadelphia. (See "Madison on Separation of Powers and Government.") The writers of the Constitution separated the federal government into three branches to carry out what they saw as the three major functions of government. The *legislative function*—passing the laws—was given to Congress; the *executive function*—carrying out or executing the laws—was given to the president; and the *judicial function*—interpreting the laws—was given to the Supreme Court.

Though nice and neat, the principle is probably unworkable in practice. The purpose of separation of powers was to allow ambition to counter ambition, to prevent any one authority from monopolizing power. Yet simply dividing the powers of government into these three branches would probably make the legislature supreme—as it had

Madison on Separation of Powers and Government

The great security against a gradual concentration of the several powers in the same department consists in giving to those who administer each department the necessary constitutional means and personal motives to resist encroachments of the others. . . . Ambition must be made to counteract ambition. The interest of the man must be connected with the constitutional rights of the place. . . . If men were angels, no government would be necessary. If angels were to govern men, neither external nor internal controls on government would be necessary. In framing a government, which is to be administered by men over men, the great difficulty lies in this: You must first enable the government to control the governed; and in the next place, oblige it to control itself.

Source: James Madison, *The Federalist Papers* No. 51.

been in the colonies. As the starter of the governmental process, the legislature could determine how, or even if, the other branches played their roles. Although Congress was accepted as the most important branch, something was needed to curb legislative power; that something was checks and balances.

Checks and balances create a mixture of powers that permits the three branches of government to limit one another. (A *check* is a control one branch has over another's functions, creating a *balance* of power.) The principle gives the branches constitutional means for guarding their functions from interference by another branch. Checks and balances mix together the legislative, executive, and judicial powers, giving some legislative powers to the executive, some executive powers to the legislative branch, and so on, to keep any branch from dominating another.

There are a number of examples of checks and balances in the Constitution. The president is given legislative power to recommend measures to Congress and to call Congress into special session, and some judicial power like the right to pardon (which presidents have sometimes used to excuse political allies from the judgment of the courts). The presidential veto gives the chief executive a primarily legislative power to prevent bills he or she dislikes from becoming law. Congress can check this power by its right to override the veto by a two-thirds vote. The Senate is given an executive power in its role of confirming presidential nominations for major executive and judicial posts, which is also the power *not* to confirm.

Further, Congress can refuse to appropriate money for any executive agency, thereby preventing the president from acting. President Obama learned this firsthand in December 2011, when Congress slipped into a large spending bill a paragraph that stripped funding for the Department of Energy enforcing standards that required the use of high-efficiency light bulbs. Conservatives had made the new standards a rallying point for complaints about government interference. Congress was unable to vote to repeal the new standards, but by using its power to remove the funds needed for enforcement, conservatives effectively eliminated it for the 2012 fiscal year.

The system of separation of powers and checks and balances are even more elaborate than this mixture of functions. The way each branch of government is set up and chosen also checks and balances its power. For example, Congress is divided into two houses, and both must approve legislation before it becomes law. Limited terms of office and varied methods of selection help keep any one person or branch from becoming too strong. The House of Representatives was to be popularly elected for two-year terms; senators were elected for six years, originally by their state legislatures (changed by the Seventeenth Amendment to popular election); the president was elected for four years by an electoral college, not a popular vote; and federal judges were to be appointed by the president, confirmed by the Senate, and to serve for life during good behavior. All these procedures were designed to give government officials different interests to defend, varied bases of support, and protection from too much interference by other branches.

The institutions that result from this dividing and mixing of powers are separate bodies that in practice *share* the overall power of government. Each needs the other to make government work, yet each has an interest in checking and balancing the powers of the others. This elaborate mechanism of separation of powers and checks and balances was certainly not designed to be the most efficient form of government—as President Obama fighting for reelection remarked in reply to a question about political gridlock. "What's frustrated people is that I have not been able to force Congress to implement every aspect of what I said in 2008. . . . That's just the nature of being president. . . . It turns out that our founders designed a system that makes it more difficult to bring about change than I would like sometimes."

True enough. The Constitution was written "to control the abuses of government"—to oblige the government to discipline itself. It set up a structure that historian Richard Hofstadter called "a harmonious system of mutual frustration."

Federalism

Federalism calls for political authority to be divided between a central government and the governments of the states. Both the federal and state governments may act directly on the people and each has some *exclusive powers*. Federalism, like separation of powers, distributes political authority to prevent power from being concentrated in any one group. It is a constitutional principle around which major political debates continue to the present day.

Actually, the men who wrote the Constitution had little choice. The loose confederation of states had not operated well, and centralizing all government powers would have been unacceptable to the major governments of the day—those of the states. Federalism, then, was more than just a reasonable principle for governing a large country separated by regional differences and slow communications. It also was the only realistic way to get the states to approve the Constitution.

American federalism involves two somewhat contradictory ideas. The first, expressed in Article VI, is that the Constitution and the laws of the central government are supreme. This condition was necessary to establish an effective government that would be able to pass laws and rule directly over all the people. The second principle of states' rights ensures the independence of the state governments: The Tenth Amendment *reserved powers* not delegated to the central government to the states or the people. These substantial reserved powers include control of local and city governments, regulation of business within a state, supervision of education, and exercise of the general "police power" over the safety of the people.

The conflict between the two principles—national supremacy and states' rights—came to a head in the Civil War, which established the predominance of the national government. That is not to say that the question was settled once and for all. Even today on issues such as gun control and immigration, state governments often clash with the federal government. Such conflicts can be expected from a constitution that not only divided the powers of government into a federal system but also set up the basis for national union.

As political issues—whether regulating the economy or protecting the environment—became national, so too did solutions increasingly center in the national government. In practice there are few domestic programs today that are solely run by the federal government. Almost all require cooperation by the states and often the cities. In the best cases, this arrangement helps adjust the programs to local conditions; in the worst, it may delay or hinder needed changes, even in a natural catastrophe. (See the case study, "Federalism Caught in a Storm: The Katrina Disaster.")

Whether harming or helping, federalism now exists far less as separate boxes of powers than as a mix of overlapping relations between the states and the federal government, sometimes called a *marblecake*, because of its swirl of different colored ingredients. This blending of relations can be seen in public education. Public schools in this country are governed by local school boards. The boards set teachers' salaries and make the basic decisions concerning day-to-day operations of a public school system. Local taxes on property in the school district are usually the major source of public school funds.

Public education in the United States is not, however, solely a local government responsibility. State governments provide a large part of the funds for local education. These funds from state taxes are partly supplied to school districts according to financial need. This equalizes local revenues from property taxes, which vary widely from poorer to wealthier school districts. In addition, state governments usually control teacher qualifications, set educational standards in public schools, and approve the textbooks used.

▋ No Child Left Behind and Federalism

The first bill sent to Congress by President Bush was the education reform called No Child Left Behind. It passed both houses of Congress and was signed by the president in January 2002. The law increased the federal government's role in education, even if it undermined the conservative position of strengthening federalism by giving more powers to the states.

The approach in No Child Left Behind was to hold states, districts, and schools accountable for student performance. The federal government would reward improved student achievement, as measured by annual reading and math tests. There were also penalties to states for failure. If after a few years these schools did not meet performance goals, federal funds would be provided to parents to help them relocate their children in other schools.

The reform's impact on education has been debatable; student scores rose in some states, while antagonism from state and local officials was apparent almost everywhere. Many, including conservative Republicans, felt that Washington was stepping over traditional lines of federalism. A number of states had difficulty providing qualified teachers in classrooms or having their students pass the required tests. President Obama supported the goals of the reform but criticized its lack of funding and flexibility for the states.

The federal government gets involved in public education through aid programs that help equalize state funding, just as state funds are used to reduce the differences among local school districts. Some "strings" are attached to these federal funds. In President Obama's education reform, "Race to the Top," the federal government made educational money conditional on school districts taking action to improve schools. Under the program, states drew up reform plans and then competed against each other for limited federal monies. Federal monies would help states achieve these goals and penalize them if they didn't. This pattern of setting standards for funding as a way of regulating public education is found in federal government activities ranging from pollution control to traffic safety on public highways. (See "No Child Left Behind and Federalism.")

The Debate over Modern Federalism

At first glance, *modern federalism* appears far different from the original creation. While the Constitution remains a limit on centralized power, the federal government has grown stronger than the framers could ever imagine. Still, most nonmilitary government services are supplied by state and local governments in a complex web of relationships with

TABLE 2.1 89,055 GOVERNMENTS IN THE UNITED STATES

Types and Numbers of Governments

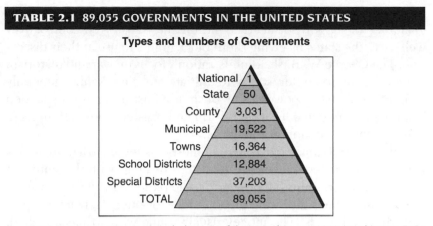

National	1
State	50
County	3,031
Municipal	19,522
Towns	16,364
School Districts	12,884
Special Districts	37,203
TOTAL	89,055

Source: U.S. Census Bureau, *Statistical Abstract of the United States*. 2012 (Washington D.C.: Government Printing Office, 2012).

Washington. In some ways, federalism makes it easier for citizens to participate in decisions because they occur closer to home. In other ways, it's more difficult because people need to keep track of separate decisions being made in a variety of places. (See Table 2.1)

Are local and state governments closer to the people, and do they therefore produce better policies, than the national government? Historically, the answer to this question has depended on how satisfied people have been with what the government does. The growth of the federal government has been fueled by big problems leading to popular demands for their solution. As the economy became national, issues like regulating banks, protecting workers, providing housing, and guarding the environment seemed beyond the states' capacities to solve. By responding to these challenges, the national government appeared both efficient and representative, certainly an improvement over state and local governments.

These liberal programs produced opponents. Business opposed encouragement for labor unions, environmental restrictions, and consumer protections that curtailed the marketplace. Wealthy people disliked paying taxes for programs that benefited non-wealthy families. Elected officials worried about expanding government spending that led to more bureaucracies. Public opinion began to shift; more people trusted state and local governments than trusted Washington and wanted the smaller governments to take the lead in solving national problems.

In the 1980s, Republican president Ronald Reagan pioneered a "New Federalism" that gave large block grants of money to states and localities to use with few controls from Washington. Democratic president Bill Clinton continued this conservative trend. Clinton's welfare reform legislation reduced federal programs and shifted more responsibility to the local level. It ended the federal government guarantee of support for needy children and transferred control over welfare to the states by giving them block grants to use at their discretion. The George W. Bush administration's focus on war and terrorism left plenty of room for states to initiate policies. While generally supportive of states' powers, the Bush administration also expanded Washington's role in education reform and resisted states' attempts to issue tougher air pollution standards.

President Obama's activism on domestic issues led to a more dominant role for the federal government in its dealings with the states. In the huge 2009 stimulus bill designed to help the country recover from the recession, the states were given money for budgets, teachers' pay, and Medicaid funds. The money usually came with strings attached. These federal requirements were made clear in education reform. Obama's *Race to the Top* program offered states the chance to compete for a pot of money, provided they changed their laws to meet higher educational standards. This "carrot" of federal spending was repeated in the Democrats' health care reform where state budgets were steered toward federal priorities in order to qualify. The Obama administration was not giving the states money to spend for their own priorities; it has an agenda.

This shift in federalism flowed from a simple fact: The states were broke. Under Obama, federal money rose to over one-third of state spending. The poor economy cut states' budgets and their ability to independently chart their own policy directions. Depending on federal money meant following federal guidelines, especially in health care and education. This was a major shift from programs in the past that allowed states to experiment in their use of federal funds. However, by 2013, the states could be heard complaining less about federal interference than about the cuts in aid from Washington's efforts to reduce the budget deficit. Even though, as the economy improved, the states were increasing the taxes they collected, they feared being forced to cut programs. Neglect by Washington was more of a worry than being overwhelmed.

Still federalism seemed alive and well. State and local governments employed some 19 million people, while the federal payroll fell to under 2 million employees. Despite politicians' speeches against expanding government, the public supported state and local authorities spending their taxes. General backing for reducing deficits didn't significantly weaken the public's wish to keep programs that provided education and needed infrastructure. And often state governments were providing the model for federal government actions in areas like gas mileage standards (California) and health care (Massachusetts).

These "laboratories of democracy" could still offer alternatives to a gridlocked government in Washington.

A century ago, the only political scientist to become president, Woodrow Wilson, wrote that the relations of the states and federal government cannot be settled "by one generation, because it is a question of growth, and every new successive stage of our political and economic development, gives it a new aspect, makes it a new question." This view of federalism as a flexible system for representing the varied interests of a large, diverse country is not far from what we have today. Actually it is not far from what the framers of the Constitution had in mind. (See "Federalism at 55 mph.")

Federalism at 55 mph

A 55 mph speed limit has been praised as policy and seldom followed in practice. It was first passed by Congress in the 1970s, during the Arab oil embargo, to conserve fuel and protect public safety. (While under federalism, Congress could not directly legislate state speed limits, it could threaten to withhold federal money from states that didn't comply.) By 1995 times had changed, and a bill raising the limit to 65 mph was before Congress. Western states, with long distances to travel, especially hated the 55 mph limit, and the newly elected Republican majority saw a popular way of getting a "paternalistic" federal government off the backs of the states.

In a vote that was seen by the press as a strong endorsement of federalism, Congress quickly repealed the 55 mph speed limit. Less noticed was the Senate vote on the same day that approved the federal government's 55 mph limits on big trucks, which were seen as more dangerous than cars. The next day the Senate voted *not* to repeal popular federal requirements that people use seat belts. Later in that session, the Senate overwhelmingly passed a bill requiring tough new state laws against drinking and driving by minors. Any state not adopting such "zero tolerance" laws would lose up to 10 percent of their federal highway funds.

Confusing? Perhaps, because federalism in practice represents a policy choice, not just an abstract constitutional principle. In real life, it must compete with other policy choices, in this case concerns for safety and the environment. This makes the modern application of federalism, as the 55 mph limit illustrates, only as consistent as the politics swirling around it.

Limited Government

The principle of *limited government* means that the powers of government are limited by the rights and liberties of the governed. This principle is basic to the very idea of constitutional government: The people give the government listed powers and duties through a constitution, while reserving the rest to themselves. This *political compact* means that government actions must rest on the *rule of law*, approved, however indirectly, by the consent of the governed. Furthermore, the Constitution sets up procedures, such as separation of powers and federalism, to ensure that the government remains limited to its proper duties and powers. For example, the president may not exercise powers given by the Constitution exclusively to Congress.

Limited government guarantees citizens their *rights against* the government as well as *access to* the government. Civil liberties and rights guarantee the openness and competitiveness of the political process, which is not only the right to vote but also the freedom to dissent, demonstrate, and organize to produce alternatives. These rights make voting meaningful. Civil liberties protect citizens from arbitrary governmental power. Under civil liberties would fall a citizen's right to a fair and speedy trial, to be defended by a lawyer and be judged by an impartial jury of his or her peers. Further, government can neither take life, liberty, or property without due process of law, nor interfere with a citizen's right to practice religion, nor invade one's privacy. In short, the people who make the laws are subject to them. (See Chapter 6 on civil rights and liberties.)

Judicial Review

An important means of keeping government limited and of maintaining civil rights and liberties is the power of judicial review vested in the Supreme Court. *Judicial review*, the last constitutional principle, is the judicial branch's authority to decide on the constitutionality of the acts of the government (local, state, and federal). The political importance of judicial review could be seen in the summer of 2012, when the Supreme Court in a narrow 5–4 ruling declared that key parts of the administration's health care reform were allowed under the Constitution. The decision had been awaited with anxiety by both sides of the debate over Obamacare because of the power of the Court to declare this major piece of legislation unconstitutional.

Although judicial review has become an accepted constitutional practice, it is not actually mentioned in the document. There was some debate in the first years of the Constitution over whether the Court had the power merely to give nonbinding opinions or whether it had supremacy over acts of the government. Most people at that time agreed that the Supreme Court did have the power to nullify unconstitutional acts of the state governments, but opinion was divided over whether this power extended to the acts of the federal government. In 1803, the case of *Marbury v. Madison* clarified this power that the Court probably already had. The Supreme Court first struck down an act of Congress, which gave a duty not mentioned in the Constitution to the Court. This power has since become a firmly entrenched principle of the Constitution, though limited by the Supreme Court's own practices and by the other branches of government.

Judicial review not only makes the Court a watchdog limiting the central government but also the guardian of federalism. The latter function, reviewing the acts of state and local governments, has historically been the Supreme Court's most important use of judicial review. Though relatively few federal laws have been struck down by the Court, hundreds of state and local laws have been held to violate the Constitution. As Justice Oliver Wendell Holmes said over 80 years ago, "The United States would not come to an end if we lost our power to declare an act of Congress void. I do think the Union would be imperiled if we could not make that declaration as to the laws of the several states." (See Chapter 5 on the judicial branch.)

How Is the Constitution Changed?

To say that the Constitution has lasted over 200 years is not to say it is the same document that was adopted in 1789. The Constitution has changed vastly; in practical ways, it bears little resemblance to the original. Most of the framers would scarcely recognize the political process that operates today under their constitution. Changes in the Constitution have been made by four major methods: formal amendment, judicial interpretation, legislation, and custom.

Amendments

Although the amendment process is the first way we usually think of for changing the Constitution, it is actually the least common method. Only 27 amendments (including the first 10 amendments, which can practically be considered part of the original document) have been adopted. (The Equal Rights Amendment and the Washington, D.C., Voting Rights Amendment were proposed by Congress but not ratified by the needed three-fourths of the state legislatures.) As those proposing an amendment to require a balanced federal budget have discovered, adopting amendments is meant to be difficult. Though the Constitution's framers recognized the need for change in their basic document, they wanted to protect it from temporary popular pressure. Hence, they required unusually large majorities for adopting amendments.

Article V of the Constitution provides a number of methods for adopting amendments. (See Figure 2.1) Amendments may be *proposed* by a two-thirds vote of each house of Congress or (if requested by two-thirds of the state legislatures) by a national convention called by Congress. They must be *ratified* by conventions in three-fourths of the states, or by three-fourths of the state legislatures (the choice is up to Congress).

The national convention has never been used; all amendments have been proposed by Congress. The most recent attempt occurred in the late 1980s, when 32 states of the needed 34 passed resolutions calling for a constitutional convention to draft a new amendment requiring a balanced budget. Only the Twenty-first Amendment, repealing Prohibition, was ratified by state conventions. The idea behind this one use of state conventions was that the state legislatures were still full of the same representatives who had passed Prohibition in the first place, and conventions seemed likely to be the fastest way to change it. A major reason that the national convention method has never been used to propose amendments is Congress's jealousy toward another body trespassing on its powers. Another is worry over how many other amendments might be proposed by such a convention. After all, the

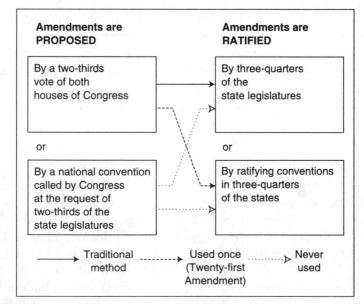

FIGURE 2.1
Amending the Constitution.

Constitution was written by an earlier runaway convention set up only to amend the Articles of Confederation.

Judicial Interpretation

If the amendment process is the least-used method of changing the Constitution, interpretations by the Supreme Court are probably the most common. Practically every part of the Constitution has been before the Court at some time or another. The justices have shaped and reshaped the document. Modern Supreme Court decisions have allowed Congress great scope in regulating the economy, prohibited legal segregation of races, allowed local communities to determine the limits of obscenity, and established "one man, one vote" as a constitutional principle governing election to the House of Representatives. The Supreme Court has also given practical meaning to general constitutional phrases such as "necessary and proper" (Article I, Section 8), "due process of law" (Amendments 5 and 14), and "unreasonable searches and seizures" (Amendment 4). No wonder the Supreme Court is sometimes called "a permanent constitutional convention."

Legislation

Although legislation is passed under the Constitution and does not change the basic document, Congress has been responsible for filling in most of the framework of government outlined by the Constitution. Congress has established all the federal courts below the Supreme Court. It has determined the size of both the House of Representatives and the Supreme Court. The cabinet and most of the boards and commissions in the executive branch have been created by congressional legislation. Most of the regulations and services we now take for granted, such as Social Security, have come from laws passed by Congress.

Custom

Custom is the most imprecise way in which the Constitution has changed yet one of the most widespread. Many practices accepted as constitutional are not actually mentioned in the document. The growth of political parties and their role in Congress, the presidential nominating conventions, the breakdown of an independent electoral college, and the committee system in Congress are just a few customary practices not covered by the Constitution.

Custom also has changed some practices that, at least on the surface, seem to have been clearly intended by the framers. The Eighth Amendment, forbidding "excessive bail," has not prevented courts from setting bail for serious offenses that is too high for the accused to raise. Although Congress has the right to declare war (Article II, Section 8), presidents have entered conflicts that looked very much like wars (Korea, Vietnam, Iraq, Afghanistan) without such a declaration. Customs also have been broken and reestablished by law. The custom that a president serves only two terms was started by Washington and cemented by Jefferson. Franklin D. Roosevelt broke the tradition with much debate by running for a third term in 1940, and then a fourth term four years later. The custom was made law in the Twenty-second Amendment, adopted in 1951, to keep FDR's example from being followed in the future.

Why Has the Constitution Survived?

How the Constitution has been changed does not entirely explain why it has survived. Indeed, many of the framers saw the Constitution as an experiment not likely to outlive their generation. Various explanations have been offered for why the Constitution has endured to become the oldest written constitution of any country.

The major reason it has lasted probably lies not in the Constitution itself but in the stability of American society. Upheavals like the Civil War, the Indian campaigns and massacres, and foreign wars all have been handled within the same constitutional structure. The Constitution has been made more democratic to include "out" groups, such as immigrants, African Americans, women, and the poor, that were originally excluded from political participation. The Constitution's emphasis on procedures has served it well through the wars and depressions as well as the peace and prosperity of various ages.

▌A British View on the Constitution's Survival

The late nineteenth-century British scholar and diplomat James Bryce believed the Constitution deserved "the veneration" bestowed on it. He thought much of its value came from the "political genius" of the Anglo-American race.

> The American Constitution is no exception to the rule that everything which has the power to win the obedience and respect of men must have its roots deep in the past and that the more slowly every institution has grown, so much the more enduring it is likely to prove. There is little in the Constitution that is absolutely new. There is much that is as old as Magna Carta.

Source: James Bryce, *The American Commonwealth*. New York: Macmillan, 1910, vol.1, p. 28.

Other explanations for the Constitution's durability focus on the document. One maintains that it is a work of genius. William Gladstone, the nineteenth-century British prime minister, described it as "the most wonderful work ever struck off at a given time by the brain and purpose of man." Incorporating centuries of English political traditions as well as the framers' own experience, the Constitution set out the principles and framework of government in concise, well-written phrases. (See "A British View on the Constitution's Survival.")

The shortness of the document (only some 7,000 words with all its amendments) is another major reason for its durability. Although it sets out the basic principles and structures of a government, the Constitution leaves much only generally stated or not mentioned at all. In a word, the Constitution is *vague*. Many of the most enduring constitutional phrases ("freedom of speech," "due process of law," "all laws which shall be necessary and proper," "privileges or immunities of citizens") have been applied differently at different times in our history. Other principles, such as majority rule and individual liberties, sometimes seem contradictory. It is left to the political players of each age to resolve the conflicts between groups claiming constitutional support. Ambiguity and flexibility have been the Constitution's major strengths in adapting to new political pressures and allowing people to reach compromises under competing principles.

CASE STUDY

Federalism Caught in a Storm:
The Katrina Disaster

On Monday morning, August 29, 2005, Hurricane Katrina hit the coast of Louisiana 63 miles southeast of New Orleans. Although missing the brunt of the storm, the city suffered one of the nation's worst natural disasters. Its levees collapsed, flooding much of the area. The failure of these flood walls reflected both shoddy engineering and an historic lack of political will to maintain them. The threat of a hurricane to a city built largely below sea level was well known, with the federal government four years before listing it as one of the three most catastrophic events

the country could face. But preparations remained, to say the least, inadequate.

In the days that followed the deluge, the response and conflicts of the different levels of government—federal, state, and local—would compound New Orleans's pain. Katrina would illustrate the inconsistencies, the politics, and the hazards surrounding modern federalism. Among the many failures was the failure of relations between leaders of the city, state, and nation.

ON THE GROUND

Katrina overwhelmed New Orleans. It left 80 percent of the city underwater, with no ground transportation, little shelter for those who lost their homes, 75,000 stranded—many on their roofs waiting for rescue—and masses of citizens, mostly poor, heading for the Superdome where food, water, and medicine were dwindling. While TV was showing the chaos and adding reports of crazed looters on the loose, local political leaders running on no sleep were trying to cope with a unique disaster. The mayor, Ray Nagin, who had waited until less than 24 hours before the storm struck to call for a mandatory evacuation, seemed shell-shocked.

On Monday evening President Bush telephoned Kathleen Blanco, Democratic governor of Louisiana. The desperate governor told the president that the worst had happened. "We need your help," she pleaded. "We need everything you've got." The vagueness in the request led the president to not respond with immediate actions. He privately regarded her as incompetent and worried that the partisan divisions between them would lead to the White House being blamed for the difficulties ahead. In the days that followed, administration spokesmen were notably upbeat in describing the situation in New Orleans as "going relatively well." Unfortunately the president was relying on a federal agency that was not up to the huge challenge.

FEMA, the Federal Emergency Management Agency, had been absorbed in the Homeland Security Agency created in a 2003 reorganization designed to elevate antiterrorist programs. This reduced the importance of disaster relief within the administration and hindered access to the White House. Further weakening FEMA was the appointment of Republican allies of the president to run the agency. Bush appointed his campaign manager as the head of FEMA, and when he resigned, the president passed on the position to a college friend with little experience in the field. Trained disaster relief experts tainted by service in the previous administration lost their jobs. FEMA was a bureaucracy crippled by cronyism.

Not surprisingly, both advanced planning and immediate relief efforts were poor. Frightened by reports of lawlessness, the head of FEMA on Monday actually advised emergency responders to *stay home* until requested by local authorities. The agency also turned down offers of support from other federal agencies because of its concern for security. Examples of incompetence were abundant. In early September, as thousands still awaited help, 600 firefighters from across the nation who had volunteered for rescue duties in New Orleans were taken to Atlanta to sit in a hotel listening to FEMA lectures on customer service and sexual harassment. "This is ridiculous," one yelled at a speaker.

At the same time, local leaders in New Orleans faced a situation where civilization seemed to have dissolved in the rising waters. Police deserted their posts or exercised authority arbitrarily, often violently. Buses were not available to transport evacuees out of the city— hundreds of school buses had been unthinkingly left in parking lots submerged by the flood—and control by local government was sporadic at best. Mayor Nagin avoided the governor in a state where the politics were described as "dysfunctional." Instead, the mayor spoke directly to White House officials about his city's needs. He used frequent news conferences to communicate to a national audience. The mayor, who was notably emotional during the days after the storm, soon left the city for Dallas for five days. Before that he had called into a radio talk show to declare to the levels of government above him, "Now, get off your asses and do something, and let's fix the biggest goddamn crisis in the history of this country."

SEND IN THE TROOPS

The need for troops to restore order and allow relief efforts seemed clear at the time. But this too got bogged down in the politics of federalism.

On Wednesday Governor Blanco had called the president requesting 40,000 troops. She expected that these would be mainly National Guard units officially under her control. The president requested that they be federalized, which would put them under the president's authority. Blanco did not think that this would help the rescue and relief efforts—which she felt that FEMA was already botching. The possibility that this would provide a public opportunity to scapegoat her for the post-Katrina mess undoubtedly figured into the calculation. Handing over responsibility for the troops to the president meant minimizing her own role. Why should she let George Bush play hero, leading the cavalry to the rescue?

The president may have had a similar view, seeing no reason why he should help a Democratic governor enhance her profile. (The issue of federalizing National Guard troops in neighboring Mississippi, where there was a friendly Republican governor, never came up.)

Though he had the authority, the president was reluctant to federalize Louisiana's troops and police without the governor's permission. Such an action would bring back memories of the 1950s and 1960s when southern governors had been forced to do that in school desegregation fights with Democratic presidents. He was also reluctant to send in regular army units because they were not allowed to perform domestic law enforcement. Mayor Nagin supported the president's increased role, but it was not a decision that the mayor could make.

Eventually, in a meeting held in Air Force One parked at New Orleans International Airport, the governor and president reached a private understanding. She refused to sign a document that would have handed over state control of the National Guard troops to the president. The president dispatched the troops anyway and Blanco maintained her authority over them. Only with the arrival of federal troops supplementing the state forces some five days after the storm could the immediate crisis be considered to have ended. It may have been that the widespread media reports of federal mismanagement of the rescue efforts motivated the president to reach an agreement.

AFTER THE DELUGE

"The infuriating, unmistakable and unnerving lesson of the continuing tragedy is the fundamental failure of government at all levels to protect its citizens, the most vulnerable chief among them."

Editorial, The Washington Post, *September 5, 2005.*

Blame for the inadequacy of the government's response to the Katrina disaster belongs on all three levels of the federal system. Neither the mayor nor the governor had adequately prepared for the disaster, nor had they plans or people in place to respond in the days following the flood. But the government in Washington cannot avoid a singular fact: It alone had the resources to meet the challenge. Whether it was troops, emergency responders, or relief supplies, the federal government had its hands on what was needed. State and local authorities were overwhelmed. They looked for support to the national government, which, because of mismanagement, as well as politics, was not in a position to quickly respond. Federalism complicated the efforts, but political leaders were ultimately responsible for the ineffective response.

WRAP-UP

Reflecting on the creation of the Constitution, we saw how the Founding Fathers drew from English political thought, the models of colonial government, and their own experiences with the Articles of Confederation in shaping the Constitution. The framers also were influenced by who they were. As a wealthy elite, they sought to establish a government that would further the public interests of the nation and their own private economic concerns. They divided into Federalists and Anti-Federalists over how strong the government should be and how individual rights would be best protected. Ratification and the addition of the Bill of Rights forged an uneasy agreement between the two groups.

The Constitution that has developed centers on four major principles: separation of powers and checks and balances, federalism, limited government, and judicial review. Although these principles remain fundamental, the Constitution has been changed vastly by four main methods: formal amendment, judicial interpretation, legislation, and custom. The changes it has undergone have enabled the Constitution to endure. Perhaps more important to its survival, however, is the stability of American society and the ambiguity of the document itself. The flexibility of the document can be seen in the modern application of the principle of federalism. Still, the question of "who's in charge" is at times not answered quickly or competently enough to prevent the disaster seen in New Orleans following Hurricane Katrina.

Does the ambiguity of the document mean that the Constitution, as a body of rules governing the American political game, is meaningless—that essentially it serves the interests of those in power, and its interpretations change only as those interests change? Perhaps. Certainly any document that has legitimized importing and enslaving most of its black residents, placing its citizens of Japanese descent in detention camps, allowing sweatshops and child labor, and presiding over great wealth alongside extreme poverty has much to answer for. Is the Constitution a grab bag of obsolete principles used to rationalize domination by the few?

As Chapter 1 made clear, politics is not primarily about words—it is about power and ideals. We can't blame a body of principles and procedures for the power or lack of power, for the ideals or lack of ideals of the players in the game. All great historical documents, from the Bible to the Constitution, have been applied very differently by leaders at different times.

More than the rules of the game, then, the Constitution stands as a symbol of the ideals of a people. But it is a symbol with power. That a president is accused of violating the law does mean that he has to answer to impeachment charges in Congress. That people have a constitutional right to elect representatives can change what laws are passed and whether the government continues an unpopular war. That the press has the right to report and publish officials' mistakes—from a Watergate break-in of opposition party headquarters to WikiLeaks pictures of war crimes—does affect whether voters keep an administration in office. Even the hypocrisy of politicians in bowing to principles they may wish to ignore shows the strength of the symbol.

Yet the meaning of the principles in the Constitution must ultimately rest on the relationships in the political game. The *right* to vote is meaningless without the *will* to vote and someone to vote for. Freedom of speech means nothing if no one tolerates or expresses informed dissent. Judicial safeguards, such as the right to a lawyer, could be lost (and indeed were ignored in the government's treatment of accused terrorists) without anyone changing a word of the Constitution. Power without principle may be blind, but principle without power is crippled.

The rules of this game, then, are not fixed or unchanging. Though written in the traditions of the past, they live in the politics of the present. They are not only historical guides but future goals as well. Therefore, they remain unfinished, as must any constitution setting out to "secure the Blessings of Liberty to ourselves and our Posterity."

THOUGHT QUESTIONS

1. How did the Constitution, as written by the framers, reflect the politics of the time and their need to resolve sectional differences? Give examples of the impact of these politics in how each branch of government is set up.
2. Could the Constitution be adopted today? How would the drafting process be different? What might be changed in the document?
3. How effective are the political structures set up by the Constitution in dealing with contemporary problems? Do the goals of efficiency and democracy in the Constitution work against each other?
4. "Americans can afford optimism partly because their institutions, including the Constitution, were conceived by men who thought tragically." Comment.
5. How important in the bungled response to the flooding of New Orleans was the federal divisions in government? Could competent leaders have overcome the obstacles in federalism?

SUGGESTED READINGS

Beard, Charles A. *An Economic Interpretation of the Constitution of the United States.* New York: Macmillan, 1935. Pb.
    The famous criticism of the framers' economic motivations in writing the Constitution.
Dahl, Robert. *How Democratic Is the American Constitution?* New Haven, CT: Yale University Press, 2001.
    An insightful, short read by a noted political scientist that discusses the problems of the Constitution and why the framers wrote it the way they did.
Eggers, Dave. *Zeitoun.* New York: Vintage, 2010, Pb.
    A novelist writes an alarming nonfiction tale of how badly, and illegally, one man was treated by law enforcement officials in the aftermath of Katrina.
Ellis, Joseph J. *Founding Brothers: The Revolutionary Generation.* New York: Vintage Books, 2000. Pb.
    Well-written Pulitzer Prize–winning stories of the flawed but fascinating fraternity of men who unexpectedly made the new American republic work.
Green, John. *The Constitution, the Articles, and Federalism: Crash Course US History #8*—YouTube, March 21, 2013. www.youtube.com/watch?v=bO7FQsCcbD8
    A bit caffeinated but a funny, quick review of at least some of the history around the drafting of the Constitution.
Hamilton, Alexander, James Madison, and John Jay. *The Federalist Papers.* New York: New American Library, 1961.
    The classic work on what the framers thought about their Constitution.

CHAPTER 3

The Executive Branch: The Presidency and Bureaucracy

Presidents are the superstars of the American political game. Although the head of just one of the three branches of the federal government, the president is the only official—along with the vice president—elected by the entire country. He (all men, so far) stands as the representative of the government and, in times of crisis, as a symbol to unite the nation. Yet the presidency is an intensely political office, the target of partisan attacks and fenced in by the powers given by the Constitution to other branches and players in the federal system of government.

At times Americans have idolized their president. He may represent the country's belief in its religious mission as "the last best hope of mankind" and is expected to act for the good of the nation. All the while he must stay popular with voters who see him as "one of the folks," both king and kin. These expectations clash with realities: the limited executive power granted by the Constitution, the reluctance of public and political opinion to follow where he leads, and the record of deceptions and mistakes by modern chief executives. The result is often presidents who disappoint.

Not surprisingly Americans swing back and forth in how powerful they want their presidents. In times of crisis, people demand strong leadership, yet this often leads to popular concerns about the consequences of that strength. In more peaceful periods, the call is heard for a less vigorous executive, an inactivity that is soon dismissed as weakness. Steering between popular impatience with delays in economic recovery or political reforms and the fear of concentrated government power, presidents need to choose. Whatever choices they make, presidents will be saddled with responsibility for the results, both good and bad. (See "Presidents on the Limits of the President.")

Modern presidents have faced this tension between great expectations and limited powers with varying success. Often they enter office by contrasting themselves with their predecessors. Underlying Richard Nixon's resignation in 1974 was the public's fear of the president's growing—and illegal—use of his authority, revealed by the Watergate scandal. Distancing himself from Nixon, a more open Jimmy Carter fell victim to the popular view that the president was too weak to solve the country's problems of American hostages in Iran, gas shortages, and inflation. Ronald Reagan brought a smiling conservatism to the office. His efforts to extend the powers of the office in order to limit the growth of the federal government seemed to achieve more, at least in raising the popularity of his Republican Party. Inheriting the optimism of the Reagan years, George Bush Sr.'s low-key concentration on governing proved popular at first and less so later on.

Presidents on the Limits of the President

Martin Van Buren

"As to the Presidency, the two happiest days of my life were the entrance upon the office and my surrender of it."

Abraham Lincoln

"I claim not to have controlled events, but confess plainly that events controlled me."

Harry S Truman

"The people can never understand why the President does not use his supposedly great power to make 'em behave. Well, all the president is, is a glorified public relations man who spends his time flattering, kissing, and kicking people to get them to do what they are supposed to do anyway."

John F. Kennedy

"Mothers all want their sons to grow up to be president, but they don't want them to become politicians in the process."

Lyndon Baines Johnson

"The presidency has made every man who occupied it, no matter how small, bigger than he was . . . and no matter how big, not big enough for its demands."

Barack Obama

"Somebody noted to me that by the time something reaches my desk, that means it's really hard. Because if it were easy, somebody else would have made the decision and somebody else would have solved it."

President Bill Clinton, with his populist charm, shaped an administration that emphasized youth and change. While bogged down in scandals and investigations, Clinton was propelled by a prosperous economy, the excesses of his opponents, and his own political skills. George W. Bush projected a more businesslike leadership that didn't quite remove the doubts about the disputed 2000 election and his intellect. The 9/11 attacks silenced dissent in a flurry of patriotism. But after winning a close reelection in 2004, Bush's popularity suffered from questionable wars in Iraq and Afghanistan, his own tough-guy image, and a financial panic that dragged down the economy. The 2008 election was a striking rebuke of his presidency.

President Barack Obama inherited presidential leadership of a nation pessimistic about the future and suffering the worst recession since the Great Depression of the 1930s. At first the new president proclaimed a sharp break with the past. He emphasized change not just in politics but in the debate over politics, emphasizing a bipartisan approach to the challenges facing the nation. Yet for all his successes—from economic recovery to comprehensive health care—he failed to bridge the divisions of a polarized politics. Obama served as a liberal pragmatic leader adapting to the very real limits that public opinion, Republican opponents, and the Constitution placed on his office. It was enough to win him reelection but not enough to overcome the gridlocked politics of the country.

This chapter is about the president and the executive branch he leads. The growth of the presidency starts from the limited powers granted to the office by the Constitution. Next, we will discuss the different approaches to being president and the various roles of the office. Then there are the departments of the federal bureaucracy under the president and the problems of controlling the bureaucracy. Finally, a case study looks at the president under the worst of circumstances, the days following September 11, 2001.

The President and the Constitution

The Constitution in Article II grants a president far less power and far fewer duties than it gives Congress in Article I. Nevertheless the opening sentence of the article ("The executive Power shall be vested in a President of the United States of America") and other broad phrases ("he shall take Care that the Laws be faithfully executed") have been used by presidents to justify enlarging their powers. As we will see, presidential practice has vastly expanded the Constitution's ideas of executive powers.

In setting requirements for the office, the Constitution states that the president must be at least 35 years old, a resident of the United States for 14 years, and a native-born citizen. The president can be removed by impeachment or, because of the Twenty-fifth Amendment, if he is disabled. His term of office is fixed at four years. Under the Twenty-second Amendment, passed in 1951, presidents are limited to two terms.

During the last months of his final term, the president often is called a *lame duck*: Because he cannot be reelected, his influence—and his accountability—are lessened. For political reasons, the term often is expanded to label presidents in their last term as being powerless, as Republicans tried to do to President Obama in 2014 following his difficulties in implementing Obamacare. Strictly speaking, only between the election in November 2016 and his successor's inauguration in January 2017 would President Obama be a lame duck.

The Electoral College

Presidents are not chosen by direct popular elections. All the votes across the United States are not added up on Election Day, with the candidate receiving the most declared the winner. Rather, presidents gain office through the *Electoral College*. Each state is granted as many electors—members of the Electoral College—as it has senators and representatives combined (the District of Columbia gets three votes). After a presidential election, the votes *within each state* are added up, and the candidate with the most votes receives *all* that state's votes in the Electoral College (except for Maine and Nebraska, which do not use this "winner-take-all" system). If any candidate has a national majority of Electoral College votes—270, which is 50 percent plus 1—he or she becomes president. If no candidate wins a majority—because several candidates have split the votes—the Constitution provides that the election will be decided by a majority vote in the House of Representatives, with each state delegation casting one vote.

Sometimes the presidential electoral system does not work very well. Back in 1800 and 1824, the House of Representatives had to decide on a president because no candidate received a majority of the vote. In 1876 Democrat Samuel Tilden lost to Rutherford Hayes when a Republican-dominated Electoral Commission awarded the Republican the election even though Tilden had won the popular vote. Then in 2000 Al Gore won the popular vote by over 500,000 votes yet lost the Electoral College, and the presidency, to George W. Bush by 271 to 267. It was an election that came down to a difference of a few hundred votes in Florida and a contested recount halted by the U.S. Supreme Court.

In an unusually close race like 2000, the messiness of an election is exposed to public view. This mess includes the states determining their own election laws as well as designing and supervising the ballots. It also includes the Electoral College.

A result of compromises at the Constitutional Convention, the Electoral College reinforces federalism by strengthening the smaller states. It also forces campaigns in the general election to focus on about a dozen large "swing" states that, because neither party is sure of dominating the vote, can determine the outcome. The Electoral College was designed to filter the prejudices of eighteenth-century voters. The development of political parties (see Chapter 7) has undercut the purpose of the college, for electors are now pledged to one party's candidate at the time of the elections. After the 2000 election, there were calls for a constitutional amendment to replace the "outmoded" Electoral College with a direct popular vote. Since many states and interests benefit from the present system, these voices for change quickly faded.

Vice President

The major constitutional duties of the vice president are to preside over the Senate and to succeed the president if the office should become vacant. (The Speaker of the House of Representatives and the president *pro tem* of the Senate are next in line.) Traditionally the vice presidency has been seen as a limited, frustrating office. John Nance Garner, Franklin Roosevelt's vice president, commented that his position was "not worth a pitcher of warm spit." But this view is out of date. Just the fact that seven vice presidents became president in the twentieth century has increased the importance of the office.

Today scholars speak of a "new vice presidency." Vice presidents such as Al Gore, Dick Cheney, and Joe Biden have played key roles in their administrations. They have represented the chief executive in visits overseas, lobbied for him in Congress, campaigned in midterm elections, and served as key presidential advisers. Al Gore was treated as a partner of President Clinton and became the president's chosen successor.

George W. Bush's vice president, Dick Cheney, was probably the most powerful in the nation's history. With long experience as a Washington insider, he made the vice president's office the center of a web of like-minded conservative officials throughout the executive branch. Cheney was known for his muscle in moving the Bush administration toward hard-line positions on national security issues, many of which became unpopular by the end of Bush's two terms.

Joe Biden took office promising to shrink the office closer to its traditional role. Biden saw the vice presidency as an "adviser in chief" to the president rather than running what Democrats referred to as Cheney's separate "shadow operation." Soon Biden was labeled the second most influential figure in the government because of his personal chemistry with the president. Biden's decades of experience in the Senate helped make him the White House's main link with Congress, especially on international issues. The successful negotiations in late 2012 between the White House and congressional Republicans to avoid the "fiscal cliff" ended up being conducted by the vice president. Less useful was the veep's tendency to speak bluntly (and "off message") to the press. In Obama's second term, Biden was widely rumored to have ambitions to succeed his boss as president, rumors that he did little to deny.

History of the Presidency

Forty-three men have been president of the United States, from George Washington, who took office in 1789, to Barack Obama, who became the nation's first African American president on January 20, 2009, and was sworn in for a second term four years later. (See Tables 3.1 and 3.2.) Between the two, the influence and duties of the presidency have expanded considerably, if not always in a pattern of constant growth.

Most members of the Constitutional Convention in 1787 did not see a *political* role for the president. They pictured the president as a gentleman-aristocrat—probably because they had George Washington in mind—who would stand above politics as a symbol of national unity. He would be selected by an Electoral College to ensure that he was not dependent on popular support. Congress, not the president, was to be the leading branch. Yet strong chief executives confronting national problems soon increased these powers, although at times less assertive presidents and popular sentiment have reduced executive power. In the twentieth century, presidential power has irregularly expanded as a result of wars and domestic crises, such as economic depression.

George Washington sent troops to put down a rebellion among farmers in western Pennsylvania who were angered by a tax placed on whiskey. Washington's action in the Whiskey Rebellion was later claimed as the precedent for a president's *residual power* (also called *inherent power*)—powers not spelled out in the Constitution but that are necessary for the president to be able to carry out other responsibilities. The third president, Thomas Jefferson, had fought against establishing a strong executive in the Constitution. Yet as president, he expanded the powers of the office. By negotiating and signing the Louisiana Purchase, gaining the approval of Congress only after the fact (perhaps inevitable in an age of slow communication), Jefferson weakened the principle of checks and balances. Congress played a minor role in doubling the size of the country and then couldn't easily reverse the president's action once it had been taken.

TABLE 3.1 PRESIDENTS OF THE UNITED STATES

Year	President	Party	Year	President	Party
1789	George Washington		1901	Theodore Roosevelt[a]	Republican
1792	George Washington		1904	Theodore Roosevelt	Republican
1796	John Adams	Federalist	1908	William H. Taft	Republican
1800	Thomas Jefferson	Democratic-Republican	1912	Woodrow Wilson	Democratic
1804	Thomas Jefferson	Democratic-Republican	1916	Woodrow Wilson	Democratic
1808	James Madison	Democratic-Republican	1920	Warren G. Harding	Republican
1812	James Madison	Democratic-Republican	1923	Calvin Coolidge[a]	Republican
1816	James Monroe	Democratic-Republican	1924	Calvin Coolidge	Republican
1820	James Monroe	Democratic-Republican	1928	Herbert C. Hoover	Republican
1824	John Quincy Adams	Democratic-Republican	1932	Franklin D. Roosevelt	Democratic
1828	Andrew Jackson	Democratic	1936	Franklin D. Roosevelt	Democratic
1832	Martin Van Buren	Democratic	1940	Franklin D. Roosevelt	Democratic
1836	Andrew Jackson	Democratic	1944	Franklin D. Roosevelt	Democratic
1840	William H. Harrison	Whig	1945	Harry S. Truman[a]	Democratic
1841	John Tyler[a]	Whig	1948	Harry S. Truman	Democratic
1844	James K. Polk	Democratic	1952	Dwight D. Eisenhower	Republican
1848	Zachary Taylor	Whig	1956	Dwight D. Eisenhower	Republican
1850	Millard Fillmore[a]	Whig	1960	John F. Kennedy	Democratic
1852	Franklin Pierce	Democratic	1963	Lyndon B. Johnson[a]	Democratic
1856	James Buchanan	Democratic	1964	Lyndon B. Johnson	Democratic
1860	Abraham Lincoln	Republican	1968	Richard M. Nixon	Republican
1864	Abraham Lincoln	Republican	1972	Richard M. Nixon	Republican
1865	Andrew Johnson[a]	Democratic (Union)	1974	Gerald R. Ford[a]	Republican
1868	Ulysses S. Grant	Republican	1976	James E. Carter	Democratic
1872	Ulysses S. Grant	Republican	1980	Ronald W. Reagan	Republican
1876	Rutherford B. Hayes	Republican	1984	Ronald W. Reagan	Republican
1880	James A. Garfield	Republican	1988	George H. Bush	Republican
1881	Chester A. Arthur[a]	Republican	1992	William J. Clinton	Democratic
1884	Grover Cleveland	Democratic	1996	William J. Clinton	Democratic
1888	Benjamin Harrison	Republican	2000	George W. Bush	Republican
1892	William McKinley	Democratic	2004	George W. Bush	Republican
1896	Grover Cleveland	Democratic	2008	Barack H. Obama	Democrat
1900	William McKinley	Republican	2012	Barack H. Obama	Democrat

TABLE 3.2 VICE PRESIDENTS OF THE UNITED STATES

Year	Vice President	Party	Year	Vice President	Party
1789	John Adams	Federalist	1908	James S. Sherman	Republican
1792	John Adams	Federalist	1912	Thomas R. Marshall	Democratic
1796	Thomas Jefferson	Democratic-Republican	1916	Thomas R. Marshall	Democratic
1800	Aaron Burr	Democratic-Republican	1920	Calvin Coolidge	Republican
1804	George Clinton	Democratic-Republican	1924	Charles G. Dawes	Republican
1808	George Clinton	Democratic-Republican	1928	Charles Curtis	Republican
1812	Elbridge Gerry	Democratic-Republican	1932	John N. Garner	Democratic
1816	Daniel D. Tompkins	Democratic-Republican	1936	John N. Garner	Democratic
1820	Daniel D. Tompkins	Democratic-Republican	1940	Henry A. Wallace	Democratic
1824	John C. Calhoun	Democratic-Republican	1944	Harry S Truman	Democratic
1828	John C. Calhoun	Democratic	1948	Alben W. Barkley	Democratic
1832	Martin Van Buren	Democratic	1952	Richard M. Nixon	Republican
1836	Richard M. Johnson	Democratic	1956	Richard M. Nixon	Republican
1840	John Tyler	Whig	1960	Lyndon B. Johnson	Democratic
1844	George M. Dallas	Democratic	1964	Hubert H. Humphrey	Democratic
1848	Millard Fillmore	Whig	1968	Spiro T. Agrew	Republican
1852	William R. King	Democratic	1972	Spiro T. Agrew	Republican
1856	John C. Breckinridge	Democratic	1973	Gerald R. Ford[b]	Republican
1860	Hannibal Hamlin	Republican	1974	Nelson A. Rockefeller[b]	Republican
1864	Andrew Johnson	Democratic (Union)	1976	Walter F. Mondale	Democratic
1868	Schuyler Colfax	Republican	1980	George H. Bush	Republican
1872	Henry Wilson	Republican	1984	George H. Bush	Republican
1876	William A. Wheeler	Republican	1988	Dan Quayle	Republican
1880	Chester A. Arthur	Republican	1992	Albert Gore, Jr.	Democratic
1884	Thomas A. Hendricks	Democratic	1996	Albert Gore, Jr.	Democratic
1888	Levi P. Morton	Republican	2000	Richard Cheney	Republican
1892	Adlai E. Stevenson	Democratic	2004	Richard Cheney	Republican
1896	Garrett A. Hobart	Republican	2008	Joe Biden	Democrat
1900	Theodore Roosevelt	Republican	2012	Joe Biden	Democrat
1904	Charles W. Fairbanks	Republican			

[a]Vice presidents who became president on the death or the resignation (in the case of Richard Nixon) of their predecessor.

Abraham Lincoln, the sixteenth president, disregarded parts of the Constitution when he led the North in the Civil War. Lincoln raised armies, spent money that Congress had not appropriated, freed slaves in the South, suspended certain civil rights, and generally did what he felt was necessary to preserve the Union. He even sent money and troops to promote a rebellion in Virginia that created West Virginia, all without involvement by Congress. Congress later approved these actions, but the initiative was clearly with the president.

This pattern of crisis leadership continued into the twentieth century. Most visible were aggressive presidents like Theodore Roosevelt, who pushed his pro-environment and antimonopoly policies, and Woodrow Wilson, who led the country into World War I. They were followed, however, by a series of weak presidents in the 1920s (Harding, Coolidge, Hoover), reflecting a national mood in the country that favored less government activity presided over by passive chief executives.

Franklin D. Roosevelt's coming into office in 1933 confronted the Great Depression of the 1930s. FDR's tenure saw a president taking virtually full responsibility for the continual shaping of both domestic and foreign policy. His administration's programs in response to the Depression (called the *New Deal*), and his command of the United States in the international role it would play during and after World War II, firmly established the strong leadership patterns we find today in the presidency. FDR influenced the shape of the office more than anyone else in the twentieth century. Thus, Franklin D. Roosevelt is called the first modern president.

Types of Presidents

This growth of the presidency has not been a straight-line expansion of presidential powers. There have been cycles in which the power of the office has waxed and waned, reflecting presidents' personalities and national politics. To simplify matters, we will discuss three general approaches that presidents have adopted toward the office and see which chief executives fit into each category.

Buchanan Presidents

The first category is called *Buchanan presidents*, after James Buchanan, known mainly for his refusal to end southern secession by force in 1860. Presidents in this group view their office as purely administrative: The president is aloof from politics and depends on leadership from Congress. Buchanan presidents adopt a *custodial* view of presidential powers: The president is limited to those powers expressly granted to him in the Constitution. Otherwise, they argue, there would be no limits on presidential power. These chief executives accept the restrictive boundaries set by public and political opinion and the weaknesses of their own party. Presidents who have followed this approach generally have been less active chief executives. They include William Howard Taft, Warren Harding, Calvin Coolidge, and Herbert Hoover—Republican presidents in the early twentieth century.

Lincoln Presidents

Second, there are the *Lincoln presidents*. In this approach, the president is an active politician, often rallying the country in a crisis. Abraham Lincoln did so in the Civil War; Theodore Roosevelt did it later when he moved to restrain the large business monopolies called trusts. In this century, the Lincoln president also originates much of the legislation Congress considers, he leads public opinion, and he is the major source of the country's political goals.

Lincoln presidents do not interpret the Constitution as narrowly as do Buchanan presidents. In their view, the presidency is a *stewardship*; its only limits are those explicitly mentioned in the Constitution. The president's powers, then, are as large as his own assertive political skills, his ability to persuade other political actors and to lead public opinion. Following this approach have been activist presidents such as Andrew Jackson, Theodore Roosevelt, Franklin Roosevelt, Lyndon Johnson, and Ronald Reagan.

Eisenhower Presidents

The first two approaches to the presidency were outlined by Theodore Roosevelt, who used them, as the energetic twenty-fifth president, to justify his own expansion of the office. Another style of presidential leadership since then is a combination of the first two called the *Eisenhower president*. While General Eisenhower was a skilled leader, he concealed his very real quiet involvement in political business. He delegated responsibility widely, which allowed others to take the blame for policy failures while he preserved his own reputation of being "above" politics. His sense of himself as a war hero seeking national unity limited his drive to maximize power in the White House. This *hidden-hand leadership* hurt Eisenhower's ability to transfer his personal popularity to his party or his chosen successor in 1960—his vice president, Richard Nixon. Many recent presidents since Eisenhower have tried to copy his pose of remaining aloof from partisan politics, with less success.

Modern Presidents

While presidents never fall into exact boxes, modern presidents have leaned toward activism. Lyndon Johnson sought not only to represent a national consensus but also to create and guide this coalition as well. President Johnson, a master politician, was known for his midnight phone calls and political arm-twisting to gain support for his proposals. Richard Nixon tried to create an image of the presidency being above politics while using his powers as president for partisan, and sometimes illegal, activities, climaxing in the Watergate scandal. After Nixon's resignation in 1974, Gerald Ford's served a restrained, brief presidency—moving over from the nation's first nonelected vice president, selected by Nixon and confirmed by Congress under the Twenty-fifth Amendment.

Jimmy Carter, though a hardworking, honest manager, was criticized for his lack of political leadership. Trained as an engineer, Carter spent time privately submerged in policy details. By the end of his term, a widespread feeling that national problems—gas lines and inflation at home, Soviet aggression in Afghanistan, and hostages in Iran—were not being solved led to the Democrat's defeat for reelection in 1980.

Ronald Reagan came to the presidency from a career as an actor and two terms as a conservative Republican governor of California. He excelled in communicating through the media while delegating broad powers to subordinates. His relaxed, sunny attitude toward the office and his advanced age (77 when he left office) led critics to accuse him of being a "nine-to-five" president. Reagan's public relations and political skills led to decreases in social programs, increases in defense spending, and large tax cuts. His hard line toward the Soviet Union may have hastened the fall of communism in Eastern Europe and Russia. His well-publicized state funeral in 2004 celebrated Reagan's popularity decades after he had been in office. (See "Hollywood and Presidents.")

Reagan's support helped elect his vice president, George Bush Sr., to the presidency in 1988. This Bush I administration had two faces—the one looking out to foreign affairs beamed with success; the domestic side paled in comparison. Foreign policy gave Bush notable victories, some of his own doing (pushing Iraq out of Kuwait), and some with a mix of others' efforts (the end of the Cold War). His claims of being the "education president" and the "environmental president" added to complaints that he neglected domestic issues. A stalled economy contributed to the loss of his 1992 reelection bid.

Bill Clinton brought a youthful zeal for campaigning to the White House plus 12 years' experience as governor of Arkansas. With Democrats in control of both houses of Congress in his first two

Hollywood and Presidents

How much are presidents part of America's mass culture? Just go to the movies.

Strong leadership was a theme in Hollywood's favorable view of chief executives, from D. W. Griffith's classic *Birth of a Nation* (1915) showing Lincoln as a symbol of peace, through the adventure story of Jack Kennedy in World War II in *PT-109* (1963), to the fantasy fighter pilot/president in *Independence Day* (1996) successfully beating back an alien invasion.

However, mostly fictional and mostly weak presidents have also surfaced. Satires have bumbling presidents in Stanley Kubrick's *Dr. Strangelove* (1964), Jack Nicholson being Jack Nicholson in *Mars Attacks* (1996), and Chris Rock in *Head of State* (2003).

With Bill Clinton came youth, good intentions, and sex appeal in Hollywood's view of the White House. In *The American President* (1995), an attractive widower turns liberal and wins the girl. *Primary Colors* (1997) tracked Clinton's campaign and flaws, with insights on the trade-offs of politics. The George W. Bush presidency showed up in the disaster film *The Day after Tomorrow* (2004) with a nasty vice president and a detached president not doing much about global warming, until it was too late. TV had the hit series *West Wing*, (1999–2006) featuring a liberal president supported by a dedicated, mostly idealistic staff struggling with Washington and each other. A more recent, more cynical view surfaced in the online Netflix series *House of Cards* (2013-14-15) where Kevin Spacey literally kills to get from Congress to the White House, manipulates a naïve president and connives his way to the presidential throne. Stay tuned.

years in office, he passed drastic deficit reductions, but his failure to overhaul health care in 1994 followed by the Republican takeover of Congress restrained his populism. A moderate "New Democrat," Clinton compromised with Republicans in areas like welfare reform while denouncing their cuts in social programs. In his second term, Clinton used the president's "bully pulpit" to push issues like race and a peace agreement in the Middle East. While handicapped by scandals—and character lapses—his public approval remained high enough to defeat Republican efforts to impeach him. Neither his popularity nor the nation's prosperity was enough to elect his vice president, Al Gore, in 2000. (See "Presidential Mama's Boys.")

The man who was elected, George W. Bush, took office as the first president since 1888 to lose the popular vote. Bush's controversial election cast early doubts on his presidency. These low expectations elevated Bush's achievements. He won broad income tax reductions,

Presidential Mama's Boys

One overlooked part of many presidents' emotional makeup has been their extraordinarily close relationship with their mothers. Harry Truman had a portrait of his mom hung in the White House, and Calvin Coolidge died carrying a picture of his mother. In Richard Nixon's Watergate farewell address, he called his mother a "saint." Lyndon Johnson declared his mother "the strongest person I ever knew." Sara Roosevelt rented an apartment in Cambridge to be near Franklin at college. Years later when some New York political bosses asked him to run for office, he responded, "I'd like to talk with my mother about it first." George W. Bush is described as inheriting his mother's decisive good versus bad instincts. A recent biography of Barack Obama concludes that he "adored and idealized his mother" and quotes him as saying, "What is best in me I owe to her."

It is no accident that most of our presidents were their mother's first son. These strong, often religious women dominated the raising of their favorite boys, pushing them to overcome the failures of their husbands. Alas, our presidents' fathers were not great role models: Truman's lost his farm in speculation; both Eisenhower's and Nixon's dads were unsuccessful storekeepers; and Reagan's dad had a drinking problem, as did Bill Clinton's stepfather. Obama was abandoned as an infant by his Kenyan father, and the president's memoir revolves around his search for a father and a missing identity.

The sons of these laid-back fathers and dynamic mothers were hardly sissies. Rather, they became self-confident men who took their mothers' belief in them and turned it into real success.

---

education reform, and Medicare expansion. By decreasing taxes and increasing government programs, Bush, not surprisingly, caused a large rise in the federal deficit.

The 9/11 attacks elevated Bush to center stage in rallying the nation for the war on terrorism. An apparent quick victory in Afghanistan bolstered his administration's aggressive and false justifications for invading Iraq. Despite questions about his "gut" judgments, President Bush won reelection in 2004 by mobilizing his conservative base, attacking the Democratic nominee John Kerry for weak-kneed leadership, and raising fears of another terrorist attack. But his second term was throttled by doubts about the continuing war in Iraq and his failure to pass domestic proposals, like Social Security reform. The Democrats' takeover of Congress in the 2006 midterm elections underlined his decreasing popularity. Wall Street's financial meltdown in 2008 and Republican lobbyists' scandals only added to the departing president's problems.

The Obama Presidency

It would be difficult to invent a less likely president than Barack
Hussein Obama. Literally an African American—the child of a Kansas
mother and a Kenyan father who abandoned his two-year-old son—
Obama was raised in modest circumstances largely by his grandparents,
yet he made it to Harvard Law School and the Illinois State Legislature.
Still in his mid-forties, he had just been elected to the U.S. Senate from
Illinois in 2004, when the talk began about a possible run for the White
House. How did this freshman senator become president? The political setting in 2008 included a battered Republican Party, an unpopular
president, and a collapsing economy, making any Democratic candidate
a likely winner. In gaining the Democratic nomination, Obama mount-
ed a disciplined insurgent campaign, raised record amounts of money,
energized volunteers nationwide, and creatively used the Internet. His
eloquent message of change was in sync with the political climate and
his own outsider persona. Obama came across as a cautious intellectual
who could both inspire and reassure audiences.

In part because he was so unlike any president who had come
before him, in part because he took office in a time of crisis, and in
part because of his own soaring rhetoric of "Change We Can Believe
In," many expected that he would transform the presidency, much like
Franklin Roosevelt during the Depression of the 1930s. By his second
term, despite accomplishments ranging from bringing the economy
back from a meltdown to passing health care reform, and an impressive
reelection vote, Obama had fulfilled neither the hopes of supporters
nor the fears of opponents.

A pragmatist, President Obama worked within the system he inherited, accepting the political boundaries set by Congress and public opinion. He set broad policy frameworks while leaving it to Congress to manage the details of financial reform or deficit reduction or immigration. Once his Democratic party lost control of the House of Representatives, he accepted paralysis in Congress and polarization in the country. His second term stressed independent executive actions in improving education, protecting the environment, and reducing foreign conflicts. Obama could take credit for diminishing the threat from radical Islam while winding down the wars in Iraq and Afghanistan. But he benefited more from an accelerating economic recovery, a diminishing deficit and the nation's energy independence, all of which he could only claim limited responsibility for.

If his second term seemed to bog down in partisan arguments over the budget, Obamacare, government missteps, and unresolved overseas negotiations, then this sense of stalled leadership was nothing new. A president was once again being blamed for national challenges that seemed beyond his capacity to resolve. As presidential scholar George Edwards notes, the political system "is too complicated, power too decentralized, and interests too diverse for one person, no matter how extraordinary, to dominate."

A President's Power Hats

The reasons behind the evolution of the presidency lie both in the people who have been president and the powers of the office. In his well-known book *Presidential Politics*, Richard Neustadt argued that essentially "presidential power is the power to persuade." Presidents, occupying an office of weak Constitutional powers, have to struggle to exercise leadership in government. A president must bargain with bureaucrats, legislators, and the public to convince them that his interests are the same as theirs. Personality skills are essential for these individuals to achieve significant changes in government policy. Not surprisingly, our great presidents are our best politicians.

But Neustadt's famous focus 50 years ago on the importance of personality has been added to by discussions on the increasing powers of the president's office. Presidents *can* create policies on their own by exercising unilateral powers that have the weight of law. Executive agreements, proclamations, national security directives, reorganization plans, and appointments have grown in the last decades. These very real powers have allowed presidents to negotiate international agreements, create administrative agencies, tighten or relax environmental regulations, and pursue the dirty details of the "war on terror," all without Congress's involvement. As unilateral actions, they have raised fears about the rise of an "imperial presidency" undermining the Constitution's checks and balances.

The vigorous use of personal persuasion and executive powers arises from a basic dilemma: people expect presidents to accomplish far more than their traditional powers permit. The public's increasing demands on government inevitably focus on the president. When a national problem arises—declining student test scores, gun violence, unemployment, global warming, or government wiretapping—the president is expected to respond. He is also legally required to handle a number of important duties, such as presenting the federal government's annual budget to Congress. In fulfilling these responsibilities, the president wears six different hats, often more than one at a time.

Chief of State

The president is the symbolic chief of *state* as well as the head of *government*. (In England, the two positions are separate: The queen is chief of state, symbol of the nation; the prime minister is head of government, exercising the real power.) As *chief of state*, the president performs ceremonial functions ranging from throwing out the ball to start the All-Star game to shaking hands with the pope when visiting the Vatican. Because of this role, many people see the president as representing the nation and as blessed with extraordinary abilities. This perception raises public expectations, often unrealistically, but also bestows a political advantage. The difficulty in separating ceremonial from political actions was evident after September 11. As chief of state, President Bush rallied the nation at patriotic and religious events.

Chief Executive

On his first day in office, President Obama issued rules making it easier for the public to get information from government agencies. The new chief executive traded a presumption of secrecy for a presumption of disclosure in releasing government documents. This proclamation of openness didn't stop the president from vigorously prosecuting bureaucrats—some six in his first term, more than all previous administrations combined—for leaking classified information to the press. Both actions showed Obama wearing a president's second hat, presiding over the huge federal bureaucracy in the executive branch. His authority as *chief executive* comes from Article II of the Constitution, which states, "The executive Power shall be vested in a President of the United States of America." Executive power in this instance means the ability to carry out or execute the laws. By 2012 this meant the president headed a bureaucracy spending $3.8 trillion a year (a record amount) and employing about 2.2 million civilians (the same as in 1990). The federal government, with revenues larger than those of the top 40 U.S. corporations combined, ranks as the world's largest administrative organization.

Presidents can issue *executive orders* that set guidelines for federal agencies and have the force of law. They do not require approval by Congress, and their increased use by recent presidents (to around 50 a year) has led to worries that executive authority has been increasing at the expense of the legislature. George W. Bush used orders to pursue the war on terrorism, including rules on wiretaps and interrogating enemy prisoners. President Obama signed executive orders when legislation was blocked by Republican votes in Congress, including work permits for young undocumented immigrants.

Presidential candidates in every election inevitably pledge to restrain, reduce, and reform the bureaucracy. They follow a bipartisan tradition of promising to get government "off the backs of the American people." Most presidents, including the current one, have found that accomplishing their political goals required an ample bureaucracy and budget. They have acted and spent accordingly.

Chief Diplomat

In his 2002 State of the Union address, President Bush aggressively condemned Iran, Iraq, and North Korea as an "axis of evil." President Obama speaking in late 2013 announced an agreement with Iran to temporarily freeze the latter's nuclear program and subject it to international inspection. It marked a notable improvement in decades of bitter relations between the United States and Iran. Both speeches illustrated the global importance of the president's role as chief diplomat. As leader of the world's only superpower, a president's words and actions matter.

Under the Constitution, the president has the power to establish relations with foreign governments, to appoint U.S. ambassadors, and to sign treaties that take effect with the consent of two-thirds of the Senate. Because of its involvement in treaties and need to approve executive appointments, the Senate has been the legislative chamber most involved in foreign affairs. Its power to approve or reject treaties has been limited because most international agreements by the United States never reach the Senate. These *executive agreements* do not require the approval of the Senate, and their use has increased to where a president may sign hundreds of them a year. Presidents argue that these agreements usually concern only minor matters and that important issues are still submitted to the Senate. The initial 2013 agreement with Iran on its nuclear program falls under this presidential power.

Modern presidents and the national security agencies in the executive branch dominate American foreign policy. Despite Congress's power to appropriate money for weapons and foreign aid, and to declare wars, the president reigns supreme in foreign relations. The restraints on a president's power in foreign affairs are far fewer than those on domestic matters.

At times this authority over foreign policy has been used to limit constitutional rights. The war on terror, overseen by both the Bush and Obama administrations, led to various infringements of civil liberties. Under Bush, phones were tapped without court orders, citizens suspected of ties to terrorism were jailed without constitutional protections, and torture was used. Obama halted some of these practices, like torture. But he approved drones to kill American citizens over seas accused of aiding terrorists, prosecuted bureaucrats who leaked classified national security information to the press, and allowed the National Security Agency to collect phone and Internet data on millions of Americans. Both presidents faced resistance by other legislative, judicial, and media players concerned about this expansion of presidential powers. But in the face of apparent threats from abroad, public opinion generally accepted this increase in executive powers.

Commander in Chief

When President Obama sent 33,000 additional American troops to Afghanistan in a "surge" in 2010 and then withdrew them two years later, he was acting as the commander in chief of the armed forces. The principle behind this presidential hat lies in *civilian supremacy* over the military: The elected head of government is in charge of the armed forces. In practice, this authority is given to the secretary of defense, who normally delegates command to military officers. This is not limited to actions abroad, as shown by President Bush's tardy use of federal troops in New Orleans to help victims of Hurricane Katrina. The importance of this role is reflected in how much of government spending the military absorbs— some $718 billion a year, or over 20 percent of the government budget.

Although the Constitution gives Congress the power to declare war, Congress has not done so since the 1940s when the United States entered World War II. Presidents, in their role as commander in chief, initiated the country's involvement in the Korean and Vietnam wars. Congress supported both actions by appropriating money for the armed forces. Criticism of the president's role in Vietnam led to the

War Powers Act of 1973 to restrict the president's war-making powers. The law, passed over President Nixon's veto, limited the president's committing of troops abroad to a period of 60 days, or 90 if needed for a successful withdrawal. If Congress does not authorize a longer period, the troops must be removed.

The effectiveness of the War Powers Act is questionable, though presidents generally feel the need to gain congressional approval for any major use of the military. In the first Gulf War (1991), President Bush Sr. implicitly honored it by seeking a congressional resolution for sending troops to recapture Kuwait. Then in October 2002, Congress, acting under the War Powers Act, authorized his son, George W. Bush, to use the military "as he determines to be necessary and appropriate" to defend the nation against "the continuing threat posed by Iraq." The president contended that as commander in chief he already was permitted to act without a formal declaration of war, but he wanted a congressional vote to reflect national unity. Some Democrats later disagreed. They argued that this resolution was not the equivalent of a declaration of war, and that they had been duped by the administration's use of faulty intelligence.

President Obama followed previous presidents in finding ways around the War Powers Act. In 2011 he asserted that the U.S. involvement in an air war in Libya did not oblige the administration to ask Congress for authorization. Obama argued that the limited nature of the mission was not the kind of "hostilities" foreseen in the legislation because American lives weren't at risk. Concern was expressed that this meant that the use of remote-controlled drones (or obliterating a country by air) was beyond the War Powers Act. In the case of Libya, Republicans in Congress objected to a Democratic president's actions. But, as in Iraq, the president prevailed. Congress and presidents of both parties have agreed to disagree on the War Powers Act.

Chief Legislator

The Constitution gives the president the right to recommend measures to Congress, but it was not until the twentieth century that presidents regularly participated in the legislative process. The president delivers a *State of the Union address* to a joint session of Congress at the beginning of every year to present the administration's legislative program. He also gives an annual budget message, an

economic message and report, and frequently sends special messages to Congress supporting specific legislation. Early in his second term, President Obama took advantage of this power to send strong messages to Congress proposing new legislation covering gun control and immigration. Historically, most bills passed by Congress start life in the executive branch.

The president's main constitutional power as chief legislator is the *veto*. If a president disapproves of a bill passed by Congress, he may refuse to sign it and return it to Congress with his objections. The president can also *pocket veto* a bill by refusing to sign it within 10 days of Congress adjourning. Congress may override the veto by a two-thirds vote of those present and voting in each house. Only about 5 percent of vetoes are overridden by Congress. In practice, the veto is used as a threat to influence a bill while it is still being considered by Congress. By the end of his first term, President Obama had only vetoed two bills, minor ones at that, which was a historically low number. He did threaten to use the veto several times, including a veto of the entire military spending bill in the summer of 2009 to pressure Congress not to fund a jet fighter, the F-22, that the Air Force didn't want but that senators from states that manufactured the plane favored.

Note that President Obama had to threaten to veto an entire spending bill to get one item removed. This is because presidents have no line-item veto. In 1996, a Republican congress passed a law allowing the president to veto sections of some money bills. Supporters hoped that this line-item veto would reduce congressional spending on projects of local importance. During its 1997 term, the Supreme Court ruled that the line-item veto unconstitutionally expanded presidential powers (*Clinton v. City of New York*). Because the Supreme Court had the last word, presidents must still accept or reject the entire bill before them.

Presidents often try to lead Congress by controlling the *national agenda*, which consists of the highest priority public issues. After introducing his proposals for immigration reform and gun control in 2013, the president gave speeches in states with large Hispanic populations and invited victims of gun violence to the White House for media events, all designed to move the public to pressure Congress. President Obama prefers to set broad goals for legislation without micromanaging the details. He succeeded in areas like economic stimulus and health reform by working through Democrats on the Hill, and in the country, to respond to his priorities.

Frequently presidents fail to gain support for their national agenda. An indifferent public, a skeptical press, and entrenched interest groups can combine to derail this strategy. With a conservative Republican party in a majority in the House of Representatives after 2010, partisan opposition to the president's legislation frequently resulted in nothing—gridlock. Beyond the two-party conflicts and despite the president's national popularity and Democratic support, agreement between independent branches of government isn't always easy. As Senate Democratic Majority Leader Harry Reid said, "I do not work for Barack Obama. I work with him."

The president lobbies the Hill for support. He pressures individual members, offers to fund pet projects for their states, and tolerates changes in his bills to allow for local congressional interests. Obama's White House also campaigned to elect Democrats, which included recruiting new candidates to run for Congress, taking polls for them, raising money, and giving them the publicity that comes from a president's visit to their states. Presidents are noted for "killing Congress with kindness"—inviting members to dine at the Camp David retreat, watching basketball games with them, and phoning their sick relatives. Such courtesies build loyalties. More forceful leverage may also prove useful.

Party Leader

A president is the head of his political party. Wearing his party hat gives him a number of major duties: to choose a vice president after his own nomination, to distribute a few thousand offices and numerous favors to the party faithful, and to demonstrate that he is trying to fulfill the *party platform*, the party's program adopted at his nominating convention. The president is also the chief campaigner and fundraiser for his party. He names the national chairperson and usually controls the national party machinery.

The president's grip on his party has traditionally been limited by the decentralized nature of American parties. Members of Congress are selected by voters in their districts and states, and they serve as long as these voters reelect them. A president has no direct power to refuse members of Congress his party's nomination. However, President Obama maintained a great deal of influence and loyalty in the Democratic Party through his strong campaign organization and extensive fundraising for his party's candidates. His 2012 reelection campaign reinvigorated his party by recruiting young people into Democratic ranks and utilizing online targeting to mobilize supporters. These efforts accelerated the modern trend in both parties toward power being centralized in their national leadership.

The Public Presidency

A major result of the president's powers and roles is his influence over mass opinion. The president's visibility, as a symbol of the nation and as a single human being compared with a frequently impersonal government, gives the chief executive a great deal of public support in the political game. The White House offers its occupant what Theodore Roosevelt called "a bully pulpit."

"Going public" has become an essential part of presidential power. A president with visible public support can increase his overall prestige within Washington as well as his influence on a specific issue. By rallying public opinion, pressure can be brought on official Washington—usually Congress—to support the chief executive.

Mobilizing public opinion behind the president results from careful planning. The White House staff sells the president's message through marketing techniques used in election campaigns. Polling of public opinion will first be used to determine which issues and arguments have the greatest positive impact. Then the topic may be presented in a nationally televised speech, or the president may hit the road to publicize his plan through meetings and media interviews. Cabinet secretaries and allies in Congress meet with targeted groups to reinforce the message. All of this can be directed from the White House staff as a coordinated national campaign. For example, late in 2011 President Obama traveled through North Carolina and Virginia (two states crucial for his reelection) on a three-day bus tour to publicize his jobs bill. Following the 9/11 attacks, President Bush used tactics he had employed in his winning election campaign to mobilize public opinion. This strategy of "going public" is key in keeping popular backing for the public presidency. (See the case study "9/11: A President's Trial by Fire.")

A president's ability to shape public opinion has its limits. Keeping voters' support, and himself and his party in office, means convincing people that his administration is solving the country's problems as well as maintaining his own popularity. Often presidents fail. Lyndon Johnson—despite domestic legislative successes—and Richard Nixon—despite foreign policy achievements—left office widely unpopular. Johnson was unpopular because of the Vietnam War and Nixon because of Watergate. In both cases, the public attention focused on them by the mass media hastened their decline. George W. Bush completed his second term confronting a public deeply unhappy with a bungled war in Iraq, an economy in rapid decline, and administration responses that seemed ineffective at home and in the rest of the world. In the fall of 2013, President Obama, confronting a public skeptical of attacking Syria for its use of chemical weapons, was forced to go to Congress and to address the nation to gain support for an action he claimed presidents already had the power to do. He never got the public backing he needed. Later, his popularity dropped further with the delays in implementing health care reforms. (See "Presidential Privacy and the Press: FDR.")

Presidential Privacy and the Press: FDR

Franklin Roosevelt, a polio victim, could not walk. He was protected by the press in ways that seem amazing to presidents in an age of on-line media. Of 35,000 press photographs of FDR in the archives, only two showed him confined to a wheelchair. When he occasionally fell in public, photographers would take no pictures, and live radio broadcasts would not mention it.

The press's rule of thumb was that a president's private life should stay private unless it seriously interfered with his job performance. But this rule extended into 1944 (the year before his death), when FDR's failing health was a legitimate concern. His hearing had deteriorated to where he had to have questions at his press conference repeated for him. Publishers like Henry Luce of *Time Magazine*—a strong Republican—refused to print photos showing the president's poor health. World War II was going on, and this was giving comfort to the enemy.

Some presidents have been luckier. President Reagan was one of the most skillful chief executives at using the media to directly reach out and touch people with a sincerity shaped by his long Hollywood acting career. President Clinton's folksy manner and detailed command of issues never quite overcame media suspicion of his honesty and ethical lapses. He personalized his presidency by appearing on informal TV talk shows and favoring less-critical non-Washington reporters—practices continued by the presidents who followed him.

Facing a severe recession and attempting to fulfill his campaign's promise of change, President Obama often traveled "to the people" to gain support for his policies. His frequent appearances included casual TV interviews (such as the *Daily Show* and the *Tonight Show*) and at least one public event a day to guarantee news coverage. Like chief executives before him, Obama claimed to represent the national interest against the "special interests" found inside the Beltway around Washington. And yet he was unable in his public outreach to bridge the deep partisan divisions that blocked solutions for a range of national challenges. His superb verbal skills were criticized, oddly enough, for speaking "in impressive paragraphs, not memorable sentences." And he candidly admitted that his mistakes had been less in policies than in his communications, or as he said, "what the president can do, that nobody else can do, is tell a story to the American people about where we are and where we are going." By his own admission, he had only partially succeeded in this.

While keeping up his standing with the public, the president must carry out the tasks of his office and the goals of his administration. In doing so, his most critical relationship is with the government bureaucracy under him, the huge organization that manages programs ranging from launching spacecraft to teaching adults to read. What makes up this bureaucracy and how the president tries to direct it focuses the rest of this chapter.

The Federal Bureaucracy

The federal bureaucracy carries out much of the work of governing. Despite the negative sound of the word, a *bureaucrat* is simply an administrator, a member of the large organization—the bureaucracy—that carries out government policies. The U.S. bureaucracy is generally competent and uncorrupt, distinguishing it from many other bureaucracies around the world. It is what makes the country well governed—with notable exceptions like the Hurricane Katrina relief efforts. The great historical growth of the national government has produced a management system unequaled in size and complexity. Whether this huge administrative organization is the servant or master of government remains open to debate.

Most of the bureaucracy is within, or close to, the executive branch. Its structure can be broken down into the executive office of the president, the cabinet departments, the executive agencies, and the regulatory commissions. (See Figure 3.1.)

Executive Office of the President

In 1939 the *executive office* was established to advise the president and to assist him in managing the bureaucracy. It has grown steadily in size and influence, and today it includes over a dozen agencies and some 1,400 people. (See Figure 3.2.) Three of the most important agencies of the executive office are the White House office, the National Security Council, and the Office of Management and Budget. The *White House office* is a direct extension of the president. Its members are not subject to Senate approval. In recent years, centralization of executive power has increased the authority of the White House staff at the expense of the cabinet officers. Denis McDonough, a career staffer, was appointed White House chief of staff at the beginning of Obama's second term. McDonough manages the staff, keeps the paperwork flowing, and serves as the gatekeeper in determining who gets access to the president. The staff, often veterans of the campaign team, perform

THE CONSTITUTION

LEGISLATIVE BRANCH

THE CONGRESS

Senate House

Architect of the Capitol
United States Botanic Garden
Government Accountability Office
Government Printing Office
Library of Congress
Congressional Budget Office

EXECUTIVE BRANCH

THE PRESIDENT

THE VICE PRESIDENT

Executive Office of the President

White House Office
Office of the Vice President
Council of Economic Advisers
Council on Environmental Quality
National Security Council
Office of Administration

Office of Management and Budget
Office of National Drug Control Policy
Office of Policy Development
Office of Science and Technology Policy
Office of the U.S. Trade Representative

JUDICIAL BRANCH

The Supreme Court of the United States

United States Courts of Appeals
United States District Courts
Territorial Courts
United States Court of International Trade
United States Court of Federal Claims
United States Court of Appeals for the Armed Forces
United States Tax Court
United States Court of Appeals for Veterans Claims
Administrative Office of the United States Courts
Federal Judicial Center
United States Sentencing Commission

DEPARTMENT OF AGRICULTURE

DEPARTMENT OF COMMERCE

DEPARTMENT OF DEFENSE

DEPARTMENT OF EDUCATION

DEPARTMENT OF ENERGY

DEPARTMENT OF HEALTH AND HUMAN SERVICES

DEPARTMENT OF HOUSING AND URBAN DEVELOPMENT

DEPARTMENT OF THE INTERIOR

DEPARTMENT OF JUSTICE

DEPARTMENT OF LABOR

DEPARTMENT OF STATE

DEPARTMENT OF TRANSPORTATION

DEPARTMENT OF THE TREASURY

DEPARTMENT OF VETERANS AFFAIRS

DEPARTMENT OF HOMELAND SECURITY

INDEPENDENT ESTABLISHMENTS AND GOVERNMENT CORPORATIONS

African Development Foundation
Broadcasting Board of Governors
Central Intelligence Agency
Commodity Futures Trading Commission
Consumer Product Safety Commission
Corporation for National and Community Service
Defense Nuclear Facilities Safety Board
Environmental Protection Agency
Equal Employment Opportunity Commission
Export-Import Bank of the U.S.
Farm Credit Administration
Federal Communications Commission
Federal Deposit Insurance Corporation
Federal Election Commission
Federal Emergency Management Agency
Federal Housing Finance Board
Federal Labor Relations Authority
Federal Maritime Commission

Federal Mediation and Conciliation Service
Federal Mine Safety and Health Review Commission
Federal Reserve System
Federal Retirement Thrift Investment Board
Federal Trade Commission
General Services Administration
Inter-American Foundation
Merit Systems Protection Board
National Aeronautics and Space Administration
National Archives and Records Administration
National Capital Planning Commission
National Credit Union Administration
National Foundation on the Arts and the Humanities

National Labor Relations Board
National Mediation Board
National Railroad Passenger Corporation (Amtrak)
National Science Foundation
National Transportation Safety Board
Nuclear Regulatory Commission
Occupational Safety and Health Review Commission
Office of the Director of National Intelligence
Office of Governmental Ethics
Office of Personnel Management
Office of Special Counsel
Overseas Private Investment Corporation
Peace Corps
Pension Benefit Guaranty Corporation
Postal Rate Commission

Railroad Retirement Board
Securities and Exchange Commission
Selective Service System
Small Business Administration
Social Security Administration
Tennessee Valley Authority
Trade and Development Agency
U.S. Agency for International Development
U.S. Commission on Civil Rights
U.S. International Trade Commission
U.S. Postal Service

FIGURE 3.1
The Government of the United States.

72

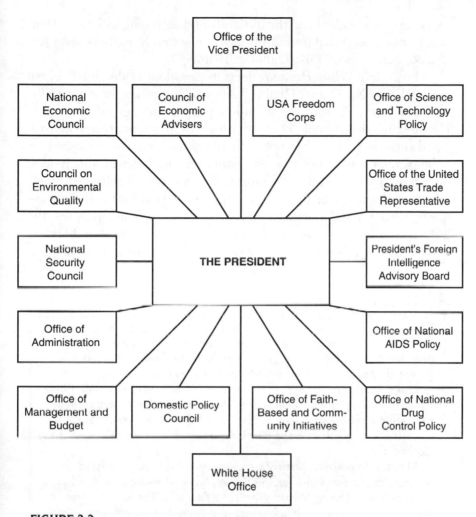

FIGURE 3.2
Some of the Offices in the Executive Office of the President.
Source: www.whitehouse.gov

a variety of tasks from speech writing and press briefings to relations with Congress and drawing up the president's calendar.

Historically, the president's staff has frequently been part of his problem in losing touch with the real world beyond the White House. Strong chiefs of staff have alienated Congress and the media by their arrogance. In the past, the president's residence has taken on the trappings of a royal castle with a "palace guard" isolating the president from dissenting voices. A special assistant to Lyndon Johnson described the staff's relationship to the president as that of a doting mother to a spoiled child—"Whatever he wants is brought to him immediately." Many people have spoken of the intimidation that comes from speaking to a president and the difficulty of disagreeing with him. That may be one reason that presidents have come to rely on their wives for frank opinions. (See "First Ladies in History.")

The present White House reflects its president's calm, intellectual personality—"No Drama Obama." After taking office, he repeatedly said that he didn't want a staff full of people who agreed with him. He mentioned the book *Team of Rivals* by historian Doris Kearns Goodwin, which describes how Lincoln assembled a war cabinet of political opponents. And to some extent Obama followed this model by naming his rival Hillary Clinton to be secretary of state as well as selecting a number of Republicans for senior positions and then allowing them the independence to manage their own departments. By 2014 two of his three secretaries of defense have been Republicans. Obama takes pride in being apolitical in seeking those who can get

■ First Ladies in History

There is no position of First Lady mentioned in the Constitution. Yet presidents' wives have often been their husbands' key advisor—the last person they talk to at night; the first person they talk to in the morning.

Dolly Madison, wife of the fourth president, was the only First Lady threatened by war. During the War of 1812, she refused to leave the White House—which the British later burned—and retreated only after she took with her the Declaration of Independence and the Constitution.

Eleanor Roosevelt, history's most active First Lady, insisted that America could not fight for democracy abroad without strengthening it at home. During World War II she flew with Tuskegee airmen to show her confidence in black pilots and toured an internment camp for Japanese Americans to press for their release.

Hillary Rodham Clinton was deeply involved in presidential policy making, from leading a major, if unsuccessful, health care reform to advocating human rights overseas. She later became senator from New York, secretary of state and, repeatedly, a serious candidate to become president on her own.

Laura Bush guarded her private life. Pro-choice and secret smoker, she quietly exercised power in the Bush White House. She increased funding for AIDS in Africa, nixed one cabinet appointment, and regularly advised her husband on his public performances.

Michelle Obama at first said she wanted to focus on being "mom-in-chief" to her two daughters and avoid a policy role. But by her husband's second term, this articulate lawyer was using her favorable public image to draw attention to the virtues of public service, the dangers of childhood obesity, and issues of fairness in society.

the job done. Contrasting himself with the Bush administration that put a high value on internal harmony, Obama stressed the rigor of a back-and-forth debate on issues. For his staff this has meant 14-hour workdays, a constant flood of demanding issues, inevitable stress, and the threat of burnout.

After breakfast with his two daughters, exercise, and a 30-second commute to the Oval Office downstairs, the president's day begins with the PDB, the *presidential daily brief*. In this meeting with staff and relevant Cabinet members, the president is updated on sensitive global intelligence reports and other issues. Obama demands significant detail and encourages outsiders' proposals that oppose his team's views. The president has described his management style as creating "space where solutions can happen." Few observers doubt the president's depth of knowledge on important policies. Whether he has found the balance between operating at too generalized a level vs. micromanaging too many issues has been a topic of debate among Washington commentators.

The *National Security Council* (NSC) was established early in the Cold War (1947) to coordinate American military and foreign policies for the president. These policies mainly involve the State and Defense Departments, which are represented on the council. (The Central Intelligence Agency, though an executive agency, also is a member of the NSC.) Presidents have varied in how much they wished to use the NSC. In President Bush's first term, National Security Advisor Condoleezza Rice became a key player, coordinating agency input to the White House and planning for the war on terrorism and the invasion of Iraq. President Obama expanded the membership of the NSC and increased its authority to set the country's international strategy. His current national security advisor, Susan Rice, is a central player in foreign policymaking, but she works for a president known for making his own decisions.

The *National Economic Council* (NEC) was established in 1993 because President Clinton decided that the United States needed an organization similar to the NSC to manage orderly economic policymaking by the executive branch. In its formal structure, the NEC includes cabinet members plus various top aides.

The *Office of Management and Budget* (OMB) was created by President Nixon in 1970 to replace the Bureau of the Budget. Departments of the executive branch submit competing claims for shares in the federal budget to OMB. Besides preparing the budget, OMB is an important general-management arm of the president. It helps control the executive branch by overseeing the agencies and their success in accomplishing their programs. Preparing and administering the annual budget, which is then submitted to Congress for approval, gives OMB tremendous power within the government. It is the largest organization in the Executive Office of the President, and its director is a member of the Cabinet. OMB has a hard-earned reputation for brutally reducing spending requests by government agencies.

The *Council of Economic Advisers* is another important unit of the executive office. Its three-member council of economic experts, appointed with Senate approval, helps the president form a national economic policy and predicts future economic developments.

Obama's *czars* are an informal term for the president's special advisors, some of whom have been confirmed by the Senate, while others have not been in positions requiring it. Sometimes referred to as *ad hoc* government (from the Latin term "for this purpose"), Obama by the end of his first term had appointed 42 "czars," each in charge of a policy area or appointed to fix an immediate problem. Examples include a climate czar—the assistant to the president for energy and climate change; a drug czar—the director of national drug control policy; and an intelligence czar—the director of national intelligence. These appointments reflect a president's powers to make and implement policies in various arenas. The tradition of special advisors dates back to the Woodrow Wilson administration during World War I. Recently critics have seen this as a presidential power grab at Congress's expense. The Republican majority in the House eliminated funds for many of Obama's czars in late 2011, but the Democratic Senate blocked the move.

The Cabinet Departments

The *cabinet departments*, created by Congress, are the major agencies of the federal government. At first there were only three (the Departments of State, War, and the Treasury); today there are 15. The expansion of the cabinet has been due largely to the growth of problems that political and popular interests wanted the federal government to deal with.

The newest cabinet department, Homeland Security, came out of the widespread frustration with the bureaucratic "turf wars" over national security both before and after 9/11. While originally pushed by congressional Democrats over the administration's objections, it was soon embraced by the Bush White House. The agency combined 22 agencies and some 170,000 employees in a cabinet department that aimed to centralize domestic security. It was the biggest government reorganization since the creation of the Defense Department in the late 1940s. The complexity of blending various agencies with different workplace cultures and physical locations behind a common mission was reflected in the agency's bungled response to Hurricane Katrina. As seen in the previous chapter's case study, FEMA, which was placed under the Department of Homeland Security, saw its budget, people, and mission of emergency assistance buried under the superagency's focus on terrorism. Reforming bureaucracy often promises more than is delivered.

Each cabinet department is headed by a secretary, who is appointed by the president with the consent of the Senate, which is usually given. Cabinet secretaries hold office as long as the president wishes. Pressures from their staff and constant involvement with the problems of their agencies may cause secretaries to act more like lobbyists for their departments than delegates of the president. This detachment leads them to play a secondary role to White House staff in shaping presidential policies. Cabinet secretaries in more than one administration have been heard complaining that they were excluded from important decisions by young White House staffers who blocked their access to the president.

The cabinet has no power as a body. How much the president uses the cabinet as a whole is strictly up to him. Although many presidents entered office promising to give the cabinet more power, it never happens. Neither Clinton nor Bush used the cabinet as a whole, except for ceremonial rallies. President Obama continued this tradition. One rare exception—illustrating the point— was in the fall of 2013 when he invited in the press to a Cabinet meeting that announced departments' plans for a government shutdown because of the failure of Congress to pass a budget for the new fiscal year. As one White House scholar, Bradley Patterson, wrote, "The Cabinet is for pictures and stories and publicity." This traditional lack of a policymaking role underlines a story about President Lincoln being opposed by his entire cabinet on an issue. He remarked, "Seven nays, one aye; the ayes have it."

A cabinet department may only be a loose umbrella over strong, independent agencies. For example, the attorney general has authority over the FBI, which is part of the Justice Department. Yet the reports on FBI missteps in tracking the Al Qaeda terrorists who hijacked American planes in 2001 and the difficulty in steering the bureau from crime detection to terrorist prevention illustrated the independence of the FBI from any administration's control. The FBI's ability to keep apart from the Department of Homeland Security showed that this autonomy was likely to continue.

Much of the work of cabinet departments involves serving the interests of clients for whom they were established in the first place. Departments like Labor (unions), Commerce (business), and Agriculture (farmers) are designed to promote and reflect their industry. Their regional offices in the field are set up to serve these clients, with

Agriculture's "extension agents," who encourage better farming practices, being the best known. Back in Washington, these departments, and others like Education and Transportation, operate like a *client agency*, lobbying for the bills and regulations that their industries need.

The Executive Agencies

Executive agencies are simply important agencies of the executive branch that are not in the cabinet. Their heads are appointed by the president with approval of the Senate, but they are not considered major enough to be part of the cabinet. Examples of these are the Office of Personnel Management (OPM), the National Aeronautics and Space Administration (NASA), the National Security Agency (NSA) and the Central Intelligence Agency (CIA).

Under executive agencies we might include *government corporations*, which began as semi-independent but have come increasingly under presidential control. Government corporations, like private corporations, perform business activities such as operating a transportation system or developing and selling electricity. They are usually governed by a board of directors, have limited legislative control over them, and allow for flexible administration. The Tennessee Valley Authority is a government corporation set up in the 1930s to develop electricity for the Tennessee Valley. The U.S. Postal Service is another, established in 1970 when Congress abolished the post office as a cabinet department and set it up as a semi-independent, government-owned corporation.

The Regulatory Commissions

Regulatory commissions are charged with regulating and making rules for certain parts of the economy. Examples are the Federal Trade Commission, which restrains unfair business practices; and the Federal Communications Commission regulating telephones, radio, Internet, and TV. The Consumer Financial Protection Bureau is a recent and controversial newcomer, set up to monitor mortgages, debt collection, and credit card abuses. It was strongly opposed by the financial industry and their conservative allies in Congress. Although the president appoints the members of the commissions and chooses who chairs them, the commissions are relatively independent of all branches of the government. They are bipartisan (members come from both parties)—the president has only a limited right to remove commissioners, who generally serve longer terms than the chief executive—and there is no presidential veto over their actions. These commissions generally have all three capacities of government: They make rules that have the force of law (legislative), administer and enforce these regulations (executive), and conduct hearings and issue orders (judicial). Their decisions can be reviewed by federal courts, while their authority and budget can be reduced by Congress.

The important Federal Reserve Board, under its first woman chair, Janet Yellen, is a special type of regulatory agency that determines general monetary policies, like short-term interest rates, for Federal Reserve Banks. Following the financial meltdown of 2008–2009, the Fed was unusually active in arranging, in cooperation with the Treasury Department, rescue packages for endangered large banks and insurance companies. The Fed chairman at the time, Ben Bernanke, ensured that enough money was in circulation until the end of his term in early 2014 to keep the slowly recovering economy from slipping into a depression. The Fed was crucial in calming panicked stock, bond, and currency markets by playing this role of lender of last resort. After the crisis, the Fed continued to boost the economy by reducing both long- and short-term interest rates. While criticized for its aggressive monetary expansion, the Fed got good marks for supporting the economy.

The logic behind these regulatory commissions was the idea that the economy required oversight on complicated matters on which Congress didn't have the technical expertise. They were made independent because their decisions were not supposed to be made on a partisan basis. But their detachment from the rest of the government has led to these commissions being pressured by the groups they are regulating. The lack of governmental controls and public pressures has led them to negotiate with, rather than regulate, important economic interests. They have been charged with serving powerful economic clients rather than exercising oversight. For example, following the Bernie Madoff scandal, the Securities and Exchange Commission (SEC) was accused of not closely regulating the financial industry. However, a few years earlier under Democratic president Clinton, the SEC had been accused of overregulation by the same business groups that now blamed lax government supervision. (See "The SEC and the Bernie Madoff Scandal.")

Problems of Bureaucracy

When most Americans hear the word *bureaucracy*, they think of incompetence and red tape, faceless administrators blindly following rules despite their impact on people's lives. Yet bureaucracies are set up to apply standardized rules, to treat people the same or at least according to some standard operating procedure (SOP). The problems with bureaucracies seem to be related to their size rather than the nature of the public or private organizations they serve. Large corporations and

▮ The SEC and the Bernie Madoff Scandal

The chief function of the SEC is to regulate the stock market and prevent corporate abuses. It was established by Congress following the stock market crash of 1929 as part of the New Deal. Governing its staff of some 3,800 are five commissioners headed by a chairman, with no more than three from the same political party.

In the last few decades, deregulation of the economy dominated Washington. Efforts were made to deemphasize government rules over business and free up the marketplace. Under Chairman Christopher Cox, appointed by George W. Bush, banks were allowed to take on more debt, and the SEC was limited in collecting penalties from corporations violating regulations. The staff was discouraged from being aggressive regulators, and morale was considered poor.

In June 2009 one of the world's largest financial frauds ended with Bernie Madoff convicted of fleecing investors of $50 billion. In Madoff's "Ponzi scheme," earlier investors were paid with money from new clients, with no money actually invested. It had gone on for years. Despite repeated complaints that Madoff's profits were impossibly high, the SEC had failed to uncover wrongdoing and had not pursued credible complaints. It was not the SEC but Madoff's own sons who alerted the FBI. Madoff was sentenced to 150 years in prison. The new Democratic administration replaced Chairman Cox.

socialist governments don't run notably more effective administrations. The complexity of any large bureaucracy makes it hard to tell who is responsible for a particular action, inhibiting public oversight.

Franklin Delano Roosevelt created the modern American bureaucracy. The only president to be elected to four terms, FDR brought the United States through the Great Depression of the 1930s and World War II. To fight the depression, Roosevelt started 30 new federal agencies, including well-known ones like the Social Security Administration and the SEC.

Later, to pay for the war, payroll deductions allowed the government to automatically collect income taxes. As a result, taxes poured into Washington at six times the rate as before the war, and the bureaucracy expanded. Federal taxes now take 15 percent of the nation's gross domestic product, much greater than under Roosevelt, but still the lowest in 60 years.

In recent decades, public distaste for the bureaucracy has helped antigovernment politicians gain positions of power. These leaders then faced the dilemma of both denouncing bureaucrats and depending on the same experts to carry out their policies. Bureaucrats have also proven useful scapegoats for failed policies. Whether in 2003 the CIA bureaucracy misjudged the presence of weapons of mass destruction in Iraq or was pressured by the Bush White House to shape its findings to support administration policies became an issue in assessing blame for the war.

At times dissenting bureaucrats have risked their careers by leaking information to the press that their superiors preferred to keep secret from the public. Torture of captured terrorist suspects, widespread abuse in U.S.-controlled Iraqi prisons, and wiretapping of Americans' phone calls and Internet mail only became known because courageous government employees released classified information to reporters who had the freedom to publish it. Secret policy battles behind closed doors in government agencies frequently result in leaks to the press and a more open public debate than high-ranking officials would prefer (See "Obama and Whistleblowers.").

Obama and Whistleblowers

In most democracies the punishment for making official secrets public is pretty mild. In Britain and Denmark, two years is the maximum prison sentence. Actual prosecutions in most European countries are rare. In Britain, since the 1989 Official Secrets Act took effect, only 10 public employees have been prosecuted and none received more than one year in prison. Aside from the United States, the only country where prosecutions are common is Russia, a nation not known for robust free speech and press rights.

In general the Obama administration has actively pursued those who reveal government secrets. As of 2013, seven of the 10 total indictments ever brought under the 1917 Espionage Act were during Obama's presidency, which means his administration has prosecuted over double the number of leakers than all past presidents combined. Included in these was Pfc. Bradley Manning, who provided more than 700,000 government files to WikiLeaks. Manning was sentenced to 35 years in prison in 2013. While officials claimed that much damage had been done to U.S. foreign policy, no specific instances of harm were ever raised at his trial.

After Manning's actions, the Obama administration launched the Insider Threat program, which requires federal employees to keep closer tabs on their coworkers and forces managers to punish those who fail to report their suspicions. In 2012, a Defense Department strategy memo stated, "Hammer this fact home . . . leaking is tantamount to aiding the enemies of the United States."

President Obama has defended his efforts: "Leaks related to national security can put people at risk. . . . So I make no apologies. . . ." In his 2008 presidential campaign, Obama's webpage asserted that whistleblower revelations were "acts of courage and patriotism, which can sometimes save lives and often save taxpayer dollars." In 2013, Obama's political webpage deleted his earlier campaign pledges to protect whistleblowers.

Rise of the Civil Service

In the federal government's first century, the usual method of choosing bureaucrats was known as the *spoils system*. Taken from the phrase "to the victor belong the spoils," the spoils system meant that victorious politicians filled government jobs with their supporters. This system of patronage became widespread during the administration of Andrew Jackson (1828–1836) and may have peaked under Abraham Lincoln (1860–1865). These bureaucrats did not need to be educated in their fields, but as the skills expected of bureaucrats became more complex and corruption grew, pressure for reform increased.

In 1881 President James Garfield was assassinated by a disappointed (and crazy) office seeker. The new president, Chester Arthur, backed by public outrage over the murder, supported the Civil Service Reform Act (also known as the *Pendleton Act*), which was passed by Congress in 1883. The law set up a bipartisan Civil Service Commission, under which government employees were chosen by merit through examinations. At first only about 10 percent of federal employees were covered by civil service, but the system has grown and now covers almost the entire bureaucracy. This has considerably diminished the spoils system and has added stability to government activity. The president today fills only about 5,000 patronage jobs, of which fewer than one-third are policymaking. While undermining the spoils system, it also has weakened presidential control of the bureaucracy; the bureaucrats know they will have their jobs long after the current administration passes into history.

Bureaucrats as Policymakers

The traditional idea of *public administration* was that *policy* and *administration* were two different functions of government. The president and Congress, elected by the people, should make policy. The unelected bureaucracy should carry it out. The goal of bureaucracy was efficiency. According to this ideal model, bureaucrats administer policy and provide their expert knowledge to elected policymakers. Today political scientists consider this traditional view inadequate, if not a bit naïve.

Political conflicts do not stop when a law is passed. They continue in implementing the law. In order to pass a bill, Congress may reach battle-scarred compromises, resulting in vaguely worded requirements. That leaves it to the administrators to referee the debate—on, say, how clean is clean water or what towns can do with their stimulus funds—in applying the law. Before the bill is passed, bureaucrats may have had an influence by their advice and information, even to the point of writing the bill with congressional staff. Afterward they may apply the law in changed political and economic situations not foreseen by those who drafted it. And, not surprisingly, bureaucracies have interests of their own, such as increasing their budget or protecting their "turf." The result is that the model of a bureaucrat as a politically neutral administrator looks like an isolated musical note in a symphony of sounds. Bureaucrats carry other tunes as well.

Bureaucracies are involved in policymaking by exercising legislative, judicial, and executive powers. For example, the Internal Revenue Service (IRS) holds hearings on tax cases, makes judicial findings, and issues regulations. These legislative and judicial powers have been delegated by Congress. In exercising executive power, federal bureaucracies draw up long-range plans and then make decisions about day-to-day operations: By what standards should schools be evaluated to get education funds? Will allowing roads harm this national forest? Should accused terrorists get constitutional protections? Decisions made by administrators in the executive branch include the government's most important policy choices.

The President and the Bureaucracy

Curiously, the bureaucracy is both an important support for the president and a major limit on his actions. The agencies of the federal government give the president access to more information than anyone else is likely to have and allow him to initiate actions to which others must react. But in carrying out his administration's policies, the

president must rely on the information, advice, and behavior of many others. Keeping control over the employees of the executive branch is a full-time job in itself. As political scientist Richard Neustadt commented, the president spends much of his time finding out what his political and bureaucratic subordinates are doing in his name.

Members of the bureaucracy may work to protect their own agencies or may respond to pressures from economic interests threatened by presidential policies. They may ignore the president's orders and delay or even sabotage him, even on trivial matters. Often executive departments have long-standing rivalries with each other: Labor versus Agriculture on food prices, or State Department versus Defense Department over national security policies. The president must judge these conflicts yet maintain the support of both sides. Cabinet officials may push their own departments' interests against those of the president who appointed them. ("Dancing with the natives," one White House aide called it.) Does the secretary of defense represent the president to the Defense Department, or the department to the president? Clearly both, but conflict often results.

Those benefiting from specific programs don't want them touched, whatever a president may want. And whether they are retired people or teachers or oil companies, these groups are usually intent on preserving their benefits. Government programs create and reward beneficiaries, who in turn lobby for continuing the program seemingly forever. President Ronald Reagan entered office promising to abolish two cabinet departments—Education and Energy. He left office having created one, Veterans in 1988, with Education and Energy still there. President Obama asked Congress in 2012 to close the Commerce Department, an overhaul that would save $3 billion. It never happened. As one congressman remarked, bureaucrats may have discovered the secret of eternal life—government programs.

However attractive we find the abstract idea of limiting the government and reducing the bureaucracy, when challenges arise—whether from hurricanes, recessions, or terrorists—Americans understand the need to act. If growth in the economy is to be restored, if Wall Street is to be regulated, and if foreign enemies are to be restrained, then government will be involved. The problems confronting America at home and abroad require leaders in government to respond. That response may be financial, political, educational, or military, but if it is to be more than words, it will call on the skills and resources that only an organization of specialists, the bureaucracy, can bring.

Especially in a crisis.

CASE STUDY

9/11: A President's Trial by Fire

It was a horrible day, for the nation and the president. On Tuesday morning, September 11, 2001, 19 terrorists linked to the radical Islamic group, Al Qaeda, took control of four California-bound jets at three East Coast airports. Using the planes as "smart bombs," they crashed into both towers of the World Trade Center and the Pentagon. (The fourth plane, United 93, apparently thwarted by passengers, dove into a field in Pennsylvania.) The huge 110-story towers imploded to the ground, thousands were killed, and a stunned nation watched the doomsday images repeated endlessly on television. The nation's airports were closed, Congress evacuated the capital, rumors of further attacks spread, and Americans struggled to regain their balance as well as a lost sense of security.

A Challenged Leader

At first President Bush had problems appearing in command. His day had begun in an elementary school in Sarasota, Florida, where he had been plugging his education program. He had waited seven minutes after the second attack before leaving the class and then took 12 hours to get back to the White House. Relying on his staff's security fears, Air Force One had taken a zigzag course, first to an air base near Shreveport, Louisiana, and then to a command post in Omaha, Nebraska, where he conducted a meeting of the National Security Council by video phone to Washington. While the secret service worried that the attacks had not ended, the president's political aides had to face another issue: How could Mr. Bush appear in control and reassure the nation from a bunker in Nebraska? Or as a *USA Today* reporter sarcastically noted, "Not since the British burned the White House in 1814 has a President been persuaded by security concerns to avoid the Capital."

Arriving back at the White House that night, President Bush addressed the nation from the Oval Office at 8:30 p.m. In his brief talk, a "somber" chief executive sitting alone at his desk assured his audience, "Our country is strong. . . . Terrorist acts can shake the foundation of our biggest buildings, but they cannot touch the foundation of America." He

declared that the government would continue "without interruption," that the search was underway to find those behind these evil acts, and that both allies and members of Congress would stand together to win the war against terrorism. He ended asking for prayers for the grieving and promised, "America has stood down enemies before, and we will do so this time."

In the coming days, the president expanded on these themes. He would be shown offering sympathy, demonstrating national unity, defining an unseen enemy, and executing a strong response. Underlying his activities was a nagging doubt: Was this commander in chief, barely eight months in office, elected by a minority of voters, with no foreign policy experience, up to the enormous task? With the nation traditionally rallying around the president in a time of crisis, many of his actions in this first week were designed to answer that unspoken question.

Congress on the day of the attacks was reminded of its physical dependency on the executive. Vice President Cheney ordered that the leaders of Congress be taken to a secure location—a resort in West Virginia. Later one Republican senator demanded that the leadership be returned to Washington, but the vice president refused. The senator pointed out that Congress was not under executive control. Cheney replied, "We control the helicopters."

THE PRESIDENT RESPONDS

On September 12, his first full day back in the White House, President Bush focused on defining the issue, rallying an international coalition, and asserting his presence in the midst of the tragedy. He escalated his language, calling the attacks "more than acts of terror; they were acts of war," thus laying the foundation for military action. He was shown calling world leaders, meeting security advisors, and discussing with congressional leaders new defense spending. The House passed a resolution of support, and administration officials, led by Secretary of State Colin Powell, sent stern public messages to other countries—"You're either with us or against us."

As the week went on, the president overcame his tentative first day. He did this in a way that only an individual chief of state could do: by personally connecting to the range of emotions felt by most Americans, from sadness to anger. He comforted victims, thanked rescue workers at the Pentagon and at the World Trade Center site, and reflected stunned feelings of outrage. On Thursday when he got off the phone after talking with New York Mayor Rudolph Giuliani, a *Boston Globe* reporter described him this way: "The president's eyes glistened and welled with emotion as he blinked to hold back tears. 'I'm a loving guy,' he said. 'And I'm also someone, however, who's got a job to do and I intend to do it. And this is a terrible moment.'"

A president's religious role as a "democratic priest-king" was displayed. The president declared Thursday a national "day of prayers and remembrance." His proclamation read, "In the face of all this evil, we remain strong and united, one nation under God." During a televised service at Washington Cathedral on September 14, Bush said, "The commitment of our fathers is now the calling of our time. We ask almighty God to watch over our nation and grant us patience and resolve in all that is to come."

At the same time he remained the commander in chief, rallying the country for what lay ahead. Even at the cathedral service, Bush talked tough: "This conflict was begun on the timing and terms of others; it will end in a way and at an hour of our choosing." Two days after the attack the president declared, "The nation must understand this is now the focus of my administration." He asked Congress to authorize the use of force against those responsible for September 11, while adding that he did not need prior approval to launch a military attack. Congress played its part by easily passing $40 billion in emergency spending. By September 15, the president had approved an antiterrorist global strategy involving intelligence, finance, diplomacy, and the military. The CIA became the lead agency in the planning to overthrow the Taliban government in Afghanistan that had harbored the Al Qaeda terrorists.

In the coming days, the president pointedly did *not* do certain things. He did not blame anyone in the government for allowing the attack. Although the hijackings represented an enormous intelligence failure, the president made clear his confidence in the CIA by meeting with its director. Bush also tried to separate the terrorists from the religion they claimed to represent. He publicly met with American Islamic leaders, declaring that the hijackers had nothing to do with peaceful Muslims. When professional baseball resumed, he went to the mound to throw out the first pitch. The president made clear that he didn't want the national agenda disrupted by terrorism. He emphasized that his education reform, No Child Left Behind, remained a top domestic priority.

A CALL TO ARMS

The climax of the country's initial response to the terrorist attack came in President Bush's speech to a joint session of Congress on September 20. Using the Capitol as the stage and Congress as his cheering chorus, a president not known for eloquence gave an inspiring speech. He issued an ultimatum to the Afghan leaders to turn over the Al Qaeda leaders responsible for the attack, and called on the nation and world to unite to destroy terrorism. "Tonight we are a country awakened to danger and called to defend freedom. Our grief has turned to anger, and anger to resolution. Whether we bring our enemies to justice, or bring justice to our enemies, justice will be done."

He framed the threat not as mere policy differences but as a challenge to America's core values. "They hate our freedoms—our freedom of religion, our freedom of speech, our freedom to vote and assemble and disagree with each other. . . . We have seen their kind before. They are the heirs of all the murderous ideologies of the twentieth century . . . they follow in the path of fascism, and Nazism and totalitarianism. And they will follow that path all the way, to where it ends: in history's unmarked grave of discarded lies."

And when Bush concluded, "In our grief and anger, we have found our mission and our moment," he was speaking for more than a generation of Americans. He was speaking of his presidency.

***

In the months and years that followed, the president's rare dominance of the political system would not last. Crippled by unpopular wars in Afghanistan and Iraq, the renewal in confidence of other branches of government, partisan foes, and a free press, the president would find his authority reduced. Though mistakes by the chief executive could be blamed for this loss of support, more importantly was a constitutional system of separated powers working as intended. The traditional limits on presidential power remained firmly in place.

WRAP-UP

This chapter has introduced the executive players in the political game—the president and the bureaucracy. We have seen how the presidency has irregularly, but vastly, grown in influence from a limited grant of constitutional powers. We have looked at three different presidential styles as well as how some modern presidents have carried out the duties of their office. The six major hats a president wears—chief of state, chief executive, chief diplomat, commander in chief, chief legislator, and party leader—show how broad and public presidential power has become. In the last century, government power has been centralized, in the federal government relative to the states, and in the presidency relative to the Congress.

The bureaucracy within the executive branch generally reinforces the president's power. Yet its size, its influence over policymaking, the economic clients it serves, its complexity, and the rivalries among agencies—from the executive office to the cabinet departments, executive agencies, and regulatory commissions—limit the president's control. In the aftermath of the 9/11 terrorist attacks, we saw a president use the powers of his office to unify, defend, and rally a country stunned by a sudden and terrible blow.

The president as both an individual and an institution will continue to play a central role in the American political game. Often presidents have seemed ineffective in managing the bureaucracy, in getting Congress to act, or in persuading the public to follow their leadership. Dissatisfaction with government often focuses on individual presidents. Many of us still look for a presidential Moses to lead us out of a wilderness of domestic and foreign troubles, which is part of the problem.

Presidents are political leaders. They hold a powerful office limited by history, law, and politics. They may disappoint us by overpromising, they may mislead us by abusing their powers, and they may do great damage to our nation and the world through their errors in judgment. But we also play a role. If we expect them to be heroes or symbols, priests or kings, we are bound to be disappointed. We may need to moderate our expectations of what presidents can do to protect our country and improve our lives. In that way we can, as citizens of a democracy, more realistically judge the leader of the executive branch of government.

◼ THOUGHT QUESTIONS

1. What are the major reasons for the growth in the power of the president? Why do you think that presidential candidates' claim to want to limit this growth and then change when they take office?
2. Do you think the president is too powerful or not powerful enough? Should a president's power expand in a crisis like that of 9/11? Should it be limited afterward? How?
3. When the executive and legislative branches are controlled by different political parties, complaints of gridlock are often heard. Is that situation closer to the framers' idea of checks and balances by separate branches? Or does it make government less responsive? Give examples.
4. How can the president gain control over the rivalries and independence of the various departments in the executive branch bureaucracy?
5. Should bureaucracies, like Agriculture and Labor, serve the interests of the clients in the economic areas they govern? What is the danger in this relationship? How can it be counterbalanced?

◼ SUGGESTED READINGS

Alter, Jonathan. *The Promise*. New York: Simon & Schuster, 2010. A sympathetic, detailed insider account of the early years of the Obama administration, its fights and frustrations.

Bacevich, Andrew J. *The Limits of Power*. New York: Holt, 2008. Pb.
A powerful argument that America's foreign policy has been hijacked "in going abroad in search of monsters to destroy." (JQ Adams)

Caro, Robert A. *The Years of Lyndon Johnson, The Passage of Power*. New York: Alfred A. Knopf, 2012.
The fourth volume in the classic biography of one of America's most brilliant politicians as he takes power following the Kennedy assassination.

Cronin, Thomas E. *On the Presidency: Teacher, Soldier, Shaman, Pol.* Boulder, CO: Paradigm, 2010.

A leading presidential scholar punctures the romantic myth of successful presidencies finding that most modern ones have failed.

Edwards, George C. *Overreach: Leadership in the Obama Presidency.* Princeton, NJ: Princeton University Press, 2012. Pb.

A sharp critique by a presidential authority of Obama's leadership style and the frustrations surrounding the powers of any president.

Pious, Richard M. *Why Presidents Fail.* New York: Rowman & Littlefield, 2008.

Nine case studies from the U-2 to Iraqi weapons of mass destruction incisively trace why presidents make similar mistakes over and over again.

Woodward, Bob. *State of Denial.* New York: Simon & Schuster, 2006. Pb.

Described by the *New York Times* as showing President Bush "a passive, impatient, sophomoric and intellectually incurious leader, presiding over a grossly dysfunctional war cabinet. . . ."

CHAPTER 4

The Legislative Branch: Congress

The Constitution puts Congress at the center of the American political game. The framers' experience with the King of England and his autocratic governors had left the framers suspicious of a strong executive. As a result, the Constitution begins with Article I giving many detailed powers and duties to Congress; Article II provides far fewer to the president.

Further, congressional powers limit those of the president. The president is the commander in chief of the military but cannot declare war or raise armies—only Congress can. The president is the chief administrative officer of the government, but there will be no government to administer if Congress does not create and fund it. He can appoint executive officials and negotiate foreign treaties only if the Senate consents. Both the raising of money through taxes and the spending of it by the government require congressional legislation. Finally, Congress has the power to impeach and then remove the president.

Through its major function of making laws, Congress creates the rules that govern the political players. Article I of the Constitution gives Congress the power to tax, borrow money, raise armies, declare war, create the federal courts, regulate commerce, coin money, and "make all Laws which shall be necessary and proper for carrying into Execution the foregoing powers, and all other Powers vested by this Constitution in the Government of the United States, or in any Department or Officer thereof."

For most of the nineteenth century, Congress did in fact shape government policies. By the end of the nineteenth century, President Woodrow Wilson proclaimed, "Congress is the dominant, nay, the irresistible power of the federal system." Wilson was later to change his mind. And, since the Great Depression and World War II, the presidency generally increased in influence compared to Congress with, occasionally, periods of weak executives and strong legislatures.

Two of the most powerful players in Congress are not mentioned at all in the Constitution—political parties and congressional committees. Both are vital for creating legislation and providing specialized instruments for doing Congress's business. Recent congresses have seen political parties becoming more important and the committees getting weaker in leading the legislature. Party leaders, especially in the majority party, are key in what the legislature does and in choosing who will become chairmen of committees.

Since the 2010 elections, Republicans have had a majority of members in the House, while Democrats have controlled the Senate with a majority there. Republican control of the House has allowed the party to block much of the legislation introduced by Democrats through their leadership of the executive branch in the person of President

Obama. Depending on one's political views, this has resulted in either gridlock with few legislative achievements or Congress restraining a free-spending liberal executive. Either way the modern Congress reflects a political fact of life: Representative assemblies depend on executive leadership to tackle major issues. The legislature remains necessary to govern but not sufficient to shape the nation's policies on its own—close to what the Constitution intended.

In this chapter we will examine the structure and activities of Congress, how it was designed, and how it actually operates today.

Makeup of the Senate and House

The Congress of the United States is *bicameral*, made up of two houses: the Senate and the House of Representatives. The Senate consists of two senators from each state, regardless of the size of the state. House members are distributed according to population so that the larger the state's population, the more representatives it gets. The Constitution requires that each state, no matter how small, have at least one representative. These provisions are the result of a political compromise between the small states—favored in the Senate—and the large states—with more representatives in the House—in writing the Constitution.

As the country has grown, so too has the size of Congress. The first Congress consisted of 26 senators and 65 representatives. With each new state added to the Union, the Senate has grown by two, so that it now has 100 members from 50 states. As the nation's population grew, the size of the House of Representatives also grew. In 1922 Congress passed a law setting the maximum size of the House at 435 members, where it remains today. In the first House, each member represented 50,000 citizens. The average representative now serves over 700,000 people.

Role of the Legislator

There are many questions about the role of a legislator, questions as old as the idea of representative assemblies. Should representatives follow their own judgments about what is best or do only what their constituents wish ("re-present" them)? What should representatives do if the interests of their district conflict with the needs of the nation as a whole? Should legislators recognize a "greater good" beyond their own voters?

Members of Congress are both *national* and *local* representatives. They are national representatives who make up one branch of the national government, are paid by the federal government, and are required to support and defend the interests of the nation. However, they are chosen in local districts or states. In running for election, legislators must satisfy *their* constituents that they are looking out not only for the national interest but for local interests as well. In controversial areas, such as cutting the defense budget by closing military bases, national views may be very different from local popular opinion. In 2010, many Democratic representatives running for reelection tried to distance themselves from Obamacare, the president's unpopular health care reform that they had supported. They were mindful of a warning heard in Congress: "You have to save your seat before you can save the world"—a reminder that usually gives local voters' opinions the upper hand.

Casework, or helping constituents solve individual problems with government agencies, is a vital part of what senators and representatives do. Most of a member's staff work not on legislation but on constituency service for their local voters, intervening with bureaucrats on behalf of voters. Given the growing role of government in people's lives and the ease of contacting congressional offices by e-mail, casework has increased. Casework gives people access to, and influence with, an impersonal bureaucracy. It certainly helps incumbents get reelected.

Casework includes assisting veterans in getting information about programs for the disabled or intervening with a government agency so a surviving child can get an overdue social security check. These are not always the most earth-shaking issues. One Georgia congressman tells a story about receiving a call from a constituent that her garbage hadn't been picked up. The congressman asked her why she hadn't called the director of the local Department of Sanitation. "Well, Congressman," she replied, "quite frankly, I didn't want to go up that high." (See "The Image of Congress.")

Who Are the Legislators?

To be a member of the House of Representatives, you must be at least 25 years old, a citizen of the United States for seven years, and a resident of the state electing you. As a senator you must be 30 years old, a citizen for nine years, and a resident of the state. State residency is a loose requirement. Hillary Clinton first won her Senate seat from New York in 2000 despite never living in the state before. Other states, like Arizona, have a five-year residency requirement to run for office.

Members of the House of Representatives (called *representatives* or *congressmen/women*) serve two year terms, and all of them need to run every two years. They are elected from congressional districts drawn up by the states. Since these districts are shaped by the party dominating state government, they are frequently constructed to be

The Image of Congress

In recent polls, just 13 percent of the public said that they approved of the way Congress was handling its job (84 percent disapproved). This was around the same support Americans gave North Korea.

Congress's lousy image is not new. In the nineteenth century, Mark Twain remarked that "there is no distinctly native American criminal class except Congress." Today Congress is seen as chaotic, polarized, and unresponsive to national needs. In part, this is true. But Congress *is* doing what the framers intended—slowing down the policy process to argue the issues of the day. The media darkens this view further by finding the fights and scandals of a few members easier to report than complicated legislation.

Ironically many congressmen intentionally worsen the image of their institution. There's a long tradition of members running *for* Congress by running *against* Congress. By pandering to negative views of Congress, members can present themselves as lonely fighters against a corrupt legislature. The result is that people dislike Congress but reelect their own incumbent congressman over and over.

one-party districts. The results are congressmen who often represent the partisans within their party, which in recent congresses has meant conservative Republicans who dominate state legislatures in turn dominate their majority party in the House. No congressional district ever crosses state borders.

Senators serve six-year terms and are elected by the entire state's population. Every two years, during national elections, one-third of the Senate seeks reelection. The other senators do not run because they are only one-third or two-thirds of the way through their terms.

The Constitution originally provided that members of the Senate would be elected by their state legislatures. This was done to remove the choice from the public and ensure that more conservative elements would pick the senators. The Seventeenth Amendment changed this in 1913, and senators now are elected by the voters of their state.

Congress has traditionally been composed overwhelmingly of white males and tends to reflect the values of upper-middle-class America. Almost half of the members of Congress are lawyers. Other common professions are business, banking, education, farming, and journalism. Women and minorities have historically been underrepresented in Congress for many reasons, including the selection of candidates by party organizations and voter apathy. Recent elections have increased the number of women, African Americans, and Hispanics in Congress. (See "The 113th Congress.")

The 113th Congress

In the 2012 elections, the Democrats increased their majority in the Senate, 54 to 45, with one independent who aligned with them (Bernie Sanders from Vermont, the Senate's only socialist). In the House, the Republicans remained the majority party but with reduced numbers, 234 to the Democrats 201. House Republicans counted 49 Tea Party members among their majority.

The two houses were among the oldest of any recent congresses, averaging 57 years old in the House, 62 in the Senate. John Dingell, Democratic congressman from Michigan, had the longest service of any member in history, having served since 1955, or almost 60 years when he announced his retirement in 2014 declaring that the House had become unproductive and "obnoxious." The Senate had its first Buddhist, Mazie Hirono (D-Hawaii), and the first openly gay senator, Tammy Baldwin (D-Wisconsin). The House had 40 African Americans, all Democrats; 33 Hispanics, 25 Democrats and 8 Republicans; and 9 Asian Americans, all Democrats. For the first time, white men are a minority among House Democrats.

Careerism—the tendency for legislators to serve in Congress as a lifetime career—still exists. The current unpopularity of *incumbents* has led some new members of Congress—calling themselves "citizen legislators"—to vow to stay in office for only a few terms. It does seem ironic that although high-level executive branch administrators and members of the judiciary may be appointed from outside fields, it is a lifetime career to become a leader in a representative assembly. The problem with careerism is that, although it may guarantee loyalty to their institution, it also may separate members from a changing society.

Popular disgust for entrenched government led in the past to proposals for *term limits* on members of Congress. Almost half the states limited the number of times their representatives and senators could run for reelection. Congress tried to pass several different measures to restrict members to 6 or 12 years in office; they all failed. Even more damaging for supporters was a 1995 Supreme Court decision (*U.S. Term Limits v. Thornton*) declaring that term limits by the states added to the qualifications for office and thus needed an amendment to the Constitution. Support has since cooled. As one senator said about Congress voting for such an amendment, "I don't think there's any way to get two-thirds of the people in this place who are willing to say good-bye to their jobs." (For another side of this issue, see "Is There Life after Congress?")

Is There Life after Congress?

There was no bigger fight in the 111th Congress than the one over health care reform. Leading the battle to make sure that reform didn't hurt their business were the nation's largest insurers, hospitals, and medical groups who spent $1.4 million *a day* lobbying Congress. Working for them were 350 former congressmen and government staff members. Many of them had worked on the committees that now had to write a new health care law for the country. These former colleagues were there to make sure that Congress didn't endanger health care interests, which make up one-sixth of the U.S. economy.

Despite various reforms, large numbers of congressmen and staff use their government positions as a stepping stone to higher paying jobs as lobbyists. The nonpartisan Public Citizen found that half the senators and 42 percent of House members became lobbyists when they left Congress. Some feared that public service had become not a goal but a door to riches in the private sector.

The drawing of House districts is up to the state governors and state legislatures, who use these powers to boost their own party and penalize the party that is out of power. In the past, *malapportionment* (large differences in the populations of congressional districts) was common in many areas of the country. Districts would be drawn up so that minority-party districts included more voters than majority-party districts. In this way, each minority-party voter would count for less. In 1960, Michigan's sixteenth district had 802,994 people, whereas the twelfth district had only 177,431. Both elected just one representative.

In addition, the art of *gerrymandering*—drawing district boundaries for partisan advantage—was practiced. The name comes from Massachusetts governor Elbridge Gerry, who in 1812 helped draw a long, misshapen district composed of a string of towns north of Boston. When painter Gilbert Stuart saw a drawing of the oddly shaped district, he penciled in claws, wings, and a head and said, "That will do for a salamander!" His editor replied, "Better say a gerrymander." The two most common forms of gerrymandering are "packing" and "cracking." *Packing* involves drawing up a district so that it has a large majority of supporters, to ensure a "safe" seat. *Cracking* means splitting up opponents' supporters into minorities in a number of districts to weaken their influence.

Such practices have long been attacked by reformers. In 1962 a Supreme Court decision (*Baker v. Carr*) held that legislative districts must be as close to equal in population as possible. Many of the worst abuses of malapportionment were ended by this and later Court

Apportionment of the U.S. House of Representatives Based on the 2010 Census

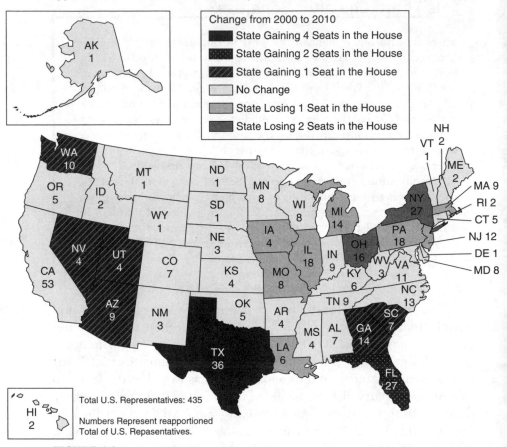

FIGURE 4.1
States Gaining and Losing Congressional Seats Following the 2010 Census.
Source: U.S. Bureau of the Census, "News Release," December 28, 2010.

decisions. But politics—including gerrymanders—remains part of drawing of districts, as seen in the conflicts following each census.

At the beginning of each decade, the Census Bureau counts the nation's population, and the House of Representatives is reapportioned to reflect the change in each state. In recent counts, including the 2010 census, the population grew and shifted toward the South and the West of the country. Because the number of seats in the House is limited by law to 435, states in the Northeast and Midwest lost seats while the south and west gained. Texas added four congressional seats and Florida gained two. New York and Ohio lost two apiece. Several midwestern and northern states lost one each, while a number of southern and western states gained one. (See Figure 4.1.)

The redistricting following the 2010 census was as partisan as ever with each party seeking an advantage from the state governments they controlled. Since Republicans controlled a majority of state legislatures and had more congressional incumbents running, they used redistricting to consolidate their majority in the House. In Texas, for example, the increase in seats was largely due to the growth of the Hispanic population. Yet since these were largely Democratic voters, Republican state legislators did their best to scatter these voters in Republican districts or consolidate them in a few overwhelming Democratic districts. Democrats in states like Illinois and New York returned the favor by combining Republican districts so that GOP incumbents had to run against each other. In some southern states, the Voting Rights Act was used by the Justice Department to ensure that minority voters weren't completely overwhelmed in the partisan battles.

Partisan redistricting probably helped Republicans retain their majority in the House in 2012 while losing the overall national vote for congress by a half million votes. Yet in states like California where control over redistricting has been put into nonpartisan commissions, the elections have not become more competitive. Despite widespread fears that gerrymanders can polarize and "fix" the results, elections are not yet fully determined by party maneuvers. Redistricting has an effect, but only a limited one, on election outcomes. (See "The Incumbent Protection Game.")

The Incumbent Protection Game

The advantages of holding office—being an incumbent—are considerable. Incumbents have wide name recognition. Just by speaking or issuing "official" statements, they can get free publicity not available to their lesser-known opponents. House members have office and staff budgets of approximately $1.4 million a year. Senators are often given considerably more, up to $3.8 million if their states are large. Both receive 32 government-paid round trips to their districts each year. And there is the *frank*, the privilege of official mailing enjoyed by Congress, under which 200,000,000 pieces of mail, much of it quite partisan, are sent free every year. The local press joins the parade by generally treating incumbents like hometown heroes. And there's always lots of "pork" to pass around.

Adding to the advantages of House incumbents is reapportionment. Changing the shape of the playing field maximizes the number of districts favorable to incumbents. Coupled with the usually low voter turnout in congressional races and the one-party dominance of most congressional districts, incumbents usually win. The average re-election rate in the House is over 90 percent; only 27 incumbents who ran in 2012 lost.

Organization of the House of Representatives

Parties are key to how Congress is organized. The *majority party* in each house—the one with the greatest number of members—chooses the officers, controls debate on the floor, selects all committee chairs, and has a majority on all committees. Until 1994 the Democrats had controlled both houses of Congress for 40 years, except for the years 1980–1986, when the Republicans ran the Senate. From 1994 to 2006 the Republicans were the majority in both houses, with a brief 18-month interim from June 2001 to January 2003, when the Democrats took back the Senate after a Republican senator left his party. Then in the 2006 midterm elections, the Democrats increased their numbers in the House by over 30 seats and became the majority party there (and in the Senate). But in 2010 Republicans used popular opposition to President Obama to win a majority in the House, and despite Democratic gains, they kept control in the 2012 elections.

In the House of Representatives, the majority party chooses the *Speaker of the House* from among its members. He or she does not have to be the oldest or longest-serving member but will certainly be well respected and is likely to have served in other party posts. During some periods, such as 1890 to 1910, the Speaker exercised almost dictatorial powers. Today's Speakers, though hardly dictators, still retain power through control over the majority party and influence how the committee system operates, including who becomes committee chairmen.

The selection of the Speaker takes place every two years, at the beginning of Congress. The majority party votes for its leader in its party caucus, and then he or she becomes their candidate for the Speaker, voted on by the entire House. Since this is one time when party discipline must hold, the leader of the majority becomes the Speaker.

In 1994 Newt Gingrich of Georgia became the first Republican Speaker of the House since 1954. He ushered in many rule changes, cutting staffs, eliminating committees, strengthening party control, and increasing the power of the Speaker. Within a few years, the limits of the Speaker's powers became apparent. Republicans lost five seats in the House in the 1998 elections, and Gingrich was pushed into resigning. Dennis Hastert, from Illinois, emerged as the Speaker in 1999, pledging more power to committee chairmen and a low-profile office.

When the GOP lost its majority in 2006, in part due to scandals among House Republicans, the Democrats elected their former minority leader as Speaker. Nancy Pelosi, a liberal congresswoman from San Francisco, became the first woman Speaker in history and the target of partisan attacks directed at Democrats in general. Pelosi was in turn replaced by Republican John Boehner of Ohio when his party became the majority in 2010. Since then Boehner has led his divided party in opposing President Obama. Confronting right-wing House members elected with Tea Party support, Boehner has not always been successful in forging unity in the House majority behind efforts to limit government programs, reduce the deficit, and defeat the Democratic president. Because of the strength of dissenters within his party, Boehner has been labeled a weak Speaker, which became apparent during the 2013 government shutdown that he had unsuccessfully tried to steer his caucus away from.

The *caucus* of each political party in the House or Senate is simply a gathering of all the members of that party serving there. (A caucus may also refer to organized groups in Congress such as the farm bloc, blacks, women, and Hispanics.) The Republican majority caucus in the House chooses a *majority leader*, who is second in command to the Speaker. The majority leader, now Eric Cantor of Virginia, works closely with the Speaker, organizes party members, and schedules legislation.

The Speaker and majority leader are assisted by *majority whips*. (The word *whip* comes from English fox hunting, where the "whipper-in" keeps the dogs from running away.) The whips help coordinate party positions on legislation, channel information between the leadership and party members, persuade wavering representatives to vote with the leadership, and conduct informal surveys on the likely outcome of votes. Being at the center of the congressional process, these party leaders possess more information than other legislators, which adds to their power.

The minority party caucus in the House, currently the Democrats, selects a *minority leader* and *minority whips*. Like the majority party's leader and whips, their duties are to coordinate party positions. When the Democrats lost their majority, Nancy Pelosi was elected to become the minority leader. She is assisted by Steny Hoyer of Maryland, the minority whip.

The Republican and Democratic caucuses in the House run their affairs in slightly different ways. The Republican Party chooses a *Steering Committee* to function as an executive committee of the caucus. The Steering Committee helps chart party policy in the House and assigns Republican members to committees. The Democrats have a two-headed executive committee. One, the *Steering Panel*, nominates committee chairs and members, all of whom must be approved by the caucus. The other, the *Policy Committee*, studies issues, writes bills, and publicizes them. Of course with a Democratic president the White House staff will be leading, or at least coordinating closely with, these committees.

Organization of the Senate

The Senate has no Speaker. The *president of the Senate* is the vice president of the United States, at present Democrat Joe Biden. He has the right to preside over the Senate chamber, which he does only on significant votes. He is allowed to vote in case of a tie. Only in rare cases, when there is a 50–50 party split in the Senate, is the vice president's vote of importance—it could determine the majority party. Now with the Democrats in the majority, the veep has mainly a figurehead position.

The honorary post of president *pro tem* (from *pro tempore*, meaning "for the time being") of the Senate is given to the senator from the majority party who has served longest in the Senate—currently Democrat Patrick Leahy of Vermont, serving his seventh term. His only power is to preside in the absence of the vice president, but he hardly ever does so. Because the vast majority of Senate work takes place in committees, the job of presiding over a Senate chamber that may be nearly vacant falls to a junior senator.

The *Senate majority leader* is the closest equivalent to the Speaker of the House. However, because the Senate is smaller and not tightly organized, the majority leader has less control over the Senate than the Speaker has over the House. The majority leader schedules debate on the Senate floor, assigns bills to committees, coordinates party policy, and appoints members of *special committees*. But senators value their independence, including a bit of detachment from their leaders' directions. Harry Reid, a Democrat from Nevada, became Senate majority leader in 2007, when the Democrats became the majority party. Number two in the Senate is the majority whip Richard Durbin, a Democrat from Illinois.

Because they are from the majority party, the chairmen of all senate committees are now Democrats. Both the majority and minority leaders are assisted by a whip, as well as assistant whips who coordinate party positions and floor strategy. In the Senate the Democrats' caucus is organized into a Steering Committee that appoints chairmen and members to committees and a Policy Committee that coordinates party strategy. Unlike the Republican organizations, the Senate Democratic leader chairs the Democratic caucus (called the *Democratic Conference*), the Steering Committee, and the Policy Committee.

Republicans are led by their Senate minority leader, now Mitch McConnell of Kentucky, with John Cornyn of Texas as the whip. The GOP has a *Committee on Committees*, which assigns members to committees, and a Policy Committee, which charts legislative tactics. The party caucus, called the *Republican Conference*, consists of all Republicans in the Senate. Unlike the Democrats where the majority leader chairs their party groups, each of these groups is chaired by a leading Republican senator.

How Congress Works

Power in the legislature has changed in recent years. Congress has gone from a system of strong committees and weak political parties to one with stronger parties and weaker committees. Members' loyalty to their party has replaced loyalty to their committee as the chief route to advancement. Committees and their chairmen generally bend with the prevailing partisan wind. This is less true in the Senate, where committees, committee chairmen, and individual senators have more independence from party leaders.

In a period of divided government with Democrats in a majority in the Senate, Republicans a majority in the House, and a Democrat reelected president, leadership can be uncertain at best. The rise of single-party districts in the House has meant that the only strong opposition many members will face is within their own party. Notably within the Republican caucus, incumbents' fear of losing their seats comes from right-wing opponents running against them in primary elections. Veteran Republican senators Dick Lugar of Indiana and Bob Bennett of Utah were ousted by Tea Party revolts within their state parties. As a result, reaching compromises with moderate Democrats in Washington may prove dangerous in facing GOP voters back home. This has weakened the clout of party leaders, as well as presidents, in overcoming legislative gridlock.

Either the House or the Senate, or both houses at the same time, may introduce legislation. The only exceptions to this rule are money-raising bills, which according to the Constitution must start in the House, and appropriations (spending) bills, which by custom also begin there. Approximately 20,000 bills are introduced in Congress each year. (See Figure 4.2.) They may be part of the president's program, or they may be drafted by individual members or by committees. They may be the result of issue networks among members of congressional committees, the executive bureaucracy, and lobbyists. These will reflect powerful alliances of interests operating in legislative arenas like military spending, health care, or tax policies.

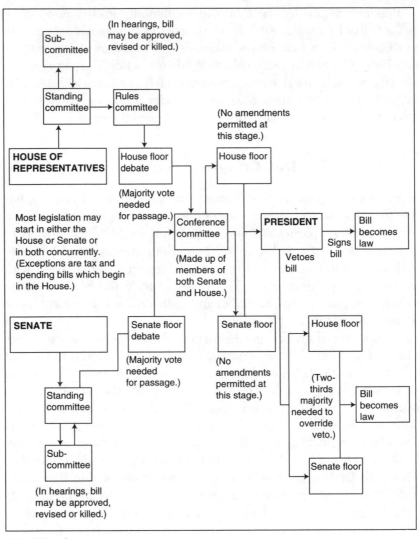

FIGURE 4.2
How a Bill (Rarely) Becomes a Law.

Further complicating matters is that the Senate and the House act separately and may amend or revise bills as they see fit. For any bill to become law, it must ultimately be passed by both houses of Congress in identical language and approved by the president or passed over his veto. Only 5 percent of the bills introduced in Congress ever become law.

The Congress operates by division of labor. Most of the work of Congress goes on not on the House or Senate floor but in committees. House committees may have anywhere from 20 to 50 representatives;

Senate committees usually have 10 to 20 senators. If they did not divide up into committees, the Senate and House would move even more slowly and deal with far fewer issues because they could consider only one subject at a time. It is difficult to imagine Congress without committees.

When a piece of legislation is introduced in either the Senate or the House, it is assigned to a committee. The committee (or, more often, one of its subcommittees) reviews the bill and decides whether to recommend it to the whole House or Senate. Between 80 and 90 percent of the bills introduced in Congress die in committee. The committee system is central to how Congress operates.

The Committee System

"Congress in session is Congress on exhibition, whilst Congress in its committee rooms is Congress at work."

—*Woodrow Wilson*

The *Washington Post* reported that on the last week of April 2004, the House of Representatives was in session for two days and one night, an average workweek. On one day they renamed a post office in Rhode Island and supported "Financial Literacy Month." On another they renamed a Miami courthouse and extended the popular repeal of the tax code's "marriage penalty." That same week, 35 U.S. servicemen died in Iraq, and CBS showed shocking pictures of Americans abusing Iraqi prisoners.

In fairness, the floor of the House is not the whole story. Floor sessions are often little more than a formality designed to make a public record. At the same time, many of the committee rooms would be buzzing with activity.

How Committees Work

There are three types of committees in Congress: standing, select, and joint. (A *conference committee* is set up in the final stages of legislation to reconcile differences between the two houses in passing a bill.) *Standing committees* are the basic working units of Congress. They were started early in the nation's history because Congress found it could do more work faster if it broke down into smaller, specialized groups. There are now 20 standing committees in the House and 16 in the Senate, most focusing on one or two general subjects.

Representatives serve on one or two standing committees, senators on three or four. Usually these committees break down into subcommittees for a further division of labor. In the 113th Congress, the House had 98 subcommittees and the Senate had 72 (see Figure 4.3).

Before any bill can be sent to the floor for consideration by the entire Senate or House, it must be approved by a majority vote in the standing committee to which it is assigned. A committee's examination of a proposed bill may

House	Senate
Standing Committees	
Agriculture	
Appropriations	Agriculture, Nutrition, and Forestry
Armed Services	Appropriations
Budget	Armed Services
Education and the Workforce	Banking, Housing, and Urban Affairs
Energy and Commerce	Budget
Ethics	Commerce, Science, and Transportation
Financial Services	Energy and Natural Resources
Foreign Affairs	Environment and Public Works
Homeland Security	Finance
House Administration	Foreign Relations
Judiciary	Health, Education, Labor, and Pensions
Natural Resources	Homeland Security and Gov'tal Affairs
Oversight and Government Reform	Judiciary
Rules	Rules and Administration
Science, Space, and Technology	Small Business and Entrepreneurship
Small Business	Veterans' Affairs
Transportation and Infrastructure	
Veterans' Affairs	
Ways and Means	

FIGURE 4.3
Standing Committees of the 113th Congress.

include holding public hearings in which interested groups, including the executive bureaucracies and lobbyists, are invited to testify. Often the actual work on a bill assigned to a standing committee goes on in one of its subcommittees. If the full committee then approves the bill, it will be sent to the floor of the Senate or House with a report describing the committee's findings and the reasons the committee thinks the bill should be passed. If the bill is not supported by the committee, it will be killed. The bill's sponsors may resubmit it in a later Congress, but if the committee involved continues to reject it, it will fail.

Select or special committees are temporary panels set up to do specific jobs and usually dissolved after they have completed them. Ordinarily, select committees do not have legislative authority and can only study, investigate, and recommend. For example, the Select Bipartisan Committee to Investigate the Preparation for and Response to Hurricane Katrina was set up in September 2005 to report back in February 2006 and then go out of business, which the committee did.

Joint committees are permanent bodies including both senators and representatives, usually set up to coordinate policy on routine matters. There are currently four joint committees; the most important is the Joint Economic Committee, which reports on the president's annual economic report. The jealousy of the two houses of Congress over their separate powers makes joint committees rare.

Committee Chairmen and the Seniority System

By the unwritten rule of *seniority*, the chair of any committee is typically the majority party member who has served longest (consecutively) on the committee. While the current congressional leadership usually follows seniority, acceptance of the party's legislative agenda is also part of the job requirements for any committee chairman and makes the OK of party leaders key to committee chairmen being appointed.

The important power of committee chairmen was apparent in 2011, when the Republicans again became the majority party in the House, allowing them to have a majority on each committee and to appoint all the chairmen. This meant control of the House agenda—the issues it would consider and those it would ignore. Not surprisingly, the House went from supporting the president on issues like health reform and climate change to opposing him. Republican House committees refused to pass his budgets and spending requests and were eager to investigate executive departments for fraud and waste.

Chairmen hire majority party committee staff, schedule committee meetings and agenda, and have something to say about the appointment of new members to their committees. Unless there is strong pressure from party leaders, chairmen usually can kill legislation they oppose. Even when a majority of committee members support legislation, the chairman can refuse to schedule a bill for hearings. That stops a bill from moving forward. A chairman's blocking power is stronger in the House than in the Senate.

The tradition of seniority is not written down in the rules of the House or Senate, and yet for most of the twentieth century, the custom was almost never broken. Then, starting in the mid-1970s, things changed. A combination of scandals and the desire of the growing number of junior Democrats for a "piece of the action" led to several committee chairs being ousted and an increase in the power of the party caucus.

When the Republicans took power in the House in 1994, party leadership was strengthened at the expense of the committees. The House Republican Conference imposed six-year term limits on chairmen, leading to some early retirements by committee chairs in 2000. GOP leaders centralized power and rewarded loyal allies with important chairmanships, with some weight given to seniority. Loyalty to the party was critical to winning the approval of the House Republican leadership. In a similar spirit Speaker Nancy Pelosi had at the beginning of the 111th Congress ignored seniority by allowing her Democratic Party's caucus to replace the chairman of the House Energy and Commerce Committee despite his seniority.

Seniority is more important in the Senate than the House. While the majority party leaders in the Senate exercise control over committees, these leaders—both Democrats and Republicans—nearly always follow the seniority rankings in determining who heads a committee or subcommittee.

The seniority system—mocked as the *senility system*—lives on. Attacked as undemocratic, it permits members who are reelected to accumulate legislative power. It has allowed minorities in the Democratic Party and less-conservative Republicans to gain positions of power. Seniority ensures that an experienced person will become chairman and has provided a predictable system of succession without constant fights over control of the chair. But party leaders of Congress, as they have gained in strength, have no longer felt the need to automatically follow a custom that limits their own influence.

Specialization and Reciprocity

Though weakened, two other informal rules support the power of committees in Congress. The first, *specialization*, is closely related to the second, *reciprocity*. Specialization means that once assigned to a committee or subcommittee, a member of Congress is expected to specialize in its work and become an expert in that area. Particularly in the House, members are not expected to follow all legislation in Congress equally or to speak out on widely varying issues. The result of this system is that committees and their individual members become experts in their own work but may not know much about other areas.

This potential problem is resolved through the practice of reciprocity. Here members look for guidance in voting on an issue outside their committee to members of committees that do specialize in it. Legislators tend to vote the way that their party's representatives on the most closely concerned committee tell them to vote. They assume that those on the committee know most about the legislation, and the members want the same support when their committee's business is involved. Specialization and reciprocity, then, are two sides of the same coin. You develop expertise in an area, and other members follow your lead in that area. You, in turn, follow the lead of others more knowledgeable than you in areas outside your expertise. Because senators commonly serve on more committees—usually four—their areas of specialization are less intense.

Assignment to a committee or subcommittee is vital to a legislator's power. This keeps committees stable and discourages "hopping" from one to another. Once members of Congress have been assigned to a committee, they will not be removed against their wishes unless the ratio between the parties should shift, which of course includes a change in the majority party as happened when Republicans won control of the House in 2010.

Major Committees in the House

Power in the House is now concentrated in the caucus and leadership of the majority party and in the senior party members of a few elite committees. In recent congresses, leaders of both parties have increasingly shaped legislation in the committees. The key committees in the House are usually those dealing with the budget. These are Budget, Ways and Means, Appropriations, and Rules.

Almost all legislation approved by committees in the House must pass through the Rules Committee before reaching the floor. The Rules Committee's name comes from its function: If the committee approves a bill for transmission to the House floor, it assigns a "rule" to that bill, setting the terms of a debate. The Rules Committee can, for example, assign a "closed rule," which forbids any amendments and forces the House into a "take it or leave it" position. As a "traffic cop," Rules has the power to delay or even stop legislation. It can amend bills or send them back to committee for revision, and it can decide where two committees have bills on the same subject, which one gets sent to the floor. Rules is directed by the majority party leadership.

The Ways and Means Committee deals with tax legislation, or the raising of revenue for the government. One former chairman called it "the Cadillac of committees." Because all money-raising bills begin in the House, any tax legislation goes first to Ways and Means, making this committee a central power in Congress. Under its chairman, Dave Camp (R-Michigan), the Committee provided a forum for opposing the Obama administration's budget deficits and for proposing tax reforms.

While Ways and Means raises money, the Appropriations Committee deals with how government spends that money. When the federal budget is presented to Congress by the president each year, it is first sent to the House Appropriations Committee and its 11 subcommittees. Because the power to tax and spend is the power to make or break programs, industries, and interest groups, and because specialization and reciprocity nudge Congress to follow the lead of its

The Prince of Pork

On reelection night the senior senator declared, "West Virginia has always had four friends: God Almighty, Sears Roebuck, Carter's Liver pills and Robert C. Byrd." Years earlier, Senator Byrd had happily set his goal: "I want to be West Virginia's billion-dollar industry." In delivering pork to his poor state in the form of federally funded projects, the senator has accomplished his goal and earned the title "Prince of Pork."

These "Byrd Droppings" fill the state, often with the senator's name attached. There is the Robert C. Byrd Locks and Dam project and the Byrd Green Bank Telescope, both with statues of the senator to greet visitors. There are two Robert C. Byrd U.S. courthouses, four Byrd stretches of highways, a Robert C. Byrd Bridge, and two Robert C. Byrd interchanges. The senator's name graces a Lifelong Learning Center, Hardwood Technology Center, Health and Wellness Center, and Institute for Advanced Flexible Manufacturing. One newspaper counted more than 30 projects named for the senator and far more that he brought to the state without his name. One critic surmised, "What next—West Byrdinia?"

As chairman of the Senate Appropriations Committee, the Democratic senator brought home 10 times the national average of legislative pork or $236 per resident. When he died in June 2010, he had become the longest serving senator in American history (1959–2010).

committees, the importance of Ways and Means and Appropriations is clear. While Appropriations is limited by the budget process on its overall spending, it can still decide where it will spend money or make cuts. Traditionally Appropriations was the place for doing favors for other members, such as passing their *pork-barrel bills*—legislation designed to produce visible local benefits, like highways and bridges. These can take the form of *earmarks*, which are parts of a bill that direct spending to a specific project usually to benefit a specific congressman. They are currently banned by Speaker Boehner. (See "The Prince of Pork.")

Major Committees in the Senate

The most important committees in the Senate (besides Budget) are Appropriations, Finance, Judiciary, and Foreign Relations. The Senate Appropriations Committee receives spending bills after they have been passed by the House. Its procedures are like its House counterpart, except that the Senate committee acts as a "court of appeals," adding money to or subtracting it from the amounts granted by the House. If passed by the House, tax legislation then goes to the Senate Finance Committee, the Senate's equivalent to Ways and Means in the House.

The Judiciary committee is one of the Senate's oldest and most important committees. Now chaired by Patrick Leahy, Democrat from Vermont, the committee has jurisdiction over federal laws, including proposed constitutional amendments. It holds confirmation hearings for federal judges, most notably nominations of justices to the Supreme Court.

The Senate Foreign Relations Committee is a watchdog over the president's dominant position in foreign policy. Its importance comes from the Senate's role in confirming appointments of high-level State Department officials, including ambassadors, and approving treaties. It has provided a place for comment and debate on administration policies, such as the dispute over Ukraine, the conflict in Syria and the negotiations with Iran. Committee membership has provided useful publicity for senators aspiring to become president, including Barack Obama, or secretary of state where its former chairman John Kerry now serves.

The Senate's Rules Committee is much less important than its House counterpart. With fewer than one-fourth as many members as the House, the problem of coordination is not as great. The Senate decided that it did not need a strong "traffic cop" to screen legislation. (See "Congressional Staff.")

Congressional Staff

Despite efforts to shrink staff, the U.S. Congress remains the most heavily staffed legislature in the world, with over 35,000 employees. Even junior congressmen can have 18 full-time staffers and 4 part-time employees. By comparison, the 650 members of the British House of Commons get by with about 1,000 employees.

Congress finds it difficult to cut staff because, other than voting, a member's staff does everything he or she does. They organize hearings, negotiate agreements with other members' staffs, research proposals, speak with voters, and promote legislation. Staffers will often initiate policies and then "sell" them to their bosses. Lobbyists understand their importance and spend most of their time cultivating relationships with them. Because staff influence is best exercised quietly, it may not be visible; yet it is always present.

On the Floor and Beyond

Once a bill has been approved by committee (and in the House by the Rules Committee), it is sent to the House or Senate floor for debate. There it is placed on a calendar. *Calendars* are the schedules for Congress. Some calendars are for routine or minor legislation, others for more important bills. There is one in the House, the "discharge calendar," that, rarely, can be used to force a bill out of committee against the committee's wishes.

In the House, floor debate is controlled by the Speaker. He or she schedules bills for consideration and then makes sure the committees deliver their bills in the correct form and at the right time. The Speaker has the right to preside over debate. House members are commonly restricted to a few minutes of speaking. The Senate, being smaller, is able to operate more informally, and senators can speak longer. Power is more widely distributed in the Senate than in the House. Even junior (new) senators often chair subcommittees. The Senate majority leader schedules bills for debate, but his control during debate is much less than the House Speaker's.

When debate on a bill has ended, it is put to a vote. A majority of the legislators present is needed for passage. Whether a bill begins in the Senate or the House, it must sooner or later be submitted to the other chamber, where the whole procedure of committee review and floor action will be repeated. Any differences between the House and Senate versions of a bill must be eliminated before it can be sent to the president for his signature or veto.

When there are differences between the two houses on the same bill, a *conference committee* is set up. This is a temporary body including both senators and representatives, created solely to iron out the differences between House and Senate versions of one bill. These differences come about because of amendments attached to the bill by one chamber but not the other, or because the two houses have passed different bills dealing with the same subject, as was seen in the financial reform bill (the Dodd-Frank Act) passed in 2010. Because the bill needed to be approved in identical language by both houses, much of the heavy lifting, and lobbying, on the bill occurred in conference committee.

The Speaker of the House and the Senate majority leader have the authority to appoint the members of conference committees. In practice they allow the chairs of the relevant standing committees to do this and typically appoint the senior members of these committees. The conference committee engages in bargaining and trade-offs to reach a compromise; once this job is finished, it is disbanded. When (and if) the conferees reach agreement, the new substitute bill is then sent back to the House and Senate floors for a yea-or-nay vote. This bill cannot be amended; it must be accepted or rejected as is. If this rule were not in force, the bill might be amended again in different ways in the House and Senate, thereby requiring yet another conference committee, and so on. (See Table 4.1.)

Party identity is still the best single predictor for how members will vote, as seen in the two parties' division on most of President Obama's legislative agenda. Of course both in committees and on the

TABLE 4.1 MAJOR DIFFERENCES BETWEEN THE HOUSE AND THE SENATE

HOUSE	SENATE
Larger (435)	Smaller (100)
Shorter term of office (2 years)	Longer term of office (6 years)
More procedural restraints on members	Fewer procedural restraints on members
Narrower constituency	Broader, more varied constituency
Policy specialists	Policy generalists
Less media coverage	More media coverage
More powerful leaders	Less powerful leaders
Less prestigious	More prestigious
Briefer floor debates	Longer floor debates
Less reliant on staff	More reliant on staff
More partisan	Less partisan

floor of Congress, members of the same political party do not always vote together, and sometimes they vote across party lines. On some measures, such as supporting President Obama's proposed bombing of Syria in 2013 for using chemical weapons, isolationist-leaning Republicans united with anti-war Democrats to oppose the president. In other cases, such as the closing of military bases, Republicans and Democrats from the same region have united to prevent the closing of their local bases. The most frequent division in Congress remains that between Republicans and Democrats.

In recent congresses, party loyalty has increased in both parties. The majority of the two parties oppose each other more often. Members now vote with their party about 80 percent of the time, whereas 25 years ago loyalty was only seen in 70 percent of the votes. The parties are both more united and more different. As Democrats continue to lose conservatives from the South, and as Republican primary voters select more conservative candidates, the parties have become polarized—fewer moderate Republicans, fewer conservative Democrats, and fewer independent *mavericks* in either party who are willing to defy their own party. As a result, recent congresses have become more partisan and harsher. (See "Nastiness on Capitol Hill.")

Despite President Obama's call for a new era of bipartisanship, it seems unlikely that this intense party division will end any time soon. For Republicans the president's policies are decidedly liberal and wrong, and his image as a post-partisan leader is just rhetoric. They

Nastiness on Capitol Hill

Thomas Jefferson recognized the importance of polite behavior in the legislature. He hoped the Senate would cool the passions of the more populist House and outlined rules to reduce personal attacks. Jefferson saw no reason that partisanship should undercut civility among legislators, which didn't stop his opponents from charging that he had fathered a child with his slave.

Recently the polarized political divisions in the country amplified on cable talk shows and the Internet have made Congress increasingly nasty. In 2009 as the president was speaking to Congress, a South Carolina congressman yelled, "You lie." In the fall 2013 budget battle, Speaker Boehner asked why Obama was willing to negotiate with Russian president Putin but not with Republicans over the debt limit. At the same time, Democratic Senate Majority Leader Reid declared that "anarchists" had taken over the GOP.

One leading political scientist, Burdett Loomis, remarked that all this hurt good policymaking, "There seems to be almost no shame. Everyone is just completely righteous right now."

view, with some justification, Obama's successes in confronting the country's economic problems as designed to cement Democrats in power. Democrats argue, also justifiably, that despite their good-faith compromises, Republicans have moved rightward, uniting in opposition. In his second term, the president has been more insistent on pushing reforms in areas of energy, immigration, and gun control often through executive orders not requiring congressional approval.

Filibuster

In the Senate, except under unusual circumstances, debate is unlimited. Senators may talk on a subject for as long as they wish, and they will not be cut off. Never-ending talk by one or a number of senators designed to delay or block action in the Senate is called a *filibuster*. The original filibuster was a type of pirate ship. Its current meaning probably comes from the image of a lone individual defying the rules. Traditionally senators filibustered by talking for several hours (sometimes reading the Bible or the Washington phone directory) before giving up the floor to an ally. Now senators don't actually have to speak; they can just announce their willingness to filibuster. Former senator Strom Thurmond of South Carolina set the individual filibuster record in 1957 by speaking against a civil rights act for 24 hours and 18 minutes nonstop. More recently in 2013 Senator Ted Cruz, Republican from Texas, filibustered for 21 hours in support of defunding Obamacare.

Rule 22 (of the Senate Rules—a set of regulations governing Senate behavior) protects the filibuster unless three-fifths of the Senate votes for an end to debate. This is the only vote in Congress based on the total number of legislators. All other votes in both the Senate and House are based on the number of members who are present and voting. Voting to end debate is called *cloture*. Because many senators, especially those of the minority party, see advantages in having the filibuster available, cloture is rarely successful.

Historically the minority party in the Senate threatened a filibuster to prevent intensely disliked majority actions. But in recent senate sessions, with Republicans in the minority, the use of the filibuster to prevent majority action has become standard behavior. Between 1917 and 1970, only 58 motions for cloture were filed, or about one a year. For the two-year Congress that ended in 2012, there were 73 cloture votes to end filibusters, or nearly one filibuster per day that the Senate was in session. This has meant that passing major legislation in the Senate requires a "supermajority," the votes of 60 members—sufficient to invoke cloture.

The result has been a "minority veto," delaying the appointment of judges and the confirmation of heads of agencies, even including former Republican senator Chuck Hagel to be secretary of defense. Despite the president's call for reform at the start of the 113th Congress, Democrats in the Senate (looking down the road to when they could be a minority) proved reluctant to limit the filibuster. Then in late 2013 Senate Democrats voted to cut off debate on executive and judicial nominees by a simple majority vote. This was called the most significant change in Senate procedures in a generation and denounced by Republicans as a "nuclear option" in undermining individual senators' power to stop "majority excesses." The ability to use the filibuster on other legislation remained in place.

Because the House of Representatives is larger and harder to manage, it has decided it cannot afford the luxury of unlimited debate. Hence, filibusters are not allowed in the House.

Presidential Veto

Even after it has been approved by both the House and Senate, a bill may still be killed by a presidential veto. The president may veto any legislation he wishes. The threat of a veto increases the influence of a president in bargaining with congressional leaders while legislation is still being drafted.

A president may not veto only part of a bill—called an item veto. He must veto it all or accept it all. But Congress has the last word: If Congress *overrides* a veto, the bill becomes law. To override a veto requires two-thirds approval of each house of Congress. Vetoes are rarely overridden. They are also rarely used by recent chief executives, especially when a president's party runs Congress. While President Eisenhower vetoed 181 bills in his two terms, Bill Clinton only vetoed 37. Before the Democrats took control of Congress, President George W. Bush had only used the veto once in six years—on stem cell research. After the 2006 elections, Bush exercised the veto 11 more times. President Obama, history's most veto-shy president, only used the veto twice in his first term.

The president must act on a bill within 10 working days. If he does not sign it within that period while Congress remains in session, the bill becomes law without his signature. If Congress adjourns before the 10 days are up and the president does not sign the bill, it does not become law—this is called a *pocket veto*.

Because the item veto was declared unconstitutional by the Supreme Court in 1998, Congress retains the advantage of *riders* in any confrontation with the president. A rider is a piece of legislation

The White House Trades for China Trade

To get members of Congress to agree with the White House often requires appealing to the interests of their district. In 2000 a bill to allow free trade with China came before Congress. It was strongly backed by the Clinton administration and eventually passed both houses. But before that could happen, the White House had to offer local deals for this national issue.

House Democrats, who generally opposed the trade agreement, were swayed by other considerations. Democrat Robert E. "Bud" Cramer voted "yes" after the Commerce Department promised to reconsider closing a weather station in his tornado-prone Alabama district. Martin Frost, a Texas Democrat, supported the bill when Northrop Grumman Corp., a major defense contractor, decided to stay in Dallas after reaching an agreement with the navy. And three other Texas congressmen supported the administration when EPA promised to quickly complete its required environmental review that was holding up the opening of a gas pipeline across southern Texas.

Source: *CQ Weekly*, May 27, 2000, p. 1250.

attached as an amendment to another bill, which may deal with a totally different issue. Commonly, the rider contains provisions that the president does not like, whereas the "parent" bill to which the rider is attached is favored by the president. Either the president vetoes the rider and thus also the main bill, or he accepts the unwanted rider in order to get the rest of the bill. These riders helped increase government spending, and for this reason many Republicans supported the item veto, even for a Democratic president. (See "The White House Trades for China Trade.")

The Budget Process

Passing laws does not automatically make anything happen. If money is needed for the government's wishes (as expressed in a bill) to be carried out, the entire legislative process must be gone through *twice*— once to pass a bill *authorizing* the activity and a second time to pass a bill *appropriating* the money to do it. The goals of the authorizing bill will not come into effect if the appropriations process does not provide the funds.

The "power of the purse" is the basic constitutional power of Congress. Historically, the *authority* to control government spending and taxes has not meant the *ability* to control them. Congress has traditionally not acted coherently on the budget. The numerous committees and decentralized power bases in Congress has meant that overall

spending (expenditures) was seldom related to taxes (revenues), and neither fit into a national economic policy. The responsibility for putting together a comprehensive government budget and national economic policy thus fell to the president. Congress struggled to change this.

In 1974 Congress passed the *Budget Act* (the *Congressional Budget and Impoundment Control Act*), which allowed Congress to propose an alternative to the president's budget. Congress could now examine all spending and tax measures and evaluate them in terms of the overall needs of the economy. The Budget Act did this in several ways.

The act set up House and Senate Budget Committees. The House Budget Committee members are drawn mainly from the Ways and Means and Appropriations committees, with one member from each of the other standing committees. Members of the Senate Budget Committee are selected in the same way as members of other committees in the Senate. The committees guide Congress in setting total spending, tax, and debt levels. Aiding the two budget committees is a *Congressional Budget Office* (CBO). The nonpartisan CBO's experts analyze the president's budget proposals and match Congress's spending decisions with the budget targets. For example, the CBO, despite a Democratic majority in Congress at the time, criticized Obama's health care reforms as adding to the budget deficit.

The budget works its way through Congress on a series of deadlines. The goal is to have a completed budget by the beginning of the government's fiscal year, October 1. The process starts when the president submits his budget to Congress in January. All the committees in Congress then submit their estimates and views of the budget to the budget committees, which gather them in a first resolution. Congress must vote on this resolution, which sets overall spending and tax levels, by April 15. The various parts of this first resolution then go back to the standing committees concerned with the particular subject or program. By mid-June the standing committees' recommendations would have gone back to the budget committees, which draw up a reconciliation bill that is then voted on by Congress. This part of the process is called *reconciliation* because it attempts to balance the separate standing committees' decisions with the targets set by the first resolution.

Throughout the 1980s, various Congressional efforts to control the budget deficit failed miserably. In 1993 President Clinton introduced an ambitious deficit-reduction package that promised to reduce the deficit by $500 billion. The White House claimed that half of the reduction would come from tax increases (mostly on the wealthy) and half from cutting government spending. Republican opponents charged the bill's numbers were suspect and that it was too "tax heavy." After considerable debate and changes by Congress, the bill was passed.

The prosperity of the late 1990s increased tax revenues beyond all predictions and aided in producing balanced budgets in 1998, 1999, 2000, and 2001. It had been 50 years since the U.S. government had this many consecutive years of national debt reduction. It did not last. President George W. Bush pushed through a $1.35 trillion tax cut that slashed government revenues, the stock market cratered, the recession continued, and the war on terrorism and in Iraq led to increased spending for defense. By 2006, the year's federal deficit was over $400 billion because of spending on hurricane relief and on the war in Iraq. It was a blunt contrast with the *surplus* of $236 billion in fiscal 2000.

Budget Deadlocks and Sequesters

With the recession of 2008 and the Obama administration's vigorous (and expensive) stimulus program to revive the economy, the federal deficit skyrocketed. It reached $1.55 trillion in 2009 and then fell to less than half five years later—still almost 5 percent of gross domestic product. The lack of agreement between the president and House Republicans led to both sides making sweeping proposals, none of which were adopted. Republicans proposed reducing government spending, especially in social programs and entitlements; the Democrats wished to raise tax revenues and close loopholes on the wealthy. Neither the threat of defaulting on the debt, the decrease in the U.S. credit rating in 2011, Obama's reelection victory, nor popular pressure for a compromise led to a "grand bargain" between the two parties on the budget.

Instead, there arose the *sequester*, harsh automatic budget cuts that sliced spending across the board by $109 billion a year, half from domestic programs, half from the military. The sequester was passed as part of the Budget Control Act of 2011 as an incentive for Congress to cut $1.5 trillion over 10 years. If Congress had passed its own spending cuts and tax increases, the unattractive sequester would have been avoided. That didn't happen, and the sequester began in March 2013.

While mandatory programs like Social Security and food stamps were excluded, everything from air force weapon purchases to emergency unemployment to national parks were included. The sequester threatened the country with increased unemployment and decreased economic growth. While government departments threatened lay-offs of their employees, many later backtracked. The Pentagon said it would have to furlough all of its civilian employees for 22 days but ended up reducing the days of unpaid leave to six. A bipartisan budget compromise signed by President Obama in early 2014 effectively ended the unpopular sequester.

Even though the budget process has not changed, only four times in almost 40 years has Congress passed its appropriations bills on time. Instead, Congress must adopt *a continuing resolution* to keep the government running for a set period of time. Even this couldn't be done in the fall of 2013 with a resulting shutdown in the federal government. The lack of a budget agreement has produced a debt that is larger, as a percentage of the economy, than at any time in U.S. history except World War II. While annual deficits were shrinking rapidly—to around $680 billion—they were expected to rise again in a few years as the baby-boom generation retires.

Other Powers of Congress

Besides these legislative powers, Congress also has several nonlegislative powers. Among them are *oversight* of the executive branch and *investigation*. Congress created the executive agencies and departments and specified their duties. It can change them at any time. Congress appropriates the funds those agencies need to perform their jobs. These powers give Congress an interest in what the executive branch is doing and the means to find out. Congress, for example, can decide who will and will not receive food stamps and can judge who will be allowed to use federal lands. In short, the annual appropriations process gives Congress the chance to ask what the bureaucracies are doing, tell them what they ought to be doing, and give money for what Congress wants and withhold money for what it does not want. When different parties control the executive and at least one house of Congress—like now—the political advantages of using these powers becomes more apparent.

The *Government Accountability Office* (GAO) is an agency created by Congress to help with its oversight function. Congress uses the GAO to examine questionable government programs or departments. Many of the stories about scandals in government that appear on shows like *60 Minutes* start life as GAO reports.

Congress has the power to investigate. If Congress, or a committee (or a committee chair), decides that something is not being done properly, an investigation may be launched. The subject might be the abuse of prisoners at Guantanamo, corporate executives' salaries, or illegal campaign contributions. In other words, Congress can investigate whatever it wishes.

Congressional investigations are not welcomed by the executive. On June 4, 2002, the House and Senate Intelligence Committees began joint hearings to investigate "why the Intelligence Community did not learn of the September 11th attacks in advance." President Bush was clearly not pleased. In 2013, the House Oversight and Government Reform Committee, with Republicans in the majority, launched an investigation of whether the IRS improperly targeted right-wing political groups and the tax deductions they received.

At times congressional investigations have proven dangerous to civil liberties. In the 1950s, Republican senator Joseph McCarthy's Permanent Investigations Subcommittee and the House Un-American Activities Committee falsely accused government officials of disloyalty and whipped up fear in the country with charges of communist sympathies. Such widespread personal attacks came to be called "witch hunts."

The Senate has the power to approve or reject most presidential appointments, including ambassadors, cabinet members, and military officers. Presidential appointments are usually routine, and the Senate tends to agree that the president has a right to have the persons he wishes to work with him. Still, the "behind-the-scenes" pressure of Senate dissatisfaction undoubtedly causes presidents not to make certain nominations in the first place. The Senate often takes a more active role in presidential appointments to the independent regulatory commissions and the Supreme Court, as shown by the public debate and divided Senate vote over the appointment of Janet Yellen to be the chair of the Federal Reserve.

Congress also has certain judicial functions. The House of Representatives has the power of *impeachment*, bringing charges against a federal official by a simple majority vote. Then, the Senate holds a trial on these charges. In the case of impeachment of the president, the chief justice of the Supreme Court presides. If two-thirds of the Senate votes to uphold the charges and to convict the official, that official is removed from office.

Impeachment is difficult, slow, and cumbersome. Several federal judges have been impeached and convicted in the past. Only two presidents were ever impeached—Andrew Johnson in 1868 and Bill

Clinton in 1998. Neither was convicted by the Senate. Richard Nixon resigned the presidency in 1974 (the only president ever to do so) in the face of likely impeachment by the House and conviction by the Senate.

The failed 1998–1999 attempt to remove President Clinton illustrated the political and constitutional obstacles to impeachment. Acting on the report of Independent Counsel Kenneth Starr, the House of Representatives in the fall of 1998 took up the question of whether the president should be impeached. Accused of perjury for lying to a grand jury about his affair with intern Monica Lewinsky and then of obstructing justice by trying to cover it up, the president benefited from personal popularity and economic prosperity throughout the scandal. Voting on party lines, a majority of the House impeached the president. But on February 12, 1999, the GOP, lacking Democratic support, could not get a two-thirds vote for conviction in the Senate. President Clinton's accusers could never quite convince the public that the president's sleazy behavior rose to the level of the "high crimes and misdemeanors" that the Constitution requires for impeachment.

Despite its difficulty, impeachment remains an ultimate check over the executive in the hands of the legislature.

CASE STUDY

The Limits of Limiting Global Warming

After years of denial, Washington seemed ready to tackle global warming. The evidence was clear. More than 2,000 scientists on the Nobel Prize–winning International Panel on Climate Change declared that carbon from burning fossil fuels was warming the planet, causing drought and rising sea levels. U.S. government agencies predicted that the Southwest would become another Dust Bowl and Florida would flood. Polls showed that three-quarters of Americans thought the government should regulate the release of greenhouse gases. In 2009 Democratic majorities in both houses and a new president agreed to make the issue a priority.

The most straightforward way of limiting carbon would be to tax it: make polluters pay. But a new tax for every activity that burns carbon-based fuels would be a political nightmare. The so-called cap-and-trade system seemed more doable.

Under cap and trade, the government would set a yearly limit on carbon emissions and then gradually tighten. It would issue

"permission slips to pollute," giving companies permits for the carbon they burned. These permits could be bought and sold. Tougher standards each year and fewer permits would lead to higher prices and consumers cutting back on carbon products. Europe had operated a similar system with mixed results.

THE HOUSE ACTS

The legislation in the House proposing to set this up was called Waxman-Markey, after Henry Waxman of California, chairman of the Energy and Commerce Committee, and Edward J. Markey (D-Massachusetts). The bill won approval from Waxman's committee, as well as Ways and Means and Agriculture committees, and after months of negotiations, was passed by the House in June by a vote of 219–212. Only eight Republicans voted for it, and the GOP denounced it as a national energy tax. Forty-four Democrats, mostly from conservative and rural districts, voted against the measure.

To get the votes needed for passage, the bill changed *who* pays the costs of cutting greenhouse gases. To satisfy Democrats from critical states, allowances were given to coal-based electric utilities, energy-intensive manufacturers, oil refiners, and the auto industry. Instead of auctioning off the cap–and-trade permits, the government gave them away, costing the Treasury some $713 billion in the program's first 10 years. Congressmen from the South protected their region's utilities by weakening the requirements for renewable energy.

In the months of horse-trading, the bill's targets for carbon use were weakened, its requirements for switching from fossil fuels were reduced, and the incentives for industries were sweetened. While some environmentalists backed the final House bill, others like Greenpeace and Friends of the Earth opposed it. Industry was split. President Obama welcomed House passage but admitted, "I think that finding the right balance between providing new incentives to businesses, but not giving away the store, is always an art. . . ." The Senate was expected to be even more difficult.

ON TO THE SENATE

The economic downturn coming out of the 2008 financial meltdown undermined support for spending money on the environment. For the White House, health care reform was a more important priority facing the Senate. Democrats were a majority in the Senate but did not have the same strong party control as the House leadership. With many senators from energy-producing states, the decentralized Senate presented new obstacles, including the need for 60 votes to overcome an almost-certain Republican filibuster.

Nonetheless, after months of meetings, Senator Barbara Boxer (D-California), chair of the Environmental and Public Works Committee, along with Senator John Kerry (D-Massachusetts), introduced a climate bill. It was similar to the House bill, but from the beginning it was in trouble. Ten moderate Democratic senators from Midwestern states sent the president a letter reminding him that their electricity largely came from burning coal, a major source of greenhouse-gas pollution. Lobbyists warned that the bill would harm the recovering economy by raising energy prices. Nonetheless, the bill, Clean Energy Jobs and American Power (S. 1733), was voted out of Senator Boxer's Committee, with all the Republican members boycotting the vote.

THE CLIMATE OUTSIDE THE SENATE

For the next several months, the issue disappeared. Health care reform absorbed the Senate until it passed both houses in March 2010. Lobbyists kept up the pressure on the climate bill. Environmentalists were being outspent by a wide margin by oil and natural gas businesses. In the first six months of 2009, anti-climate bill groups spent over $82 million lobbying Washington, while groups on the other side spent under $19 million. Despite this, a Washington Post–ABC News poll found that 52 percent of Americans supported cap and trade.

On April 21, 2010, an oil drilling rig leased by British Petroleum exploded in the Gulf of Mexico, causing the worst oil spill in U.S. history. Unlike past disasters, like the 1990 sinking of the supertanker Exxon Valdez, this environmental horror had little political impact. The dismal economy and the public's fears of more expensive gasoline trumped other concerns.

Yet the president used the powers of his office to act on the climate. By executive order, President Obama required all federal agencies to reduce their greenhouse-gas emissions in buildings and vehicles. As the nation's largest consumer of energy, the federal government was leading by example. May 2010 saw the EPA release its final greenhouse-gas regulations, forcing power plants and refineries responsible for 70 percent of all emissions to use the best available technology to minimize these gases. The EPA promised to begin enforcing this by January 2011.

Congress was put on notice that the executive branch would act on global warming with or without legislation.

THE SENATE PULLS THE PLUG

Responding to weak Senate support, Majority Leader Harry Reid in early July introduced a "utility first" energy bill. It cut pollution from utilities (some 40 percent of the nation's carbon use), leaving aside transportation, agriculture, and other polluting sectors. This scaled-down version of the House bill required utilities to provide 15 percent of their power from renewable sources by 2021. Electric companies argued that this approach discriminated against them. However, reducing the bill's scope meant losing its intensely committed supporters without picking up any neutrals or opponents.

Weeks later, Senator Reid announced the bill's failure. "We know that we don't have the votes." The bill was abandoned. The president and environmentalists stopped pushing for it. There were quicker, if less comprehensive, solutions available in executive action by EPA to regulate carbon. Given the Republican unity in polarizing issues that the Democrats were introducing, the votes in the political center were simply not there.

Little effort was put into mobilizing the public around the law's global benefits. The loudest voices misrepresented the science of climate change, spread fear about loss jobs, and focused on the costs of these changes to particular industries and regions. They argued for doing nothing, and that's what happened.

CONCLUSION

The climate bill fell victim to the struggle between national goals and intense regional interests. Curbing the use of carbon was difficult for members who may have recognized climate change as a problem but had voters to represent. Energy interest groups from these regions stressed jobs over the planet's long-term viability. In the House, their representatives limited the overall targets, obtained for them rich compensation for changing their energy use, and got the costs shifted to consumers. In the Senate, because of the greater power given to individual senators and the lack of party control, even these compromises failed.

America's decentralized politics may offer other solutions to the challenges of global warming. Some 29 states have created their own renewable energy standards. A regional cap-and-trade program has been operating in 10 Northeastern and mid-Atlantic states. President Obama set a goal of cutting greenhouse-gas emissions 17 percent by 2020, and in summer 2013, he directed the EPA to create carbon standards for power plants. His plan didn't require congressional approval, neither did his administration's agreement with the auto companies setting higher fuel efficiency standards. It was the biggest step the U.S. government has ever taken toward cutting greenhouse gas emissions. Between 2010 and 2012, greenhouse gas emissions from power plants declined by 10 percent, reflecting their switch from coal to natural gas.

Action by Congress is, fortunately, not the only path to protecting the environment.

■ WRAP-UP

The U.S. Congress consists of two houses, the Senate and the House of Representatives. Two senators are selected from each state, and they serve for six years. Representatives are allocated to states according to population; they serve for two years. The Senate, with 100 members, is smaller, more informal, and more prestigious than the House, with its 435 members. The House, because it is larger, is more tightly controlled by party leaders. Since the 2010 elections, Democrats have been the majority party in the Senate, while Republicans have had a majority in the House.

The House and Senate operate separately, but before any legislation can be sent to the president for signing, it must be passed in identical language by both. In the House floor debate, the agenda for legislation, and even committee priorities, are controlled by the majority party. The Speaker of the House works closely with the majority leader and whips. The Senate has no Speaker; floor debate is managed by the Senate majority leader. Each chamber also has minority leaders and minority whips.

While much of the work of the House and Senate goes on in committees and subcommittees, party leadership has in recent years become more important than committee leaders. The committee chairmen (who are always from the majority party) do exercise considerable power. Despite some exceptions, chairmen are usually chosen on the basis of seniority—longest consecutive service on the committee. The majority leadership in the House has become influential in this decision, but the leaders in the Senate defer to seniority. The focus on the budget and the deficit along with members following specialization and reciprocity has raised the importance of the taxing and spending committees. The persistent lack of partisan agreement on budgets and deficits has led to gridlock, government shutdowns, and automatic cuts by sequester.

All legislation, other than revenue-raising and appropriations bills (which must start in the House), can be introduced in either the House or the Senate. It is then assigned to the relevant committee for review. If approved by committee, a bill is sent to the floor of the House or Senate (going through the Rules Committee in the House). When approved there, the bill goes to the other chamber for a similar process. If the House and Senate pass different versions, they will be ironed out by a conference committee. When both branches of Congress have approved the same bill, it is sent to the president. The president may sign it, veto it, pocket veto it, or allow it to become law without his signature. If he vetoes it, Congress may try to override the bill by a two-thirds vote in each house. The difficulty of passing major legislation, such as the climate bill to reduce greenhouse gases, comes out clearly in our case study. (See "The Limits of Limiting Global Warming.")

Congressional procedures seem complex and confusing because they *are* complex and confusing. Congress has been criticized for being slow, unresponsive, and even unrepresentative. Certainly, its procedures involve time-consuming duplication. The filibuster in the Senate, the fragmentation of power into committees, and the parties' polarization sometimes frustrate majority wishes. But they have not stopped Congress from quickly acting in an emergency, as seen in the weeks that followed the banking panic in the fall of 2008. Congressional complexity also doesn't stop voters from changing Congress through elections.

If Congress is sometimes slow to solve national issues, it may be because the country's leaders and people do not agree on either the problems or the solutions. If Congress bogs down in party disputes or struggles to reach a watered-down compromise, it may be because a country as large as the United States includes strongly opposing opinions that the Congress reflects. If special interests receive special treatment, this may simply be an accurate reflection of these players' political power.

Congress was not set up to make government more efficient. It was designed to represent the wishes of the people governed, to be the political game's democratic centerpiece. Congress acts best not when it acts least but when it reflects the public on which America's government rests.

THOUGHT QUESTIONS

1. How can Congress be made more responsive to public opinion? Does the increased party leaders' control over Congress bring the legislature closer to the public? Further away? Or does it not make any difference?
2. Think about the "unwritten rules" of seniority, specialization, and reciprocity. How do these rules help Congress operate? What are their drawbacks?
3. Congress is generally unpopular, whereas individual members are popular and usually reelected. Why does the institution suffer while incumbents shine?
4. How does Congress know what to do? Did recent elections give Congress a clear direction for policy? Or did they just reflect an uncertain polarized nation?
5. If you were a member of Congress, how would you have voted on the legislation to halt global warming, assuming that it may hurt your state's economy? How would you explain your decision to voters?

SUGGESTED READINGS

Caro, Robert A. *Master of the Senate: The Years of Lyndon Johnson*. New York: Alfred A. Knopf, 2002.
   The third volume of this masterful biography of Lyndon Johnson dissects the U.S. Senate in the 1950s and LBJ's powerful presence. The first 100 pages is an excellent history of the Senate.
Fenno, Richard E., Jr. *Home Style: House Members in Their Districts*. Boston: Little, Brown, 1978.
   Still the classic study of how representatives act in front of their most important audience—the folks back home.

Kaiser, Robert G. *Act of Congress*. New York: Alfred A. Knopf, 2013.
  A detailed and surprisingly hopeful account of how Congress can support policy over politics in voting for a financial reform bill, the 2010 Dodd-Frank Act.

Kennedy, John F. *Profiles in Courage*. New York: Harper & Row, 1956. Pb.
  The future president wrote these prize-winning profiles of members of Congress who stood up to the popular pressures of their time and sacrificed their careers to do what was right.

Lessig, Lawrence. *Republic, Lost*. New York: Hachette Book Group, 2011. Pb.
  The subtitle reads "How Money Corrupts Congress," which sums up this lawyer's indictment of the legislature.

Mann, Thomas E. and Norman J. Orenstein. *It's Even Worse than It Looks*. New York: Basics Books, 2012.
  According to these authors dysfunction in Congress comes in part from intensely opposed political parties, but mostly from a Republican party that has polarized to the right.

CHAPTER 5

The Judicial Branch: The Supreme Court and the Federal Court System

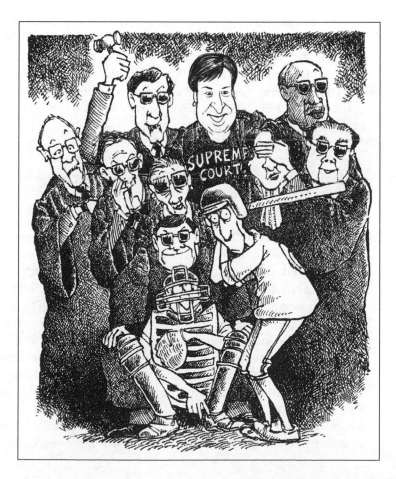

Article III of the Constitution gets right to the point in providing for the judicial player: "The judicial Power of the United States shall be vested in one Supreme Court, and in such inferior courts as the Congress may from time to time ordain and establish." When the Supreme Court upheld President Obama's contested health care reform law in the summer of 2012 in a close 5 to 4 ruling, we were reminded of the Court's central importance to constitutional government. The public attention given to this decision echoes in other pressing political conflicts including civil liberties, campaign finance, and presidential power; disagreements that the Court is called on to resolve.

Following the directions of the Constitution, Congress set up two major levels of federal courts below the Supreme Court—federal district courts and courts of appeals. It also established several special federal courts as the need for them has arisen. The federal court system is responsible for judging cases involving the U.S. Constitution and federal laws.

Paralleling the federal court system are the state courts. Each state has its own judicial system to try cases that come under state law (though state courts may also deal with cases under the U.S. Constitution and laws). Issues involving the Constitution may be appealed to the U.S. Supreme Court. In this chapter, we will focus on the federal court system and particularly the Supreme Court; state courts are set up in much the same way.

Federal Court System

U.S. District Courts

At the base of the federal system are the courts of *original jurisdiction*— the *U.S. district courts*. Except in a few special instances, all cases involving federal law are tried first in district courts. There are 89 district courts in the United States and another 5 in the U.S. territories, with at least 1 federal district court in each state. The larger, more populous states have more district courts. New York, for example, has 4 district courts. Each district has between 1 and 28 judges, for a total of 678 district judges in the country. These judges preside over most federal cases, including civil rights cases, controversies involving more than $10,000, antitrust suits, and counterfeiting cases. The large volume of cases they handle (over 250,000 annually) has led to long delays in administering justice. At one time, it took four years to complete a civil case in the Southern District of New York.

Courts of Appeals

Above the district courts are the *U.S. courts of appeals* (sometimes called by their old name, *circuit courts of appeals*). These courts have only *appellate jurisdiction*; that is, they hear *appeals* from the district courts and from important regulatory commissions, like the Federal Trade Commission. If you took a civil rights case to your district court and lost, you could appeal the decision and have the case brought before a court of appeals. The United States is divided into 13 courts of appeals. There are 12 geographic *circuits* (11 plus 1 in Washington, D.C.), and 1 U.S. Court of Appeals for the Federal Circuit dealing with appeals from special federal courts like the U.S. Claims Court. Each of the 13 appeals courts has between 6 and 28 judges, depending on the volume of work. Usually three judges hear each case. One hundred and seventy-nine circuit court judges handle almost 55,000 cases a year. These are the final courts of appeal for most cases. The Supreme Court hears only about 80 cases a year. (See Figure 5.1.)

Special Federal Courts

Special federal courts have been created by Congress to handle certain cases. The *U.S. Claims Court* deals with people's claims against government seizure of property. The *U.S. Court of Military Appeals*

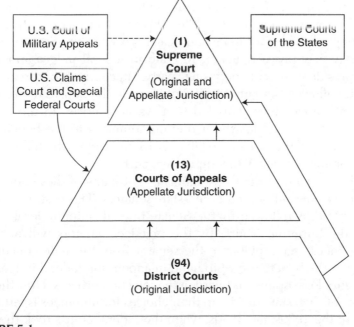

FIGURE 5.1
Federal Court Structure and the Flow of Cases to the Supreme Court.

(often called the *GI Supreme Court*), composed of three civilians, is the final judge of court-martial convictions. The U.S. Supreme Court can review only certain types of military cases.

The Judges

All federal judges, including Supreme Court justices, are nominated to the bench by the president and must be confirmed by the Senate.

Under the Constitution, federal judges hold office for life "during good behavior" and are removed only by *impeachment*. This has rarely happened. However, in October 1989, the Senate impeached a Florida judge (who is now a Florida congressman), Alcee Hastings, in a controversial bribery case. To further protect them from political pressures, judges' salaries cannot be reduced while they're in office.

Despite these protections, the appointment of judges is a very political matter. Judges almost always are selected on a party basis, usually as a reward for their political services. One commentator called the judiciary "the place to put political workhorses out to pasture." In this partisan spirit, 87 percent of Bill Clinton's appointments to federal judgeships were Democrats, while 89 percent of George Bush Sr.'s were Republicans. This motivation carries over to the Senate, where one party may prove reluctant to confirm federal judges appointed by a president of the opposing party. Recently the threat of a filibuster allowed the minority Republicans in the Senate to block the president's appointees. This led to a "vacancy crisis" in the federal courts as the Senate delayed acting on nominees to the bench. The Senate changed the rule in the fall of 2013, forbidding the filibuster on judicial nominees below the Supreme Court.

Adding to a president's problems is that many of these nominees require the consent of their home-state senators. This custom, *senatorial courtesy*, is followed by the Senate in confirming federal judges below the Supreme Court. By the practice, senators will not vote for nominees unacceptable to the senator from the state concerned. This gives the Senate the whip hand in appointing federal judges and makes sure local opinion is heard in the selection process. How the two senators of each state divide up their choices for nominees is left up to them. In the 1960s and 1970s, when the federal courts took the lead in enforcing controversial racial integration, senatorial courtesy made

◼ Presidents and the Court

Less than six months after taking office, the new president had a chance to nominate Judge Sonia Sotomayor to the Supreme Court. The popular enthusiasm for the first Latin woman justice may have obscured her record as a moderate judge who was probably not as liberal as Barack Obama. Historically, justices have a way of disappointing the president appointing them.

Theodore Roosevelt said of famed justice Oliver Wendell Holmes: "He has the backbone of a banana." President Eisenhower was so angered at Chief Justice Earl Warren's rulings that he called Warren's appointment "the biggest damn-fool mistake I ever made." The controversy set off by the Warren Court's activism led President Nixon to appoint Warren Burger as chief justice to replace Earl Warren when the latter retired in 1969. Nixon hoped that the four justices he had appointed, including Burger, would inspire greater political restraint in the Court. However, the Burger Court, in *U.S. v. Nixon* (1974), unanimously ruled that President Nixon had to surrender to the special Watergate prosecutor the White House tapes of his conversations about illegal activities. The president, who resigned shortly afterward, was certainly not pleased by this example of the Court's independence.

the appointment of liberal judges in the South politically difficult for a president.

The president's power to influence the makeup of one of the three branches of the government is extremely important, though it may be restricted in practice. (See "Presidents and the Court.")

By the end of Clinton's second term, he had appointed 373 federal judges, including 65 of the 179 appellate judges. Similarly, George W. Bush finished his eight years in office having appointed a total of 324 judges, 261 to district courts, 61 on courts of appeals, and two Supreme Court justices. Some scholars have argued that Democrats like Clinton stressed diversity over ideology, often picking moderate minority and female judges that didn't necessarily reflect the president's own political philosophy. On the other hand, Republican presidents are more ideological, with conservative credentials given priority over diversity in filling judicial vacancies. In appointing Justices Sotomayor and Kagan, President Obama opted for female candidates who were not necessarily the most liberal choices on his short list.

A majority of the current Supreme Court has been appointed by Republican presidents. In 2005 President Bush had the unusual opportunity to appoint two justices to the Court, John G. Roberts as chief justice and Samuel A. Alito Jr. as an associate justice. Both replaced

Republican-appointed justices. Alito took the seat of Sandra Day O'Connor who, in 1981, became the first woman on the Supreme Court. Roberts replaced Chief Justice William Rehnquist, who had been elevated to that post from his seat on the Court when Warren Burger resigned in 1986. At that same time, President Ronald Reagan nominated an equally conservative Antonin Scalia to be the first justice of Italian descent. Reagan's 1988 selection of Anthony Kennedy, after the Senate had rejected Robert Bork, aimed at pointing the Court in a conservative direction. President Bush's 1990 appointment of a moderate New Hampshire judge, David Souter, was later considered a mistake by many conservatives.

Four justices have been chosen by Democratic presidents. Bill Clinton selected Ruth Bader Ginsburg in 1993 and Stephen G. Breyer in 1994, while Barack Obama appointed Sonia Sotomayor in 2009 to replace David Souter, who resigned. In May 2010 President Obama nominated Elena Kagan, dean of Harvard Law School, to the Court, replacing Justice John Paul Stevens. All these Democratic-appointed justices have been considered moderates when they were appointed and have generally voted as part of the Court's liberal wing. Justice Ginsburg, for example, has focused on gender issues. She and Justice Breyer vigorously dissented from the Court's decision to stop the vote recount in the 2000 Florida presidential election, allowing George W. Bush to become president.

Senate confirmation of justices, once a fairly gentlemanly affair, turned nasty in the late 1980s. President Reagan's 1987 nomination of Robert Bork set off fierce opposition from liberals offended by his views on civil rights, abortion, and privacy. After a flurry of personal attacks (now called "borking" by conservatives), Bork was rejected by the Democratic Senate. This unusually public politicizing of the confirmation process continued with President Bush's nomination of conservative Clarence Thomas in 1991. Unlike Bork, Thomas had fewer qualifications, which ironically gave opponents less of a "paper trail" to criticize. Despite the dramatic televised testimony of Anita Hill (accusing him of sexual harassment), Thomas was confirmed, though by the smallest margin of approval (52–48) in more than 100 years.

The confirmation hearings in 2005 and 2006 of Chief Justice Roberts and Justice Alito looked mild by comparison. Although partisan in their questioning of the nominees, Democratic senators seemed relieved that the appointees were not as conservative as other candidates might have been. Although most Republican senators opposed Justice Sotomayor in 2009, her hearings were also restrained, perhaps because a supportive Democratic majority made her confirmation a given. Similarly, Elena Kagan became the fourth woman to serve as a justice in August 2010 with most Republicans opposing her in a 63–37 Senate confirmation vote. Recent appointees have also been better briefed on how to deal with televised Senate hearings than they were in the past. On hot-button issues, like abortion, the nominees duck and weave repeated questions without firmly expressing a position. This tends to produce confirmations of less substance and more theater.

Jurisdiction

Jurisdiction refers to the matters over which a court may exercise its authority. The jurisdiction of the federal courts falls into two broad categories: In the first group, it depends on the *subject of the case*; in the second, on the *parties to the case*, no matter what the subject. The federal courts have jurisdiction over all subjects related to the Constitution and over treaties of the United States. (Admiralty and maritime cases involving international law are also included.) Jurisdiction determined by parties includes cases involving ambassadors and other foreign representatives, controversies in which the United States is a party, and controversies between two or more states or between a state or citizen of the United States and a foreign citizen or state. The federal court system's last and largest source of cases is suits between citizens of different states.

This definition does not mean that the federal courts have the *only* jurisdiction over such cases. Federal courts have *exclusive jurisdiction* in some cases, such as cases involving crimes against the laws of the United States. However, in other cases, they have *concurrent jurisdiction*, shared with state courts. For example, some suits between citizens of different states may be heard by both federal and state courts.

U.S. Supreme Court

Composed of a chief justice and eight associate justices, the *Supreme Court of the United States* sits on the summit of the federal court system. (See Table 5.1.) Although Congress is allowed to set the number of justices on the Court, the number has remained at nine since 1869. The Supreme Court has some *original jurisdiction* (cases that can be presented first to the Court), but most of the cases it hears are appeals of lower court decisions, which involve its *appellate jurisdiction*. If a case is lost in both the district court and the court of appeals, it could still heard by the Supreme Court.

Actually very few cases reach the Supreme Court. Of more than 10 million cases tried every year in American courts (federal and state), some 7,400 petitions for review are taken to the Supreme Court.

TABLE 5.1 THE SUPREME COURT, 2014			
JUSTICE APPOINTED	DATE OF BIRTH	APPOINTED BY	DATE
John G. Roberts Jr. (chief justice)	1955	Bush II	2005
Antonin Scalia	1936	Reagan	1986
Anthony Kennedy	1936	Reagan	1988
Clarence Thomas	1946	Bush	1991
Ruth Bader Ginsburg	1933	Clinton	1993
Stephen G. Breyer	1938	Clinton	1994
Samuel A. Alito Jr.	1950	Bush II	2006
Sonia Sotomayor	1954	Obama	2009
Elena Kagan	1960	Obama	2010

In the 2012–2013 term, the Court issued opinions in 79 cases. The other petitions are affirmed or reversed by written *memorandum orders*. The majority of the cases that come to the Court do so in the form of petitions (written requests) for a *writ of certiorari* (*certiorari* means to be informed of something). A writ of certiorari is an order to the lower court to send the entire record of the case to the higher court for review. Lawyers losing in a lower court could petition for this writ. It is granted when four justices of the Supreme Court feel that the issues raised are important enough to merit a review. Many of these involve constitutional issues. The Court denies 90 percent of these applications. This procedure rests control over the appeal process in the hands of the Supreme Court, keeping a maximum number of cases in the lower courts.

The Final Authority?

The prominence of the Supreme Court in American history rests on its "final" authority over what the Constitution means. Yet a ruling of the Court has not always been the last word. The Court itself has reversed its decisions, as will be seen in our Case Study, "Separate but Equal?" at the end of the chapter. If the Court interprets a law in a way Congress does not like, Congress can simply rewrite the law. In 1990 Congress passed a Civil Rights Restoration Act that extended civil rights protection to all programs of colleges accepting federal aid. The act overturned a Court ruling that limited this protection. Amendments to the Constitution also have reversed decisions by the Court. An 1895 Court decision striking down the federal income tax was overturned by the Sixteenth Amendment in 1913, which allowed income taxes.

The strength of the Court's "final" authority is also tempered by the other branches of government and by public opinion. Despite the

Court's popularity, the public's acceptance of a decision is not always guaranteed. In civil rights cases, for example, police stopping black drivers because of illegal racial profiling, or in civil liberties cases like Christmas displays in public buildings, local communities have ignored the Court's interpretation of the Constitution. Congress and the president have taken their turn in interpreting vague parts of the Constitution to meet the demands of the public and the needs of those in power. The president's right to involve the country in the Vietnam and Iraq wars without a declaration of war would seem to fly in the face of the war-making powers given to Congress by the Constitution. Yet without a challenge by Congress, the president's interpretation of the Constitution stood.

Despite this shared role in changing the Constitution, the Supreme Court, through its rulings, repeatedly explains and applies the Constitution, breathing life into 200-year-old words. A brief history of the Court will show how.

Early Years of the Court

The Supreme Court was neglected in its first years. It did not start life as the powerful institution we know today. No cases at all were brought to the Court in its first three years. Many leaders, such as Patrick Henry and Alexander Hamilton, refused appointments to the Court. Having been overlooked when Washington, D.C., was first planned, the Court had no building or chamber provided. Court sessions were held in places like basement apartments.

Under the leadership of John Marshall (who served as chief justice from 1801 to 1835), the Court's influence greatly increased. (See "Chief Justice John Marshall.") Two landmark decisions marked this growth in power. The first announced the Court's *judicial review*, the power not only to declare acts and laws of any state and local government unconstitutional but also to strike down acts of any branch of the federal government. The second major decision established the principle of *national supremacy*—that the U.S. laws and Constitution are the supreme law of the land and state laws that are in conflict with federal laws cannot stand.

Judicial Review and National Supremacy

Marbury v. Madison (1803) clearly established the principle of judicial review. In this case the Supreme Court, for the first time, struck down an act of Congress. The case shows Chief Justice John Marshall as a shrewd politician.

Chief Justice John Marshall

"Marshall found the Constitution paper and he made it power."

—James A. Garfield

John Marshall served as the fourth, and arguably greatest, chief justice from 1801 to 1835. He applied his genius to a single mission: building the government of a united nation. Raising the limited prestige and power of the Supreme Court was necessary so that it could serve that mission. Marshall shaped constitutional law so that it too could preserve a strong central government into an unlimited future. For Marshall, the Constitution must serve its goal of creating a lasting union. This underlines his famous phrase, "We must never forget that it is a *constitution* that we are expounding."

Thus, Marshall acted more like a statesman than a judge. In his major decisions on judicial review and national supremacy, he was not strictly interpreting and applying the law. Marshall was establishing principles for a growing nation. Interestingly, his lack of legal training— less than three months of law classes, and poorly attended at that— may have helped him. Rather than deciding cases like a lawyer, he acted like a legislator breaking with the past. His experience in General Washington's starving army at Valley Forge may have provided his most important lesson by reminding him of the price of disunity.

When Marshall died in Philadelphia, citizens rang the Liberty Bell in his honor. It cracked and has never been rung again.

Shortly before leaving office, President John Adams (who had nominated Marshall to the Court) appointed a number of minor judicial officials in order to maintain the influence of his party in the coming administration of his opponent, Thomas Jefferson. When Jefferson took office, he discovered that the commission of William Marbury had not actually been delivered. Jefferson ordered Secretary of State James Madison to hold it up. Under a section of the Judiciary Act of 1789, Marbury sued in the Supreme Court to compel delivery of the commission. Marshall was then confronted with deciding a case between his political allies and his enemy, Jefferson, who as president was determined to weaken the power of the conservative Supreme Court.

What Marshall did was to dismiss Marbury's case, ruling that the section of the Judiciary Act under which he had sued was unconstitutional (the act allowed the Supreme Court original jurisdiction in a case not mentioned by the Constitution). By doing so he clearly asserted that the Supreme Court, on the basis of *its* interpretation of the Constitution, could limit the actions of Congress. At the same time, the Court supported Jefferson's argument that he did not have to deliver the commission. How could the president object?

Another early decision established that states could not interfere with the functioning of the federal government. In this case, *McCulloch v. Maryland* (1819), the state of Maryland attempted to tax the Baltimore branch of the unpopular Bank of the United States, established by the federal government. Chief Justice Marshall, speaking for a unanimous Court, ruled that the federal government, "though limited in its powers, is supreme within its sphere of action." Marshall also found that although the Constitution did not specifically allow Congress to create a bank, Article I, Section 8 gave Congress the power to make all laws "necessary and proper" for carrying out its authority. *Implied powers* based on this clause were used later in broadly expanding the duties that Congress could undertake.

In 1857 came the famous *Dred Scott* case (*Dred Scott v. Sandford*). Here, the Court ruled that a slave (Dred Scott) was not automatically free because his owner had taken him to a state not allowing slavery. Congress, the Court said, had no right to interfere with property rights guaranteed by the Constitution. The Court went on to say that the Missouri Compromise (1820), which had attempted to resolve the slavery issue by dividing the new western territories into slave and free parts, was invalid. In terms of constitutional development, this unpopular decision supporting slavery was the first time an act of Congress of great importance was struck down by the courts. As such, the *Dred Scott* case marked a critical expansion of judicial powers. Many concluded that the Court had gone too far.

The Court after the Civil War

The end of the Civil War signaled the end of the major political conflict dominating the first 75 years of the Republic—*states' rights* versus *federal powers*. With federal unity achieved, rapid national growth began. The resulting economic expansion and the unrestrained growth of giant monopolies created a new demand for government regulation of the economy. The Supreme Court became more active, and judicial power was greatly enlarged. In just nine years (1864–1873), 10 acts of Congress were struck down, compared with only two acts in the previous 74 years.

Not only was the Court more active, it also was more conservative. Many liberals viewed the Court as an instrument for protecting the property rights of the rich and ignoring popular demands for government regulation.

This trend continued into the twentieth century, when the Court found itself up against the growing power of the executive branch. The presidency was widely felt to be the most effective place in the government to regulate the social and economic changes brought about by the post–Civil War industrialization. But the Supreme Court continued to resist the expansion of government's regulatory power, even though much of the legislation it struck down (such as minimum wage and child labor laws) was widely popular. Between 1890 and 1936, the Court declared 46 laws unconstitutional in full or in part.

It was President Franklin D. Roosevelt who caused the Court's policy to change. He fought the Court's opposition to his New Deal measures by threatening to expand the Court with new judges of his own choosing, the so-called *court-packing* bill. Although Roosevelt's plan was unsuccessful and aroused a storm of public and congressional opposition, it may have accomplished FDR's purposes. In 1937 the Court backed down—the famous "switch in time that saved nine"— and turned away from economic policymaking.

Mid-Twentieth-Century Courts

Beginning in 1937, Supreme Court decisions over the next 50 years showed three major trends. These trends peaked in the decisions of the Warren Court (led by Chief Justice Earl Warren) in the 1950s and 1960s and have been eroded in the decisions of more recent, more conservative courts.

First, the Court invalidated much less federal legislation than it had in the 50 years before the New Deal. Generally only a few federal laws were held unconstitutional, and in most of these cases, the legislation struck down was not very significant. In a second area, the Court avoided protecting private property rights. The Court, during this time, was not greatly concerned with guarding economic interests from government policymaking.

The Court showed more positive interest in a third area—increased judicial protection for civil liberties. While reducing property rights in importance, the Court sought to preserve and protect the rights of individuals against the increased powers of an expanding government. *First Amendment freedoms* of speech, press, religion, and assembly were developed and extended by these liberal/moderate Supreme Courts. With Earl Warren as chief justice (1953–1969), the Supreme Court moved to liberalize reapportionment, racial discrimination, and the rights of defendants in criminal cases.

In decisions dealing with reapportionment, beginning with *Baker v. Carr* (1962), the Warren Court established the principle of "one man, one vote" for election districts. The Court ruled that districts must contain roughly equal populations—which still allowed parties to draw boundaries to their advantage. In other decisions, eliminating racial discrimination, the Court led the nation in cutting back racism in schooling, voting, housing, and the use of public facilities.

Another major interest of the Warren Court, the rights of criminal defendants, saw the Court throw the protection of the Bill of Rights around people accused of crimes by state and federal authorities. The Court insisted on an impoverished defendant's basic right to a lawyer, declared that illegally seized evidence cannot be used in state criminal trials, and held that suspects must be advised of their constitutional right to silence and to have a lawyer before questioning. This last area, summed up as the *Miranda* decision (*Miranda v. Arizona,* 1966), is familiar to all fans of TV detective series. (See "Miranda: Pop Culture and the Court" in Chapter 6.)

The Supreme Court under Warren Burger (1969–1986) was not as liberal as the Warren Court but not as conservative as many conservatives had hoped. On the liberal side, the Burger Court legalized abortions except in the last 10 weeks of pregnancy, declined to stop publication of the Pentagon Papers (official papers on the government's planning for the Vietnam War unofficially leaked to the press), and drastically limited capital punishment.

In more conservative directions, the Burger Court allowed local communities, within limits, to define obscenity and ban those works considered pornographic.

Perhaps the most important changes the Burger Court made were in the rights of the accused. Here the Court allowed the police broader powers in searching without a warrant—deciding, for example, that persons detained on minor charges (like traffic violations) may be searched for evidence of more serious crimes (like possession of drugs). The Court also permitted illegally obtained information to be used at a trial and allowed the police to continue their questioning after a suspect claimed the right to silence. However, the Burger Court left the *Miranda* decision in place.

The Rehnquist Court (1986–2005)

When Chief Justice William Rehnquist died in 2005 at the age of 80, he had served on the Court for 33 years and as its chief since 1986. His appointment as chief justice came from President Ronald Reagan's hopes for a more conservative, more restrained court. These hopes were only partly fulfilled.

While Rehnquist was a skillful leader noted for his wit and informality, he never was able to create a "Rehnquist Court" in the same defining way that there had been a "Warren Court." He was often found in the minority, positioned firmly to the right of the Court's majority, on issues like affirmative action, abortion, religion, property rights, and campaign finance. The courts he presided over were deeply split. Both the independent-minded jurists (described as "nine scorpions in a bottle") and the polarized nation they served made it hard for Rehnquist to win converts to his own conservative philosophy.

Consequently the Rehnquist Court, lacking a conservative majority, did not dramatically break with past Court rulings. In areas like civil liberties, the Court zigged and zagged with little of the clear direction that Rehnquist's Republican backers had hoped for. In its abortion rulings, for example, the Court placed few limits on the practice while affirming it as a woman's basic right. In major decisions affecting race and religion, the Court was cautiously conservative. Its landmark 2003 decision on affirmative action at the University of Michigan upheld the practice in college admissions. (See "Affirmative Action in Michigan" in Chapter 6.)

The Rehnquist Court's activism was most apparent in its rulings concerning federalism. Here the Court was willing to overturn laws of Congress and decisions by executive agencies in order to guard the rights of the states. The Court's modest revolution of federalism limited the power of Congress while protecting the rights of the states. In *United States v. Lopez* (1995), the Court ruled that Congress had exceeded its authority to regulate interstate commerce by passing a law intended to keep guns out of schools. This marked the first time in 60 years that the Court had limited Congress's power to regulate interstate commerce. Previous courts for most of the nineteenth century and since the New Deal had used the Commerce Clause to expand federal power. The Rehnquist Court reversed this precedent in order to restrain the federal government.

The Court showed a pragmatic ability, as one law professor put it, "to split the difference and avoid drawing bright lines." This led varying majorities in the Court to overturn student-led prayers at public high school football games yet to allow partial-birth abortions because they are the most medically appropriate way of terminating some pregnancies. Arguably the Court's most critical ruling was in *Bush v. Gore* in 2000, where the Court split on partisan lines, stopped a vote count in Florida, and made George W. Bush president. Their decision may have avoided a national crisis as Rehnquist suggested, but the weakness of the majority's legal arguments also stained the Rehnquist legacy. (See "*Bush v. Gore.*")

The Court under Rehnquist spoke less in the areas of race and individual rights, where modern Courts before it had made their mark. Instead, Rehnquist focused on a federal government—including Congress—that his Court viewed as too big, too powerful, and too out of control. This emphasis on federalism has continued under his successor as chief justice, John Roberts.

The Roberts Court (2005–)

In the beginning, Chief Justice John G. Roberts Jr. appeared to be in charge but not in control. Even with President Bush appointing Samuel Alito to replace more moderate Justice Sandra Day O'Connor in 2006, the Court only gradually changed. The Roberts Court was divided between its conservative and liberal justices. But it was led by a shrewd conservative strategist as chief justice, who wrote incremental opinions that nudged his Court to the right in the major cases before it.

Issues of race brought out the chief justice's skepticism about government efforts to promote equality. *Community Schools v. Seattle School District* (2007) saw Roberts in a 5–4 majority limiting the use of race to promote diversity in school. In a much-quoted phrase, he wrote, "The way to stop discrimination on the basis of race is to stop discriminating on the basis of race." Similarly in *Ricci vs. DeStefano* (2009) involving reverse discrimination in New Haven, Connecticut, the Court restricted affirmative action by support-ing the results of exams even when they were racially unbalanced in favoring white firefighters. In a 2013 decision, the Court avoided ruling on a University of Texas program that admitted the top 10 percent of state high school graduates. Instead, the Court gave priority to "race-neutral alternatives" before turning to race in admissions decisions; this was seen as raising barriers to affirmative action.

In other areas of voting rights, business practices, and campaign finance, the Roberts Court moved toward conservative positions. In a 2013 5–4 decision, the Court struck down the heart of the Voting Rights

Bush v. Gore

The reaction matched the decision itself. "Judicial lawlessness," said a writer in the *Washington Post*; "Comparable to Dred Scott," thundered both Alan Dershowitz of Harvard Law and black activist Jesse Jackson. A Columbia law professor predicted increased cynicism about the courts. What the Supreme Court had done in their December 12, 2000, ruling, *Bush v. Gore*, was to decide the outcome of the presidential election. Five Republican-appointed justices decided that Republican George W. Bush would be the next president of the United States.

By a 5–4 decision, the Supreme Court, in a reversal of its usual support for federalism, overturned the Florida Supreme Court and halted further counting of the state's disputed presidential votes. This effectively ended 35 days of arguments in the nation's closest presidential election, which had focused on whether to allow hand recounts of Florida's vote. Bush, who had narrowly won the state votes, resisted further counts. Al Gore, who had won the nation's popular vote, thought recounting votes overlooked by machines would give him Florida's electoral votes and the election. The legal fights in the lower courts had brought the case to the Supreme Court.

The majority ruled that the different standards in Florida counties for counting punch-card ballots (the so-called hanging and dimpled chads) created problems of due process and equal protection of the law. In other words, a valid vote in one county wouldn't necessarily be valid in another one. Some of the dissenting justices agreed that there were problems but thought they could be corrected and the counting resumed. The majority, recognizing the limits of their opinion, added that it would only apply in this case. The dissent by John Paul Stevens implicitly criticized the majority for serving partisan interests: "Although we may never know with complete certainty the identity of the winner of this year's presidential election, the identity of the loser is perfectly clear. It is the nation's confidence in the judge as an impartial guardian of the rule of law."

Act of 1965 that required states in the South with a history of voting discrimination to get approval from the Justice Department before altering their election laws. "Our country has changed," the Chief Justice wrote for the majority. In *Citizens United v. Federal Election Commission* (2010), the Court boldly overturned precedents and congressional reforms by removing almost all restraints on corporation spending to influence elections. One law professor who studied the Court's business rulings called it "the most pro-business court in the modern era."

On the other side of the ledger, two of the Roberts Court's most publicized recent decisions angered conservatives. In upholding the constitutionality of President Obama's health care reform, a deeply divided Court held that Congress could require Americans to either obtain health insurance or pay a penalty. The Chief Justice joined the 5–4 majority in this 2012 "Obamacare ruling" in support of the individual mandate. The next year, 2013, the Court struck down the federal Defense of Marriage Act (DOMA) and effectively allowed same-sex marriages in the states that had chosen to grant them. In complicated and divided rulings, the Court not only allowed federal benefits for such unions but also left in place laws banning same-sex marriages around the nation.

These last cases are a reminder that labels like "conservative" risk simplifying complex judicial decisions. The chief justice has spoken of his judicial philosophy as one of "modesty and humility." But he and his court are more willing to change the law in a conservative direction than he admits. Legal scholars and reporters mostly agreed with Jeffrey Toobin writing a few years ago, "In every major case since he became the nation's seventeenth Chief Justice, Roberts has sided with the prosecution over the defendant, the state over the condemned, the executive branch over the legislative, and the corporate defendant over the individual plaintiff." (See "The Chief Umpire: John Roberts.")

"The Least Dangerous Branch of Government"?

Despite its great power of judicial review, the Supreme Court remains the weakest of the three branches, as Alexander Hamilton predicted in his famous quote. The Court must depend on the other parts of the government to enforce its opinions. Its authority to cancel actions of the rest of the federal government is in fact seldom used and strictly limited. These limits are found both within the Court and within the political system.

Internal Limits on the Court

Most of the limits on the power of the Supreme Court are found in the traditional practices within the Court. For starters, a long-held interpretation of the Constitution requires that an actual case be presented to the Court for it to exercise judicial review. The Court cannot take the lead in declaring laws unconstitutional. It cannot give advisory opinions. Justices must wait for a real controversy brought by someone actually injured by the law to make its way through the lower courts.

The Chief Umpire John Roberts

"And I will remember that it's my job to call balls and strikes, and not to pitch or bat."

—John G. Roberts Jr.

"It's hard to see home plate from right field."

—Senator Richard J. Durbin (D-Illinois)

When John Roberts first became a nominee for the Supreme Court, he embraced modest goals for a judge. A judge was to be an umpire, not a player, he stressed at his confirmation hearings. "Umpires don't make the rules. They apply them." And he emphasized his limited role: "Nobody ever went to a ballgame to see the umpire." His stated lack of a judicial philosophy ("I am not an ideologue,") and a respect for precedents set by previous Supreme Courts left the expectation of a restrained, articulate new leader of the Court. But that seems to be only half the story.

Appointed at age 50, Roberts was considerably younger than his colleagues and was expected to serve for decades. Well known in Court circles, he had served as a young law clerk of Chief Justice Rehnquist and as a private lawyer representing corporate clients before the Court. Roberts's early career included service in the Reagan administration, where he wrote strong defenses for conservative positions. These credentials were enough to secure the support of President George W. Bush. After Roberts's public bow to moderation during Senate hearings, he ended up on the right in most of the major cases before the Court. Despite the chief justice's critical support in 2012 upholding the president's health care reform, Barack Obama probably didn't regret his vote as senator opposing Roberts's nomination. He said at the time, "It is my personal estimation that he has far more often used his formidable skills on behalf of the strong in opposition to the weak."

Years may pass after a law is put on the books before the Court can rule on it. (The Supreme Court's *Dred Scott* decision struck down a law—the Missouri Compromise—passed 37 years before.)

Its refusal to resolve political questions is another important restraint on the Court. A *political question* is an issue on which the Constitution or laws give final say to another branch of government, or one the Court feels it lacks the capability to solve. Political questions often crop up in foreign relations. The justices of the Court lack important secret information, they are not experts in diplomacy, and they recognize the president's dominance over foreign affairs. Consequently, a federal court in December 1990 used the doctrine of political questions to avoid deciding whether President Bush Sr. could use force against Iraq without congressional approval. Similarly, a dozen years later the courts were equally reluctant to interfere with his son's decision to attack Iraq.

The Supreme Court has narrowed or expanded its definition of a political question at various times. For many years, the Court used this doctrine of political questions to refuse to consider reapportionment of state legislatures and congressional districts. In 1962 the Court reversed its position forcing state legislatures to draw boundaries to create districts with more nearly equal populations (*Baker v. Carr*). In the 2000 presidential election, the Court could have avoided deciding *Bush v. Gore* by declaring that it was more appropriate for state courts or Congress to resolve—a position consistent with the Court's support for federalism—but it did not. A political question, then, is whatever issue the Supreme Court wants to avoid.

Just as the Supreme Court avoids political questions, so too it avoids *constitutional issues*. The Court will not decide a case on the basis of a constitutional question unless there is no other way to dispose of the case. The Court will not declare a law unconstitutional unless it clearly violates the Constitution. It will assume that a law is valid unless proved otherwise. Although we have stressed the role of the Court in applying the Constitution, the vast majority of its cases deal with interpretations of less important federal and state laws.

A final internal limit on the Supreme Court is that of *precedent* or *stare decisis* ("to stand by the decision"). Justices generally follow previous court decisions in cases involving the same issue. Recent abortion cases have illustrated the reluctance of the Court to reverse precedents, in this instance *Roe v. Wade* (1973), which legalized abortion. Yet as the conservative majority on recent opinions has shown, at times the Court will not follow precedent if it feels the prior cases did not follow the Constitution or the justices' own political leanings. *Citizens United* has been pointed to as a case that dealt with a minor political movie but was turned into a landmark ruling by the Roberts Court that wanted to undermine campaign finance laws and precedents. Usually the Court likes to appear consistent with precedent even when changing the law.

What these limits on its power mean is that the Supreme Court avoids most of the constitutional questions pressed upon it. "Delay" is the Court's favorite tactic when, for both political and legal reasons, the Court wants to duck an issue that is too controversial, on which the law is uncertain, or where there is no political consensus. The Court may simply not hear the case, or may decide it for reasons other than the major issue involved. An example of this judicial avoidance occurred in 2004, when the Supreme Court refused to rule on the constitutionality of the phrase "under God" in the Pledge of Allegiance. The Court cited procedural reasons for not deciding on this inflammatory issue in an election year. Knowing the difficulty of enforcing a ruling against strong public opinion, the Court generally avoids such a confrontation.

This self-imposed restraint may make the use of judicial review scattered and long delayed, but the Court has maintained its great authority of judicial review by refusing in most instances to use it.

External Limits on the Court

The Supreme Court's external limits come from the duties the Constitution gives to other parts of the government, especially to Congress. Congress has the right to set when and how often the Court will meet, to establish the number of justices, and to restrict the Court's jurisdiction. This last power has been used to keep the Court out of areas in which Congress wished to avoid judicial involvement. For example, in passing the 2006 Detainee Bill allowing the president to detain terrorist suspects without various constitutional rights—like indefinite detention without a trial—Congress stripped the courts of jurisdiction over these cases. Nevertheless, such legislation can still be challenged in court. Congress may pass legislation so detailed that it limits the Court's scope in interpreting the law. Finally, the Senate has the duty of approving the president's nominations to the bench, and Congress has the seldom-used power to impeach Supreme Court justices.

These limits on the Court underscore the weakness of that body. With no army or bureaucracy to enforce its decisions, the Supreme Court must depend on the rest of the government to accept and carry out its decisions. (President Andrew Jackson, angrily disagreeing with a Supreme Court decision, is supposed to have exclaimed, "John Marshall has rendered his decision; now let him enforce it!") Yet with few exceptions, the Court's decisions have been accepted and enforced. When opposed, this weak, semi-isolated branch of government has usually overcome resistance. Why?

Strengths of the Court

The Supreme Court relies on three major supports: (1) its enormous prestige, (2) the fragmented nature of the American constitutional structure, and (3) the American legal profession, which acts like the Court's constituency.

The Court's *prestige* is unquestionable. Despite public dissent to many of its decisions in areas like civil liberties and abortion, the Court retains its high public standing. Opinion polls have shown that the position of a judge is one of the most respected in our society. This respect is due not only to the quality of many judges but also to the public image of an elevated judicial process. Anyone who has watched televised criminal trials is familiar with the qualities of theater in the legal process: the judge sitting on a raised platform dressed in robes, the formal speeches addressed to "your honor," the use of Latin phrases, and the oath on the Bible. Nor does the Supreme Court tarnish its image by actively attempting to shape its public relations. After the controversial 2000 Florida election decision, no justice felt the need to explain the *Bush v. Gore* opinion in the press, and yet the Court's popularity remained high. (See "The Court's Supreme Popularity.")

These customs creating a somber impression of dignity mask the fact that a judge is simply an administrator resolving public controversies. The Supreme Court, which presides over this judicial system, has added prestige because it is seen as the guardian of the Constitution and often is equated with that document in people's eyes.

An added strength of the Court comes from the *fragmented nature of the American system of government*. With powers separated among the three branches of the federal government, and federalism dividing power between the states and federal government, conflict is inevitable. This division of power creates a need for a referee; the Supreme Court fills that role.

In acting as a referee, the Court is hardly neutral. Its decisions may reflect the justices' partisan loyalties. They are certainly political in determining who gets what, when, and how, and to enforce them, the Supreme Court needs political support. The other players might not give this support to decisions they strongly disagree with. Consequently, the Court's rulings generally reflect the practices and values of the country's dominant political forces. As a referee, the Court enforces the constitutional rules of the game as practiced by the political game's most powerful players, of which it is one.

A final source of support for the Court is the *legal profession*. There are more than one million active lawyers in the United States. Lawyers occupy all the major judicial positions, and more lawyers than any other occupational group hold offices in national, state, and city governments. There are an estimated 80,000 lawyers, or one of

▮ The Court's Supreme Popularity

One of the ironies of American democracy is that the least democratic branch is also the most popular. People usually show more confidence in the Supreme Court than in the two elected branches of government. Some reasons for its public support lie in the general view that the Court carries out its duties in a disinterested way, that the justices are people of wisdom, and that the Court both protects and reflects the Constitution. Another explanation lies in the very invisibility of the Court's activities. As a scholar of the Court remarked, the public likes its politics done quietly and without an appearance of partisanship. The Court generally does this. (See Figure 5.2.)

However, recent polls have shown a decline in the Court's popularity, in part because it has been viewed as an increasingly partisan institution and in part because of its rulings on controversial issues like the 2000 presidential election, gay marriage, and health care reform.

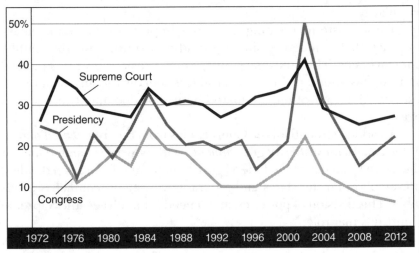

FIGURE 5.2
Public Confidence in the Supreme Court. A higher percentage of the public has consistently said it has a "great deal of confidence" in the Supreme Court than in the presidency or Congress.

Source: Harris Interactive http://www.harrisinteractive.com/NewsRoom/HarrisPolls/tabid/447/mid/1508 /articleId/1068/ctl/ReadCustom%20Default/Default.px

Source: The Harris Poll, *www.harrisinteractive.com*; compiled from Harris Poll data by John R. Hibbing and James T. Smith for their article "What the American Public Wants Congress to Be" in *Congress Reconsidered*, seventh edition, Lawrence Dodd and Bruce I. Oppenheimer, editors (Washington: Congressional Quarterly Press, 2001).

every 12 residents, in Washington. Perhaps the number of lawyers explains why so many political conflicts, including sex scandals and presidential elections, end up as legal issues. Other countries manage with far fewer lawyers and far fewer issues winding up in court.

Some scholars argue that lawyers use their domination of elected offices to pass laws and regulations that create new demands for their skills. The American Bar Association (ABA), with half the lawyers in the country as members, reviews nominees to the bench, and its comments on candidates' fitness influence whether they are appointed. Because of their own commitment to law, as well as some similarity in educational and social backgrounds, lawyers generally back the Court.

The Court as a Political Player

In applying the Constitution and laws to the cases before it, the Court clearly makes political choices. In arriving at decisions on controversial questions of national policy, the Supreme Court is a player in the political game. The procedures may be legal and the decisions may be phrased in lawyers' language, but to view the Court solely as a legal institution is to ignore its important political role.

"We are under the Constitution, but the Constitution is what the judges say it is," declared former chief justice Charles Evans Hughes. In interpreting the meaning of the Constitution, each Supreme Court must operate within the political climate of its time. Judges read not only the Constitution but also the newspaper. The Court must rely on others, especially the executive branch, to enforce its rulings. The Court cannot ignore the reactions to its decisions in Congress or in the nation because its influence ultimately rests on the acceptance of these decisions by the other players and the public. Generally, the Court's opinions are not long out of line with the dominant views in the legislative and executive branches. (See "The Court Waits for an Election.")

Judicial Activism versus Judicial Restraint

The question of how the political and legal power of the Supreme Court should be applied has centered on whether judicial authority should be active or restrained. How far should the Court go in shaping policy when it may conflict with other branches of the government? The two sides of this debate are reflected in the competing practices of *judicial restraint* and *judicial activism*.

Judicial restraint is the idea that the Court should not impose its views on other branches of the government or on the states unless there is a clear violation of the Constitution. Judicial restraint calls for a passive role in which the Court lets the elected branches of the government lead the way in setting controversial policies. The Constitution is constructed or interpreted as close to the intent of the framers

▋ The Court Waits for an Election

Civil rights decisions have never been far removed from politics. Here is an example of the Court keeping an eye on the political arena in a landmark case:

"Why doesn't the Supreme Court pass the school desegregation case?" asked one of Chief Justice Vinson's law clerks in 1952. *Brown v. Board of Education of Topeka, Kansas,* had arrived on the Court's docket in 1951, but it was carried over for oral argument the next term and then consolidated with four other cases and reargued in December 1953. The landmark ruling did not come down until May 17, 1954.

"Well," Justice Frankfurter explained, "we're holding it for the election"—1952 was a presidential election year.
   "You're holding it for the election?" the clerk persisted in disbelief. "I thought the Supreme Court was supposed to decide cases without regard to elections."

"When you have a major social political issue of this magnitude, timing and public reactions are important considerations, and," Frankfurter continued, "we do not think this is the time to decide it."

Source: David M. O'Brien, *Storm Center: The Supreme Court in American Politics.* New York: W.W. Norton, 1993.

as possible and practical. The Supreme Court intervenes in political conflicts only with great reluctance. Felix Frankfurter and Oliver Wendell Holmes Jr. are two famous justices of the Supreme Court identified with judicial restraint. Frankfurter argued that social improvement should be left to elected officials of the federal and state governments. The Court, he declared, should avoid conflicts with the other branches of the federal government whenever possible.

Judicial activism takes the approach that the Supreme Court should be a creative partner with the legislative and executive branches in shaping government policy. Judicial activists seek to apply the Court's authority to solving economic and political problems ignored by other parts of the government. In this view, the Court is more than an umpire of the American political game: It is an active participant. The Supreme Court under Earl Warren practiced judicial activism. In its rulings on reapportionment, civil rights, and the right to counsel, the Warren Court boldly changed national policy.

It is important not to confuse judicial activism versus restraint with liberal versus conservative. Although twentieth-century activist justices, such as Earl Warren and Thurgood Marshall, took liberal positions on issues like race and dissent, this was not always so. John Marshall's court was both activist—in establishing judicial review—and conservative—in protecting private property rights. The conservative

Supreme Court during the 1930s attempted to strike down most of Franklin D. Roosevelt's New Deal program as unconstitutional. On the restraint side, justices Frankfurter and Holmes were political liberals, yet both believed it was not wise for the Court to dive into political battles to support positions they may have personally backed.

In recent times, judicial restraint and conservatism have overlapped. Conservative jurists, under the banner of *strict constructionism*, have viewed modern courts as stretching the Constitution for liberal ends, and thereby ignoring the intentions of the framers. They point to the vast expansion of federal power to regulate the economy, which liberal courts have ruled acceptable under flexible interpretations of the Constitution. However, when the Burger Court found abortion to be constitutional in *Roe v. Wade*, it brought this legal debate to a contemporary boil.

Critics of the decision point out that in other countries elected representatives have legalized abortion. In America this change in policy was done by unelected judges who found a right to abortion in constitutional phrases, hidden for centuries, ". . . completely unknown to the drafters. . . ." as Rehnquist put it. One reason why the debate over abortion may have turned more bitter in this country than elsewhere is because many Americans believe that the courts are "legislating from the bench."

But the conservative judges, now in an uneasy majority in the Supreme Court, also face a dilemma. Abortion has become a legally accepted practice, embedded in decades of court rulings and legislation. To overturn it based on a strict reading of the original written Constitution would boldly place the Court in the midst of polarizing political fights. Indeed in a number of conservative rulings, such as *Citizens United*, the Court's majority aggressively overturned laws passed by Congress and precedents of previous Courts—hardly acts of judicial restraint.

CASE STUDY

Separate but Equal?

I still have a dream, a dream deeply rooted in the American dream—one day this nation will rise up and live up to its creed, "We hold these truths to be self evident: that all men are created equal." I have a dream . . .

When Martin Luther King Jr. spoke these words 50 years ago at the end of the 1963 March on Washington, he was addressing a nation awakening to its failure to live up to its own ideals. Making racial equality a constitutional principle as well as a political reality took the struggle of many groups for many years. In this the Supreme Court played a role. By first approving racial segregation in the nineteenth century and later abolishing it in the mid-twentieth century, the Court was key in shaping relations between the races. The changing, powerful position of the judiciary in the evolution of the legal doctrine of "separate but equal" demonstrates how central the Supreme Court is to America's politics, history, and dreams.

POLITICAL BACKGROUND OF SEGREGATION

The end of the Civil War and the emancipation of the slaves did not offer black people the full rights of citizenship, nor did the passing of the Thirteenth Amendment in 1865 (which outlawed slavery), the Fourteenth Amendment in 1868 (which extended "equal protection of the laws" to all citizens), or the Fifteenth Amendment in 1870 (which guaranteed the right to vote to all male citizens regardless of "race, color, or previous condition of servitude").

Between 1866 and 1877, the "radical Republicans" controlled Congress. Despite becoming a bad memory for the white South, *Reconstruction* was a racially progressive period when blacks won a number of political rights. In 1875 Congress passed a Civil Rights Act designed to prevent any public form of discrimination—in theaters, restaurants, transportation, and the like—against blacks. Congress's right to forbid a *state* to act contrary to the Constitution was unquestioned. But this law, based on the Fourteenth Amendment, assumed that Congress could also prevent racial discrimination by private individuals.

The Supreme Court disagreed. In 1883 it declared the Civil Rights Act of 1875 unconstitutional. The majority of the Court ruled that Congress could pass legislation only to correct *states'* violations of the Fourteenth Amendment. Congress had no power to enact "primary and direct" legislation on individuals—that was left to the states. This decision meant the federal government could not lawfully protect blacks against most forms of discrimination. In other words, white supremacy was beyond federal control.

With this blessing from the Supreme Court, the southern states passed a series of laws legitimizing segregation. These laws included all-white primary elections, elaborate tests to qualify for voting, and other racial restrictions. (See "American Apartheid.")

American Apartheid

In the South during the late nineteenth and early twentieth centuries, Jim Crow laws (taking their name from a blackface minstrel song) were passed to prohibit blacks from using the same public facilities as whites. These state laws required segregated schools, hospitals, prisons, restaurants, toilets, railways, and waiting rooms. Some communities passed "sundown ordinances" that prohibited blacks from staying in town overnight. Blacks and whites could not even be buried in the same cemeteries.

There seemed to be no limit to the absurdity of segregation. New Orleans required separate districts for black and white prostitutes. In Oklahoma, blacks and whites could not use the same telephone booths. In North Carolina and Florida, school textbooks used by black children had to be stored separately from those used by white children. In Birmingham, Alabama, the races were specifically prohibited from playing checkers together.

SEPARATE BUT EQUAL

Segregation was given judicial approval in the landmark case of *Plessy v. Ferguson* (1896). Here, the Court upheld a Louisiana law requiring railroads to provide separate cars for the two races. The Court declared that segregation had nothing to do with the superiority of the white race, and that segregation was not contrary to the Fourteenth Amendment as long as the facilities were equal. The doctrine of "separate but equal" in *Plessy v. Ferguson* became the law of the land in those states maintaining segregation.

In approving segregation and establishing the "separate but equal" doctrine, the Court was undoubtedly reflecting white attitudes of the time. To restore the South to the Union, the new congresses were willing to undo the radicals' efforts to protect blacks. It was the southern black who paid the price—exile halfway between slavery and freedom. Just as the judiciary was unwilling to prevent these violations of civil rights, so too were the executive and legislative branches.

Plessy v. Ferguson helped racial segregation continue as a southern tradition. For some 40 years, the "separate but equal" doctrine was not seriously challenged. "Separate" was strictly enforced; "equal" was not. Schools, government services, and other public facilities for blacks were clearly separate from tax-supported white facilities but just as clearly inferior to them. One can argue that the Supreme Court did not even support its own doctrine during this period.

By the late 1930s, the Court began to look more closely at so-called equal facilities. *Missouri ex. rel. Gaines v. Canada* (1938) held that because Missouri did not have a law school for blacks, it must admit them to the white law school. In *Sweatt v. Painter* (1950), a black (Sweatt) was denied admission to the University of Texas Law School on the grounds that Texas was building a law school for blacks. The Court examined the new school carefully, found that it would in no way be equal to the white one, and ordered Sweatt admitted to the existing school.

Thus the *Plessy* doctrine of "separate but equal" was increasingly weakened by judicial decisions. By stressing the "equal" part of the doctrine, the Supreme Court was in fact making the doctrine impractical. (Texas was not likely to build a law school for blacks equal to its white one.) These decisions also reflected the Court's change after 1937 from making economic policy to protecting individual rights.

Still, the Court did not overrule *Plessy*. It was following precedent. Paralleling the rulings of the Supreme Court were the actions of the executive branch and some northern states that were increasingly critical of racial segregation. In 1941 President Franklin Roosevelt issued an executive order forbidding discrimination in government employment. And President Truman abolished segregation in the army in 1948. Congress, however, dominated by a conservative seniority system and blocked by southern filibusters in the Senate, was unable to pass civil rights measures. Nonetheless, public attitudes toward segregation were changing, and the Court's rulings were reflecting that change.

THE END OF SEPARATE BUT EQUAL

In 1954 the Supreme Court finally reversed *Plessy v. Ferguson* in *Brown v. Board of Education*, even while denying it was overturning the precedent. The Court held that segregated public schools violated the "equal protection of the laws" guaranteed in the Fourteenth Amendment. "Separate but equal" had no place in public education, the Supreme Court declared. Drawing on sociological and psychological studies of the harm done to black children by segregation, the Warren Court's unanimous decision stated that, in fact, separate was "inherently un-equal." This finding was the beginning of the end of *legal segregation*.

The Court backed up its new equal protection stand in areas other than education. In the years following the B*rown* decision, it outlawed segregation in interstate transportation, upheld legislation guarantee-ing voting rights for blacks, reversed convictions of civil rights leaders, and often protected civil rights demonstrations by court order. These decisions, though they stirred up opposition to the Court (including billboards on southern highways to impeach Earl Warren), helped a political movement apply pressures to wipe out racial discrimination. Civil rights groups were active in these cases, which shows how results sometimes can be gotten from one part of government (the courts) if another part (the Congress) is unwilling to act.

Congress finally joined in by passing ever-stronger Civil Rights Acts in 1957, 1960, and 1964. Both political parties had gained a heightened appreciation for the black voter, especially the large numbers who voted in northern cities. The 1964 act, coming after continuing pressure and agitation by civil rights activists, was the first comprehensive legislation of its kind since 1875. The act prohibited discrimination in public accommodations (such as hotels, restaurants, and gas stations) involved in interstate commerce and in most busi-nesses, and enforced equal voting rights for blacks.

The Court acted to encourage and to force all levels of the govern-ment—federal, state, and local—as well as the private sector to move toward full equality. The Supreme Court's support of busing to end the segregation of schools caused by housing patterns aroused opposi-tion in northern cities like Boston. By the 1980s President Reagan was calling *affirmative action* "reverse discrimination" against white males, yet affirmative action expanded beyond discrimination against African Americans to include vague goals of cultural diversity and racial "bal-ance." It was also applied to groups from the Middle East and Latin America, with little historical claim to its benefits. As the programs spread, judicial and public support for affirmative action waxed and waned. In recent decisions, the Supreme Court has narrowed affirma-tive action programs that fell under its strict scrutiny. The current chief justice, John Roberts, has declared that the time has come for the Court to restrict broad government remedies for discrimination. (See also "Affirmative Action in Michigan" in Chapter 6.)

Still, racism remains. And for this, the Supreme Court as well as the rest of the political system must share responsibility. The Supreme Court struck down civil rights acts of the Reconstruction era and failed to protect the rights of African Americans between 1883 and 1937 when they were most trampled on. And it was the Court that made "separate but equal" the legal justification for white supremacy. Even today the

Court has viewed housing patterns—a major cause of segregated public schools—as largely beyond its authority. The Court's effort to put
equal rights before the eyes of the nation was in many ways merely an
undoing of its own past mistakes.

Throughout this history of "separate but equal," the Court has
acted politically as well as legally and morally. At times the Supreme
Court held back efforts at reform, at other times it confused them, and
at still others it forced political and social changes toward constitutional ideals more rapidly than many wished. Yet the Court never acted
apart from the political game, and in the past, it was a central force in
moving the nation toward a dreamer's vision of racial equality.

WRAP-UP

The federal court system consists of U.S. district courts, courts of appeals,
special federal courts, and the U.S. Supreme Court. Although very few of
the cases tried in the United States ever reach the Supreme Court, it retains
its position as the "final authority" over what the Constitution means. Nevertheless, the Court's decisions have changed over the years, usually by the
Court itself, in part reflecting the changing political climate. Our brief history of the Court showed this, as did the case study of "separate but equal,"
where the Court first allowed racial segregation and then gradually reversed
its position.

The practices of judicial activism and judicial restraint are two sides of
the debate over how far the political involvement of the Court should go.
The Supreme Court is limited by a number of its own practices and, most
important, by its dependence on other parts of the government to enforce
its decisions. The Court's respect for these limits, as well as its great prestige,
has given it the strength to overcome most resistance. Recent criticism of its
decisions, from both conservatives and liberals, on issues like health care,
campaign finance, and affirmative action, has run up against solid support for
the Court.

Secure within its limits and resting on public respect, the Supreme Court
of the United States remains a unique political player. No other government
can boast a long-held tradition that gives "nine old men" (and women, now)—
nonelected and serving for life—the duty of overturning the acts of popularly
elected officials. Through this power of judicial review, the Court is deeply involved in setting national policy, limiting how the political game is played, and
bringing pressing social issues to the attention of the people and their leaders.
Whether the Supreme Court protects constitutional liberties or ideological
allies depends on who are the justices, how they interpret the law, and which
political forces prevail in the nation.

THOUGHT QUESTIONS

1. How did the Supreme Court become so important to our system of government? Would John Marshall be pleased or surprised?
2. Are Supreme Court justices influenced too much by their own conservative or liberal philosophies? Give some examples.
3. Why did the courts take the lead on civil rights for minorities? Isn't this issue more appropriate for the elected officials of the government?
4. Do judges deserve to be more popular and more respected than other government officials? Why or why not?
5. Why have recent chief justices had so much trouble gaining a clear direction from the Supreme Courts they led? Does this reflect the nation's political polarization?

SUGGESTED READINGS

Branch, Taylor. *Parting the Waters: America in the King Years, 1954–1963.* New York: Simon & Schuster, 1988.
The Pulitzer Prize–winning account of the civil rights movement with a focus on Martin Luther King Jr.

Burns, James MacGregor. *Packing the Court: The Rise of Judicial Power and the Coming Crisis of the Supreme Court.* New York: Penguin Press, 2009.
A warning by an eminent historian that the power of judicial review has often been used against "the progress of history."

Greenhouse, Linda. *The US Supreme Court: A Very Short Introduction.* New York: Oxford University, 2012, Pb.
The noted *New York Times* reporter puts her experience to work in briefly showing the Court at work.

King, Gilbert. *Devil in the Grove: Thurgood Marshall, the Groveland Boys, and the Dawn of a New America.* New York: Harper Perennial, 2012. Pb.
A Pulitzer Prize story of violence and injustice in the South of the 1940s and how the case was fought through the judicial system by a future Supreme Court justice.

Lewis, Anthony. *Gideon's Trumpet.* New York: Vintage Books, 1966.
A short story that traces the development of a case from a Florida jail to the U.S. Supreme Court.

Sotomayor, Sonia. *My Beloved World.* New York: Alfred A. Knopf, 2013.
An engaging autobiography of the rise from poverty to the Supreme Court by the first Hispanic woman justice.

Toobin, Jeffrey. *The Oath: The Obama White House and the Supreme Court.* New York: Doubleday, 2012.
A revealing look at the ongoing rivalry between a conservative Court and a liberal administration.

CHAPTER 6

Civil Rights and Liberties: Protecting the Players

Civil rights and liberties protect the political players and the American people. They limit government conduct, for example by requiring officials to follow due process of law, and describe some of the goals of the republic, such as allowing the greatest possible freedom of speech. They guard citizens against discrimination because of their gender, age, sexual preference, and race; protections that Americans didn't have a half century ago.

The U.S. government is shaped by the Constitution and Bill of Rights so that certain rules govern the relationships between citizens and their government, and other rules govern the relationships between groups of people. These rules rest on two principles: The government must not violate the civil rights and liberties of the people, and the government must protect people from those who would violate their rights.

This chapter focuses on how the courts and others protect civil rights and liberties. We will see what these rights and liberties are and how the protections in the Bill of Rights have expanded through American history. We will discuss the different players involved in applying these protections. A case study on terrorists and liberties shows the political pressures these rights face in an atmosphere of fear. (See the case study, "Fighting Terror, Guarding Liberties.")

What Are Civil Liberties and Rights?

Civil liberties are protections against government restrictions on freedom of expression. Civil liberties are those First Amendment rights of freedom of speech, petition, assembly, and press that protect people against government actions that would interfere with their participation in democratic politics. This definition includes Fifth Amendment and Fourteenth Amendment guarantees of due process of law in courtroom proceedings and government agencies. The underlying principle here is that ours is a government of laws rather than of arbitrary action.

Civil rights are protections for some groups that because of their race, religion, ethnicity, or gender may be discriminated against by others. Civil rights include the protections of the Fourteenth Amendment to the Constitution, recognizing that all citizens are entitled to be treated equally under the law. No members of a racial, religious, or economic group may claim or receive privileged treatment by virtue of group membership, nor may any group be discriminated against by others or by government officials.

Our daily lives are full of issues of civil rights and liberties. Civil liberties involve your rights as a college student: Can school authorities suspend a student for making critical remarks about homosexuals?

Establish a "civility" code barring "hate speech"? How about your right as a citizen to be informed: Can the government on national security grounds prevent a newspaper from publishing a story? Can it require reporters to reveal their sources to prosecutors investigating a crime? Is a government agency allowed to collect e-mail and phone records on millions of citizens because they are looking for contacts with accused terrorists? Can corporations spy on their employees? (See "Cartoons and Colleges in a Delicate Time.")

Everyone is affected by civil rights issues: Will you, as a woman, receive equal pay for equal work? As a Mexican American, will you be discriminated against in hiring and promotion? Will affirmative action programs designed to make up for past discrimination against minorities and women lead to "reverse discrimination" against you as a white male?

These debates have inflamed our national politics. In recent elections, a same-sex couple's right to marry and a gun owner's Second Amendment right to defy local gun control laws have lit the fire of conflict. Congress regularly grapples with civil rights issues: proposals to bar discrimination against the disabled, limits on federal insurance for birth control, and laws making it easier to prove discrimination against women at their jobs. To understand these current issues, let's look at the past.

Cartoons and Colleges in a Delicate Time

A student group at New York University (NYU) in 2006 planned to hold a panel discussion called "Free Speech and the Danish Cartoons," to debate the controversial Danish cartoons of Mohammed, which, after publication in Europe, had sparked protests and rioting in Muslim countries. Shortly before the meeting, the NYU administration ordered the group either to not display the cartoons or to not allow anyone from off campus to attend. The group refused. Their meeting was held in front of a row of blank easels.

At Century College in Minnesota, a geography teacher posted the cartoons on a public bulletin board and had them repeatedly torn down, until college administrators asked her not to post them again. She followed her employers' request but asked, "If we can't talk about this controversy at a college, where are we supposed to talk about it?" (The South Park cartoon TV show was censored by its network when it tried to broadcast an image of Mohammed in a scene.)

Nat Hentoff, a writer on First Amendment issues, quoted Justice Oliver Wendell Holmes as a challenge to universities dealing with this controversy: "If there is any principle of the Constitution that more imperatively calls for attachment than any other, it is the principle of free thought—not free thought for those who agree with us, but freedom for the thought that we hate."

Expanding the Bill of Rights

The Bill of Rights applied only to the national government when it was added to the Constitution in 1791. The Congress that passed these first 10 amendments had no intention of restricting the activities of state governments or any private individual or group. Since the early twentieth century, however, the protections of the Bill of Rights have gradually been extended to cover actions of state and local officials as well as individuals and organizations. To do this, the federal courts have relied on the *Fourteenth Amendment*. That amendment, ratified in 1868, reads in part: ". . . nor shall any State deprive any person of life, liberty or property, without due process of law, nor deny to any person within its jurisdiction the equal protection of the laws." The two key, if vague, phrases are "due process" and "equal protection."

The *equal protection* clause has been used to prevent state officials from discriminating based on race or sex. It has also prevented discrimination by private individuals when that action (1) is aided by state action such as a law; (2) furthers a state activity such as an election, or the activities of a political party; or (3) involves a fundamental state interest such as education or public safety. Therefore, the equal protection clause has been used to strike down state laws segregating students by race in public schools. It has been used to put an end to the "whites only" primaries that the Democratic parties in Southern states used to hold prior to the general elections. It was even used to halt the hand recounting of votes in Florida in the 2000 election, when the Supreme Court declared that different methods for counting votes would deprive citizens of equal protection. Though individuals may practice racial, religious, or gender discrimination in inviting guests to their homes, they cannot discriminate in private schools because education involves a fundamental state interest. And private clubs that serve the public are now considered places of public accommodation. If they discriminate in selecting members on the basis of race or gender, they may lose certain tax advantages.

The *due process* clause of the Fourteenth Amendment applies to state and local governments. To say that states must act according to due process of law raises a basic question: What does "due process" mean? This issue of fair procedure involves the extent that Bill of Rights protections should be "incorporated" into the language of the Fourteenth Amendment so as to apply to the states. On one side of the debate over due process are the *partial incorporationists*. They believe that only some of the Bill of Rights should be included in the meaning of "due process" in the Fourteenth Amendment, mainly those procedures guaranteeing fair criminal trials and *First Amendment freedoms* of religion, speech, and press. Which rights are to be incorporated? Those that are considered *preferred freedoms*—that is, the liberties necessary for a democracy to function—which, in the words of Justice Louis Brandeis, form the essence of "a scheme of ordered liberty." But not everything in the Bill of Rights is considered fundamental by partial incorporationists.

On the other side of the debate are the *complete incorporationists*. They believe that the entire Bill of Rights was incorporated into the Fourteenth Amendment. Thus, there is no need to consider which rights to apply. When a case comes before them, they incorporate the entire Bill of Rights and use it as a limit against state action.

Consider the case of a prisoner held in a state prison who sues the warden in federal court. The prisoner argues that two months of solitary confinement for a mess hall riot is a violation of the Eighth Amendment prohibition against "cruel and unusual punishment." Partial incorporationists first must decide whether or not the Eighth Amendment should be incorporated into the Fourteenth Amendment as a limitation on state prison officials. They might argue that it applies only to criminal trials in state courts and that prison discipline does not involve any "fundamental rights." Full incorporationists would automatically incorporate the Eighth Amendment into the Fourteenth Amendment: There would be no question that the amendment applied to state prison officials. The judge would decide only the question of whether two months of solitary confinement qualified as "cruel and unusual punishment."

Full incorporation has never been embraced by the Supreme Court. Yet, in the past 90 years, the effect of numerous federal court decisions has been to include almost all of the Bill of Rights into the Fourteenth Amendment. In recent years this has covered an individual's right to bear arms, applying the Second Amendment against state laws. While states may still ignore a few parts of the Bill of Rights, such as a jury trial in civil cases, most of the rights not incorporated are not very important.

Civil Liberties: Protecting People from Government

For the framers of the Constitution, the greatest danger to citizens lay in the abuse of government power. For this reason, the most important civil liberties are those that protect citizens from their government.

Most of these "preferred freedoms" are recognized—not given or created—in the *First Amendment*, which states:

> Congress shall make no law respecting an establishment of religion, or prohibiting the free exercise thereof; or abridging the freedom of speech, or of the press, or the right of the people peaceably to assemble, and to petition the Government for a redress of grievances.

The First Amendment's "rules of the game" are essential for democracy to work. They enable people to keep informed, to communicate with each other and with their government without fear. Remove these protections, and it would be difficult for political players to operate. The press, interest groups, and even members of Congress would find their ability to "go public" and organize to change government policies restricted. The political party that lost an election might be prevented from getting out its message, making it impossible to contest the next election. The Bill of Rights, along with separation of powers and checks and balances, is designed to protect a people with a healthy fear of governmental power. Note that the Constitution protects rights that Americans already have. It does not *grant* them.

Supreme Court justice Oliver Wendell Holmes once wrote that a democratic society needs competition among ideas as much as an economic marketplace needs competition among producers. "When men have realized that time has upset many fighting faiths," he wrote, "they come to believe . . . that the ultimate good desired is better reached by free trade in ideas—that the best truth is the power of the thought to get itself accepted in the competition of the marketplace." Put another way, how can you be sure your opinion is correct unless you are willing to test it against different opinions? And how can wrong opinions ever be changed, even when held by a majority, unless there is freedom for other opinions to be expressed?

Fundamental to Holmes's thinking is the belief that good ideas would drive bad ideas out of the market and that the public will reject the false in favor of the true. Given the awesome power of modern communications, and the ignorance about politics shown by many, these calculations may not always be true. Propaganda sometimes overwhelms reason; the demagogue may defeat the democrat. But it is hard to see how restricting speech can better protect freedom, though other countries disagree. (See the box, "Other Democracies Dissent on U.S. Freedoms.")

A look at recent thinking about four of the most important civil liberties—freedom of speech, freedom of religion, the right to privacy, and due process of law—will help us understand how the Bill of Rights protects Americans.

Other Democracies Dissent on U.S. Freedoms

- *England, South Africa, the Netherlands, Australia, and India have laws banning hate speech.*
- *In Canada and Germany, it is a crime to deny the Holocaust.*
- *A French court fined an animal rights activist for criticizing a Muslim ceremony where sheep were slaughtered.*
- *The Egyptian protesters who burned American flags in Cairo in the summer of 2012 would have been protected in the United States by the same government they were attacking.*

In most democracies of the world, denouncing other races, displaying ethnic hatred, or urging discrimination against religious minorities will result in the speaker being fined or imprisoned, but not in the United States.

Under the First Amendment, even false, provocative, or hateful speech about minorities and religions is protected. There is only one justification for making such speech a criminal offense—the likelihood of immediate violence. This high hurdle to suppressing speech in part reflects the nation's emphasis on the individual, as well as Americans' historic fear of allowing their government to decide what speech is acceptable. Other countries like Canada, Germany, South Africa, India, and Israel use the law to promote social harmony. Given each of these states' histories, one should pause before criticizing any nation for either banning or allowing, hate speech.

Source: From Adam Liptak, "Unlike Others, U.S. Defends Freedom to Offend in Speech," *The New York Times*, June 12, 2008.

Freedom of Speech

The First Amendment guarantee of freedom of speech has been widened to apply to state governments under the Fourteenth Amendment. "Speech" has also been deepened by court decisions to include not only speaking but also gesturing, wearing buttons and armbands, raising signs, and leafleting passersby. The Supreme Court has upheld laws that make conspiracy to overthrow the government by force a crime. But it has struck down convictions of communists based only on their membership in the Communist Party because the government was infringing on their freedom of association. Just believing in the violent overthrow of the government, or giving a speech about revolution, is not a crime, nor is membership in an organization that believes in the violent overthrow of the government. The courts insist that if the government puts terrorists in prison, it first prove that they took concrete action to commit violence.

The First Amendment not only protects your right to say what you believe; it also prohibits the government from forcing you to say what you do not believe. In 1943, during World War II, schoolchildren who were Jehovah's Witnesses refused to say the Pledge of Allegiance on the grounds that they would be worshipping "graven images" (the flag), violating their religion. The Supreme Court overturned their suspension from school by state officials, and Justice Robert Jackson wrote, "No official, high or petty, can prescribe what shall be orthodox in politics, nationalism, religion, or other matters of opinion, or force citizens to confess by word or act their faith therein." Americans have the freedom to refuse to say what we do not believe.

The Supreme Court has protected what is called *speech plus*. This involves symbolic actions, such as wearing buttons or even burning flags. In one case, an antiwar student during the Vietnam War who entered a courthouse with the words "Fuck the Draft" written on the back of his jacket was held in contempt by a local judge. The Supreme Court reversed the decision. One justice pointed out, "While the particular four-letter word being litigated here is perhaps more distasteful than most others of its genre, it nevertheless is often true that one man's vulgarity is another's lyric."

The First Amendment provides no protection to speech that directly leads to illegal conduct or that might be illegal conduct by itself. Shouting "fire" in a crowded theater (when there is no fire) is not considered speech but rather a reckless action that the state may punish. Writing or speaking damaging lies about a person (libel and slander) is not protected, and you can be sued. Making or selling child pornography is not protected speech and does not involve freedom of expression, and you go to jail for it. When an individual directs abuse or "fighting words" at someone, particularly a police officer, convictions for disorderly conduct will be upheld by the courts.

Schools can limit speech that would be allowed in other settings. In a 2007 5–4 decision (*Morse v. Frederick*), the Supreme Court permitted schools to punish a student for speech that promotes illegal drug use. The Alaskan high school student had unfurled a banner that read "Bong Hits 4 Jesus" at a gathering to watch the Olympic torch relay pass in front of his high school. The student wanted to make a statement about his First Amendment rights in front of TV cameras. Though the banner was "cryptic," both his principal and a majority of the Supreme Court saw it as promoting drugs. As such, schools had the right "to safeguard those entrusted to their care from speech that can reasonably be regarded as encouraging illegal drug use," according to Chief Justice Roberts.

In a controversial 2011 case, the Supreme Court protected hateful protesters at military funerals (*Snyder v. Phelps*). Members of the tiny Westboro Baptist Church had demonstrated at military funerals, including this one for a marine killed in Iraq, contending that God was punishing the United States for tolerating homosexuality. Chief Justice Roberts said that even hurtful signs reading "Thank God for Dead Soldiers" required protection "to ensure that we do not stifle public debate." Speech "cannot be restricted simply because it is upsetting or arouses contempt," he said writing for an 8–1 majority.

Internet communications have been a fertile field of conflict over questions of public policy and free speech. At the urging of religious groups, several senators had downloaded hard-core pornography from the Internet. The result has been a back-and-forth debate between the elected branches and the Supreme Court over what can be allowed online. The Communications Decency Act of 1996 punished making "indecent" or "patently offensive" material available to minors over the Internet. But in 1997 the Supreme Court struck down the act as overly vague, ruling that free speech protections apply just as much to online systems as they do to books and newspapers. Congress tried again in 1998 in the Child Online Protection Act, which penalized Internet material posted for "commercial purposes" that was "harmful to minors." A 5–4 Supreme Court didn't like this law any better (*ACLU v. Ashcroft*, 2002). Justice Kennedy wrote for the majority, "There is potential for extraordinary harm and a serious chill upon protected speech."

Since the 9/11 attacks, the Justice Department has asked Internet companies to keep records on their e-mail users. Whether it is for child pornography, terrorism, or general law enforcement, this data retention has led to an obligation by business to retain all information on all customers. Paralleling this expansion of government interest in online communications is the development by computer companies of technological tools to filter information on the Web. Depending on your viewpoint, this filtering technology is either a parent's tool for controlling their children without government involvement or a censoring device limiting this most democratic of media.

Freedom of Religion

The Constitution provides that there will be no religious test for office, prohibits the establishment of an official religion by Congress, and allows the "free exercise of religion." Yet there has never been a complete "wall of separation" between church and state in the United States. The armed forces have chaplains paid for by Congress, the

Supreme Court chambers have a mural of Moses giving the Ten Commandments, and the dollar bill states, "In God We Trust."

The question of freedom of religion inevitably gets mixed up in the constitutional prohibition against the establishment of religion. To allow students to pray in school, a position favored by a large majority of Americans, may seem to be simply an issue of the free exercise of religion. But if most children in the class are Protestant, should the prayer be Protestant? And, if so, which denomination? Will other children feel like outcasts, even if they are excused from saying the prayer? Administrations have tried to clarify the legal limits of religion in public schools and to distinguish between what teachers cannot do and what students can do. (See "Dos and Don'ts on Religion in Public Schools.")

While Americans strongly support freedom of religion, most believe that the government must not favor one religion over another. Balancing these competing values is difficult, and the courts have become less rigid in separating government activities from religious practices. In 1995 the Supreme Court ruled against the University of Virginia for refusing to fund a student publication because it had a Christian orientation. In 2002 the Catholic Church argued—unsuccessfully—in court that it was shielded from suits against priests for child abuse by the First Amendment protection of religious freedom. In a significant decision on religious liberty, the Supreme Court in 2012 ruled that

Dos and Don'ts on Religion in Public Schools

Department of Education guidelines on religious activity in schools:

Permitted:

- Student prayer by individuals or groups
- Student-initiated discussions on religions
- Reading the Bible
- Saying grace before meals
- Wearing religious clothing or symbols
- Religious activities before or after school

Forbidden:

- Prayer endorsed or organized by teachers or administrators
- "Harassing" invitations to participate in prayer
- Teaching or encouraging a particular religion rather than teaching about religion
- Denying school rooms to religious groups

employment discrimination laws did not apply to churches' right to hire or fire a minister of their choice. For the Court the Constitution clearly kept internal church affairs, including who should be their teachers of religion, off limits to the government.

How to recognize the religious feelings of the people, while not hindering religious freedom or favoring one group over another, is a delicate matter. In many states religious facilities are exempt from property taxes, religious employers do not have to obey labor laws protecting employees, and religious day care centers and drug-treatment clinics do not have to be licensed by the state. Abuses have been reported. Some groups argue that the constitutional wall separating church and state is needlessly high by, for example, forbidding Christmas displays on public property. Perhaps—but former New York governor Mario Cuomo observed, "I protect my right to be Catholic by preserving your right to be a Jew, or a Protestant, or a nonbeliever, or anything else you choose."

Right of Privacy

". . . the right to be let alone—the most comprehensive of rights and the right most valued by civilized men."

—Justice Louis Brandeis

Do citizens have privacy rights against intruding government officials? Though nowhere mentioned in the Constitution, the First, Fourth, and Ninth Amendments are sometimes read by the courts as creating a "zone of privacy" that shields individuals from government spying on their phones and computers, homes, and bedrooms.

In June 2013, the *Guardian*, a British newspaper, reported that the National Security Agency had for the last seven years conducted a secret effort monitoring millions of phone calls and e-mails within the United States. While aimed at foreigners suspected of being security threats, the program, called Prism, swept up the records of Americans without a court-approved warrant normally required for domestic spying. These reports confirmed earlier newspaper stories of antiterrorist monitoring of communications that had begun shortly after the 9/11 attacks. Since 2008, the so-called FISA Amendments Act allowed the government to conduct blanket surveillance of foreigners authorized by Congress and approved by the secretive Foreign Intelligence Surveillance Court (FISC).

A disenchanted government contractor, Edward Snowden, had leaked the information about the program and later fled to Russia, where he was granted asylum. President Obama refused to end the mass data collection, declared that no one was listening to citizens' phone calls, and announced modest reforms to increase the public's confidence in the government's concern for people's privacy. Civil liberties critics charge that these are basically window-dressing and that Obama has expanded the surveillance he inherited and given it bipartisan acceptance. Monitoring of telephone and Internet data of citizens has now become an entrenched practice of government.

Some recent privacy issues have centered on sexual conduct. The state, according to the Supreme Court, cannot prevent couples from using contraceptive devices, nor can states forbid abortions in the first trimester of pregnancy. However, state regulations have been upheld that make it difficult for women to use abortion services without informing their spouses or waiting 24 hours after "family counseling."

The 1996 Defense of Marriage Act (DOMA), signed by President Clinton, defined marriage as exclusively between one man and one woman and said that states could not be forced to recognize same-sex marriages authorized in another state. In early 2004, President Bush endorsed a constitutional amendment that would restrict marriage to two people of the opposite sex, but the difficulty of the amendment process made the proposal more of a campaign slogan than a likely constitutional change. Since then, attitudes toward homosexual rights have changed considerably. By the early 2010s, polls consistently showed that a majority of Americans supported same-sex marriage. During his first term, President Obama sought to expand rights for gays and lesbians. He signed bills ending the military's "Don't Ask, Don't Tell" program and expanded hate crimes protections to homosexuals. In 2011, Obama ordered the Justice Department to stop defending DOMA in court. The following year, before beginning his reelection campaign, he fully endorsed same-sex marriage.

Today same-sex marriage remains an issue in flux. Thirteen states and the District of Columbia allow it, but a majority of states continue to ban it in their state constitutions. In *U.S. v. Windsor*, the Supreme Court overturned DOMA's definition of marriage, allowing the federal government to recognize same-sex marriages in states where it is legal. The Court has yet to rule that same-sex couples have a constitutional right to marry.

Due Process Rights

The Fifth Amendment and the Fourteenth Amendment can be called on to prevent national and state governments from depriving persons of their lives, liberty, or property without due process of law. Due process guarantees involve fundamental procedural fairness and impartial rulings by government officials, especially in (but not limited to) criminal courtrooms. In criminal trials, the right to due process includes the right to free counsel if you cannot afford a lawyer; the right to have your lawyer present at any police questioning; the right to reasonable bail after being charged; the right to a speedy trial; the right to confront and cross-examine your accuser and witnesses testifying against you; the right to remain silent; the right to an impartial judge and a jury of your peers, selected without racial bias; and the right to appeal the decision to a higher court if you believe legal errors were committed by the judge.

These rights were granted in federal criminal trials under the Fifth and the Sixth amendments. As a result of Supreme Court decisions over the years, these rights also have been established for state criminal trials. In the 1970s the federal courts began to require some of these procedures in noncriminal settings. Students could not be suspended from high schools or public universities without certain kinds of hearings. People on welfare could not be purged from the rolls without receiving "fair hearings." Recent more conservative courts have limited this right, declaring in 2011 that the states did not need to provide lawyers for poor people in civil cases (*Turner v. Rogers*). Whether these rights extend to wartime situations and people accused of terrorism is now an ongoing debate. (See the case study, "Fighting Terror, Guarding Liberties.")

Consider the case of a student who has participated in a disruptive campus demonstration against the war in Afghanistan. She is told by university officials that she will be suspended for a semester. Surely she would want all the due process guarantees she could obtain in order to prove to these officials that they are wrong. Obtaining one due process right often leads to others. Once the college decides that students are entitled to a hearing, students may demand the right to an attorney. The attorney will insist on written transcripts and an appeals process. A fair hearing procedure and the presence of lawyers can encourage informal, often less-expensive, settlements.

These due process rights support First Amendment political freedoms. It does little good to give people the right to protest if officials can retaliate by cutting off essential services to protesters. Students or workers who are politically involved need legal protection from unfair action by school administrators or employers. Due process protects them. It also protects officials. By requiring them to meet standards of fairness and procedure, authorities gain legitimacy for their decisions.

Civil Rights: Protecting People from People

Protecting people against state action is only half the game. Civil rights involve the national government in the protection of minorities (or women, who are a majority) against actions by state and local governments or by private individuals and organizations.

Civil rights involve discrimination based on race, religion, gender, age, sexual preference, or national origin. A group that believes it is being discriminated against may try to obtain satisfaction from elected officials or may turn to the judiciary. African Americans may find it difficult to rent apartments because landlords discriminate against them. To combat this, many states and the national government have passed fair housing laws making such discrimination illegal. Presidents have signed executive orders banning racial discrimination in public housing and in private housing financed through federal mortgage programs.

Civil rights issues are not always clear-cut. Free speech advocates may find that exercising that right runs up against minority groups perceiving harassment. (See the box, "Conservative Bake Sales.") Affirmative action programs sometimes have placed groups in opposition to one another. The woman who supports affirmative action in order to get a job may be in conflict with the African American who believes that these programs were designed primarily to redress

■ Conservative Bake Sales

On a pleasant fall day a few years ago, conservative student organizations held "affirmative action bake sales" on college campuses across the country. Brownies were sold at varying prices: Black and Hispanic students were charged less than Asian and white students. Supporters described the sales as satire designed to draw attention to the discrimination involved in affirmative action. Many university administrators were not amused.

At William and Mary, for example, the president denounced the bake sale there as "inexcusably hurtful" and "abusive." The sale was halted because it "did not meet the administrative requirements we routinely impose on such activities." A lawyer for the student group remarked, "One can hardly imagine such tactics being used to shut down a protest that administrators found more to their liking politically." At the University of Washington, the College Republicans holding the sales were attacked by other students.

Elsewhere, universities defended the sales. An Indiana University administrator remarked, "It is exactly the kind of dialogue that should be encouraged on college campuses." Back at William and Mary, after press coverage, a second bake sale was allowed two months after the previous one was halted.

wrongs committed against blacks. As the late civil rights leader Dr. Kenneth Clark remarked, if women, blacks, Latinos, and Asians are all given affirmative action preferences, almost three-quarters of the population would be protected. These programs have fueled charges of "reverse discrimination" by white men not covered.

However valid their arguments, critics who point out the racial nature of these programs don't necessarily support policies and spending that address poverty, illiteracy, and unemployment. If greater resources were targeted on inner city public schools, fewer programs giving advantages to the graduates of these schools might be needed. In this evolution of future efforts to remedy these social ills without the public disfavor of racially based programs, the courts, too, will play a role.

Which People Need Protection? Suspect Classifications

The Fourteenth Amendment declares the right to "equal protection of the laws." However, the government may pass laws applying to some citizens and not to others, or applying different criteria to different classes of people. For example, working people with low incomes may receive money from the government—in the form of the earned-income tax credit—and pay taxes at a lower rate. Upper income people provide the government with most of its income by paying taxes at higher rates than others, at least in theory.

What limits are placed on government classifications of people? Hardly any, if the classifications involve wealth. The laws dealing with economic issues are routinely approved by the judiciary, under the doctrine of *presumptive legislative rationality*. Courts assume that the lawmakers know what they are doing when they make such classifications. On the other hand, if lawmakers apply racial, religious, or national origin classifications, the courts subject these to "close scrutiny" because these are *suspect classifications*. Here the burden of proof is on the government to demonstrate that the classification is not, on its face, unconstitutional.

Governments must, when the law or action touches a "suspect class," prove a compelling state interest for their action. The courts begin their scrutiny with the assumption that the action violates the equal protection guarantee, and it is up to the lawmakers to prove otherwise. Racial classifications always are considered suspect and almost always are struck down.

Gender classifications are not suspect. To them the court applies a "middle test," stricter than standards for wealth and income but looser than standards for race. While courts have struck down many gender classifications, they have upheld some: Women are not registered for the military and, because they give birth, may get different medical benefits than men.

Race as a Suspect Classification

In 1896 the Supreme Court supported state actions that segregated the races. We saw that *Plessy v. Ferguson* (1896) upheld the right of Louisiana to enforce racial segregation in railway cars. "Equal protection of the law" was misshapen into the doctrine of "separate but equal": After all, the African American Plessy would travel in a separate railway car but would reach his destination at the same time and on the same train as a white person. Then in the 1954 landmark case *Brown v. Board of Education*, the Supreme Court held that schools segregated by race were unequal and violated the Fourteenth Amendment. After *Brown*, courts struck down most laws based on racial categories and made race a *suspect classification*.

But do racial classifications always violate the Fourteenth Amendment? Are there circumstances in which classification by race is a valid use of governmental power? Courts have upheld racial classifications when used to eliminate prior state-sponsored segregation. In devising plans to desegregate schools, for instance, administrators took into account the race of students attending schools, as well as their teachers. To make desegregation work, blacks would have to attend schools that had previously been all white.

Affirmative action programs permit racial classifications. An affirmative action program in schools allows admissions officers to take race and ethnicity into account in awarding places in the entering class. An affirmative action program in employment usually requires employers to make efforts to match the racial and gender numbers in their workforce with the pool of qualified workers in their areas. In 1978, in the *University of California Regents v. Bakke*, the Supreme Court upheld the principle of affirmative action, holding that it was a "state interest" to provide for diversity among medical students at the University of California. At the same time, the Court held that the use of numerical quotas for minorities was a violation of the equal protection clause.

Recent supreme courts have grown more skeptical of affirmative action programs. As we saw in the last chapter the current chief justice has been reluctant to approve programs to promote racial balance, declaring himself "more faithful to the heritage of *Brown v. Board of Education*," which he sees as banning assigning schools by race. While not declaring all affirmative action programs unconstitutional, courts have made it clear that there had to be a "compelling interest" to relieve a specific case of discrimination and that the remedy had to be "narrowly tailored." In the 2013 *University of Texas* case, the Roberts Court sent the decision back to the lower court, making it clear that states would need to show "a *real need* for affirmative action programs to diversify student enrollment."(See "Affirmative Action in Michigan.")

Recent administrations have paralleled this lukewarm trend toward affirmative action. The Clinton administration's Justice Department issued guidelines for federal agencies that led to reducing or eliminating 17 affirmative action programs. President Bush publicly opposed affirmative action and supported the cases against the University of Michigan. One member of his administration denounced affirmative action as "a corrupt system of preferences,

Affirmative Action in Michigan

In *Grutter v. Bollinger* (and a parallel case in the college), the Supreme Court heard arguments about the University of Michigan's admission policies intended to boost minority enrollments. A white student argued that because less-qualified minorities were admitted to the law school, she was denied a place. The university said that race-conscious admissions were a constitutional and limited way of ensuring "educational diversity." Opponents, including the Bush administration, argued that this was in fact a racial quota and that diversity could be reached through other methods. Using race violated white students' constitutional right to equal treatment under the law.

On June 23, 2003, the Court supported the law school's affirmative action program as a flexible, narrow way of promoting diversity in their student body. At the same time they rejected the undergraduate admissions program that awarded points based on race, regardless of individual merits. The Supreme Court supported the *Bakke* decision (1978) that race could be a factor in admissions but worried that what was once a temporary "catch-up" remedy to discrimination was becoming permanent.

After the Michigan ruling, the state's voters passed a constitutional amendment in 2006 banning the use of race in college admissions. This was thrown out in 2012 by a federal appeals court. In Spring 2014 the Roberts Court in a 6–2 decision supported the Michigan referendum that banned affirmative action in higher education. While the majority maintained that they were only ruling on the right of voters to democratically decide against racial preferences, the opinion was consistent with the current Court's steady march toward rejecting affirmative action.

set-asides and quotas." Even the first president who actually benefited from these programs only gingerly supported them. Obama declared that affirmative action "hasn't been as potent a force for racial progress as advocates will claim and it hasn't been as bad on white students seeking admissions or seeking a job as its critics say."

Public opinion, which was negative toward the programs a few years ago, seems more mixed today. Polling data are unreliable because the results depend on the wording of the questions. In a CBS poll, support for affirmative action programs stood at 53 percent. However, when mention is made of "preferential treatment" for minorities, support dropped by half. Yet the consequences of eliminating affirmative action also concern the public. The banning in California of the use of race in college admissions led to a drastic 57 percent drop in black applicants and a 40 percent decline in Hispanic high school seniors accepted for admission to Berkeley. This led some opponents of affirmative action to question their criticisms and puzzle over these "unintended consequences." In other arenas, like the military and corporations, affirmative action programs appear to be a permanent fixture, whatever their popularity.

Is Sex Suspect?

In the nineteenth century, women and children were widely exploited. They worked 14-hour days in factories, seven days a week, for low wages in unsafe conditions (of course men did too). In the late nineteenth century, a coalition of women's rights advocates, labor organizers, and public health professionals demanded that government protect women and children through wage and hour regulations. Some states passed these laws, known as *protective legislation*. The Supreme Court, which opposed state efforts to regulate industry, held many of them to be unconstitutional.

But protective legislation did not stop with factory conditions. State legislatures further "protected" women by restricting their opportunities to enter professions. In 1873 the Supreme Court upheld a decision by the Illinois courts that prevented Myra Bradwell from becoming a lawyer. "The natural and proper timidity and delicacy which belongs to the female sex," a justice wrote, "evidently unfits it for many of the occupations of civil life." Under this reasoning, women were denied the right to enter businesses, serve on juries, sign contracts, or work at all if they were pregnant. Former Supreme Court justice William Brennan observed that this "romantic paternalism" put women "not on a pedestal, but in a cage."

Throughout the twentieth century, these restrictions on women were chipped away. By the 1970s, women's groups had attacked the remaining "protective" laws in federal courts, arguing that gender should be considered a suspect classification. The Supreme Court responded by striking down many laws involving gender, including professional and educational requirements that discriminate against women. It has ruled that men have an equal right to sue for alimony, that the drinking age must be the same for both sexes, and that unwed fathers have rights in deciding whether a baby is put up for adoption. But the Court has not held that gender classifications are suspect.

In fact the Supreme Court has allowed state laws granting certain tax benefits to widows but not widowers. It upheld a state law permitting men but not women to serve as guards in a maximum security prison. It let stand a lower-court decision permitting single-sex schools to continue to receive federal funds. The Court has also upheld gender classifications when used for approved purposes such as an affirmative action plan. No challenges to single-sex bathrooms have succeeded.

The federal courts do retain part of the protective movement, the one that involves sexual harassment. The Supreme Court has recognized a pattern of harassment that exists, which makes it difficult for women to work in a hostile environment. In 1998 the Court held employers liable for a supervisor's behavior even if it did not know of the misconduct. Congress gave women who have been harassed on the job the right to sue in federal court for damages. In 2013 Congress passed, and Obama signed, a new Violence against Women Act that provides funds to investigate and prosecute domestic violence and sexual assault. For the first time, it included explicit protections for lesbian, gay, bisexual, and transgender (LGBT) victims of domestic violence.

Despite these crosscurrents, it is likely that more sex-based classifications will fall as a result of present standards applied by the courts.

Actors in Civil Liberties and Rights

Many players act on civil liberties and rights. Within the government, the courts have been the most important, although Congress's laws and the executive's actions affect these issues. Outside the government many organizations champion the rights of particular groups, pressuring officials with tactics like lobbying, publicity, and boycotts. The politics of civil liberties and rights involves struggles of group against group, as well as group against government, in ongoing attempts to strike a balance among competing claims.

Judges

Judges have taken the lead in protecting and expanding civil rights and liberties. Activist judges, who along with other supporters of civil liberties are called *civil libertarians*, issue decisions in *class action suits* in which lawyers bring a case to court not only for their individual clients but also on behalf of everyone in a similar situation—perhaps millions of people. Judges may rely on court-appointed experts to do the research needed to resolve complicated social issues. To decide a case, they may use not only previous cases and laws but also the equity powers of the judiciary.

Equity is used to prevent permanent damage in situations not covered by existing law. Suppose my neighbor, Jones, decides to cut down a tree in his yard. I see that the tree will crash into my house. My legal remedy is to sue Jones after my house is damaged. My equitable remedy is to obtain a court injunction that prevents Jones from cutting down the tree. Activist judges use equity powers to overcome the effects of discrimination. Take a school district that has been segregated by race. Requiring that the system ignore race may not have any effect if housing segregation exists so that schools will still remain segregated. Some federal judges have applied equitable remedies: They have required that the school districts take into account racial imbalances and come up with plans to overcome these imbalances.

Other judges show greater restraint in civil liberties and civil rights cases. They follow precedent rather than expand constitutional protections. They place great weight on the policies of Congress, the president, and state legislatures, even when these restrict civil rights and liberties. These judges will presume that elected officials are acting lawfully unless proven otherwise. Because elected officials are directly accountable to voters, these unelected judges hesitate to impose their own views. (See pp. 153–55 for more on activist and restrained judges.)

The Justice Department

Historically the Department of Justice has played a key role in protecting civil rights and liberties. Its lawyers in the U.S. attorney's offices in each judicial district may prosecute persons, including state or federal officials, accused of violating people's civil rights. Under Republican presidents since Ronald Reagan, the Justice Department pulled back from support of civil rights groups. The department opposed busing plans to overcome segregation of schools, opposed some affirmative action hiring plans, and argued that job discrimination cases should be limited to the individuals involved and not cover patterns of employment.

President Clinton entered office calling for civil rights enforcement. He appointed the nation's first female attorney general, Janet Reno, as well as liberal judges and U.S. attorneys. The Republican takeover of Congress in 1994 and the unpopularity of affirmative action programs led to Clinton's more lukewarm stance toward civil rights. George W. Bush, elected with little black support, steered a conservative course toward civil rights. He opposed affirmative action, which he equated with quotas and racial preferences. But he supported "affirmative access" such as the Texas 10 percent plan, where students graduating in the top 10 percent of their high school class were automatically admitted to a state university. The Bush Justice Department was only modestly active in civil rights enforcement.

The nation's first black president was, as we saw, ambivalent toward controversial affirmative action programs, perhaps understandably. His Justice Department under a black attorney general, Eric Holder, has emphasized the educational benefits of diversity and encouraged universities to achieve their desired levels of diversity without explicitly considering an applicant's race. Overall the use of race and ethnicity in college admissions has declined sharply.

"Private Attorneys General"

Various organizations have been created to support the rights of individuals and groups. These are called *private attorneys general* because they act not for the government but for groups bringing court cases against the government or against other groups. For example in 2011 the Supreme Court rejected an effort on behalf of a million female workers to sue Wal-Mart in what was the biggest class-action discrimination case in history. Such efforts are funded by foundations, wealthy donors, and individual members' dues.

The largest of these groups is the *American Civil Liberties Union* (ACLU). The ACLU has a national staff and 50 state chapters handling more than 6,000 cases each year. The ACLU was organized in the 1920s to defend against the hysteria of "red scares" (a period when socialists were persecuted) and has fought against wiretapping, surveillance, and "dirty tricks" by law enforcement agencies. It is especially active in First Amendment freedom of speech, press, and religion issues. Recently it has opposed the FBI's aggressive assault on citizens' privacy rights and has defended the due process claims of those swept up in the war on terrorism.

The NAACP's Legal Defense and Educational Fund, Inc. (LDF) began in 1939 with one lawyer, Thurgood Marshall, who later became the first black person on the Supreme Court. In the past, the LDF concentrated on school desegregation, but today its dozens of lawyers focus on discrimination in employment and housing, and abuses in the judicial system. The largest legal organization for women is the National Organization for Women (NOW) Legal Defense and Education Fund, which works for women's employment rights and against biased legislation.

The Foundation for Individual Rights in Education (FIRE) is a conservative/libertarian nonprofit that defends students and faculty confronting restraints on their freedom of speech on college campuses. The Council on American-Islamic Relations (CAIR) is a major Muslim organization involved in encouraging a greater Muslim presence in the media and government, in promoting a positive image of their religion and in defending civil liberties cases of people accused of terrorism.

Legal Strategies

These organizations use a range of tactics. Their research attempts to find a pattern of discrimination for a large class of people. They offer their services to individuals suffering discrimination whose rights have been violated. Such people cannot afford the hundreds of thousands of dollars it takes to pursue a case to the Supreme Court, so the assistance of the "private attorneys general," almost always provided free, is crucial. Civil liberties lawyers choose, from a large number of complaints, a *test case* for their arguments. Such a case offers the group its best shot because the violation is so obvious, the damage so great, and the person making the case so appealing.

These groups hope that their case eventually will wind up in the Supreme Court as a *landmark decision*—one that involves major changes in the definition of civil rights and liberties. Often similar cases will be filed in different courts, hoping for conflicting constitutional interpretations that will "force" the Supreme Court to rule on the issue. Such a decision creates a new precedent, such as the right to counsel in a state trial, which is then enforced by lower federal and state courts. After the landmark case is announced by the high court, the lawyers from these organizations then must bring dozens of cases in federal district courts to make sure that rights affirmed by the Supreme Court are obeyed. (For an example of a landmark decision, see *Brown v. Board of Education* in Chapter 5.)

Obeying the Courts

These private organizations ask judges to do several things. First, they may ask that a law or executive order be declared unconstitutional, or that actions of private individuals be found to violate the law or the

Constitution. Second, they may ask that a right be protected by judicial action. Of these, the most important are the *injunction*, which prevents someone from taking an action to violate someone else's rights, and the *order*, which requires someone to take a specified action to ensure another's rights.

In the event of noncompliance with a judicial injunction or order, the judges may issue a citation for contempt of court. Civil contempt involves the refusal to obey a court order granted to a party in a case and can lead to imprisonment. The court also may find someone in criminal contempt of court for disrupting the court or showing disrespect for the court's enforcement powers. This too may lead to prison or a stiff fine.

The orders of a federal court are enforced by federal marshals, backed up by the state's National Guard (which may be brought into federal service by proclamation of the president) or by federal troops under the orders of the president. In 1957, for example, when Governor Orval Faubus of Arkansas refused to obey a federal court order to desegregate Little Rock Central High School, President Dwight Eisenhower took control of the Arkansas National Guard away from the governor. Federal troops were used to protect black students at the school.

In writing their orders, federal courts can act as administrators over state agencies. At one time in the 1970s, federal judges in Alabama were running the state highway patrol, the prison system, and the mental hospitals because the governor refused to obey federal court orders guaranteeing equal protection and due process of law by these agencies.

Sometimes state officials do not wish to comply with the spirit or letter of court orders. Consider the landmark decision of *Miranda v. Arizona* (1966), in which the Supreme Court held that once an investigation by police focused on an accused, that person had to receive the following warning:

> *You have the right to remain silent.*
> *Anything you say may be used against you in a court of law.*
> *You have the right to be represented by an attorney of your choice.*
> *If you cannot afford an attorney, a public defender will be provided for you if you wish.*

At first, there was only limited acceptance by police of the new rules of the "cops and robbers" game. After all, unless there was a federal judge in every patrol car, voluntary compliance was the only practical way such a rule could be implemented. Some departments ignored the order; others gave only part of the warning.

Miranda: Pop Culture and the Court

"You have the right to remain silent" is how the *Miranda* warning begins. It was also how Chief Justice William Rehnquist began his decision upholding *Miranda*. The chief justice was reflecting the fact that TV had made *Miranda* a part of pop culture. Detective shows from *Dragnet* to *Law and Order* repeated this warning endlessly. It was delivered so frequently that these by-the-book TV cops made it a bit of a joke.

When the Supreme Court had to rule on Congress's effort to overturn *Miranda v. Arizona* (1967), it had to deal with a warning that had become part of the nation's culture. In *Dickerson v. United States* (2000), Chief Justice Rehnquist, speaking for a 7 to 2 majority, ruled that *Miranda* "announced a constitutional rule," which Congress was not free to replace with a case-by-case test. The Court noted that *Miranda* had become an accepted national norm for making an arrest legitimate. The justices had found it difficult to overturn both the Constitution and the culture.

The courts gained compliance through the *exclusionary rule*: They threw out evidence obtained illegally, including confessions where *Miranda* warnings had not been given. The Supreme Court, while continuing *Miranda*, has narrowed the exclusionary rule, allowing evidence if police officers "acted in good faith," even if they did not follow all due process rules. (See the box, "Miranda: Pop Culture and the Court.")

Public Opinion and Civil Liberties

Public support for civil rights and liberties cannot be assumed. A majority of the public, for example, does not believe that evidence should be thrown out in state criminal trials on "legal technicalities," which is what the *Miranda* rule requires. Some years after 9/11, when Americans were asked whether it was more important to investigate terrorist threats even if that intrudes on personal privacy, or for the federal government not to intrude on privacy even if that limits its ability to investigate these threats, 65 percent backed aggressive investigation. On whether to permit wiretapping overseas calls without a court warrant if needed to catch terrorists, 57 percent approved. Most Americans do not expect to need the Bill of Rights protections because they are not criminals or terrorists or illegal immigrants. While the American idea of freedom includes freedom from their government, this view does not comfortably apply in fearful situations of economic or political crises. (See "Uncle Sam: Enemy of Civil Liberties?")

Uncle Sam: Enemy of Civil Liberties?

Freedom in general receives broad public support, but that doesn't mean people defend civil liberties for unpopular causes. Throughout U.S. history, there are uncomfortable reminders of government actions that seem to violate the Bill of Rights.

Not many years after the ink had dried on the Constitution, Congress passed the Alien and Sedition Acts of 1798. Aimed at the opposition party, these acts promised heavy fines and imprisonment for those guilty of writing or speaking anything false, scandalous, or malicious against any government official. Such a broad prohibition today would put an end to most political campaigns. The slavery issue in 1840 led Congress to pass the "Gag Rule," preventing anti-slavery petitions from being received by Congress (thus violating a specific First Amendment right).

Violations of civil liberties continued into the twentieth century. Five months after the United States entered World War I, every leading socialist newspaper had been suspended from the mails at least once, some permanently. During World War II, Japanese Americans along the West Coast were forced into internment camps based solely on their national origins. The Smith Act of 1940, which is still on the books, forbid teaching or advocating the violent overthrow of the government. In 1951, Communist Party leaders were convicted under it for activities labeled "preparation for revolution." This "preparation" involved teaching works like the *Communist Manifesto*, which today can be found in any college library. Ten defendants were sentenced to five years in prison.

More recently, the FBI infiltrated the anti–Vietnam War movement, wiretapped civil rights leader Martin Luther King Jr., and got into a shoot-out with a right-wing family at Ruby Ridge, Idaho. In 2011 American citizens Anwar al-Awlaki and his 16-year-old son were killed by drones in Yemen for encouraging jihad against the United States in public speeches. No one had accused him of firing a shot. Down to the present, government respect for civil liberties remains a sometime thing.

But it is because the rights of politically unpopular groups have been violated that judicial protection becomes necessary. Where support by local leaders does not exist and community sentiment runs against the decision, as with the ban on prayer in the public schools, compliance may be spotty. Often a Supreme Court ruling signals the start—not the end—of political debate. In the case of abortion rights, the Supreme Court decision (*Roe v. Wade*) affirming the right to abortion was followed by congressional and state laws cutting off public funding for abortions and requiring parental consent for teenagers.

The legitimacy of judicial action supporting civil liberties and rights never rests on its popularity. The federal judiciary is not elected and does not directly answer to the people. It is accountable to the Constitution that attempts to secure the rights of the people against governmental action. The judiciary protects these rights. Low levels of approval for some of its decisions are often to be expected. If anything, it is a sign that the system is working as a check on popular excesses.

Realistically for the courts to operate in the political game, and for their decisions to be enforced, they must function within the bounds of public opinion and the cooperation of other parts of the government. This is not automatically given, as the following examples of civil liberties in an age of terrorism illustrate.

CASE STUDY

Fighting Terror, Guarding Liberties

The enemy has declared war on us. And we must not let foreign enemies use the forums of liberty to destroy liberty itself.

—George W. Bush

They that can give up essential liberty to obtain a little temporary safety deserve neither liberty nor safety.

—Benjamin Franklin

Two Asian men with box cutters were taken off an Amtrak train in Texas on September 12, 2001, and held in isolation for three months without being brought before a court or being given a lawyer. Both were eventually cleared of any involvement with terrorism.

After 9/11, defending the country against terrorism and defending the Constitution's civil liberties seemed in conflict. George W. Bush, acting under his powers of commander in chief, took a number of aggressive actions. Without approval from Congress or the courts, the executive branch locked up over 1,200 people either for violating immigration laws or as material witnesses—though the real motive was to investigate their links to terrorism. (The attorney general refused to release their names, claiming, without a trace of humor, that he was protecting their privacy.) Secret deportation hearings were ordered for suspected terrorists. The administration held to a firm position in terrorist-related cases: no judicial review, no right to counsel, no public disclosure, no open hearings. A federal appeals court later ruled these secret hearings "undemocratic" and "in complete opposition to the society envisioned by the Framers of our Constitution."

Historically presidents during wars have found ways around civil liberties, and the Supreme Court usually goes along. Recent presidents' actions look mild compared to their predecessors: Abraham Lincoln detained thousands of rebel sympathizers, Woodrow Wilson banned antiwar publications during World War I, and Franklin D. Roosevelt interned tens of thousands of Japanese Americans in World War II. The courts avoided intervening in these clear violations of civil liberties, and public opinion supported them.

The men who wrote the Constitution wanted a strong president for protection against foreign attacks. But did wartime needs override fundamental rights like representation by a lawyer who could argue against detention before a civilian judge? The Bush administration claimed that these were military decisions that the Constitution gave to the executive branch alone. And, later, when the Obama administration attempted to return to constitutional procedures, it faced strong political and popular opposition.

A TERRORIST AND DUE PROCESS

In the year following the 9/11 terrorist attacks, the case *Hamdan v. Rumsfeld* brought up core civil liberties issues and the role of the courts in reviewing government actions.

Hamdan, a Saudi national, was captured in Afghanistan and, along with other prisoners, was taken to Guantanamo Bay in Cuba. When Hamdan said he was born in Louisiana and was therefore an American citizen, he was declared an "enemy combatant," taken to Norfolk, and held incommunicado in a navy jail. His father and a public defender tried to get access to him, but the government said that for reasons of national security he could not have visitors.

A federal district judge in Norfolk (an appointee of another Republican president, Ronald Reagan) ruled that Hamdan had a right to see a lawyer. The judge described the situation as "the first where an American citizen has been held incommunicado and subjected to an indefinite detention in the continental United States without charges, without any findings by a military tribunal, and without access to a lawyer." The Court of Appeals ruled against the judge, twice asking him to reconsider his decision, giving greater consideration to the executive branch's right to wage war. But the court also questioned the administration's "sweeping proposition" that "any American citizen alleged to be an enemy combatant could be detained indefinitely without charges or counsel on the government's say-so."

The issue was not whether the government could detain an "enemy combatant." This had already been allowed under precedents from World War II. The issue was whether the executive could lock up U.S. citizens it *says* are enemy combatants and refuse them the opportunity to tell their side of the story to a court, to a lawyer, or to the public. Could they be held in solitary confinement for months or even years without a hearing? Does this accused citizen have the right to be heard?

The government responded to the appeals court by giving the district judge a two-page declaration of why Hamdan was an "unlawful enemy combatant" entitled to neither constitutional protections nor international prisoner-of-war status. The government declined to give the judge any further information. The federal judge was not impressed: "I do think that due process requires something other than a basic assertion that they have looked at some papers and therefore they have determined he should be held incommunicado. Is that what we're fighting for?"

In the summer of 2004, the U.S. Supreme Court ruled in the *Hamdan* case against the government's claim of sweeping executive power. The Court declared that an American citizen detained as an enemy combatant had a due process right to a hearing to challenge his detention. Many observers thought that the abuses by the American military revealed at Abu Ghraib prison in Iraq had shown that the executive branch could not be trusted with such an extensive claim to power. Media exposure of torture produced a climate of public opinion that made it politically easier for the Supreme Court to limit presidential powers, even in wartime.

In September 2004, after nearly three years in solitary confinement, Yasser Hamdan was released from custody and flown home to Saudi Arabia. He was required to renounce his American citizenship. What were the compelling national security concerns that led the executive branch to fight his release all the way to the Supreme Court? Never revealed.

GUANTANAMO, CONGRESS, AND OBAMA

Whether a president has the power to label people, including American citizens, enemy combatants and imprison them indefinitely without trial continued to be debated. In the past when such claims were made, the war lasted a limited time. Now in a war with neither a clear beginning nor end, the concern was that these claims by the executive would shape civil liberties for the indefinite future. That is what worried a majority on the Supreme Court, as Justice O'Connor wrote in the *Hamdan* case, "A state of war is not a blank check for the president when it comes to the rights of the nation's citizens."

In the fall of 2006, Congress passed a bill that generally approved the president's power over terrorist suspects. It authorized the president to define enemy combatants (including American citizens) and to imprison and interrogate them indefinitely, and it stripped the courts of jurisdiction. The detainee bill answered critics who complained that the president was acting without congressional approval. But the law clearly undermined *Hamdan v. Rumsfeld* and continued the practices of detention. This was made clear to President Obama in his unsuccessful efforts to shut down the Guantanamo detention facility in Cuba.

During his first week in office, President Obama had signed an executive order to close Gitmo within one year. He declared that his action was meant to restore "core constitutional values" of due process. Five years later, in 2013, the office responsible for closing the prison was itself closed. Guantanamo remained open. Congress, reflecting popular opposition, had blocked all attempts to close the prison and put the inmates on trial.

President Obama initially attempted to acquire a prison in Illinois as Gitmo's replacement. This ran into not-in-my-backyard opposition and fear of terrorists. The House Armed Services Committee in May 2010, with a Democratic majority, prohibited bringing these prisoners to detention centers in the United States. The next year, the plan to prosecute 9/11 mastermind Khalid Sheik Mohammed in federal court fell apart. New York wanted no part of this trial, and so he was returned to Guantanamo. The *Washington Post* declared that this marked "the effective abandonment of the president's promise to close the military detention center."

A renewed attempt was made in 2013 to transfer those detainees cleared for release to third countries. Of the 166 prisoners left at Gitmo, 86 had been cleared for release. The House of Representatives voted for restrictions on moving any detainees, which included preventing the president from using funds to return them to Yemen. Many congressmen simply didn't want to think about the issue, in part because, as one congressman put it, the Republicans had been masterful in tying support of Guantanamo with being tough on terror. The president's argument that the base was expensive, unnecessary, and unconstitutional was no match for scare tactics.

The Patriot Act

The Patriot Act sped quickly through Congress on October 25, 2001. It was hyped as key to the antiterrorism war—the attorney general at the time declared that repealing any part of it would "disarm" the United States. It was then extended in 2006 and in 2011 by overwhelming majorities in Congress.

The act strengthened law enforcement. It allowed the FBI and CIA to share evidence. It made it easier for the FBI to ask federal judges to force businesses (including libraries and bookstores) to turn over records in terrorism probes and to delay telling people that their homes and offices were being searched. It also allowed "roving" wiretaps, under court order, to listen to electronic devices.

President Obama was criticized for signing a four-year extension to many Patriot Act sections in 2011. These included the "roving wiretap" power, allowing federal authorities to listen in on conversations of foreign suspects. Another section gives the government access to a wide range of personal material of suspects and came to be known as the "library provision." A third section, known as the "lone wolf" provision, gives the government the authority to investigate foreigners with no known affiliation with terrorist groups. All of these government powers require an order from secret federal courts.

WRAP-UP

Civil rights and liberties are constitutional protections granted to all citizens. They protect people against violations of their rights by other people or by the government. Civil liberties refer to rights—such as freedom of speech and religion and guarantees of due process of law—which allow people full participation in a democratic political system. Civil rights guard groups against discrimination by other groups. Historically, both sets of rights have been deepened as to what they cover and widened as to whom they cover.

Using the Fourteenth Amendment concepts of "equal protection of the laws" and "due process of law," the courts have applied the Bill of Rights to the states as well as the national government. Freedom of speech has expanded to include freedom of expression, including symbolic speech. Privacy rights now include protection for consenting adult sexual behavior but not necessarily freedom from government wiretapping. Due process rights cover bureaucracies as well as states' criminal justice systems. Civil rights similarly have been widened with the use of suspect classifications to deal with racial prejudice. Although the strict scrutiny test does not apply to gender classifications, a large number of laws containing "protective" gender classifications have been removed from the books.

Helping the process along have been activist judges and private attorneys general, whose test cases have changed the law, sometimes dramatically and sometimes slowly. The cases of terrorism and civil liberties illustrate how difficult it is to support constitutional protections for unpopular individuals and groups.

Civil rights and liberties do not just protect individuals. They also defend our system of government. These well-tested values balance and restrain the drives and ambitions of leaders. They give us standards by which to judge the actions of these players. They underline the historical truth that majorities err, that leaders can mislead. These rights may grant "freedom for the thoughts that we hate," but they also restrain the "tyranny of the majority."

Although the Bill of Rights is written in inspiring and absolute language—"Congress shall make no law"—these rights are seldom applied that way. Judges weighing civil liberties and rights (and students as well) are influenced by the political climate of the times. First Amendment freedoms are easier to support when we agree with the views being advanced. Conservatives may not be quite as upset by violations of free speech when police rough up Occupy Wall Street protestors. Liberals may not see an issue of individuals' privacy being undermined when they read about secret government spying on citizens' emails by a Democratic administration. But each citizen's understanding and support for these freedoms is the most important defense for these liberties. As Judge Learned Hand wrote, "Liberty lies in the hearts and minds of men and women; when it dies there, no constitution, no law, no court can save it."

THOUGHT QUESTIONS

1. How can individual citizens support civil liberties? Do they?
2. Some people believe that the Bill of Rights could not be passed in Congress today. Do you agree? Which of the first 10 amendments would be the most controversial?
3. Should affirmative action be used just to remedy the effects of racial discrimination? Or should it be used for broader goals in promoting a more diverse society? Should affirmative action be applied on a basis of social class to help any person in poverty?
4. Do you think that the threat of terrorism will cause a long-term decline in popular support for civil liberties in the United States? How would you prevent this from happening?

SUGGESTED READINGS

Cole, David, ed. *Securing Liberty*. New York: IDebate Press, 2011, Pb.
    Six debates over the balance between security and liberty in post-9/11 America.
Friendly, Fred W. *Minnesota Rag*. New York: Vintage Books, 1982.
    A delightful account of a famous case of freedom of the press.
Hentoff, Nat. *Living the Bill of Rights*. New York: HarperCollins, 1998.
    Entertaining flesh-and-blood examples of how Americans from Justice William O. Douglas to an Alabama homecoming queen have fought for their civil liberties.

Lewis, Anthony. *Freedom for the Thought That We Hate*. New York: Basic Books, 2008.

This former *New York Times* columnist writes a "biography of the First Amendment" with considerable praise for the brave judges who protect it.

Scahill, Jeremy. *Dirty Wars: The World Is a Battlefield*. New York: Nation Books, 2013. Pb.

A journalist with *The Nation* probes the wars America has waged since 9/11, often in secret. Also a movie.

Walker, Samuel. *Presidents and Civil Liberties from Wilson to Obama*. New York: Cambridge University Press, 2013, Pb.

A historian's account of the troubled relationship between presidents of both parties and the civil liberties that they often ignore or violate.

CHAPTER 7

Voters and Political Parties

S o far we have only discussed half of the political game: the institutions of government. Equally important are the "players" outside of government. Don't assume that they have less power than those within the government. That will be determined by the skills and resources of the participants as well as the nature of the issue. The next two chapters will discuss four nongovernmental players—voters, political parties, interest groups, and media—and how they influence American politics.

In this chapter we will first look at voters—who they are and who they are not. What leads some to vote and participate in politics and others to not do either? Political parties, whatever their shortcomings, are a critical link between voters and government. The history of the party system, its functions, and how well it performs its tasks today are the key topics. The case study at the end—the Barack Obama campaign's use of the Internet—shows how candidates and their parties identify, persuade, and mobilize voters, and win elections.

Voters

Who Votes?

"Who votes in America?" seems like an easy question. Citizens who are 18 and older (because of the Twenty-sixth Amendment lowering the voting age) and who have satisfied their states' residency requirements can vote. But in presidential elections, around 40 percent do not vote; in elections between presidential years, at least 60 percent don't show up to vote. The good news is that turnout seems to be improving. The bad news is that popular disgust with government and state officials raising barriers to voting may be reversing the trend.

In the 2012 election 58.2 percent of those eligible voted. This was almost 4 points down from the 2008 election, where 131 million voted, some 62 percent of those eligible, a small increase from 2004. Recent presidential elections have seen the highest turnouts since 1968, when Richard Nixon beat Hubert Humphrey in the swirl of controversies over the Vietnam War. (See Figure 7.1.) In 2012 women voted at a 4-point higher rate than men, the same as 2008. Hispanic turnout fell 2 points to 48 percent. Voting by blacks rose to 66.2 percent from 64.7 percent in 2008, while white voting declined to 64.1 percent from 66.1 percent. This marked the first time in American history that black turnout has been higher than white turnout. (See Figure 7.2.)

Much lower voting rates exist in nonpresidential elections, and that has had a significant impact on partisan divisions in Washington. In 2010, 41 percent of eligible voters turned up at election booths, a figure only slightly higher than the 2006 midterms. Midterms, with

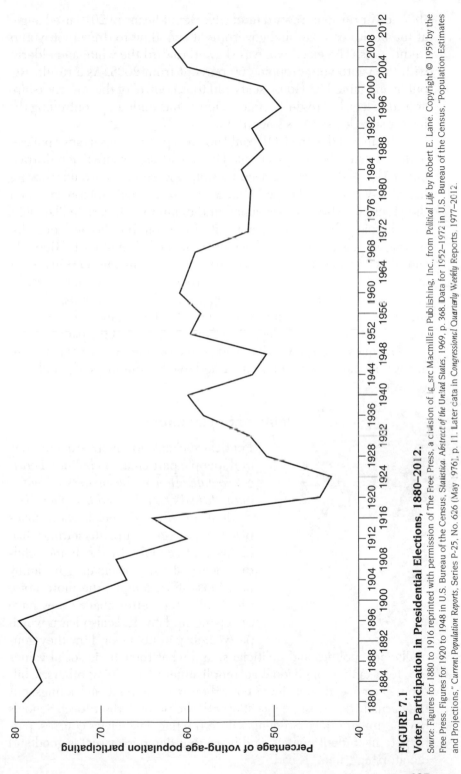

FIGURE 7.1

Voter Participation in Presidential Elections, 1880–2012.

Source: Figures for 1880 to 1916 reprinted with permission of The Free Press, a division of Macmillan Publishing, Inc., from *Political Life* by Robert E. Lane. Copyright © 1959 by the Free Press. Figures for 1920 to 1948 in U.S. Bureau of the Census, *Statistical Abstract of the United States*, 1969, p. 368. Data for 1952–1972 in U.S. Bureau of the Census, "Population Estimates and Projections," *Current Population Reports*, Series P-25, No. 626 (May 1976), p. 11. Later data in *Congressional Quarterly Weekly Reports* 1977–2012.

their lower turnout, reward intensity. Republicans in 2010 used anger at the health care law and government spending to drive their voters to the polls. The electorate was skewed toward the white and elderly, with the youth vote dropping 60 percent from 2008. As a result, Republicans gained 63 House seats and took control of the governorships and state legislatures in 12 states. Democrats ended up controlling the fewest state legislatures since 1946.

This meant that the GOP could not only pursue conservative policies in the 24 states they now controlled but could also ensure that redistricting of House districts, overseen by state governments, would work for their party. So even though Democrats won 1.7 million more votes for the House in 2012, they remained in the minority. In a state like Ohio, for example, Obama won 51 percent of the vote but, because of redistricting, its congressional delegation remained three-fourths Republican. This drawing of safe districts means that in 2014 only 35 House seats are actually competitive. These one-party districts create more partisan representatives who don't have to appeal to *independents* or members of the other party to keep their seats. In the GOP case, incumbents worry more about primary challenges from the right wing of the party.

The questions grow. What leads some people to vote? What influences how they vote? And what has led to large numbers of people not voting?

Political Socialization

Political socialization helps explain how, or if, people participate in politics. *Political socialization* is the *process of learning political attitudes and behavior.* The gradual process of socialization takes place as we grow up, in settings like family and schools. In the home, children learn about participating in family decisions—for example, the more noise they make, the better chance they have of staying up late. Kids also learn which party their parents favor, how they generally view politics and politicians, and what their basic social values are, for example, individual accomplishment or helping others. Children, of course, do not always copy their parents' political leanings, but they usually do. Most people stay with the party of their folks. Schools have a similar effect. Students salute the flag, take civics courses, participate in student politics, and learn that democracy (us) is good and dictatorship (them) is bad.

People's social characteristics also affect their participation in politics. Whether a person is male or female, religious or not, black or white, rich or poor, and a Northerner or Southerner will affect her or his political opinions and behavior. These views are reinforced by a person's peer group (friends and neighbors), and by the communities we live in that tend to echo our political beliefs. The influence of religion and ethnic background can be seen today in the "politics of identity," where people find meaning in politics from participating because of their religion, gender, or ethnic group. These intensely felt loyalties have brought new voters to the polls and increased involvement in public affairs. But they have also polarized politics. Activists opposing each other on issues like abortion or taxes, or even health care reform, may see the other side not as political adversaries but as wrong, even evil. The issues being debated take on symbolic importance that elevates them beyond the normal give-and-take of policymaking. Compromise, a pillar of traditional American politics, becomes an act of betrayal for the leaders who attempt it.

Class and Voting

Class may be just as important in shaping people's political opinions and behavior. The term *social class* refers to a *group's occupation and income, and the awareness it produces of their relations to other groups or classes in the society*. In general we can speak of three broad, overlapping categories: a working class, a middle class, and an upper class. The *working class*, which covers the majority of people in a society, receives the lowest incomes and fills "blue-collar" jobs in factories and farms, as well as "white-collar" positions like clerical and secretarial jobs in offices. The *middle class* consists of most professionals (like teachers and engineers), small businesspeople, bureaucrats, and some skilled workers (say, those earning $50,000 a year). The *upper class* (often called the *elite* or *ruling class*) is composed of those who run our major economic and political institutions and receive the highest incomes for doing so.

At least as important as these "objective" categories that political scientists use is the "subjective" way in which people in these classes view their own position. Whether union members or teachers or housewives see themselves as members of the working class or the middle class will influence their political attitudes. An important fact about class in the United States is that class identification is quite weak. People either do not know what class they are in or do not think it is important. Most Americans see themselves as members of the middle class no matter what "objective" class they are placed in.

Class as reflected in education, income, and occupation, however, does influence people's attitudes on a variety of issues. Studies have shown that people in the working class tend to be liberal in wanting greater economic equality and more social welfare programs. This liberalism on economic issues contrasts with their ideas on civil liberties. Here, people of lower income and education tend to be intolerant of dissenters and not supportive of minority views or different styles of behavior, such as homosexual rights. (Obama won only 36% of white voters without college degrees.) Wealthier Americans are more supportive of tax cuts and less supportive of measures like Medicare and Social Security that provide economic security. The upper classes are more conservative in their economic views and more liberal on issues such as free speech and respect for civil liberties. Class attitudes on political questions, then, are both liberal and conservative, depending on the type of issue.

Government policies and economic growth may also affect classes differently. The prosperous 2000–2007 business cycle was the first in which the nation's middle-class families had less real income at the end than when they started. By June 2013 their income had dropped even further. Compared to December 2007, when the economic slump began, median household income had declined 6 percent—or $3,400. During and after the economic recession, those with lower incomes had steeper declines in income. This included African Americans, Southerners, people who did not attend college, and households headed by people under 25. As President Obama said in 2013, "Nearly all the income gains of the past 10 years have continued to flow to the top 1 percent. The average C.E.O. has gotten a raise of nearly 40 percent since 2009. The average American earns less than he or she did in 1999."

Studies by political scientists have revealed that government policymakers are more responsive to wealthy groups than they are to the poor. When the opinions of the poor and the middle class differed from those of the well-off, the views of the poor ceased to have any apparent influence. If the wealthy strongly favor a policy change, it is substantially more likely to happen. When the middle class strongly supports a policy change, it had hardly any more chance of happening than when they strongly opposed it. As Jacob Hacker and Paul Pierson conclude in *Winner-Take-All Politics* (2010), there is "a startling disconnect in American politics, a chasm between voters and policymakers."

The problem with figuring out how characteristics of race, class, and religion influence a person's political behavior is that so many of them overlap. If we say that blacks vote less than whites, are we sure that race is the key category? We also know that poorer people, those with less education, and those who feel they have less effect on their government also are likely to be nonvoters. These categories include the majority of blacks. But we do not yet know which is more important in influencing behavior, and so even the historically "true" statement that blacks vote less may conceal as much as it reveals. We also have to examine whether blacks with more income or education also vote less—which they do not. And by 2012 black voting rates rose to 66 percent, higher than white turnout. We might then conclude that race is not as important in voter turnout as class or education—or a black presidential candidate.

Who Doesn't Vote?

Pollster: *Do you think people don't vote because of ignorance or apathy?*
Nonvoter: *I don't know and I don't care.*

The difficulty of answering the question of why people do not vote ought to be clear. As the charts indicate, turnout varies with education, income, race, gender, and age, and it changes over time. (See Figure 7.2.) Studies have shown that nonvoters most often are from the less educated, nonwhite, rural, southern, poor, blue-collar, and very young of the American population. Voters most often come from the white, middle-aged, college-educated, urban or suburban, affluent, white-collar, and female groups. These are only broad tendencies, with a great many exceptions. *Generally, people with the biggest stakes in society are the most likely to go to the polls*: older individuals and married couples, and people with more education, higher incomes, and good jobs.

In the 2012 election (according to the Pew Research Center), nonvoters favored Barack Obama over Mitt Romney by a wide margin, 59 percent to 24 percent. About half of nonvoters identified as Democrats, while only a quarter leaned toward the Republicans. Nonvoters were far less likely than voters to follow public affairs. They were also younger, less educated, and less affluent than likely voters. More than a third (36%) were under 30, compared with just 13 percent of voters. While most voters are married, most nonvoters are not. Hispanics were 21 percent of nonvoters, which is three times the percentage of Hispanics among voters (7%). Nonvoters were generally more liberal on a range of issues—favoring health care reform, withdrawing from Afghanistan as soon as possible, and supporting activist government. On social issues like gay marriage, abortion, and the impact of immigrants, nonvoters' opinions did not differ much from those of voters.

Americans, voters or not, are poorly informed about politics. Some two-thirds of American adults could not name all three branches of government, and one-third could not name even one. Less than half of voters know the name of their representative in Congress. There is no doubt that the less income you have, the less likely you are to vote or participate in politics. During the lead-up to the 2008 primaries,

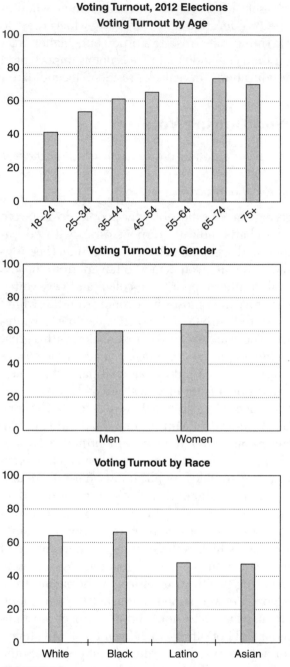

FIGURE 7.2
Presidential Voting Turnout of Eligible Voters by Age, Gender, Race Educa-
tion, Income, and Marital State, 2012.
Source: http://www.census.gov/population/www/socdemo/voting.html

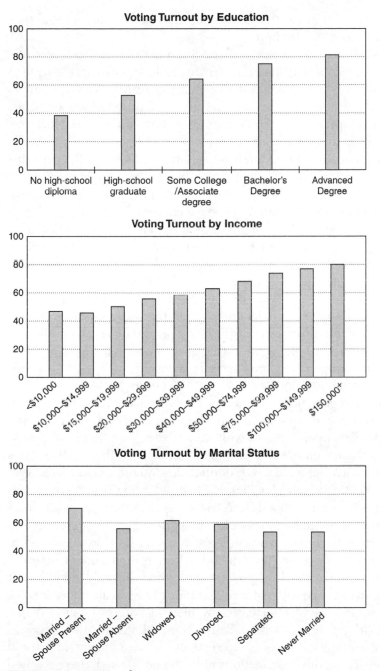

FIGURE 7.2 (continued)

66 percent of those who were "having an easy time financially" said they were likely to participate in the primaries, compared to only 49 percent of those who said times were tough. In the months before the 2012 election, less than half of registered voters (45%) said they were

paying a lot of attention to the campaigns, while 20 percent said they had paid almost no attention.

Class differences in voting reflect differences in economic security. Low-income people who face immediate challenges like finding a job or paying bills may view politics as an expensive luxury. Class differences in political socialization also have an effect. Children of working-class parents, perhaps because of poor education, grow up believing that they can have little influence on politics ("You can't fight city hall"). At the same time, because of the disadvantaged reality they and their parents face, they tend to have a not-so-favorable image of political leaders. These children end up being both more resentful and more passive toward politics. Middle- and upper-class children have a higher regard for political leaders and are taught in their schools to value participation in politics. They are encouraged to participate and are led to believe that the political system will respond favorably to their involvement. Of course, political leaders are more likely to listen to people with a similar background and education as theirs—upper middle class. Because political leaders do in fact respond to the wealthy—because they are organized and financial contributors—people from the middle and working class are not likely to feel that government is listening to them.

Electoral barriers to voting are increasingly playing a role in lower turnout. State registration laws—some that require 50 days of residency and periodic registration—are, at least, inconvenient. Making registration and voting two separate acts on different days clearly cuts out the "last-minute shoppers." States with same-day registration have consistently led the nation in voter participation. Four of the top five states in voter turnout in the 2012 presidential election offered same-day registration. Politicians have long known that older, inefficient voting machines in poor neighborhoods lead to long lines at the polls, more votes being disqualified, and more people being discouraged from voting. Recent elections have seen partisan legislatures passing laws designed to discourage eligible voters. (See the box, "Voting Rights under Attack.")

Until recently, the U.S. government stood virtually alone in not helping citizens cope with voter registration. The so-called *motor voter* legislation made registration easier by allowing voters to register when they got drivers' licenses. The assumption behind the 1993 law was that the easier it was for people to register, the more likely they would be to vote. Yet in the first elections after the law passed, there seemed to be little impact on either registration or voting. Fewer people registered to vote in 1996, and even fewer voted. It took until the 2004 election for both registration and voting numbers to surge, and then it was for partisan reasons having little to do with ease of registration. Government can make voting easier by making Election Day a national

▎Voting Rights under Attack

In 2010, Republicans took majority control of many state legislatures. Following these victories, more than a dozen states passed new laws making voting more difficult. These laws required that voters show photo IDs at the polls, reduced the days allowed for early voting, and put new restrictions on voter registration drives. In 2011, Ohio passed a law eliminating early voting on Sundays, while Florida eliminated it on the Sunday before Election Day. Maine voted to stop allowing people to register to vote on Election Day—a practice credited with enrolling some 60,000 new voters in 2008.

Voting access was limited in southern states in 2013 after the Supreme Court invalidated part of the Voting Rights Act. The law had required states, mostly southern, with a history of discrimination to clear any changes in their election laws with the Justice Department. After the 5–4 Court ruling removed the Justice Department's role, many states quickly altered their laws. Within hours of the ruling, Texas officials said that they would begin enforcing a strict photo identification requirement for voters, which had been blocked by a federal court on grounds that it would disproportionately affect black and Hispanic voters. Meanwhile, North Carolina approved a strict voter-ID requirement, along with the elimination of the first seven days of early voting and same-day voter registration.

Republicans argued that the new laws were necessary to prevent voter fraud. Democrats pointed out that voter fraud is rare and charged that the laws will discourage eligible voters—especially those who are poor, young, and African American, all of whom tend to vote for Democrats.

holiday, as it is in many European countries, or letting people vote on Saturday or by mail. Culture may explain why some states rank near the top in voting turnout. Places like Minnesota and Maine have close-knit rural communities where personal communications among neighbors reinforce a traditional belief that they have a duty to vote. Rules encouraging voting help, but they're not everything.

Explanations

The objective categories describing nonvoters—younger, less educated, lower incomes—may conceal as much as they reveal. The term *nonvoters*, after all, covers more than half of the American population (Note: This counts not just *eligible* voters.) and a great deal of variety. For example, surveys have shown that while nonvoters tend to be less affluent, 43 percent have incomes over $30,000. Nonvoters are significantly younger than voters, but one-quarter of nonvoters are 45 years old or older. When people in a census survey were asked why they didn't vote in 2012, some 19 percent said they were too busy; 15.7 percent reported they were not interested. Almost 13 percent did not like the candidates or campaign issues, while 5.5 percent had problems with registration. Of nonvoters responding, 14 percent claimed they were unable to vote because of an illness or disability.

The ability to generalize about nonvoters gets cloudier in examining negative feelings toward government. While it is true that nonvoters feel alienated from government, this is also true for voters. In one study of a recent election, about two-thirds of the population felt that to some extent "most elected officials don't care what people like me think." The percentage for nonvoters was exactly the same. Nonetheless, mistrust of government has grown in recent years. This may have a cumulative effect, especially on the views of young people as they form their impressions of government and their own roles as citizens.

This lack of *political efficacy*—a sense that government will respond to people's needs—among both voters and nonvoters has several explanations. That people "don't think it makes any difference" in whether they participate may come in part from the way they were socialized or brought up. People may not consider politics relevant to their lives, identify with a political party, understand the political system, follow news about public affairs, or some combination of these. The less informed people are about politics, the less relevant it appears to their lives. And, in fact, government may not be responsive.

This lack of confidence in government has grown. In the early 1960s, three out of four Americans responded to survey questions by saying they trusted Washington all or most of the time. Today it is just the opposite: Three out of four no longer trust the government. There has been much debate over the causes of this lack of trust. In the 1960s, the government was remembered for having rescued people from the Great Depression and winning World War II. Since then the issues have gotten more complex and the victories fewer. Poverty, crime, discrimination, and terrorism are just some of the problems that government is now expected to solve—and has not. Other institutions like the family, church, and school have all weakened in their ability to speak to many of society's ills. The media, with their blustering talk shows and skeptical reporting, have been blamed for turning people off politics. And, at least prior to 9/11 and the 2008 financial meltdown, the argument was heard that big issues like the Great Depression or Vietnam were not around to shock people into getting involved in political issues.

The government is not exactly blameless in this cycle of distrust. At least beginning with Vietnam and Watergate, leaders have misled. President Clinton, with half-truths about his personal life from avoiding the Vietnam draft to not avoiding Monica Lewinsky, reinforced popular prejudices. George W. Bush benefited from the initial patriotic rallying after 9/11, but that was followed by the Iraq invasion justified by imagined weapons of mass destruction and nonexistent ties to Al Qaeda. TV images of American leaders squirming to avoid responsibility for torturing prisoners or for painting an unrealistically rosy picture of the war increased public disillusionment. The high expectations raised by President Obama's outsider campaign of hope and change left many disillusioned when he embraced unattractive compromises and presided over administrative missteps that come with leading a large, divided government.

Presidential elections have traditionally been seen as a major vehicle for gaining public participation. In the past they have also been faulted for going on far too long and for focusing on only a dozen or so key states for intensive activities and advertising. Press coverage that is negative about candidates and absorbed with horse-race stories—stressing "who's ahead?"—may minimize issues and maximize cynicism. Yet Barack Obama's candidacies are reminders that the appeal and ideals of a leader can encourage a surge of participation. Obama attracted young people to his campaign, and they in turn made a difference in his being elected. But their reduced numbers in the most recent elections raise doubts about how long lasting this involvement will turn out to be. (See "Is the Vanishing Young Voter Vanishing Again?").

Voting is not the only way of participating in politics. Recent years have seen an increase in personal politics—concerning gender, the

Is the Vanishing Young Voter Vanishing Again?

For years complaints were heard that young voters were invisible on Election Day. They voted less, scholars said, because they moved more, married and bought homes later in life, and had no strong identity to either political party—all factors that erode the voting habit. While young people are no more cynical than older ones about politics (equal percentages believe most politicians are crooks), young cynics vote almost 40 percent less than older ones. Most young voters do not consider it a civic duty to vote, while older voters, especially senior citizens, overwhelmingly do.

Not surprisingly, they vote less than the population as a whole. And yet the youngest voters (18–24) were the only age group to show a significant increase in voting in 2008, 49 percent compared to 47 percent in 2004. But younger voters still had the lowest voting rate, while older citizens had the highest. By 2012 youth turnout was down again, with only 41.2 percent voting mostly for Obama. Disillusionment with elections and with Congress was up among the young, taking a toll on their participation. In 2008 43 percent of young voters had said they were politically active; four years later, it was only 22 percent.

environment, energy, food, health, and relationships. In the home, in dorms, at work, and constantly online, politics flourishes among friends, parents, children, and strangers. Individuals engage in politics by wearing a "Thank You for Not Smoking" button, by teaching younger relatives to read nutrition labels at the supermarket, or by trying to get their families to live "green" by turning down the thermostat or by eating less meat. Women and minorities may do politics just by showing up in jobs where they were rarely seen in the past. Teens blog to protest severe drug laws, march for funding for breast cancer research, or join their church group cleaning up a local park.

Professor Michael Schudson has made the argument well: "The changes that have made the personal political have been profound, arguably more so than the slackening of voter turnout."

And isn't this politics—people influencing others on public issues?

Political Parties

A *political party* is an organization that runs candidates for public office under the party's name. Although the framers of the Constitution worried more about factions and interests, they were well aware that parties could soon develop. George Washington, in his famed farewell address, warned against "the baneful effects of the spirit of party." Despite his advice, parties soon arose, and for good reasons.

The national government, as we have seen, is based on a system of dividing or *decentralizing* power. Political parties, on the other hand, are a method of organizing or *centralizing* power. The Constitution decentralized power in separate branches and various states to avoid the development of powerful factions that could take over the government. This decentralization of power, however, created the need for parties that could elect officials loyal to each other who could then effectively govern.

For the rest of the chapter, we will ask and answer the following questions: What are the functions of parties? How have they historically developed? How are they organized? What are the consequences of our two-party system? How important are parties today? Do these parties have a future?

Party Functions

What do political parties do? Political parties throughout the world organize power in order to control the government. To do so, American parties (1) contest elections, (2) organize public opinion, (3) put together coalitions of different interests, and (4) adopt policy changes proposed by smaller political groups.

First, parties *contest elections*. They organize voters in order to compete with other parties for elected offices. Parties and their candidates recruit people into the political system to work on campaigns. Parties provide people with a basis for making choices. People who identify with one of the political parties overwhelmingly vote for their party's candidate. In the 2012 election, 92 percent of Democrats voted for Obama and 93 percent of Republicans chose Mitt Romney. (Democrats were 38% of the electorate, while Republicans were 32%.) In addition, when parties contest elections, they express policy positions on important issues that *educate* voters. Most people are not ordinarily involved in politics. They rely on elections to keep them informed.

Second, parties *organize public opinion*. Despite the variety of views within them, parties give the public a limited channel of communication to express how they think government should operate. At least, voters can approve of the party that has been holding office by voting for it, or they can disapprove by voting for the opposition. The 2008 election gave voters the opportunity to show their disapproval of a president who was not even on the ballot. In 2012 President Obama's performance in office was the key issue.

Third is building *coalitions*. Parties put together, or *aggregate, various interests*. The Democratic and Republican parties organize different regions, ethnic groups, and economic interests into large coalitions for the purpose of winning elections. When Barack Obama campaigned in 2008 in the Ohio primary, he promised to renegotiate a trade treaty, NAFTA, that he had previously favored. This was an effort to cement the support of union workers behind his candidacy. Gathering special interests under the broad umbrella of a party label is an important function of American parties. This can be seen clearly at the presidential level, where elected candidates often claim a *mandate*, or the widespread national support needed to govern.

Finally, the two major parties *adopt changes* or popular reforms proposed by third parties or protest movements. If third parties or political movements show that they have considerable support, their programs are often incorporated, though usually in more moderate form, by one of the major parties. President Obama in running for re-election in 2012 saw the growing public and political acceptance of gay marriages. So after "struggling" with the decision and recognizing that a majority of his supporters supported this position, unlike four years before, he switched from backing civil unions to endorsing the right to marriage for gay and lesbian couples.

The Rise of Today's Parties

The *Federalists* and *Anti-Federalists*, the groups that supported and opposed the adoption of the Constitution, were not organized into actual political parties. They did not run candidates for office under party labels. There were, in fact, no political parties anywhere in the world at the time. Popularly based parties would evolve in the United States. At the time, what did exist were networks of communication and political activity competing on opposite sides of a great dispute—ratification. The framers preached against political parties. Thomas Jefferson, who founded what would become the Democratic Party, wrote a bit hypocritically that "if I could not go to heaven but with a party, I would not go there at all." Being called a "party man" was a stain against the political honor of this revolutionary generation. Yet as soon as these radicals had to operate a national government, they ran into problems. They confronted separate executive and legislative branches, a complex brew of checks and balances, and a fragmented federal system of states. Not surprisingly, they reached out for parties to help organize this unwieldy divided government. (See "Political Parties around the World.")

After the Constitution was ratified, the Federalist faction grew stronger and more like a political party. Led by Alexander Hamilton, secretary of the treasury under President Washington, the Federalists

Political Parties around the World

One hundred years ago, political parties were confined to Europe and North America. Elsewhere they were weak or nonexistent. Now parties are found everywhere in the world. Generally they are better organized with far more members than in the early twentieth century.

In spreading worldwide, parties have adapted to local forms. In Africa parties sometimes formed around a tribe, with party leadership drawn from chiefs' families. In Asia membership in modern parties is often dominated by religious groups or by ritual brotherhoods. Many parties in less-developed countries are partly political, partly military.

The organization of parties mirrors their political system. In Great Britain, where Parliament acts as both the legislative and executive branches of government, parties are centralized and powerful. Members of Parliament choose the party leaders, and even if they should attain a position in government, it is dependent on party support. So in 2007 the British Labor Party pressured Prime Minister Tony Blair to resign. This was despite his leading his party to three general election victories, the latest two years before he resigned. The party's officials acted without any input from voters.

championed a strong national government that would promote the financial interests of merchants and manufacturers. After Jefferson left Washington's cabinet in 1793, an opposition party formed under his leadership due to the behind-the-scenes politicking skills of James Madison. The new *Democratic-Republican Party* drew the support of small farmers, debtors, and others not benefiting from the financial programs of the Federalists. Under the Democratic-Republican label, Jefferson won the presidential election of 1800, which, because it was the first peaceful transition from one party to another, may have been the most important election in American history. Jefferson's party continued to control the presidency until 1828. The Federalists, without power or popular support, died out.

At the end of this 28-year period of Democratic-Republican control, the party splintered into factions. Two of these factions grew into new parties, the *Democrats* and the *Whigs* (first called the *National Republicans*). Thus, the Democratic Party, founded in 1828, is the oldest political party in the world. The early Democratic Party was led by Andrew Jackson, who was elected president in 1828. Jackson spread power down into the party ranks by using a national convention (first created by a third party and then adopted by the Democrats) to nominate presidential candidates. Under Jackson, the Democrats became known as the party of the common people. The Whigs, like the old Federalists, were supported by the wealthier conservative groups: bankers, merchants, and big farmers.

In 1854, a *coalition* (a collection of interests that join together for a specific purpose) of Whigs, antislavery Democrats, and minor parties formed the *Republican Party*. One of the unifying goals of this new party was to fight the expansion of slavery. The Republicans nominated a *dark horse* (a political unknown), Abraham Lincoln, on the third ballot for president in 1860. The Democrats were so deeply divided over the slavery issue that the southern and northern wings of the party each nominated a candidate. Against this divided opposition, as well as a fourth candidate, Lincoln won the election in the electoral college with less than a majority of the popular vote but more than any other candidate—in other words, a *plurality* of the vote.

Maintaining, Deviating, and Realigning Elections

For 155 years, the Democratic and Republican parties have dominated American politics. Their relative strength and the nature of their support have shifted back and forth. We can put this history into categories by looking at three types of presidential elections: maintaining, deviating, and realigning elections. *Maintaining elections* keep party strength and support as they are. *Deviating elections* show a temporary shift in public support for the parties, usually caused by the unusual popular appeal of a candidate of the minority party. *Realigning elections* reflect a permanent shift in the popular base of support of the parties and a shift in the strength of the parties so that the minority party emerges as the majority party. The president who emerges from a realigning election, whether a Lincoln or a Franklin Roosevelt, has a fresh national coalition behind him, able to change the course of the nation's history.

Most presidential elections between 1860 and 1932 were maintaining elections. The Republicans (or GOP, for *Grand Old Party*) kept the support of a majority of voters, and controlled the executive branch, in all but 16 of those 72 years. When the Democrats did gain control of the presidency, they held office for only short periods. The two elections of Democrat Woodrow Wilson in 1912 and 1916, for example, were caused by temporary voter shifts in party support and by splits within the Republican Party.

The social and economic earthquake called the Great Depression of the 1930s destroyed the Republicans' majority support and contributed to a realignment in the two-party system. Under Franklin Delano Roosevelt, the Democrats became the majority party, representing labor, the poor, minorities, the cities, immigrants, eastern liberals, and the white South. This *New Deal Coalition* kept majority support in the country at least through the Democratic administrations of John F. Kennedy and Lyndon Johnson in the 1960s. Democrats dominated Congress through most of the period until 1994. During this time, the party gradually weakened in the face of growing Republican voting strength in the South and the West and among the white suburban middle class.

Beginning in 1968 and continuing through the two elections of Ronald Reagan in 1980 and 1984 and beyond, a rolling Republican realignment occurred. The social disruptions of the 1960s led to divisions within the Democrats' New Deal Coalition, to the advantage of the Republican Party. The independent presidential candidacy of segregationist Alabama governor George Wallace exposed a traditionally Democratic white working class alienated from a party they felt to be too pro–civil rights and too anti–Vietnam War. Wallace's conservative *populism* claimed that pointy-headed bureaucrats and ivory-tower liberals were promoting government programs that helped minorities by taxing the white majority. Rising crime and taxes symbolized this alienation. Republicans saw the chance to steer blue-collar voters away from blaming the country's problems on their traditional New Deal enemy of Wall Street and Big Business to the new liberal-elite targets found in Georgetown, Hollywood, and Harvard.

Riding this wave of conservative populism, with a smattering of racism, Republicans were elected president in five of the six elections before 1992. The southern and western states were consistently voting for Republican presidential nominees, the youth vote shifted to the GOP, and polls of party identification showed almost as many Republicans as Democrats. Despite dominating the presidency, the GOP marketed themselves as the anti-government, anti-taxes party.

Political crosscurrents allowed the Democrats to capture the presidency in the Bill Clinton elections of 1992 and 1996. Having a gifted southern candidate who could run as a moderate "New" Democrat helped, as did a certain public weariness over 12 straight years of Republican presidents. A changing electorate increasingly refused to identify with either party—almost one-third of voters declaring themselves independents. The emergence of Ross Perot as a nonparty presidential alternative in 1992 exposed the weakness of the two major parties. The Texas billionaire, for a short time that summer, outpolled both Democratic and Republican candidates. Perot's 20 percent of the vote in 1992 helped Clinton defeat the incumbent George H.W. Bush.

The Elections of 2000–04 and 2008–12: Whose Realignment?

The two elections of Bush's eldest son, George W. Bush, in 2000 and 2004 convinced many that a Republican realignment had occurred. After all, by 2004 Republicans were in control of the three branches of the federal government. Democrats, who had dominated Congress for almost all of the 62 years up to 1994, had failed to win a majority in the House of Representatives for six straight elections, from 1994 to 2004. They had been a minority in the Senate for most of these 10 years. While Democrats could claim equal numbers of voters as Republicans could, and independents seemed to favor the Democrats, it did not seem to matter. The country might be divided; the government was not.

Much of the explanation for this lay in one region: The South had switched parties. Since 1980 the South had consistently voted for Republican presidential nominees. The only Democrats to win the presidency after 1960 and until 2008 were from the South—Johnson, Carter, and Clinton. The 1994 election marked the first time that a majority of Southerners voted Republican for Congress. It was this realignment in the South as well as an effective party organization that led to a GOP majority in both houses of Congress in 1994. Bringing together small-town religious believers with Wall Street financial clout, conservatives shifted the party to the right. Republican leaders delivered cultural populist speeches on the values of faith and family, while more concretely delivering pro-business economic and tax legislation. After the 9/11 attacks in 2001, the Republican president could add to this cultural and economic clout by stressing the dangers of terrorism, especially if "cut and run" Democrats were put in power.

None of this seemed to matter in the 2008 elections. The Democrats in 2006 had already recaptured control of both houses of Congress, gained a majority of governors, and made substantial gains in state legislatures. Popular opinion had turned bitter toward the war in Iraq, the administration's ineptness after Hurricane Katrina, and the corruption displayed by lobbyists and members of Congress. More voters declared themselves Democrats than Republicans, and the quarter of the population that called themselves independents voted Democratic by better than 3 to 2. And then there was Barack Obama, with all his star qualities.

Paralleling Obama's 2008 victory, students of realignment discovered a more politically liberal America. Ruy Teixeira and John Judis wrote about the rise of an "emerging Democratic majority" produced by a postindustrial economy devoted to ideas and elevating professionals like teachers and IT workers. This new majority was made up of those with college degrees; minorities—African Americans, Latinos and Asian Americans, women—particularly working, single, and college-educated; and young people. All these groups flocked to Obama.

Meanwhile the Republicans were divided and demoralized. The culture wars that conservatives waged for decades (against homosexuality, pornography, abortion, etc.) no longer found a place on the agenda of these rising liberal groups. Much like the president, they were progressive and pragmatic on civil rights, lifestyle choices, religion, regulation of business, the environment, immigration, and foreign policy. Both wounded and bonded together by the economic crisis, they supported ambitious government initiatives to correct a damaged, unfair economy. And these groups were not only shifting to the Democrats; they were also growing in numbers, especially Hispanics and young professionals. And yet the 2010 congressional elections, as well as the state-level votes placing Republicans in charge of a majority of legislatures and governorships, pushed the pause button on this argument. At the least, the rising Democratic coalition didn't emerge for this vote, which might indicate something less than a permanent realignment in the two parties.

The 2012 elections continued the argument, just as it continued divided government in Washington. The Democrats drove their coalition to the polls, which gave them a majority of voters. Governor Romney retained almost 60 percent of the white vote, reflecting the diminished Republican base of support. And yet any Democratic realignment seemed more gradual and less comprehensive than those of the past. With GOP control of the House, manipulation of electoral barriers (like gerrymandering and turnout) and entrenched interest group opposition, few drastic policy changes were likely in Obama's second term. And since realignments are defined by both a permanent shift in party control and policy reforms, some hesitation seemed appropriate in prophesizing this one—especially when parallel predictions for a new Republican majority were being made just two presidential elections ago.

Polarizing the Parties: The Growth of Partisans

The differences between the two major parties lie in both image and reality. The image of the parties is usually based on a stereotype of people who support the parties. Typical Republicans are white, middle and upper-middle class, and Protestant; they are educated and, with the rise of the "gender gap," are less often women. They support business, organized religion, law and order, a hard-line policy in foreign affairs, and limited government intervention in the economy but more involvement in enforcing moral values in people's lives. They call themselves conservatives. (See Table 7.1.)

Typical Democrats are members of a minority, ethnic, or racial group; belong to a labor union; and are working-class, non-Protestant, and urban residents, or professionals with liberal views. They support social welfare measures to help the poor at home, government regulation

---

TABLE 7.1 HOW TO TELL A LIBERAL FROM A CONSERVATIVE

Here are some of the political beliefs likely to be preferred by liberals and conservatives.

	LIBERALS	CONSERVATIVES
On Social Policy:		
Abortion	Support "freedom of choice"	Support "right to life"
School prayer	Opposed	Supportive
Affirmative action	Favor	Oppose
On Economic Policy:		
Role of the government	Government can be a regulator in the public interest	Government messes up free-market solutions
Taxes	Want to tax the rich more	Want to keep taxes low
Spending	View government as offering solutions to national issues	View government as expanding and spending too much
On Crime:		
How to cut crime	Believe we should solve the problems that cause crime	Believe we should support the police
Defendants' rights	Believe we should respect everyone's civil liberties	Believe we should not let criminals escape justice

of big business, more equal distribution of wealth, and more internationalist, less aggressive foreign policies, except perhaps in favoring trade restrictions to protect jobs. The majority of Democrats are female (55 percent). Blacks, Latinos, Asian Americans, and Native Americans make up 46 percent of the party. While labeled liberals, they prefer to be called progressives.

Not surprisingly, the reality is more complex than the image. Leaders of the Democratic and Republican parties do disagree on major issues, more often than party members. Party *followers*, not actively involved with the party, tend to be more moderate (or indifferent) than *leaders* on issues. A number of voters straddle the positions of their parties, for example, Democratic union members who favor expanded liberal social programs at home but stronger military actions abroad. Democratic and Republican party members often agree more with each other than with their party leaders, though the numbers of strong partisans have grown in both parties.

Another complicating factor in party differences is that each party is a coalition of often differing groups. The Democrats include, for example, liberal, black, urban, working-class supporters from the northern industrial cities and moderate, white, wealthy, educated suburbanites from the West. The GOP includes moderate business leaders and retirees from the East and small-town religious fundamentalists/conservative farmers from the South and Midwest.

Because of their conservative cultural and religious beliefs, white, working-class Southerners and Westerners have increasingly voted for Republicans. (If only whites had voted in 2006, the Republicans would have won a majority of seats in Congress.) Despite what seems like the white working class's economic self-interest in government programs—job training, money for education, and expanded health care—identification with conservative positions on abortion, school prayer, and gay marriages has outweighed liberal concerns for increased public services funded by higher taxes on the wealthy. Cultural populism and anger at government elites has been more important than economic resentment of corporate elites. This working-class conservative populism has been used by Republican strategists to polarize voters and win elections.

Obama's victories revived the counter argument that voters remain moderate. Because the party elites were so ideological and angry with each other, they had in the past forced voters to make extreme choices. Bush Republicans in winning presidential campaigns had pursued a "base" strategy of mobilizing their core voters and adopting emotionally polarizing positions to get their partisans to vote. But in both 2008 and 2012 Obama and his two Republican opponents John McCain and Mitt Romney, had each run in opposition to the extremes in their parties. They had preached in the general election—if not practiced by their campaigns—reaching across the red-state (Republican) and blue-state (Democratic) divisions. As Obama said repeatedly, "We have the chance to build a new majority of not just Democrats, but Independents and Republicans ... we can change the electoral math that's been all about division and make it about addition."

And ultimately the ability to win elections is the key measure by which parties judge the policies and strategies they adopt.

View from the Inside: Party Organizations

Historically American parties have been weak national organizations. Traditionally there have been few ties knitting various local parties together, and fewer still binding them into a coherent countrywide organization. The late twentieth century saw the rise of candidate-centered campaigns, media dominance over political communications, and the importance of money raised from interest groups and spent on advertising, all further undermining the classic functions of parties.

The current national parties seem to have made a comeback. They have centralized their organizations by controlling campaign technology, strategy, and fundraising. American parties may appear weak and locally based when compared to the strong centrally run parties of other countries. But the two national parties are far from powerless, and they now appear to be gaining strength.

Machines—Old and New

Particularly in the last half of the nineteenth century, many local American parties were so tightly organized that they were called *political machines*. Party machines had a party *boss* (leader) who directly controlled party workers at the city or district levels. Local leaders obeyed the boss because he handpicked party nominees and distributed patronage jobs, political favors, and money to loyal supporters. While an effective instrument for managing a precinct or city government and assuring immigrants a political network to respond to their needs, machines had a well-deserved reputation for corruption. Until his death in 1976, Richard Daley Sr., mayor of Chicago for more than 20 years, kept firm control of a strong Democratic Party machine. Daley's machine acted as an informal government and social service agency, meeting the immediate needs of urban citizens. Chicago's party organization has declined (despite Mayor Daley's son, also Richard Daley, serving as mayor from 1989 to 2011), and political machines, in general, have gone the way of the dinosaur. (See "Machine Politics.")

Machine Politics

When Richard M. Daley retired from being mayor of Chicago in 2011—after six terms in office—he and his father, Richard J. Daley, had been mayors of the city for 43 of the last 56 years. They were big-city bosses who ruled as kingmakers. While in office the two Daleys headed a family institution that ran America's third-largest city. Chicago became known as the City That Works, which meant an expanding skyline of new buildings as well as corruption scandals.

The senior Richard Daley ran the city through his control of the local Democratic Party. He provided his party supporters with jobs on the public payroll, and they gave him the votes he needed to stay in office. President Kennedy's 1960 close election victory was helped by Mayor Daley delivering critical votes from Illinois, some of which were rumored to have come from graveyards.

Opponents to the Daleys could expect to fight City Hall such as shutting off microphones at City Council meetings for those who tried to say something that annoyed the mayor. Another example of machine politics arose in an election when the owner of a small restaurant put up a sign that advertised the campaign of Benjamin Adamowski, who was challenging Mayor Daley Sr.'s reelection. The local Democratic precinct captain approached the restaurant owner and asked him to take down the sign. He refused.

A couple days later the city building inspectors paid a surprise visit to the restaurant that cost almost $3,000 in plumbing repairs.

Political machines lost much of their leverage early in the twentieth century when three things happened: (1) local, state, and federal agencies took over distributing benefits (like welfare) to the poor; (2) civil service reforms made most city jobs require competitive exams; and (3) direct primaries turned the party's nomination into an election contest any candidate could enter and win.

Modern machines have appeared that allow political leaders to use the new technologies of fundraising and direct-mail campaigns to raise and give away money to party colleagues. These *leadership PACs* can cement loyalty to their creators and promote their ambitions for higher office. While they have been around since the 1970s, former Speaker Newt Gingrich is credited for starting the model for this fundraising machine. GOPAC was Gingrich's political action committee that raised millions for Republicans and aided his rise to House Speaker. Congressional leaders in both parties are now expected to have a leadership PAC to raise money. Typically, committee chairmen raise funds from interest groups with issues before their committees. They then spread the wealth to more junior party members of their committees.

Recent White Houses have been accused of using their young campaign staff to form modern political machines. Labeled a "permanent campaign," many of the media advisers and organizers who shaped the president's march to the White House found jobs in the party's national committee. But now they pushed for the president's budget and health care reform packages and, ultimately, his reelection. Obama added a new wrinkle to this model in forming Organizing for America (OFA) within the Democratic National Committee. OFA relies on a 13-million-strong e-mail list, calls volunteers to go door to door, and mobilizes grassroots support through the Internet—techniques that are borrowed from Obama's election campaigns.

American Party Structure

Picture the American party structure as a pyramid. Local political organizations or clubs are at the bottom, county committees are above them, and state committees are above the county. (See Figure 7.3.) The national committee of each party is over them all with the national conventions the ultimate elected authority. The strength of the party, which had traditionally been at the bottom, has now gravitated toward the top.

As a result of the welfare, civil service, and primary election reforms, most local parties have few resources with which to maintain

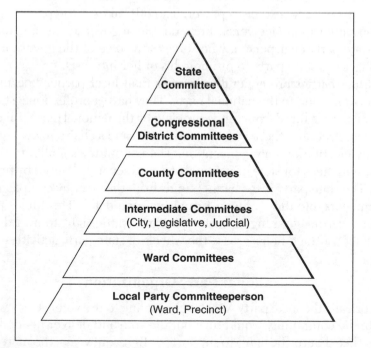

FIGURE 7.3
Typical State Party Organization.

a strong organization. Local parties range from virtual disorganization to still-powerful operations, with most parties falling closer to the pole of weakness. In much of the United States, a handful of officials meet occasionally to carry out the essential affairs needed to keep the party going. The party revives only around elections to support candidates generally selected by their own efforts.

What do the party's officers do in nonelection years? Their duties primarily depend upon whether they are the *in-party* or the *out-party*. The party that is out of office tries to show that it is still alive by operating booths at county fairs and issuing press releases. However, political activity takes money, which out-parties have difficulty raising without the clout of a member in a powerful public office. Systems for collecting regular contributions have been only modestly improved by going online. State parties typically sponsor "Jefferson-Jackson Day" dinners (Democrats) or "Lincoln Day" dinners (Republicans). The current Republican National Committee (RNC) has emphasized funding grassroots activities and expanding the GOP voter base. But as the minority party, the RNC's $300 million annual budget was going largely to just keeping national staff hired and party offices operational.

One would guess that the in-party—the party with more of its own members in important government positions—has more power than the out-party. This ain't necessarily so. The public official, rather than the party, actually exercises power. The official uses the party organization rather than vice versa. For example, a governor usually names the state party chairperson, who serves as a voice of the governor and manages the state party to promote his or her interests.

State parties are generally stronger than local parties because of their connection to the national party. They have a professional staff of several people hired from funds supplied by the national party. Like the national structure, there is a state committee and a chairperson, all chosen by election or state convention. The committee's ability to select party nominees for state or national offices is severely limited by primaries. The state party may channel funds from the wealthy campaigns of incumbents into those of new, promising candidates. This builds party loyalty. Patronage, ranging from placing a traffic light to awarding a building contract, helps grease the wheels of state party activities.

National Party Organization

Historically the local party was the closest link to the voter. Party workers in the community would turn out the vote and deliver needed services (like that traffic light) to supporters. In recent years, the increased reliance on modern campaign technology (including microtargeting and social networks) has blended with the use of local volunteers going door to door—frequently carrying handheld computers plugged into campaign data banks. The management of these canvassers and other party functions have been centralized and placed in the hands of professionals in the national organization and outside consultants, known as "hired guns." These efforts have complemented the campaigns run by the staffs of well-financed candidates.

Each party is officially governed by its *national committee*. The national committee consists of representatives chosen from all the state party organizations and various other party groups. The committee is led by the *chairperson*, who is often unofficially chosen by the party's presidential nominee every four years but is formally elected by the national committee. When the president leads the party, it is dominated by the White House and used as an instrument for promoting his policies and his reelection, often at the expense of candidates for other offices who don't get the same attention from the party. The chair of the Democratic National Committee (DNC), Florida congresswoman Debbie Wasserman Schultz, was chosen by Obama as chair of the DNC in 2011, and selected without dispute. The chair of RNC, Reince Priebus, ran for the office in a contested vote and was elected by 168 members of the central committee. That's the difference a party's control of the White House makes.

Under these authorities is the party's *professional staff*. These professionals have gained power through their understanding of the modern technology of campaigning and the complicated laws overseeing how money is raised and spent. The Republican staff has been larger than the Democrats' because the Democrats contract out much of their work, such as Internet fundraising, to campaign consultants. In both fundraising and organization—until the Democrats' recent electoral successes—the Republicans had done a better job of strengthening their party than the Democrats.

Fundraising

There are two things that are important in politics. The first is money and I can't remember what the second one is.
—Mark Hanna, Republican boss, 1895

In the 2012 elections, the two parties and their committees raised record amounts of money, over a billion dollars each. Democratic Party committees raised $1.06 billion, which continued the historic reversal of 2008 and recorded more money in party coffers than the Republicans, who were credited with $1.02 billion in 2012. These

TABLE 7.2 A CONTINUING CLIMB

PARTY FUNDRAISING FOR ELECTION CYCLES (IN MILLIONS)

	2000	2004	2008	2012
Democrats	$520	$731	$961	$1.068
Republicans	$716	$893	$920	$1.023

PRESIDENTIAL CANDIDATES' FUNDRAISING

SEPARATE FROM THE PARTIES, THE CANDIDATES THEMSELVES HAVE INCREASED THEIR FUND-
RAISING OVER THE PAST THREE PRESIDENTIAL CYCLES (IN MILLIONS):

	2000 (GORE V. BUSH)	2004 (KERRY V. BUSH)	2008 (OBAMA V. MCCAIN)	2012 (OBAMA V. ROMNEY)*
Democrats	$133	$328	$745	$715
Republicans	$193	$367	$368	$446

*Both candidates in 2012 declined matching funds during the primaries and the public funding
grant offered by the government during the general election.

Source: http://www.opensecrets.org/pres08/index.php; http://www.opensecrets.org/parties/
index.php?cmte=&cycle=2008; http://www.opensecrets.org/parties/index.php?cmte=&cycle=2012;
http://www.opensecrets.org/pres08/index.php?cmte=&cycle=2012

amounts showed a continuing trend of ever-increasing money being
raised in each election cycle. (See Table 7.2.) Both parties' totals reflected their large pool of small donors and their increasing use of
online technology. The Democrats could more than match the GOP in
the money race because of their revitalized organization, their control
of the Senate and the popularity of their presidential candidate.

These funds were used to support the party's candidates through
expensive campaign technology and, most importantly, advertising.
Besides increasing party loyalty among their candidates, the funds
were spent on media and mail campaigns to reach and register potential voters. Throughout most of the last decade, the Democrats have
been the majority party, but the Republicans have had the advantage in
money and technology. That seems to have changed with Democrats
now dominating across the board. The power of both national committees is likely to increase as the formerly weak parties use these funds to
strengthen their central organizations.

President Obama's election victory was aided by his own campaign's
fundraising operation. Apart from his party's efforts, Obama raised some
$715 million versus Mitt Romney's $446 million. (Not quite the record
$745 million the president raised in 2008.) His campaign relied on both
bigger donors and smaller donors nearly equally and pulled in donations
largely over the Internet.

Money Talks, Nobody Walks

By providing a back door for wealthy interests, campaign money has been involved in many political scandals. One that emerged a few years ago involved an aggressive businessman, the late Charles H. Keating Jr., and five senators of both parties.

These "Keating Five" had attempted to intervene with the Federal Home Loan Bank Board to protect Lincoln Savings and Loan from regulatory penalties. Mr. Keating was the bank's owner and, not accidentally, had contributed over $1.3 million to the five senators' campaigns. Each of the senators claimed the intervention amounted to constituent service because Lincoln S&L had assets in their states. The S&L failed anyway, costing taxpayers some $2 billion in deposit insurance costs. Mr. Keating ended up in jail.

Afterward Keating himself raised and answered the question "whether my financial support in any way influenced several political figures to take up my cause. I want to say in the most forceful way I can, I certainly hope so."

Neither candidate accepted government *matching funds* for the primaries, which give qualifying presidential candidates a dollar-for-dollar match as long as they obey spending limits. Also, for the first time, neither major-party candidate accepted the government's general election grant, which were part of campaign reforms that attempted to restrict private money in electing a president. Obama, in 2008, became the first major-party candidate since the system was created to reject public money in the general election. For now, both programs are essentially dead. (See "Money Talks, Nobody Walks.")

The large increase in both fundraising and spending by the two political parties for their campaigns has set off justifiable alarms of whether democracy can withstand this flood of money. It is also easy to lose perspective, forgetting that a large and wealthy country is choosing its leaders. And in the same election year (2012), an American corporation on its own, hamburger-flipping McDonald's, spent more on advertising than *both* political parties spent on everything.

The National Convention

Much of the public attention the party receives comes at its *national convention*. Held during the summer before the presidential election, the national convention is attended by delegates chosen by the state parties in various ways. In late summer of 2012, the Republican convention in Tampa Bay, Florida, had 2,286 delegates, followed by the Democratic convention in Charlotte, North Carolina, with 5,556 delegates. The convention adopts a platform, elects the party's presidential nominee, and acts as the party's highest governing body assembled every four years.

The *party platform* actually is written by a platform committee and then approved by the convention. In the document, the party declares its—or more to the point its presidential candidate's—views and promises on many issues. If the party is in power, the platform will boast of the party's achievements. If the party is out of power, the platform will criticize the policies of the incumbent. The platform will emphasize the party's differences with the other major party and minimize the divisions within the party. Since the goal of the platform is to win elections, it may fudge on controversial issues.

Frequently, groups of convention delegates will organize into factions in order to press for statements to be included in the platform representing their minority political views. In 2000 a group of women at the Republican National Convention pressed unsuccessfully for *planks* (parts of the platform) supporting abortion rights. Platforms are important in reaching compromises among groups within the party before the election. Party platforms are surprisingly accurate in predicting what a president will actually try to do when in office.

Early in the 1970s—beginning with the Democrats trying to recover popularity from their disastrous 1968 convention in Chicago—party reforms led to greater popular participation in the nominating process. Until these reforms, about 40 percent of convention delegates were chosen in states with *presidential primaries*—elections usually limited to registered voters from that one party. The rest were chosen by *caucuses*—party meetings dominated by party leaders and active members. Since then, 70 percent of delegates have been chosen by voters in primary elections.

The names of the candidates for president are placed in nomination toward the end of the convention. A roll-call vote of the delegates is then taken. The final party nominee for the office of president is elected by a simple majority vote. In 1924, the Democratic convention took 103 ballots before it was able to reach a majority decision. In recent decades, the presidential nominee has been named on the first ballot, reflecting the popular vote in the state primaries and caucuses. Conventions today can be described as *approving* or *ratifying* the candidate selected by the party voters. The delegates, who are mostly pledged to a candidate, do not make the choice themselves.

The presidential nominee chooses a vice presidential running mate, who is then formally approved by the convention. The selection of a vice president has been justly described as "an anti-democratic aberration." It is frequently a hurried choice, as shown in the 2008 selection by John McCain of Sarah Palin and John F. Kennedy's choosing Lyndon B. Johnson in 1960. It is also a decision worthy of a monarch, with no public debate or input from convention delegates. Only "a heartbeat away from the presidency," the veep is selected by the presidential nominee meeting with a few advisors behind closed doors.

A main goal of the selection is to improve the chances of winning election by *balancing the ticket*. In 1988, Michael Dukakis, a liberal New England governor, chose Lloyd Bentsen, a Texas conservative, to be the Democratic vice presidential nominee. Similarly, Dick Cheney's long public service was seen in 2000 as compensating for George W. Bush's lack of government experience. Arkansan Bill Clinton's 1992 choice of Senator Al Gore from the neighboring state of Tennessee was unusual in putting two Southerners on the ticket but reinforced the campaign's image of youth and change. In 2008 Joe Biden was seen as a party regular with long service in the Senate, who provided a reassuring contrast to the younger, less experienced presidential nominee. Sarah Palin, on the other hand, was a first–term, young, female governor of Alaska who, it was hoped, would light a fire in the GOP's base. In 2012 Paul Ryan, a conservative Wisconsin congressman, was similarly seen as bolstering Mitt Romney among indifferent party regulars.

The national convention is the exciting starting gate for the fall presidential campaign. That is why Barack Obama gave his acceptance speech in Denver in 2008 in front of 84,000 people in an NFL stadium, on a stage built to resemble the White House—then add 24 American flags as a backdrop to Stevie Wonder's singing. The nominee's speech set a convention record by attracting 38 million viewers watching on 10 TV networks, marking a successful launch of his general election campaign.

View from the Outside: The Two-Party System

Despite the occasional calls for a third political party, the United States retains a *two-party system*, in which two parties dominate national politics. In a *one-party system*, a single party monopolizes the organization of power and the positions of authority. In a *multiparty system*, more than two political parties compete for power and elected offices.

From the Civil War until at least the election of Dwight D. Eisenhower to the presidency in 1952, the 11 southern states of the Civil War Confederacy had essentially one-party systems. These states were so heavily Democratic that the Republicans were a permanent minority. The important electoral contests took place in the primaries, where blacks were excluded and where factions within the party often competed like separate parties. Multiparty systems also have existed in the United States. When former wrestler Jesse Ventura (loosely connected to the Reform Party) was elected governor in 1998, Minnesota could be said to have a three-party system, or did until he left office in 2003. Maine's senator, Angus King, was elected in 2012 in a three-candidate race as an independent but then caucused with Senate Democrats.

Causes of the Two-Party System

There are four main reasons for the continued dominance of two parties in the United States. One is the *historic dualism* of American public conflicts. The first major political division among Americans was dual, or two-sided, between Federalists and Anti-Federalists over adopting the constitution. It is said that this original two-sided political battle established the two-party tradition in this country. This dominance is more than just tradition. It has been reinforced by state laws passed by legislators from the two parties that confront third parties with high barriers to qualify for a place on the ballot.

The second reason is the *moderate views of the American voter*. Even with the recent rise of strong partisanship in both political parties, American politics tends toward the center in national presidential elections. Socialist parties on the left or conservative ones on the right have had a difficult time winning broad support. Americans may be moderate because their national parties force them to choose between two traditionally moderate parties, or American parties may be moderate because Americans do not want to make more extreme political choices. While the congressional parties tend to be more polarized because the states and districts they represent are often dominated by a single party, the national parties still need to win over moderate voters to gain the White House.

Third, the *structure of our electoral system* encourages two-party dominance. We elect one representative at a time from each district (or state) to Congress, which is called election by *single-member districts*. The winning candidate is the one who gets the most votes, or a *plurality*. (A majority of votes means more than 50 percent of the votes cast; as mentioned earlier; a plurality simply means more votes than anyone else.) Similarly, in presidential elections, the party with a plurality in a state gets all the electoral votes of that state. This winner-take-all system makes it difficult for minor-party candidates to win elections, and without election victories, parties fade fast. And voters don't want to "waste" their vote on losing minor parties.

Many European countries with multiparty systems elect representatives by *proportional representation*. Each district has more than one representative, and each party that receives a certain number of votes gets to send a proportionate number of representatives to the legislature. For example, in a single-member district a minor party that received 10 percent of the vote would not be able to send its candidate to Congress. In a multimember district the size of 10 congressional districts, however, that 10 percent of the vote would mean that 1 out of 10 representatives sent from the district would be a minor-party member. And in a parliamentary system, these minor parties might have a chance to gain a cabinet position in a coalition government formed by their aligning with a larger party—a situation that doesn't exist in a presidential system. In Europe and elsewhere, this has preserved radical parties holding views challenging mainstream opinion.

Finally, the Democratic and Republican parties continue to dominate national politics because they are flexible enough to *adopt some of the programs proposed by third parties*, and thus win over third-party supporters. The Socialist Party in America, even during its strongest period, always had difficulty achieving national support partly because the Democrats were able to *co-opt*, or win over, most of organized labor with pro-labor economic programs. The Republican Party lured voters away from Alabama governor George Wallace's American Independent Party by stressing law and order and ignoring civil rights in its 1968 presidential campaign. After seeing the disastrous results for Democrats of Ralph Nader running in 2000 (winning just enough votes in Florida to give George W. Bush the state), the 2004 Democratic presidential candidate John Kerry made clear his support for some of the populist themes of Nader's positions.

For all these historical and structural reasons, the odds are against either the emergence of a stable third party or an independent candidate being elected president. Operating as an umbrella over the broad political center, the two-party system has kept radical groups from winning power. This has meant that dissenting opinions traditionally received little consideration from voters and kept the two parties from taking extreme positions. It also meant that there was little room for third parties, except at the political fringe.

But Do the Two Parties Have a Future?

Neither major party can claim to be loved by the public. Before Obama, no Democratic presidential candidate had won a majority of the votes since 1976. The rise of conservatism led to the popular rejection of the Democratic Party's core ideology—that government could be an effective instrument to improve the lives of working people. As seen in the harsh, lengthy debate over health care reform,

large numbers of Americans remain more worried about big government's flaws than hopeful of its solutions.

Barack Obama was initially praised as the nation's first post-partisan, post-American, post-racial president, and therefore as the new Lincoln, the new Kennedy, even a new, if inside-out, Reagan. He spoke about building a grand coalition that could lead a future majority-minority country. Yet as centrist as his words were, Obama still had to retain the backing of his party's liberal base while keeping their expectations realistic. If those political tasks weren't daunting enough, there were a few inherited messes to deal with such as the global economic meltdown, wars in Afghanistan and Iraq, record deficits, global warming, Chinese and Russian rivals, millions without health care, immigration, and so on. Even those unwilling to support the president might feel some sympathy.

Republicans faced their own dilemmas. Their last administration of George W. Bush left behind a legacy of an economy in collapse, huge budget deficits and a leadership widely regarded as long on arrogance and short on competence. The Republicans' conservative base shrunk to a core that appeared to be too white, too old, and too male to grow into a winning majority of voters. Pressured by Tea Party 'mavericks', GOP conservatives closed down the government for 16 days in 2013 and seemed ready to block any efforts at governing that did not promote their anti-government rhetoric. An internal tug of war threatened to tear the party apart. Tea Party dissenters saw Republican defeats as just deserts for having betrayed traditional principles and called for more orthodoxy in opposing the New Deal programs that composed the modern federal government in Washington. The moderate wing spoke of building a "Big Tent" of ideas that would welcome growing groups like the young, the suburban, the minorities, and the college-educated, to whom radical conservatism held little appeal. The party's leadership vacuum deferred any agreement on strategies other than a unified opposition to the president's proposals.

Actually the two parties remain close in popular support. The pragmatic voters whose decisions swing elections are neither extreme nor particularly partisan in their political beliefs. The Democrats have revived less because of their own agenda than because congressional Republicans had stretched partisan attacks about as far as a broad range of moderate and independent opinion could stomach. These voters are still holding the two parties to account. However polarized American politics may sound and however partisan congressional votes appear to be, both parties will seek a majority coalition allowing them to control the two elected branches of government. For this to happen, both should expect to be judged by a decisive band of voters in the traditional way—on their performance in office.

CASE STUDY

The 2012 Reelection—Obama's Online Operation

Obama's reelection campaign was like running for Chicago alderman with the help of nerdy kids who spoke a math language no one else understood.
—Jonathan Alter, *The Center Holds*, 2013.

No part of Barack Obama's two successful campaigns for the presidency was showered with more praise than his use of the Internet. Many called it decisive in his 2008 primary victory over Hillary Clinton and in beating John McCain in that year's general election. In 2012 online data was increased and integrated across the entire campaign and again was given much of the credit for the president's electoral victory over Mitt Romney. Observers concluded that Obama's use of the Internet changed American politics in the same way John Kennedy's use of television did in 1960. The costs and benefits of this change for American democracy have not yet been added up.

ONLINE ORGANIZING

Obama's victory in 2012 testified to its online success in organizing, fundraising, and targeting voters.

The 2012 digital reelection campaign for President Obama was a more organized, top-down effort than the 2008 campaign that had brought him to power. "You had databases all over the place," said one Democrat about that first campaign. None of them talked to each other. Unlike the ad hoc arrangements of 2008, the reelection team aimed to integrate their databases and direct resources across a universe of voters and volunteers. So 2012 started by trying to create a single system that could merge information from polls, field workers, and consumer databases as well as voter files from the 2008 campaign.

The digital operation aimed to serve the campaign's strategy of persuading voters through personal relationships. This resulted in opening twice as many field offices as Mitt Romney's campaign in the crucial swing states. The strategy also called for integrating more than 13 million Obama supporters on the campaign's e-mail list with databases to produce a unified platform for millions of voters in battleground states. The dream was to match 25 million Facebook "likes" of Obama with voter rolls and door-to-door contact information to persuade supporters to vote.

The campaign never quite succeeded in this dream. But the pieces they ended up with were good enough. The Obama team was able to customize a Facebook app so that an Obama supporter with real friends (not Facebook friends) in crucial states could be identified. In the final weeks before the election, these supporters around the country were sent pictures of their friends in swing states along with a message to send them with a click of a button. Since the message came from a real friend, it was thought to be more credible and more effective.

In fact, this "targeted sharing" became, in campaign lingo, a "monster success."

Facebook targeted sharing allowed the campaign to reach youthful voters, who were mostly unreachable by phone. Called "Dashboard," it became a new social network allowing volunteers to join Nurses for Obama, Veterans for Obama, and other subgroups. By Election Day 600,000 supporters had used Facebook to contact half a dozen friends each in battleground states. Of these 3.5 million potential voters who were reached in crucial states, almost 1 million took action, such as registering to vote. This incredible response rate made digital persuasion a successful get-out-the-vote tool. It is likely to change future elections from the presidency on down.

Internet Fundraising

"We are going to measure every single thing in this campaign," declared campaign manager Jim Messina. Fundraising called for multiple tests. What appeals would work and at what time of day? What movie star making what pitch? Who would donate money online or by mail? Predictive profiles were drawn up. Models were constructed by the number crunchers predicting what types of people would be persuaded by what kinds of messages. If women aged 40–49 would listen to an appeal from actor George Clooney and the chance for a small dinner party, then that was the demographic that would get the online offer. Assumptions were backed up by real numbers. Dozens of different fundraising appeals were sent out each day. Sometimes Michelle Obama's e-mails performed best. Sometimes Joe Biden did better. And so more than 4 million people donated almost $1 billion. It wasn't magic; it was numbers.

The campaign's most noted innovation in tech fundraising was the "Quick Donate" app. This let supporters give money through their mobile phones or by responding to a link in a text message. After completing a one-time signup to store their credit card information, they could donate directly, multiple times. Donors using it ended up giving more often and three times as much as conventional contributors. Staffers called it "drunk donating" because impulsive supporters were moved by poll numbers or opponents' attacks to spontaneously contribute. The one-click system raised $75 million for the campaign.

Targeting with Big Data

These techniques could be directed to everything from online ads and humorous get-out-the-vote videos to analyzing specific demographic and regional groups. The polling and voter-contact data were processed nightly to account for changing trends. When poll numbers favoring Obama started to slip, the campaign could tell whether these were their voters or just likely Romney supporters returning home. With polling data on some 29,000 people in Ohio alone, the campaign could immediately check on various groups' thinking during the election and allocate resources accordingly.

Targeting ads at groups of voters, like single Cleveland women under 35, required complicated modeling to shape the message and the programs where they could be reached. Data directed the campaign to more efficient, if more unconventional, ways of getting their message to persuadable voters. Obama made a surprise first-ever presidential appearance on the social news website Reddit, giving an ask-me-anything session. Why? "Because a whole bunch of our turnout targets were on Reddit."

Ads were no longer driven by a bunch of guys in a room saying, "We always buy time after the local news." The era of Big Data had arrived.

CONCLUSION

There is no denying the success of Barack Obama's campaign in using the Internet to target and mobilize supporters to win reelection. These techniques of victory, however, may undermine the bridge-building message of unity that brought the president to national attention. His biracial background gave him a claim to the white Kansas heartland as well as the minority communities of Chicago. And he introduced himself to the country as a unifier, denouncing those who "like to slice and dice our country into red states and blue states," ignoring that there's the United States of America. This rhetoric was not applied where the rubber hit the road in his election campaigning.

Just in terms of presidential travel, Obama as of mid-2013 had visited the crucial swing states of Ohio 39 times and Florida 30 times. In seven states, including Arkansas and the Dakotas, he had not visited at all as president; in another six, including Mississippi and Kansas, he had visited just once. His near absence from more than 25 percent of America's states reflects a cool-eyed political calculation. But it also deepens the alienation of whites, rural residents, and older voters dominating there. Obama won using online systems to target and increase his votes in cities and among minorities and young voters.

The president cannot be blamed for the polarized politics in which he was elected. His campaign utilized those divisions. Unfortunately calculating national unity may require more than Big Data.

Sources: http://swampland.time.com/2012/11/07/inside-the-secret-world-of-quants-and-data-crunchers-who-helped-obama-win/print/
http://techpresident.com/news/23104/help-digital-infrastructure-obama-wins-re-election
http://www.wired.com/opinion/2013/06/did-hipster-technology-really-save-the-obama-campaign/
http://techpresident.com/news/23159/how-obama-america-made-its-facebook-friends-effective-advocates
John Harwood, "Dissent Festers in States That Obama Seems to Have Forgotten," *The New York Times,* June 20, 2013.

■ WRAP-UP

Voters are the most numerous and most representative players in the political game. In elections voters choose who is to run the government, and legitimate that choice. Many factors, like political socialization, party membership, gender, religion, race, and class, influence how people vote or even *if* they vote. While participation in politics takes place outside of voting, nonvoting and mistrust of Washington have in the past posed serious questions about the representative nature of American democracy. Recent elections bringing more people to the polls, especially the young, may arguably be improving both the process and results.

The political parties provide a major link between voters and elected officials. Historically the parties have evolved into a two-party system, with the Democrats and Republicans dominating elections for the last 155 years. Though the national parties in the past have been weakly organized, recent changes have strengthened the national organizations. Candidates organize their own national campaigns to compete for their party's presidential nomination. They jump into a lengthy process of state caucuses and primaries, media debates, fundraising, and finally nominating conventions, where the two major parties put their labels on candidates to run in the general election in the fall. These candidates may also make creative use of the Internet, the model of which can be seen in Barack Obama's successful 2008 and 2012 presidential campaigns.

The major parties have been subjected to internal polarizing forces pushing them to extremes, while independent public opinion seemed largely indifferent to the ideas dominating the partisan agendas. However, both parties still have a few cards left to play as seen in the excitement generated around elections. This flexibility has always been critical to the survival of the two-party system. American parties have adapted to the demands of newly mobilized groups, whether feminists or fundamentalists, blacks or bloggers. A willingness to honestly grapple with the pressing national challenges of the day, both at home and abroad, will allow them to continue as vital links between the people and their government. Not to do so will lead to questioning their role in the political game and to the continuing apathy of citizens turned off by party politics.

■ THOUGHT QUESTIONS

1. If you voted in the last election, what influenced the way you voted? Can you relate your political views to your family, religion, region, or class background?
2. If you did not vote, what led you not to vote? What would motivate you to vote in the future? Do you participate in politics even if you do not vote?
3. How have the Internet and modern technology connected people to the campaigns of elected officials? What has been gained and what has been lost, compared to traditional methods?

4. How important is money in elections? Would you do anything to change the role of money in campaigns?

5. Have recent election campaigns become nastier and more partisan? Did anything you learn from a recent campaign change your vote?

■ SUGGESTED READINGS

Alter, Jonathan. *The Center Holds*. New York: Simon & Schuster, 2013.
An experienced reporter's detailed and favorable account of the politics and the personalities leading up to Obama's reelection victory.

Douthat, Ross and Reihan Salam. *Grand New Party*. New York: Doubleday, 2008.
An effort to reform and rescue the Republican Party from the despair following George W. Bush and the 2008 election disasters.

Fiorina, Morris P., et.al. *Culture War?* 3rd ed. New York: Longman, 2011, Pb.
A skeptical examination of "the myth" of a polarized America by one of the country's leading political scientists.

Frank, Thomas. *What's the Matter with Kansas?* New York: Metropolitan Books, 2004.
Subtitled "How Conservatives Won the Heart of America," this book by a liberal Kansan describes in personal detail how his state journeyed from economic populism to social conservatism.

Halperin, Mark and John Heilemann. *Double Down*. New York: Penguin Press, 2013. Pb.
Page-turning insider gossip of the 2012 presidential elections by two experienced reporters.

Judis, John B. and Ruy Teixeira. *The Emerging Democratic Majority*. New York: Simon & Schuster, 2004. Pb.
Takes hard data to predict the dawn of a new era of "progressive centrism" fueled by the fastest growing areas of the country.

Kenski, Kate, Bruce Hardy, and Kathleen Hall Jamieson. *The Obama Victory*. New York: Oxford University Press, 2010, Pb.
A comprehensive look at how media, money, and messages shaped the 2008 presidential election.

Schudson, Michael. *The Good Citizen*. Cambridge, MA: Harvard University Press, 1998. Pb.
A coherent history of Americans' participation in public affairs with some surprisingly positive conclusions about the state of modern citizenship.

Stimson, James A. *Tides of Consent: How Public Opinion Shapes American Politics*. Cambridge, United Kingdom: Cambridge University, 2004. Pb.
How a small part of public opinion democratically and pragmatically decides elections in America.

CHAPTER 8

Interest Groups and the Media

SPECIAL INTERESTS

The last two players—interest groups and the media—are blamed for much of what is wrong with the American political game. "Special interests" are viewed as the rich and powerful pulling strings behind the scenes of the puppet officials they bribe. Media, more visibly, are seen distorting politics by being too simplistic, too negative, too liberal, or too conservative, depending on your leanings. On the other hand, many political scientists conclude that these two players are popular scapegoats: Their power is overrated, the harm they do overstated. Whatever conclusions we reach, both players are central to understanding today's politics.

The Constitution has little to say about either. The First Amendment guarantees freedom of the press and the right "to petition the Government for a redress of grievances," which protects these players briefly, if profoundly. The profound part is that both interest groups and media offer legitimate channels of access to the government. Interest groups provide tools for people with common concerns to bring their views to the attention of those in power. The media are two-way communications links (and participants as well) by which people keep themselves informed about government and vice versa. As instruments of power, the two change the game they play. Who they are, what they do, and how interest groups and media shape and are shaped by politics are central to what follows.

Interest Groups

In his classic study *Democracy in America* in 1835, Alexis de Tocqueville was impressed that Americans constantly joined all kinds of groups. The Frenchman thought these "associations" were essential to why democracy worked in the United States. The groups kept a balance between the state and the individual, offering a buffer between a large powerful government and small, powerless individuals. By doing this they preserved individuals' rights. As he put it,

> An association for political, commercial or manufacturing purposes, or even for those of science and literature, is a powerful and enlightened member of the community . . . which, by defending its own rights against the encroachments of government, saves the common liberties of the country.

Tocqueville's endorsement of the political importance of diverse group interests made him the father of what would later be called pluralism (see Chapter 9).

Though Tocqueville included local government when he wrote about associations, today we speak of *interest groups* as people organized to pursue a common interest by applying pressure on the political process. In the last chapter, we saw that American parties are not structured very well for representing specific interests. Interest groups fill this gap.

Our parties and the electoral system are organized by geography. Senators and representatives represent us on the basis of the state or the district in which we live. But within one region there are important and distinct group interests. Members of various religions, races, incomes, or economic associations may have different political concerns. Interest groups give Americans with common causes a way to express their views to decision makers. While interest groups may try to influence elections, unlike parties, they do not compete for public office. Candidates may be sympathetic to a certain interest, or even be a member of that group, but they will not run for election representing that group.

Interest groups usually are more tightly organized than political parties. They are financed through contributions and/or dues paid by members. Organizers communicate with members through newsletters, e-mails, and conferences. Union members, for example, will receive regular correspondence from their leadership informing them about political activities, policies, and candidates they should support.

Types of Interest Groups

The most important groupings are economic interests, including business, professional, labor, and agriculture. James Madison, in *The Federalist Papers* No. 10, expressed the fear that if people united on the basis of economic interests, all the have-nots in society would take control of the government. This clearly has not happened. The most influential groups generally, but not always, spend the most money. *Business groups* have a common interest in making profits, which also involves supporting the markets that makes profits possible. The Chamber of Commerce, the National Association of Manufacturers, and the National Small Business Association are well-known business groups. Powerful companies, like Exxon and General Electric, act as interest groups by themselves. (See the case study "Google: The Rise and Rise of a Washington Lobby.")

Business groups are seldom united on one side of an issue. Competitors within an industry extend their rivalries to the political arena. Microsoft lobbied the Justice Department to look into Google's Book Search project and was reported to hold "screw Google" meetings in Washington to plot strategy for getting regulators to investigate their competitor's business. Associations representing railroads and trucks regularly battle over transportation policies. Even when a political conflict is reported as business opposing, say, environmentalists, a closer look will reveal business groups on both sides of the issue. The battle over *Obamacare* saw Wal-Mart favoring the requirement that businesses provide health insurance to employees, while the National Federation of Independent Business opposed this mandate for coverage. Most contested major political issues show splits in the business community.

Professional groups include the American Medical Association, the National Association of Realtors, and the American Bar Association, all of which have powerful lobbies in Washington. *Labor unions*, like the International Brotherhood of Teamsters and the unions that make up the American Federation of Labor and the Congress of Industrial Organizations (the AFL-CIO), are the most important financial supporters of the Democratic Party. In many urban Democratic districts, Election Day will find the local labor unions and the local party practically merging to turn out voters. Labor leaders, who tend to stay in power longer than most politicians, are powerful political figures in their own right. Although there have been recent signs of revival, the influence of organized labor has declined, along with its membership, over the last 50 years.

Agricultural interests have a long history of influential lobbying. The American Farm Bureau Federation, the National Farmers Union, and the National Grange are powerful groups in Washington. Specialized groups, like the Associated Milk Producers, Inc. (AMP), strongly lobby farm legislation.

Some interest groups are organized around ethnic, social, or political concerns. Groups like the National Association for the Advancement of Colored People (NAACP) and the Urban League focus on economic and religious constituencies within the black community that they represent in national forums. The American Israel Public Affairs Committee (AIPAC) is a powerful advocate of close ties with Israel and attempts to influence American foreign policies in the Middle East.

Interest groups may organize people sharing similar social or political ideas. The Sierra Club lobbies in Washington to protect the environment but is considered more moderate than Greenpeace, a group of environmental activists who take direct action on issues like clear-cutting old-growth forests. People for the Ethical Treatment of Animals (PETA) has 2 million members who fund the nonprofit corporation that opposes factory farming, animal testing, and cruelty to pets. The *Tea Party* is a populist, conservative movement aiming to reduce the federal budget deficit and the size of government. Founded in 2009, it has remained a decentralized network of activists running candidates in Republican primaries and relying for finances on wealthy donors.

Lobbying

Lobbying is when individuals or interest groups pressure the government to act in their favor. Interest groups today maintain professional staffs of lobbyists or hire consulting firms in Washington, D.C., to promote their concerns. These lobbyists include former members of Congress or the executive branch who are knowledgeable in a particular area and personally connected to decision makers. When Senator Phil Gramm of Texas retired from the Senate in 2003, he joined the Wall Street firm of UBS Warburg for an annual salary of over $1 million. The former Republican chairman of the Senate Banking Committee had coauthored a bill a few years before that permitted banks to merge with securities firms, a law that UBS lobbied for and allowed them to purchase a brokerage for $12 billion. On the Democratic side, Chris Dodd, a senator from Connecticut, retired in 2011 and now earns approximately $1.5 million a year (a 762 percent raise) as the chief lobbyist for the movie industry. Such transitions barely cause a ripple in Washington, where getting a job from interests that

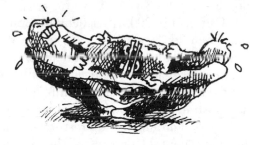

Is There Life after Congress?

Lobbyists had no bigger fight in the 111th Congress than health care reform. Leading the battle to make sure that reform didn't hurt their business were the nation's largest insurers, hospitals, and medical groups, who spent $1.4 million *a day* lobbying Congress. Working for them as lobbyists were 350 former congressmen and government staff members. Many of them had worked on the committees that now had to write a new health care law for the country.

Despite various reforms, large numbers of congressmen and staff use their government positions as a stepping stone to higher paying jobs as lobbyists. The nonpartisan Public Citizen found that half the senators and 42 percent of House members became lobbyists when they left Congress. This revolving door to riches also may influence their behavior while they are still working for the public. Jack Abramoff, a former lobbyist convicted of illegal activities, made the point after he emerged from prison.

"When we would become friendly with an office and they were important to us, and the chief of staff was a competent person, I would say or my staff would say to him or her at some point, you know, when you're done working on the Hill, we'd very much like you to consider coming to work for us. Now the moment I said that to them or any of our staff said that to them, that was it. We owned them. And what does that mean? Every request from our office, every request of our clients, everything that we want, they're gonna do. And not only that, they're gonna think of things we can't think of to do."

once lobbied you is a common practice. (See the box "Is There Life after Congress?")

Some 13,000 lobbyists spent $3.3 billion lobbying Congress and federal agencies in 2012. While lobbyists are required to register and are limited to a $100 cap in gifts to public officials, the disclosure rules governing lobbying are not considered strict. The Center for Public Integrity took a survey of state lobbying laws and found that only three states had lobby disclosure rules that were as weak as those applying to Congress. At times both political parties have promised reform and transparency of lobbying. Neither promises nor laws have diminished the growing impact lobbyists have on what Congress does and doesn't do. (See Figure 8.1.)

During his 2008 presidential campaign, Barack Obama vowed that lobbyists "won't find a job in my White House." After the election this prohibition moderated quite a bit. In November 2008 Obama announced that he would allow lobbyists on his transition team as long as they worked on issues unrelated to their lobbying. The Obama administration went on to hire at least 50 lobbyists, granting waivers in order to get around its own restrictive rules. According to the *National Journal*, about 11 percent of the president's top staff have lobbied within five years of their appointments for organizations ranging from Goldman Sachs to Mothers against Drunk Driving. During any given

Total Lobbying Spending		Number of Lobbyists*	
1998	$1.45 billion	1998	10,406
1999	$1.44 billion	1999	12,933
2000	$1.56 billion	2000	12,536
2001	$1.63 billion	2001	11,382
2002	$1.82 billion	2002	12,115
2003	$2.04 billion	2003	12,913
2004	$2.18 billion	2004	13,167
2005	$2.42 billion	2005	14,071
2006	$2.62 billion	2006	14,496
2007	$2.86 billion	2007	14,837
2008	$3.30 billion	2008	14,196
2009	$3.50 billion	2009	13,789
2010	$3.55 billion	2010	12,966
2011	$3.33 billion	2011	12,712
2012	$3.31 billion	2012	12,432
2013	$2.38 billion	2013	11,935

FIGURE 8.1
Money Spent on Lobbying (Does not include money spent on campaign contributions)
Source: http://www.opensecrets.org/lobby/index.php.

The Five Commandments of Lobbying

In meeting with elected officials, lobbyists follow a set of "informal rules" helpful to anyone lobbying Congress:

1. *Demonstrate a constituent interest.* One of the best ways to ensure attention is to show the impact on the representative's voters.
2. *Be well informed.* Officials want information in return for the time and attention they give.
3. *Be balanced.* Compromise is inevitable in legislation. Lobbyists who present both sides leave the official with the impression that they have looked at all sides of the question and then arrived at a conclusion.
4. *Keep it short and sweet.* The challenge is to present the relevant information in the shortest time and in the most memorable way.
5. *Leave a written summary of the case.* It relieves officials of the necessity of taking notes and ensures that the correct information stays behind.

week, press reports suggest that lobbyists are frequent visitors to the Obama White House.

Direct lobbying usually takes place quietly in congressional committees and executive bureaucracies. Although lobbying the legislature gets most of the publicity, lobbyists devote more attention to executive agencies in influencing their regulations. It is said that the real decisions of government are made among lobbyists, executive bureaucrats, and congressional committees—the so-called *iron triangle*. Lobbyists provide information about their industries to committees and bureaucracies. They argue their position with congressional staffers or have their powerful clients or influential grassroots supporters speak directly with decision makers. Knowledge of the issues, personal contacts, and frequent attendance at campaign fundraisers place lobbyists in a position to be heard. (See the box "The Five Commandments of Lobbying.")

Indirect lobbying may involve massive numbers of letters looking as if they had been individually written. Modern phone technologies allow lobbying firms to contact sympathetic voters and connect them directly to their member's office. The Internet can be used to produce a flood of e-mails and at times cause congressional computers to crash. More subtle lobbying efforts involve "nonpolitical" public relations campaigns. Oil companies respond to criticism about oil spills with advertising showing their concern for the environment. Lumber companies do not discuss clear-cutting forests but instead show commercials of their employees planting trees. Op-eds, letters to the editor, and radio commentaries can be quietly funded by private interests.

Spending for these communications is an effort by interest groups to *control the narrative* on public issues. Lobbyists attempt to shape the public discussion of an issue in a way most sympathetic to the interests they represent. This means using popular national goals and symbols to promote narrower, less attractive objectives. Wall Street lobbyists never speak of lower taxes as a way for the wealthy to have more money to spend. Instead, tax relief becomes a means of controlling government spending, reducing unemployment, or promoting economic growth. Gun groups denounce laws restricting the sale of automatic weapons as a constitutional issue, not as reducing the profits of the gun dealers who pay for their organizations. Minorities will promote affirmative action programs as improving education for everyone rather than a preferential advantage only for their group.

Often interest groups try to persuade others to join them in a *grassroots campaign*. They will form a *coalition* of different groups, using a letterhead name, such as Americans for Free Trade, which is invented for the campaign. Using money from private interests, such as Japanese corporations opposing trade restrictions, the lobbyists managing the campaign will recruit American labor unions, businesses, and citizen groups to sign up. This is designed to give Congress the impression that much of the voting public supports their position. These campaigns mobilize local leaders from a congressman's district, encourage employees to write their member of Congress, and entice allied businesses to join the coalition. Such efforts may merely produce Washington's famed "smoke and mirrors"—the illusion of broad popular support for what is, in fact, a narrow interest group spending lots of money. Congress, the press, and the public seem to be getting better at telling the difference.

The essence of grassroots lobbying is voters contacting their representative or senator. This demonstrates intensity and constituents' support, reflects the issue's local impact in the member's home region, and reminds elected officials of the political pain that awaits a wrong decision. Personal lobbying of this kind is applied to members of Congress while they are visiting their districts. Organizations with a national membership, such as the American Association of Retired Persons (AARP) and the National Rifle Association (NRA), can effectively lobby Congress just by contacting their association members. Single-issue groups like AIPAC and pro- and anti-abortion groups can use their members' intense feelings on narrow issues to influence legislators. These "passionate minorities" are usually the only voices representatives hear on a policy. Elected officials know that their position on these hot-button issues will directly affect these activists' votes and campaign contributions.

Lobbying scandals are a recurring Washington ritual and throw the usually quiet system of lobbying into a harsh public light. Much of the critical commentary about Washington's "business as usual" is well deserved. But the overwhelming number of lobbyists are not the fly-by-night wheeler-dealers that political cartoonists present in the newspapers. They are experts skilled in both substantive areas of public policy and in the process of passing legislation. They often represent big business, but they also work for unions, environmentalists, local governments, human rights groups, and universities. They bring detailed information on issues to the attention of busy legislators and their staffs, they publicize overlooked national problems, and they help outsiders navigate a complex, often unresponsive government. In a modern world of specialists, lobbyists are experts in influencing government decisions for their clients' benefit and thereby helping the system operate. They are neither the cause of most of the country's political problems nor the solution. Perhaps regrettably, they have become, in twenty-first century America, a needed tool of governing.

Campaign Contributions

Money has been called the mother's milk of politics. Unlike milk, however, money in elections is combustible and controversial. By contributing money to a political campaign, interest groups can reward a politician who has supported them in the past and encourage support in the future. In most presidential and congressional elections, financial support goes overwhelmingly to the winning candidate, largely from law firms, uni-  versities, and investment bankers. The Democrats, despite pleading poverty in the past, received millions in funding from labor unions and special-interest groups like trial lawyers. The Republicans were the recipients of money from large corporations. However, one should note that the organizations themselves did not donate directly to candidates. The money came from individuals and their families, as well as political action committees (PACs). The quantities of money in American elections continue to grow. (See Table 8.1.)

What does this money buy? At the least, *access*, the right to talk to the elected official. A campaign contributor may say, "I don't want any special promise from you; all I want is the right to come and talk to you

TABLE 8.1 OBAMA'S TOP 10 DONORS IN 2012	
The organizations themselves did not donate; rather, the money came from the organization's PAC(s), its individual members or employees or owners, and those individuals' immediate families.	
University of California	$1,212,245
Microsoft Corp	$ 814,645
Google Inc	$ 801,770
US Government	$ 728,647
Harvard University	$ 668,368
Kaiser Permanente	$ 588,386
Stanford University	$ 512,356
Deloitte LLP	$ 456,975
Columbia University	$ 455,309
Time Warner	$ 442,271

Source: OpenSecrets.or https://www.opensecrets.org/pres12/contrib.php?id=N00009638

when I need to." This seemingly modest request is critical. Access is power. A former congressman offered this perspective:

> You have to make a choice. Who are you going to let in the door first? You get back from lunch. You've got fourteen phone messages on your desk. Thirteen of them are from constituents you've never heard of, and one of them is from a guy who just came to your fundraiser two weeks earlier and gave you $2,000. Which phone call are you going to return first?

As we saw in the last chapter, the money raised and spent in political campaigning has increased. Clearly this increase in funds has affected Congress. One representative remarked, "It is a simple fact of life that when big money enters the political arena, big obligations are entertained." There also may be relatively little that can be done to block the impact of money and the creative ways that campaigning politicians use to get it. As one lobbyist skeptically concluded, "Trying to cleanse the political system from the evils of money is like writing a law ordering teenagers not to think about sex. . . . You don't need a law, you need a lobotomy."

There is another side to the Washington money game. Few contributions to politicians' campaigns start as the idea of the contributor. Most money is donated at the request of an elected official. With this comes the implicit, and sometimes explicit, threat that without the contribution, the donor will not get much help from the member of Congress or from the White House. Shortly before a recent election, a Republican leader met with lobbyists and told them to give to GOP candidates or they could expect their "two coldest years in Washington." One senator bluntly put it: "I've had people who contribute to my campaign, and they get access; the others get good government." Of course, giving money does not guarantee that the representative will vote the right way. A lobbyist who had just seen his bill voted down and was shortly thereafter approached for another contribution said, "It's almost like blackmail. They ask for money from you as they're screwing you to the wall."

One change in the role of interest groups in elections has been the rise of *PACs (political action committees)*. PACs are organizations set up by private groups such as businesses or labor unions to influence the political process by raising funds from their members. The big expansion in PACs occurred in the late 1970s as an unexpected result of campaign finance reforms. These laws, backed by labor, put strict limits on individual donations and provided for public disclosure. Before this legislation, money could legally go into campaigns in large amounts as individual donations from wealthy corporate leaders. There was thus little need for business PACs.

The reforms backfired. Instead of reducing the influence of large contributors, the reforms increased them. Corporations and trade associations organized PACs, bundled individual contributions together to represent their industry, and more effectively channeled their money and influence into campaigns. Even these limits placed on contributions by PACs have been overcome. Recently PACs have become less important; groups that have no limits on what they can raise from individuals or businesses have risen in importance.

Citizens United and Its Aftermath

Reformers have long sought to reduce private money in elections, arguing that donors of large sums gain unfair influence over elected officials. Others have viewed reform as limiting citizens' protected First Amendment free speech rights. Identifying money spent on politics with free speech, they have fought restrictions on private contributions to elections.

Because campaign finance laws raise important First Amendment questions, the Supreme Court has been involved. For nearly four decades, the Court argued that while money *is* a form of protected speech, the government had a legitimate role in reducing corruption in elections. As a result, the Court allowed restrictions on contributions to candidates and parties; corporations and unions were barred from contributing to federal candidates, while individuals were limited in the amounts they could contribute.

Despite these restrictions, wealthy interests found ways to inject money into campaigns. Throughout the 1980s and 1990s, businesses, unions, and individuals took advantage of a loophole allowing unlimited contributions to political parties for the purpose of "party-building"—so-called *soft money*. While these funds could not technically back candidates, it was usually apparent whose candidacy the funds—often ads—supported.

After soft money was banned in 2002 by the Bipartisan Campaign Reform Act (BCRA), wealthy donors began directing their efforts through 527 groups. These tax-exempt organizations were able to raise and spend unlimited sums so long as they did not coordinate with (or endorse) a candidate for federal office. BCRA did forbid these groups from using corporate or union funds on ads that even mentioned a federal candidate's name 30 days before a primary or 60 days before a general election.

These limits came crashing down in January 2010 in the *Citizens United* decision. The Supreme Court ruled that the First Amendment prohibited the government from restricting independent political spending by corporations and unions. While these groups could still not contribute directly to candidate campaigns or parties, or coordinate with them, they could spend unlimited sums of their own money on advertisements for or against a candidate, and at any time before an election. BCRA was finished.

President Obama warned that *Citizens United* would "open the floodgates for special interests, including foreign corporations, to spend without limit in our elections." He wasn't far off.

So-called independent expenditure committees were allowed to collect unlimited money from unions, corporations, and individuals to spend advocating or denouncing candidates. In 2010, almost 80 of these *Super PACs* emerged, spending some $90 million. The most active Super PAC was American Crossroads, led by former president George W. Bush's advisor Karl Rove, which spent over $21 million to defeat congressional Democratic candidates. In the 2012 presidential race, candidate-centered Super PACs emerged. Mitt Romney's PAC, Restore Our Future, raised over $153 million, while Priorities USA Action, a pro-Obama Super PAC, raised $79 million. These organizations could not coordinate with the campaigns, but many of their leaders had close ties with the candidates. For example in 2012, Rahm Emanuel, President Obama's first chief of staff, quit the president's campaign in order to raise money for Priorities USA.

The *Citizens United* ruling caused reformers of campaign finance to focus on transparency. Accepting that corporate funds could not be restricted, reformers sought to at least strengthen disclosure rules. Many of the groups empowered by the *Citizens United* ruling do not have to disclose the names of donors. In *McCutcheon vs. FEC (2014)* the Court did require donors' names to be disclosed but, more importantly, it removed overall limits on funds to candidates and parties. So while contributions

per candidate were still limited to $2,600 for each election, there was no limit on the total amounts anyone could give to all candidates and party committees. This might shift some big donors back to parties from Super Pacs, it certainly increases the expectation that very few donors will be contributing very large amounts of money to future campaigns.

To no one's surprise, the amounts of campaign money have skyrocketed in recent decades. In 1974 interest group donations to congressional candidates totaled $12.5 million. By the 2012 election, groups were spending at least $609 million on congressional races. At present the average cost of winning a House seat is $1.7 million, and for the Senate the figure is $10.5 million, both numbers are record amounts and certain to increase in coming elections. This meant that a winning Senate candidate between January 1, 2010, and Election Day 2012 needed to raise $14,350 each and every day. These figures included safe seats where little money had to be spent by incumbents, despite the undisputed fact that those already in office collect most campaign funds. Spending more money than an opponent did not guarantee victory, but it certainly helped.

Do Groups Interests Overwhelm the Public Interest?

Politics: The conduct of public affairs for private advantage.
—Ambrose Bierce

The idea that interest groups and their lobbyists dominate politics is widely accepted today. What the framers of the Constitution saw as multiple voices harmonized by the institutions of government has become to some a haggling marketplace where special interests negotiate laws, regulations, and the use of public money. Political power, especially that of corporations, has become a tool for avoiding laws you do not like and passing laws you do like. Whatever the public purposes proclaimed in the laws, just below the surface lies the real spirit of lobbying—"universalized ticket fixing."

Despite newspaper headlines to the contrary, political scientists have traditionally downplayed the influence of lobbyists. Many studies have found that lobbyists have little success in persuading members of Congress to change their minds. Even money, in the form of campaign contributions, can seldom be tracked down as motivating congressional votes. Lobbyists for their part have a natural tendency to overstate their influence—to boast of their successes, forget their failures, and attract more paying clients. But a congressman's support for a major corporate employer in his state or for lower taxes or for same-sex marriage may have little to do with the activities of lobbyists.

When lobbying by an interest group targets major policies, it needs public support. Lobbyists gain this backing by presenting their narrow cause as consistent with the national interest. This link to public policies is very influential when it is done over a long period of time in hearings, through news advertising, and in promoting a narrative over the airwaves. Its impact can be seen when gun owners make gun control a violation of civil liberties or environmentalists make forest clearcutting an issue of global warming. Of course members of Congress must see the lobbyists' cause as helping their own career prospects, especially their chances for reelection.

Washington seems dominated by intense groups mobilized to gain or keep particular advantages. Policies that concentrate benefits on powerful groups and disperse the costs on an unaware public are easiest for Congress to support. Tax breaks for some Wall Street banks, subsidies for large shipping companies, and less regulation for this or that industry are issues that receive focused attention from a few lobbies and the informed attention of practically no one else. A decentralized government with many points of access, embracing the values of a wealthy market economy, rewards those able to bring power and money to bear on narrow policy arenas.

There is little argument about the vast increase in the volume of lobbying. With some thousands of lobbyists now working Washington, it would seem foolish to argue that they do not have an impact on American politics. They are in the main hired by wealthy interests to influence how public officials treat their clients. The leaders of these interest groups are not people who are throwing away their money on activities that produce no benefits for their industry or organization. When compared to the relative decline in political parties, it seems fair to conclude that the major channel through which private interests influence American politics are lobbyists.

This rise in lobbying has increased demands on government. Corporate executives, veterans, farmers, realtors, doctors, retirees, and university administrators push their claims for the resources of government. As the benefits provided by government increase, more groups organize to protect what they have or to get more. This results in what Jonathan Rauch has called *hyperpluralism*, too many groups making too many demands on government. Groups demand benefits, but these subsidies strengthen the groups and encourage them to preserve the programs and relationships that keep them in business (often called *crony capitalism*) until a paralyzed government begins to choke on the demands placed on it. There are too many narrow interests—and their lobbyists/lawyers/PR consultants—to overcome. Programs serving a general interest get less support, whereas those helping special interests keep their hold on public resources—forever.

Reforms to reduce the influence of wealthy, powerful interest groups have failed. Their lobbying, their control of modern technologies, and their dominance of campaign contributions have increased. Government is held hostage by narrow groups resisting all changes not benefiting them. Average Washington deal making is not available to average Americans. The frustration and distance the public feels toward their political leaders becomes understandable.

Nonetheless, lobbyists have not yet completely rigged the game.

As witnessed in recent elections, politicians still get elected on platforms calling for change. And whether it is Barack Obama in his first campaign for president telling 'the lobbyists in Washington that their days of setting the agenda are over" or Tea Party candidates in 2010 denouncing incumbent Republican senators, elections are still won and lost on factors beyond the control of a few lobbies. It didn't hurt the president's ability to speak out that he could use online technology to reduce the obligations from special interests' money. And the ability of Tea Party conservatives to mobilize rural populist discontent depended on numerous volunteers' support. Other players limit lobbyists as well. The press investigates their cozy deals, the civil service is generally competent and committed to their agencies' programs, and networks of youthful activists often elbow their issues into the public arena. And as we will see, new forms of communications from radio talk shows to Internet blogs are frequently upsetting lobbyists' backroom handshakes.

The outcomes of the political game remain unpredictable. Lobbyists' ability to defang reforms depends on their success in convincing the public, press, and politicians that what they want these audiences should also want. Their influence ultimately depends on the resistance, acceptance, or indifference by other players as well as public opinion. Any explanation of the political game based solely on the dominance of a few wealthy interests is unlikely to understand the surprising directions that American politics has taken, and will take in the future. Some of these unexpected twists and turns will involve our last player—the media.

Media

The media are the only private business that the Constitution singles out for protection. The First Amendment prohibits any law "abridging the freedom of speech, or of the press." But like any business, the media are subject to the ups and downs of the private marketplace. And since the turn of the new century, they have been in crisis because of the rise of the Internet. Advertisements that once provided four-fifths of the money for newspapers and magazines, and almost all the money for TV and radio, are now ending up online.

How then will this "fourth branch of government" fulfill its vital functions in the political game?

These critical roles include the following:

First, media are the channels through which those in power talk to the public. Whether a new policy is being launched, a crisis responded to, or government announcements made that need distribution, political leaders depend on the media to relay the information to the rest of us. Second, and less obviously, media are the way that those in power talk to each other. If an official in the Department of Agriculture thinks the subsidy for corn-based ethanol is being poorly run (and the White House disagrees), he might communicate that to Congress by leaks to a reporter that become an article in the *Washington Post*.

Third, news media are a watchdog. Media investigate whether elected officials and others are abusing their privileges, showing favoritism to cronies, or not keeping their campaign promises. Media try to hold those in power to legal and ethical *standards* such as honesty, consistency, and transparency. Fourth, news media provide feedback so officials can learn whether their policies are working. While the full impact of a complex program may not be clear for a long time, news stories allow an immediate response. For example, a few years ago Congress required single mothers to get jobs in order to continue to receive welfare support for their children. If welfare mothers are suffering or their children are abandoned, it will be journalists who will report it so that officials know.

Finally, news media provide channels through which the general public can bring its needs, demands, and views to the attention of officials. This "voice of the people" function can be seen in reporting on the full extent of the destruction left by Hurricane Katrina in 2006, the despair created by the economic recession of 2008–2009, or the failure of Obamacare to effectively launch in 2013. The news media furnish the street-level observations that enable authorities to assess the situation, get some idea of what the public expects them to do, and respond accordingly.

In this half of the chapter, we will answer the following questions: What are the media? What do the media do? Who controls the media? How do the media influence politics, and how do other players influence media content?

What Are the Media?

Media are those means of communication that permit messages to be made public. Media such as television, radio, newspapers, and the Internet provide important links connecting people to one another. But these are links with an important quality: They have the ability to communicate messages to a great many people at roughly the same time. We will concentrate on television, newspapers, and the Internet. (See Figure 8.2.)

Ninety-percent of American households own at least one TV. Actually, the average TV-owning household has 2.8 TV sets (for only 2.5 people!). The abundance of TVs and the powerful impact of pictures are why television dominates the mass media—as well as dominating American kids, who watch some three hours of TV a day. TV's political influence varies greatly. There is the exceptional event, like the Sarah Palin–Joe Biden vice presidential debate in October 2008, watched by almost 70 million Americans—considerably more than the 57 million average for the three presidential candidate debates that year.

Just how closely people follow presidential campaigns, even hotly contested ones, is inconsistent. One poll in 2000 found that only half of voting-age Americans thought about the election or could recall even one news story about it. The 2008 election, on the other hand, which offered the first African American presidential candidate and the first serious female presidential candidate (Hillary Clinton), was set against the backdrop of two wars and a looming economic crisis, and propelled by record campaign spending of nearly $1 billion, saw dramatically higher levels of political awareness. In a 2009 poll, nearly 85 percent of college freshmen said they had discussed politics "frequently or occasionally."

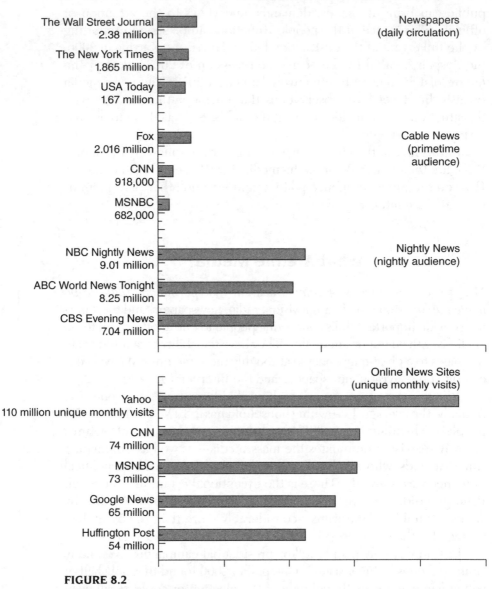

FIGURE 8.2
Audience for Media News, 2013.
Sources: Magazine Publishers of America; Audit Bureau of Circulations, Nielsen Media Research.

Thanks to the growth of cable and satellite systems—which have much more capacity than the over-the-air signals of traditional TV broadcasting—the average household now gets 104 channels, including round-the-clock news and talk on CNN, MSNBC, and Fox News. However, the most-watched TV newscasts remain the half-hour evening programs produced by the three traditional broadcast networks—CBS, NBC, and ABC. These networks rely on local stations to relay their signals to households. Some of these stations are owned by the networks. Some local stations the networks don't own but contract with; they are called *affiliates*. Each of the broadcast networks has over 200 affiliates that enable them to reach a truly national audience with their programming and in turn sell national advertising. This arrangement with local affiliates allows the networks to sell time at stratospheric rates—none higher than a 30-second ad during the 2014 Super Bowl that cost $4 million.

In recent years, the dominance of the three networks over TV news has been reduced, as has the overall importance of TV news, including local news. Traditional national network newscasts still out-draw cable for audiences: The 24 million people who watch the three evening network newscasts are several times the number who watch cable news at any moment in prime time (8 to 11 at night). Fox News' *top-rated* news program, *Bill O'Reilly*, draws a measly one-quarter of the viewers of the *least* popular evening network news program—CBS Evening News. (See Figure 8.2.)

Even though more people watch the 30-minute network news shows, Americans are increasingly relying on news available round-the-clock. In the 2008 election, cable replaced traditional TV for the first time as the most often cited source of political news. Online news also grew in influence. In September 2012, the Romney campaign was damaged by a video of him at a fundraiser, where he declared that 47 percent of Americans "are dependent upon government, who believe that they are victims. . . . My job is not to worry about those people—I'll never convince them that they should take personal responsibility and care for their lives." When the video went viral on YouTube, it had 3.38 million views within one week. The damaging video had more hits than Romney's acceptance speech at the Republican convention.

Whatever the problems of the TV industry, the most dramatic decline in American media has been that of daily newspapers. Circulation of metropolitan papers has been declining for decades—and that decline has been accelerating. In recent years newspaper circulation was falling nearly 5 percent annually. The money picture was even worse, largely because of changing conditions in the economy. Advertisers shifted their spending to cheaper targeted sites on the Internet, which promised better results than scattershot advertising in the general media. Newspaper revenue has fallen consistently year after year, reaching a low of $38 billion in 2012, despite new ventures into e-commerce.

The result: fewer newspapers. Metro papers in Denver, Seattle, Philadelphia, San Francisco, and Minneapolis closed. Those newspapers that remain are employing fewer journalists and are spending less on covering political news. Some 600 newspapers had their own D.C.

bureaus in 1985. *Half had been shut by 2008.* The three main TV networks had 110 journalists covering Washington in 1985; by 2009 they had 46. From city commissions to county councils to state legislatures to Congress, governments now have fewer reporters keeping an eye on them.

The newspapers that remain vary in size and quality, from the prestigious *New York Times*, carrying national and international news collected by its own reporters, to small-town dailies that relay crop reports and cover local fires but provide sketchy coverage of national events reprinted from the wire services. (*Wire services* are specialized agencies like the Associated Press [AP], Bloomberg News, and Reuters that gather, write, and sell news to media that subscribe to them.) Historically much of the news reaching us through TV and radio originated in stories done by the reporters of major newspapers.

This decline in the number of newspapers and their competitiveness is nothing new. In 1900, there were 2,226 daily papers in the United States. A century later, while the population had more than tripled, there were only 1,647. (As of 2012 the figure was 1,382.) The same period saw a decline in the cities with competing newspapers. In 1920, there were 700 cities with competing daily papers. Currently there are fewer than a dozen. Of major American cities, only New York has three separately owned dailies, all of them in financial trouble.

Then there is the *Internet*. While the Internet—which started out in the late 1960s as a U.S. military project to create a computer network that could survive a nuclear attack—is still young, vast numbers of people already rely on it as a principal news source. A 2012 Pew survey showed that 39 percent of people got their news online, while 55 percent look to television and only 29 percent got it from newspapers. Increasingly people are getting their news online, most often from trusted brand names, including legacy newspapers (e.g., The *New York Times*) and TV networks (e.g., CNN). The rapid growth of mobile is a key factor driving the move to digital news, with users frequently combining different devices and traditional sources.

Online news is exploding in importance. Numerous sites offer national news reported by their own staffs (Politico.com, Talking PointsMemo, CNN.com, Slate) or offer commentary about news they select from elsewhere (*Huffington Post*, InstaPundit). There is also a wave of local citizen-run sites that track city and neighborhood news. All of this was possible because the number of U.S. Internet users hit 255 million in 2012—81 percent of Americans.

By 1998, the scandal involving White House intern Monica Lewinsky showed the Internet in the first full political bloom. The news of President Bill Clinton's sexual affair with the young woman first surfaced that January on a website run by a freelance reporter appropriately named Matt Drudge. Throughout the controversy, tens of thousands of people were debating impeachment and more sordid aspects of the scandal in newsgroups and chat rooms. The customary news cycle for newspapers or evening news—geared to the hours of the working day—was replaced by a nonstop flow of information and rumors surfacing 24/7 on the Internet. The mainstream press struggled to catch up. Whether the scandal showed the Internet as a positive expansion of public debate or just the cyberbabble of an electronic mob was less clear, even now.

The spread of mobile telephones that can transmit images, and the growing popularity of social networks such as Twitter, which enable people to share short messages with thousands of others simultaneously, have affected news coverage. Every newsroom inside Washington's Beltway is wired to Twitter, giving users the power to communicate directly with journalists and to question (or harass them) over their coverage. Reporters at present look over their digital shoulders for the reaction of a wired audience. American media's meek acceptance of the Bush administration's deceptive justifications for invading Iraq in 2003 would be more difficult now in an age of instant and massive Twitter responses. Overseas, Facebook and Twitter were important to the Arab Spring 2011 uprisings in Tunisia and Egypt, where they were used to organize protests and spread discontent. News is increasingly participatory—more people than ever have their hands on the tools of mass communications.

What Do the Media Do?

The media provide three major types of messages. Through their *news reports, entertainment programs*, and *advertising*, the media help shape public opinion on many things—including politics. In news reports, the media supply up-to-date accounts of what journalists believe to be the most important, interesting, and newsworthy events, issues, and developments. But the influence of news reports goes well beyond relaying current facts. The key to this power is *selectivity*. By reporting certain items (President Obama's daily workout) and ignoring others (President Franklin Roosevelt's inability to walk), the media suggest to us what is important. Media coverage gives status to people and events—a national television interview or a *Time* magazine cover creates a "national figure."

There are limits. Few people pay attention to political news. Most people reading the newspapers are interested in the sports, comics, and local events. Those under 30 are unlikely to listen to or watch political news. What they find out about politics comes when it is relayed to them by friends, downloaded video reports, or sketches from the *Daily Show* that they get from YouTube. This is not because they do not have enough time. Young people spend more time watching sports, celebrity news, and entertainment programming on television than do adults over 30. The more young viewers ignore coverage of politics, the less they know about their government. And, perhaps, the less they care. (See the box "The *Daily Show* and Political Journalism.")

News reports perform two important functions: agenda-setting and framing. *Agenda-setting* means presenting national priorities— what should be taken seriously, what should be taken lightly, and what can be ignored altogether. "The media can't tell people what to think," one expert put it, "but they can tell people what to think *about*." The attention the media give to the deficit, climate change, or the war in Syria will affect how important most people think these issues are. What are the headlines on the front-page of the morning newspaper or what leads the evening news, makes some events, issues, or people seem more significant than others.

Framing defines problems, suggesting *how* we should see issues. Media coverage can present, or frame, an issue in many ways. Is crime

The *Daily Show* and Political Journalism

While the popularity of television news has declined in recent years, late night comedy, especially Comedy Central's *Daily Show*, has become a major source of political news, especially among young people. The *Daily Show* uses factual content, making its humor understandable only if the viewer knows the news. Host Jon Stewart weaves his satire around footage of current events and conducts live interviews with political figures.

Admirers of the program point to its willingness to confront hypocrisy in politics as evidence of its commitment to journalism. The program is at its best when combing the Internet for historical materials that expose politicians as liars. During the 2012 presidential campaign, Stewart and Stephen Colbert ran a series exposing the absurdity of the campaign finance laws. Colbert became a candidate for president, while Stewart ran a Super PAC committed to him, allowed to raise unlimited funds but forbidden to "coordinate" with Colbert's campaign. The two would do funny segments that broadcast instructions over TV to each other, which, while legally not considered "coordination," accomplished the same thing, much to the glee of both comedians.

linked to unemployment, to lax gun control laws, or to not enough police? How the problem is understood may influence whether the solution is a jobs program, restrictions on buying automatic weapons, or more cops. Linguistics professor George Lakoff points out that President George W. Bush spoke frequently about *tax relief*, which meant tax cuts. "Relief," of course, implies that taxes are a painful headache or illness that someone needs to cure. Alternatively, such cuts might increase the deficit or slash social programs, but this was not part of the frame. Media scholar Kathleen Hall Jamieson has written, "Frames tell us what is important, what the range of acceptable debate on a topic is, and when an issue has been resolved."

Entertainment programs offer amusement while giving people images of "normal" behavior. That doesn't mean actions on television always offers socially acceptable models. Some fictional characters, such as Walter White of *Breaking Bad*, engage in immoral business practices that bring wealth and power. Such media programs may substitute for learning from reality's more complex experiences and become as important as real life. As one analyst of television observed, "If you can write a nation's stories, you needn't worry about who makes its laws. Today, television tells most of the stories to most of the people most of the time."

Finally, most programs and news are built around a constant flow of *advertisements*. Television programs are constructed to reach emotional high points just before the commercials so that the audience will stay put during the advertisement. Newspapers devote almost two-thirds of their space to ads rather than to news, which led one English author to define a journalist as "someone who writes on the back of advertisements." Ads, especially television commercials, present images of what the audience finds pleasing about themselves. Accompanied by compelling symbols, commercials offer viewers comfort, good looks, and amusement. They may change what we expect in other arenas, including politics. TV's emphasis on entertaining visuals may alter how we look at our political leaders and how they present themselves: Instead of a public debate over issues, we find a competition between visual images. In this case, the medium has changed the message of politics. (See the box "Mixed Media Messages.")

Reliance on advertising means that the media must attract the right audiences—not only people who are *interested* in what's being presented but also people who are *interesting* to advertisers. A few years ago, TV network news found that its audience was too old for the advertisers it wanted to sell to. Hoping to appeal to a younger

Mixed Media Messages

During the 1984 presidential campaign, Lesley Stahl, a CBS reporter, prepared a critical commentary on how President Reagan used television. Her blunt report charged the president with manipulation, if not hypocrisy. She reported that he will appear at the Special Olympics or the opening of a senior housing facility, but no hint was given that he cut the budgets for subsidized housing for the elderly. He also distanced himself from bad news, Stahl reported. After he pulled the U.S. Marines out of Lebanon in the aftermath of a disastrous October 1983 bombing of their barracks in Beirut—which killed 241 U.S. and 58 French military personnel—he flew off to his California ranch, leaving others to make the announcement.

To illustrate her piece, Stahl put together Reagan's video clips: Reagan greeting handicapped athletes, cutting the ribbon at a home for the elderly, and relaxing on his ranch in jeans.

Stahl believed it was toughest piece she had ever done about the Reagan administration and worried about their reaction. To her surprise, however, a White House official soon called and praised the story!

Stahl was shocked. The official then stressed that the story contained nearly five minutes of seemingly flattering pictures of the president. Convinced that viewers paid little attention to the actual content of the story, the White House appreciated the free advertising.

Stahl then realized that the official had a point and broke into laughter.

Source: Based on Hedrick Smith, The Power Game (New York: Random House, 1988), pp. 413–14.

demographic—especially women of childbearing age—avid consumers of many goods and services—the news programs expanded their coverage of education, marriage, health care, and other concerns of interest to growing families. In that way, the agenda of newsworthy topics shifted because of marketing goals—leading conservative critics to accuse the network news of a liberal bias because of their change in emphasis.

Media and the Marketplace of Ideas

The framers of the Constitution believed that a free flow of information from many voices was basic to democracy. Opinions in the press would compete with one another without restraint in a "marketplace of ideas." That phrase has since been expanded to include radio and television. The principle remains the same, as Judge Learned Hand wrote:

> Right conclusions are more likely to be gathered out of a multitude of tongues than through any kind of authoritative selection. To many this is, and always will be folly; but we have staked upon it our all.

The ability of media to fulfill this goal of presenting a variety of opinion representing the widest range of political ideas has, to no one's surprise, been limited in practice. It is limited by (1) *the media themselves*, (2) *the government*, and (3) *the public*.

As businesses, media are operated, bought, and sold to make money for their owners. Profitability, not public service, has led to the concentration of media ownership; owners sought to operate more cheaply and reach larger audiences by controlling larger markets. That has encouraged an increase in control by *chains*, which are companies that combine media in different cities under a single owner. More than 80 percent of U.S. newspapers are owned by *chains*, and the country's 10 largest ownership groups control 179 magazines. Clear Channel Communications, the largest U.S. radio broadcaster, owns 900 local stations.

Mergers and acquisitions during the 1990s left major media outlets concentrated in fewer corporate hands than ever. Disney purchased ABC for $19 billion, Westinghouse paid $5.4 billion for CBS, and Time Warner bought Turner Broadcasting, including CNN, for $7.5 billion. Earlier NBC had been acquired by General Electric. In May 2000, the combination of Viacom (which owned Paramount Pictures, Blockbuster, MTV, Nickelodeon, and Simon & Schuster, among others) with CBS created the second-largest media company in the world. But this was soon surpassed. In 2001 America On Line acquired Time Warner, the largest media corporation. Ten years later, it bought the *Huffington Post* for $315 million. Consolidation continued with the 2007 purchase of Dow Jones & Co., publisher of the *Wall Street Journal*, by Rupert Murdoch's News Corp., which owns Fox News, the *New York Post*, and many other newspapers and satellite systems throughout the world. The *Christian Science Monitor* concluded, "The bulk of what we see, hear, learn, sing, play, rent and consume will shortly be controlled by a dozen corporate entities." (See the box "Rupert Murdoch and Politics.")

In the past, federal regulators prevented such mergers, arguing that monopolies over information did not serve the public interest. Organizations like the Consumers Union have opposed these mergers, believing that the results will be soaring cable rates, shrinking entertainment options, and sensationalism in news coverage. The increasing bankruptcies and declining profitability in the news business has led to

Rupert Murdoch and Politics

Rupert Murdoch is the Australian-born media baron whose U.S. holdings include the *Wall Street Journal*, the *New York Post*, and the Fox Network. Fox News, a 24-hour cable news network created in 1996, has appealed to an audience that considers other U.S. news sources as tainted by a liberal bias. Its most popular commentators—Bill O'Reilly and Sean Hannity—are strongly conservative, and its slogans, "Fair and balanced," and "We report, you decide," are seen as backhanded criticisms of its competitors, especially CNN.

But Murdoch's political leanings throughout his career have followed his corporate interests more than his personal politics (which he describes as libertarian). In Great Britain, where he bought the *Times* in 1981, he backed the Conservative Party under Prime Minister Margaret Thatcher until its popularity declined. Then he moved his support to the Labor Party. He was able to survive the 2011 hacking scandal in Britain, where his newspapers were found guilty of phone tapping, police bribery, and improperly influencing politicians.

In the United States, Murdoch was equally flexible. All 175 Murdoch-owned newspapers worldwide came out in favor of the Iraq war. But as the war and President Bush's popularity declined, Murdoch's enthusiasm waned. By 2008 Murdoch declared himself a fan of Barack Obama. Moderating his political image helped Murdoch in his 2007 takeover of Dow Jones, the Bancroft family-owned company that published the *Wall Street Journal*—the second-biggest U.S. newspaper. Family members were apprehensive about Murdoch. But his emergence as a pragmatic centrist—rather than a right-wing ideologue—helped him overcome their resistance, close the $5 billion deal, and make him America's most powerful media owner.

more flexibility in allowing nonprofits or wealthy benefactors to maintain important publications. In a recent effort to save a distinguished, if unprofitable, newspaper, the *Washington Post* was sold to Amazon.com founder Jeff Bezos for $250 million in 2013.

Beyond the arguments concerning the *quality* or variety of views that are broadcast, there is no question that the *quantity* of information has increased. One breakthrough in delivering news was CNN (Cable News Network), with 24-hour coverage. Started in 1980 by Ted Turner, few people believed there would be enough demand for such a station, and it was jokingly called "Chicken Noodle News." CNN went on to become a success, and in times of crisis it has become the channel of choice for political leaders and news junkies. Less popular C-SPAN provides continuous coverage of both houses of Congress, and many community cable stations provide similar coverage of state and local governments.

The impact of the Internet on political information and public involvement has been overwhelming; the consequences are more debatable. The online world offers a deluge of information as well as ready access to those in power. It affords virtual means for creating activist networks focused on climate change, or protecting gun rights or challenging harassment in the workplace. And it provides instant channels for mobilizing these opinions into the public arena. It is a free, decentralized media available to everyone.

Yet this enormous increase in communications has not provided an unblemished advance of democracy. In-depth press investigations of government have declined along with the numbers of reporters who used to write them. Extremist opinions and conspiracy theories are amplified in online echo chambers helping to recruit members into fringe groups and polarize the country's politics. Not surprisingly, public confidence in elected representatives has plummeted to all-time lows. This same government uses surveillance technology to secretly monitor its own citizens, not to mention a few foreign allies. Media corporations exploit their customers' e-mails and online searches to shape consumer choices. Individual privacy and independent choice are increasingly out-of-date concepts. The online world offers a huge space to both expand Americans' freedoms and restrict them. Stay connected [#basicsamericanpolitics] to see which trend wins.

Media and Government

Government and media in the United States have long been dance partners in an unsteady waltz. In the early years of the republic, the press was consciously partisan. Newspapers were sponsored by political parties to appeal to their voters and grateful for fat printing contracts once their party got into power. In the 1830s, printing by machine allowed mass circulation newspapers that could be hawked on street corners for a fraction of the price papers had cost until then. These "penny papers" now depended on advertising for most of their revenues, and advertisers wanted to reach customers, no matter what their political views. The Civil War increased the demand for human interest stories and up-to-date news unaffected by party loyalties. By the end of the nineteenth century, advertisers and publishers—not politicians—bankrolled newspapers.

Still, the media continued to benefit from government aid. But now the press was helped through subsidies and support for new technology, notably the telegraph and later the radio (developed by the U.S. Navy). Still later came microwave, satellite communications, and the Internet. In the twentieth century, federal regulation under the Federal Communications Commission (FCC), created in 1934, generally took a pro-industry stance in restricting entry to broadcasting competitors. Regulators steadily weakened the public service requirements broadcasters had to meet, and now license renewals—which come every six years—are usually a formality. The media have long been exempted from a host of government laws and antitrust regulations, including making sure that minimum wage and child labor laws did not apply to newspaper delivery boys. Plus, they benefit from an important subsidy from practically all government agencies—free information for the press through public affairs offices.

For campaigning politicians, the media are both opportunity and adversary. Two-thirds of the money in presidential races goes to advertising. Campaigning politicians live and die by media coverage. Some of their activities have been called *pseudoevents*—not real news at all, but happenings that are staged solely to be reported. One example seen in every election year is when presidents of both parties take campaigning local candidates for rides on Air Force One with television cameras aboard. While coverage has been increased by the rise in media outlets such as cable and blogs, the quality of political news has not necessarily risen with the increase in quantity. One study showed that the average *sound bite*—a video clip of a candidate speaking—had declined from 42 seconds in 1968 to just over 7 seconds today. Emphasizing the quick and dramatic in public affairs is not the same as insight and analysis.

Examples of government leaders informally pressuring media are numerous. Presidents try to get on the good side of the media by giving favored reporters exclusive "leaks" of information and by controlling information going to the public. Press conferences have been used by presidents since Theodore Roosevelt to give the media direct contact with the chief executive. Though disliked by recent presidents, such conferences, when broadcast, can allow presidents to present their views directly to the public. Franklin Roosevelt's radio "fireside chats" were a brilliant way of personally reassuring people during the Great Depression. Television and politicians can also make uneasy partners. In 1960, presidential candidate Richard Nixon's streaky makeup, dull suit, and unshaven looks made a poor impression—and may have cost him the election—in the first-ever televised debate with his opponent, John F. Kennedy.

Presidents work with experts to perfect their public images. As a former movie actor and television personality, the late Ronald Reagan was known as "the Great Communicator" due to his unrivaled skill of looking and sounding absolutely forthright. President Clinton was an intelligent, articulate media celebrity. But Clinton's press relations

The President's Lite-News Strategy

President Obama was answering plenty of questions from the media during his reelection campaign. The problem for the national press was they weren't asking them. Instead, the president was showing up on *Entertainment Tonight*, *People* magazine, and local FM radio stations, talking sports, regional food, and his favorite work-out songs. The national media was frozen out, leading NBC News's Chuck Todd to complain that the White House's disregard for the press had "reached a new low."

Obama's response to the press criticism was that the concerns of the national press corps and the American people were wildly different. He was trying to reach an audience that didn't follow the daily back-and-forth of political campaigns. He was also benefiting from the public's widespread mistrust of the press, which made it easier to ignore mainstream reporters. Even opposition Republicans thought Obama's low-risk media strategy was smart. GOP campaigners agreed with the Obamians—the press was unhappy; voters didn't care.

—Based on "Obama's Soft-Media Strategy," *Politico*, August 17, 2012.

came to a screeching halt at the feet of Monica Lewinsky, where the scandal displayed the president's negatives—questionable honesty and womanizing. George W. Bush was not as good as Clinton in public performances, but then he didn't have to defend his private life, and he usually followed the message of the day. He also avoided unscripted press conferences, favored less critical reporters from outside Washington, and frequently garbled his few question-and-answer media sessions.

Barack Obama developed a reputation as an orator and writer even before he became a presidential candidate. As a campaigner, he was widely admired for his verbal skills, to the point where his adversaries tried to use his "glibness" against him, with mixed results. He stands as his administration's most capable spokesmen. And yet he avoids press conferences, holding only 79 in his first term, the lowest since Reagan was president. Obama clearly prefers not submitting to tough questioning by Washington reporters, favoring "soft news" interviews discussing sports and music in informal settings. (See the box "The President's Lite-News Strategy.")

Media and the Public

The "definition of alternatives is the supreme instrument of power," wrote political scientist E. E. Schattschneider. "Definition of alternatives" means the ability to set limits on political discussions, to define what is politically important and what is not, and to make certain solutions reasonable and acceptable and others not. Media, to a great extent, have this power in presenting what passes for "common sense." Who influences the exercise of this power is another question.

Certainly media managers (editors, newscasters, producers, reporters) have a vital role in shaping political views. Advertisers, by buying space in some programs or papers or blogs and not in others, affect the messages sent out to the public. The owners of media, whether online sites, television networks, cable operators, or newspaper chains, play a part in selecting who runs their day-to-day operations and the general "slant" of the media they own. Corporate interests were likely considered when NBC withdrew support in 2013 for a four-hour miniseries on Hillary Clinton after external protests and threats by the Republican Party not to allow NBC to televise the next round of candidate debates.

People have a right to expect that the press will fulfill the major political functions described at the beginning of this section, particularly (1) telling the public what their leaders are doing and (2) serving as a watchdog to hold leaders accountable. The demands of the marketplace, by turning news into profitable entertainment, have limited the media's ability to fulfill either political function.

The public does not have to be passive. By watching or not watching certain programs, by buying or not buying publications, and by demanding or not demanding that dissenting voices be heard, the public can have a hand in shaping media output. The rise of talk radio, social media, and community-based programs on public access channels shows that flexibility and diversity are still possible in today's media.

CASE STUDY

Google: The Rise and Rise
of a Washington Lobby

On a cold day in January, Google held what *Washingtonian* magazine called "the swankiest office party Washington has seen in years." The celebration of their new large offices was done in a Googley way— drinks of vodka and cranberry juice in test tubes called YouTubes, massage chairs, and a game room featuring foosball. The office was located in one of the capital's rare "green" buildings. But whatever the "new media" touches, the party announced Google's entrance into a very old profession.

Google had become a political lobby. In 2008 CEO Eric Schmidt and other Google colleagues donated over $800,000 to Obama's campaign, ranking the company as one of the Democrat's top five contributors. (Schmidt was appointed to the President's Council of Advisors on Science and Technology and met with him in the White House.) The following year, the company spent $6 million lobbying 13 different government agencies, one of the highest totals in the tech industry. By 2010 Google had 30 full-time staffers in Washington, including former White House advisors. Google argues that its Washington presence is different from other businesses—a "lobby shop–think tank hybrid"—educating the government about the impact of new technologies. A spokesman for the nonprofit Center for Responsive Politics concluded a little differently, "They're one of the big boys now."

Whatever the spin, Google had, in a decade, gone from a political nonentity to a significant lobbying force. How and why?

THE GROWTH OF THE GOOD GUYS

In January 1996, two Stanford University PhD students, Larry Page and Sergey Brin, began a research project to improve Internet searches. The two "techies" concluded that a search engine that ranked websites by how many other sites linked to them, rather than the industry standard of how many times a word is found on a website, would provide better search results. For example, if a user searched for "cars," the top search results would not be those sites simply mentioning the word "cars" most often but rather those that had the largest number of sites mentioning "cars" *link to them*. They dropped their graduate studies to work full time on their system.

Using seed money of $100,000, Page and Brin established Google, Inc. in September 1998. By June 2000, Google officially became the world's largest search engine. In 2001 the founders shrewdly surrendered some of their authority to corporate veteran Eric Schmidt, who they hired as CEO. In 2004 Google went public with a market value of over $23 billion.

Before this an engineer, Amit Patel, had walked into a conference room where Google met with clients and wrote "Don't Be Evil" on a whiteboard. Patel's simple slogan became the firm's informal motto and reflected Google's self-image that they were "the good guys." Staff were permitted to devote 20 percent of their time to their own creative projects. The company aimed to be carbon neutral, to strive to "do good things for the world" even if it meant forgoing "some short-term gains." Google prided itself on not being conventional.

It was also ambitious. It expanded to include Gmail, Google Calendar, Google Store, Google Video, and Google Maps. It acquired the popular YouTube in 2006 and outbid Microsoft the next year to purchase DoubleClick, an online ad network. Its Android operating system was designed to run on mobile smartphones. And it expanded overseas, notably launching Google China in 2005.

A dozen years after being incorporated, Google's market dominance brought accusations about its monopoly power, often from competitors, and grumbling about privacy concerns from civil liberties groups. Its rapid growth meant entering different industries, from software to telecommunications, and bumping up against business competitors and government policymakers. Google's leaders were not so naïve as to go naked into these battles. They recognized the need for influence in Washington.

THE LOBBYING PULL

One lesson learned was the so-called, "Microsoft mistake." The story goes that Bill Gates, the nerdy head of that software giant, had in his company's early years ignored all things political. If the government left him alone, he would leave the government alone. For years Microsoft had virtually no lobbying presence in Washington. Then one morning Bill Gates woke up to find that his company was accused of being Public Enemy No. 1—a Monopoly. Bill Clinton's Justice Department in 1998 filed an antitrust lawsuit charging the company with illegal bundling of Internet Explorer into its operating system. The anti-trust action threatened to break up the company just like AT&T was divided into the "Baby Bells." The costly battle that followed bloodied the company's reputation. Properly instructed in the ways of Washington, Microsoft proceeded to hire the town's best-connected lawyers and lobbyists.

"The entire tech industry has learned from Microsoft . . . Washington and its policy debates are important. We can't ignore them." This was the head of Google's Washington office underlining the firm's desire to avoid Microsoft's misfortunes. The dangers of not hiring lobbyists was reinforced in the early 2000s, when Google co-founder Sergey Brin had trouble getting meetings with members of Congress when he came to DC—even after the site had become the world's most popular search engine. In 2003 Google established a DC office. (See the box "A Washington Shakedown.")

Political scientists have pointed out that when groups with sufficient resources feel that their political or economic interests are endangered, they will organize to influence a government that can change the rules of the game. Firms use lobbyists to monitor the policy agenda, push for favorable concessions, and fight off competitors. In a "spiral" of activities, competing businesses feel the need to match each other—as well as countering efforts by citizen groups, labor unions,

A Washington Shakedown

Satirist Michael Kinsley described the political arena confronting new hi-tech companies. *"It's a vast protection racket, practiced by politicians and political operatives of both parties. Nice little software company you've got here. Too bad if we have to regulate it, or if big government programs force us to raise its taxes. Your archrival just wrote a big check to the Washington Bureaucrats Benevolent Society. Are you sure you wouldn't like to do the same"*?

—*Los Angeles Times,* Op-Ed, April 5, 2011.

and political interests. Lobbying has become in modern America a normal expense of doing business for large enterprises like Google.

THE BUSINESS OF LOBBYING COMPETITORS

Google's Washington presence focused on its intense rivalry with Microsoft. An advertising partnership with Yahoo! in 2008 was defeated after Microsoft lobbied against it. Google returned the favor by helping launch an antitrust complaint to the Justice Department arguing that Microsoft's Vista operating system discriminated against Google software. The inquiry resulted in Microsoft changing its design to allow the Google search option.

The Washington fights between the rival cyberspace giants heated up. It took intense lobbying before Google won approval from the Federal Trade Commission (FTC) in May 2010 to buy a mobile ad service firm, AdMob, for $750 million. The next year Google faced a challenge from the FTC investigating whether the firm had been favoring its own web services in search results by downgrading competing firms. Pushing for this investigation was Fair Search, a coalition of Internet companies, including Microsoft. Google's top lawyers responded by arguing that rivals Apple, Microsoft, and Oracle were intentionally increasing the cost of Google's Android system by buying patents that would make it more expensive for its phones to run the system. The press reported that Microsoft was holding meetings with other tech firms to get Washington regulators to scrutinize their competitor.

Google also sought to protect its public image, especially around the issue of privacy. Lawsuits before the courts in 2013 accused Google of scanning Gmail messages and employing users' words and likeness in advertisements. Gmail, it appeared, had become Google's "secret data-mining machine," to create user profiles and to provide targeted advertising unrelated to the transmission of e-mails. Eric Schmidt had not shown much sensitivity to critics' concerns about privacy when he declared, "If you have something that you don't want anyone to know maybe you shouldn't be doing it in the first place."

Conclusion

One inevitable step after another led Google to become an influential Washington lobby. From a small hi-tech startup, Google expanded to become the world's premier search engine and a major media corporation. That meant dealing with competitors, the government, the public, and the wider world. That, in turn, required experts in public relations and lobbying who could promote the company's interests in these arenas. By 2013 Google was spending over $18 million a year on lobbying, making it one of the 10 biggest lobbyists. A Washington operation was not just a cost of business; it was the price of success.

Wrap-Up

Both interest groups and media are bridges over which people and players can reach the political game. Interest groups provide the means for business, labor, professional, or citizens' organizations to make their views known to government officials. They unify people with common concerns to bring pressure on decision makers through grassroots campaigns, fundraising, lobbying, or publicity. Those interest groups with the most resources tend to be the most effective. Reforms to limit the influence of wealthy interests have been notably unsuccessful.

Media seem to be everywhere. As both a communications tool and an economic asset, media affect politics. Through news reports, entertainment, and advertisements, media shape the national agenda and frame the nation's leading issues and personalities. What is and is not broadcast and printed establishes political figures, sets priorities, focuses attention on issues, and largely makes politics understandable to people. The media in turn are affected by the corporations that own them, the advertisers that pay for their messages, the managers who run them, the sources who supply them with news, and the public that looks, reads, and listens to what they offer. Technology has increased the variety of media outlets and led to the merger of many of them under giant corporate banners. New forms of communications, like the Internet, have flourished, while traditional media, like newspapers, seem endangered.

Political leaders influence—and are influenced by—media in numerous ways. They grant them licenses if they are television and radio stations, are sources for the news about government and its policies that media reports, and shape information in ways favorable to their interests. Media give government feedback on programs, act as a watchdog exposing their foibles, and provide a voice for people to express their opinions. Campaigning candidates spend much of their days seeking free access to media or raising the money for ads. As a player and a communications link, the media are among the political game's most powerful, complex, and controversial forces.

Interest groups and media offer the potential for wide public participation. The rise in interest groups and the explosion of media outlets provide opportunities that could be used by a broader public. But it is the public itself that is likely to be used—by players enhancing their own political and economic positions. Interest groups, through lobbying campaigns, mobilize parts of the public to support their narrow interests. Media offer the public news-as-entertainment and track their online uses for the commercial benefits that come from claiming a large audience. The public is the object of their efforts, not the shaper. These instruments of power remain largely in the hands of the powerful.

THOUGHT QUESTIONS

1. Which interests are represented best by American interest groups? How would you reform interest groups so that groups that are now poorly represented would have a greater voice?
2. Do you think that President Obama's initial dismissal of lobbyists in government was realistic? Why did his policy change?
3. By making news entertaining, are media putting their commercial needs ahead of the goal of an informed public? Are public education and media entertainment contradictory goals?
4. How would you "save" newspapers? Some have suggested running them as nonprofit foundations? Or are they just economic dinosaurs that should be allowed to go extinct?
5. Do you think Google should be expected to act differently toward Washington than any other major corporation? How important are the values of the owners and managers in shaping the social and political goals of a business?

SUGGESTED READINGS

Interest Groups

Berry, Jeffrey M. and Clyde Wilcox. *The Interest Group Society*. 5th ed. New York: Longman, 2009. Pb.

A concise overview of how, and how much, interest groups influence American politics.

Buckley, Christopher. *They Shoot Puppies, Don't They?* New York: Grand Central Publishing, 2013. Pb.

A funny, smart novel about a desperate lobbyist almost starting a war with China just to get Congress to buy a client's top-secret product.

Graetz, Michael J. and Ian Shapiro. *Death by a Thousand Cuts*. Princeton, NJ: Princeton University Press, 2005.

An insightful case study of the campaign that turned the estate tax on multimillionaires' properties into an issue of fairness for ordinary people.

Kaiser, Robert G. *So Damn Much Money*. New York: Alfred A. Knopf, 2009, Pb.

Tracks the career of a liberal do-gooder becoming Washington's leading lobbyist. You can find out how universities were first in line for congressional pork.

Rauch, Jonathan. *Demosclerosis: The Silent Killer of American Government*. New York: Times Books, 1995. Pb.

Argues that what ails the body politic are too many interest groups clogging the arteries of government.

Media

Auletta, Ken. *Googled: The End of the World as We Know It*. London: Penguin Books, 2010. Pb.

A detailed account of how the Google wave washed over the media and the world.

Cook, Timothy E. *Governing with the News*. 2nd ed. Chicago: University of Chicago Press, 2005. Pb.

Traces the history of the media as a political institution joined at the hip with the government it negotiates with and serves.

McChesney, Robert and John Nichols. *The Death and Life of American Journalism*. Philadelphia: Nation Books, 2010.

An argument that journalism is a public good that needs government subsidies to survive.

O'Connor, Rory. *Friends, Followers and the Future*. San Francisco: City Lights, 2012, Pb

As the subtitle says: *How Social Media Are Changing Politics, Threatening Big Brands, and Killing Traditional Media*.

Street, John. *Mass Media, Politics and Democracy*, 2nd ed. London: Palgrave Macmillan, 2011. Pb.

A British scholar expertly analyzes the bias in modern media presentations of politics.

CHAPTER 9

Who Wins, Who Loses: Pluralism versus Elitism

I s American politics clear now? Or have we spent so much time describing the players and rules, the terms and institutions, that we have lost sight of the game? In this last chapter, we will step back from analyzing the trees to take a look at the woods. Put another way, we will ask basic questions: Who (if anyone) is running the game? Who wins, who loses? Who plays and who just watches?

It should not be surprising that there is no single accepted answer to these questions. Rather, there are at least two competing approaches to an answer. The traditional one, supported in some form by most political scientists and most of the players in the political game, is *pluralism*. Its competitor, the *elite* school of thought, has attracted supporters on both the right and left who are critical of the American political game. Recent views have modified and attempted to close the gap between the two sets of ideas.

Pluralism

Pluralism is a group theory of democracy. According to pluralism, society contains a variety of groups with access to government officials, and these organizations compete and cooperate to influence policy decisions. Although people as individuals do not usually have much power in politics, they can gain influence through their membership in what de Tocqueville called "associations." These groups bargain among themselves and with government institutions. The compromises that result become public policy.

Four key concepts make up the pluralist argument: *fragmentation of power, bargaining, compromise*, and *consensus*.

Fragmentation of power is the pluralists' way of saying that no one group dominates the political game. Power is divided, though not equally, among a large number of groups—labor unions, corporations, nonprofits, religions, ethnic populations, and many others. To gain their goals, the groups must *bargain* with each other. Within this bargaining process, the government, though it may have its own interests, acts essentially as a referee. The government will make sure the rules of the game are followed and may intervene to help groups that consistently have less power than their opponents. It also is to the advantage of all the groups to follow the "rules of the game," because the bargaining-compromise method is the most effective way to win changes.

The result of this bargaining process is inevitably a series of *compromises*. Because no single group dominates, each must take a little less than it wants in order to gain the support of the others. This accommodation is made easier because both the interests and the membership of the groups overlap. Groups disagreeing on one issue know that they may need each other's support in the future on another issue. Individuals may be a member of two groups with different views on an issue. Their membership in both will tend to reduce the conflict between them. A black doctor may be an official of the American Medical Association (AMA), which opposes expanded programs of government-sponsored health care, but also be a member of the National Association for the Advancement of Colored People (NAACP), which supports these programs. His overlapping memberships may sway this doctor to moderate the positions of the groups and encourage them to compromise with each other.

Underlying this bargaining-compromise process is a *consensus*— an agreement on basic political questions that reasonably satisfies most groups. This agreement on the rules of the game, and also on most of its results, is the basic cooperative cement that binds society together. Aspects of this consensus in American society are the general agreement on the importance of civil liberties, on equal opportunity for all citizens, on the necessity for compromise, and on the right of citizens to voice their political views. The pluralists maintain not only that there is widespread participation (open to all who wish to organize) in political decisions but also that the decisions themselves, and the procedures by which they are reached, have a consensus in society behind them. Government decisions, in the pluralist universe, essentially reflect the compromises reached by the major groups in the political system.

The picture that pluralism presents is of a process of bargaining among organized groups and also between these groups and various parts of the government. The bargaining results in a series of compromises that become public policy and determine who gets what, when, and how. A widespread consensus on the rules and results of this process keeps the political game from descending into unmanageable conflict.

Examples of Pluralism

Pluralists have no difficulty pointing to examples of the bargaining-compromise process. When major environmental groups decided that a new law regulating air pollution was needed, they formed a Clean Air Coalition to lead the fight. Helped by environmental lobbyists, the coalition raised funds from members of wealthy groups like the Environmental Defense Fund and the Sierra Club. Big oil and insurance companies, tired of fighting lawsuits brought under what they considered unrealistic regulations, reluctantly lobbied for compromise proposals. They also worried about public opinion, which strongly supported the environmentalists' health arguments over business' cost objections. The press weighed in with editorials and generally favorable coverage. The government's Environmental Protection Agency (EPA), making sure its concerns were covered, supported the bill with studies and testimony. The appropriate committees of the House and Senate, reacting to substantive arguments, political pressures, and, yes, fundraising, approved a bill that became the Clean Air Act. Pluralists would say the law reflected the relative power of the various groups as well as the compromises they reached.

A classic study supporting the pluralist model is Robert Dahl's book on politics in New Haven, Connecticut, *Who Governs?* Dahl examined several important issues, such as urban development and public education, to see who made the key decisions. He concluded that the people influential in education policy were not the same as those involved in urban development or transportation or political nominations. Dahl concluded there was not just one economic and social elite wielding political power in New Haven. In a later book, *On Democracy*, Dahl updated and argued the virtues of democracy, and under what conditions it exists in modern societies. (See "The Pluralist View.")

Criticisms of Pluralist Theory

Pluralism has run into numerous criticisms. One argument condemns pluralism for emphasizing *how* the political game is played rather than *why* people play it. Critics say that the pluralists do not give enough importance to how benefits really are distributed. A consensus supporting equal opportunity is not the same as actually having equality. A system of democratic procedures may simply conceal the powerful having their way. The argument often goes on to say that there can be no political equality without social and economic conditions being equal for all. Critics of pluralism ask, "What good are the rules of the game to the majority of people who never get a chance to play?"

Other critics point out that pluralists believe that groups will balance off each other, producing a self-regulating stable system. But what if everyone sees the value in forming a group to gain more benefits from the government? Political inflation leads to so many competing groups making so many demands that the government begins to choke on unnecessary programs that—since no one wants to pay more taxes—can only be funded by ever-higher budget deficits. This *hyperpluralism* is for some observers a more accurate, if more pessimistic, portrait of current American politics than is traditional pluralism.

The Pluralist View

The fact is that the Economic Notables operate within that vague political consensus, the prevailing system of beliefs, to which all the major groups in the community subscribe. . . . Within limits, they can influence the content of that belief system; but they cannot determine it wholly (p. 84).

In the United States the political stratum does not constitute a homogeneous class with well-defined class interests (p. 91).

Thus the distribution of resources and the ways in which they are or are not used in a pluralistic political system like New Haven's constitute an important source of both political change and political stability. If the distribution and use of resources gives aspiring leaders great opportunities for gaining influences, these very features also provide a built-in throttle that makes it difficult for any leader, no matter how skillful, to run away with the system (p. 310).

Source: Robert A. Dahl. *Who Governs?* New Haven, CT: Yale University Press, 1961.

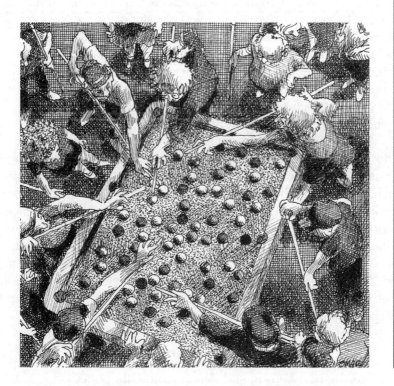

Elite

Many of those disagreeing with pluralism believe that an *elite* approach more realistically describes American politics. Supporters of this concept see society as dominated by unified and nonrepresentative leaders often called the *power elite*. This elite occupies the important decision-making positions while encouraging powerlessness below. Those in power do not represent the diversity in society. Instead, they look after their own interests and prevent dissenting views from surfacing. American politics is not a collection of pluralist groups maintaining a balance of power among themselves but an elite of economic, political, and military leaders in unresponsive control of the political game.

This elite rules the country through the positions that its members occupy. Power does not come from individuals or pluralist groups but from *institutions*. Thus, to have power you need a key role in a leading institution of the society—you have to be the chief executive of a Fortune 500 corporation, a cabinet secretary, or a full admiral in the navy. The argument broadens to a criticism of society's social classes, which limit who can climb up to these leadership positions. They are open only to the rich and the powerful, the *ruling class* of the country, whose names can be found in major newspapers' society columns and whose children go to the "right" schools. This influential class controls the country's economy and uses political power to preserve the status quo, that includes their own privileges.

The results of this elite control, needless to say, are different from the pluralist outcome. Political decisions, rather than representing a consensus in society, merely represent the *conflict* within it. Society is held together not by widespread popular agreements but by force and control: the control the elite has over the majority. The only consensus that exists is that some have power and others do not. From this pessimistic viewpoint, politics is a constant conflict between those with power (who seek to keep it) and those without power (who seek to gain it). The policies that result from this political game reflect the conflict between the elite and the majority, and domination of the more than 99 percent by the less than 1 percent.

Elite Examples

One of the best-known, and denounced, elite policy organizations is the Council on Foreign Relations. It was founded after World War I by what would loosely be called the Eastern Establishment—socially connected, New York–based bankers, lawyers, and academics. One study found that 23 of the country's largest banks and corporations had four or more directors who were members of the council. Its members played crucial roles after World War II in creating the International Monetary Fund, the World Bank, and the United Nations. Its journal, *Foreign Affairs*, is a must-read for foreign policy decision makers, many of whom are members of the council. Its discussion groups bring together leaders from business, government, universities, and the military. To those in the council, it is a policy-oriented group analyzing issues and producing broad leadership understanding of American foreign policy challenges. To critics of the elite, it looks more like an old boys' network dividing up jobs and deciding issues among themselves.

A noted study of elite control in the United States, *The Power Elite*, was written by Columbia University sociologist C. Wright Mills, who maintained that American politics was dominated by a unified group of leaders from corporations, the military, and politics. Continuing the Mills tradition, William Greider's *Who Will Tell the People?* studies Washington politics in the 1990s. Greider sees a policymaking elite working with wealthy economic interests to pass and implement laws and regulations to protect the big corporations. Even reforms of the system are "fixed." Parties and media, rather than mobilizing citizens around authentic national reforms, manipulate them to promote elite interests. The answer to the question that begins Greider's book, "Who speaks for the people?" is "No one."

David Rothkopf expands Mills and Greider to the world in *Superclass: The Global Power Elite and the World They Are Making*. The book identifies roughly 6,000 individuals (mostly men, but Angelina Jolie is in) who have "the ability to regularly influence the lives of millions of people in multiple countries worldwide." Through their membership on boards of corporations, universities, think tanks, and foundations, they network with each other. Their loyalties are more to each other than to any particular nation. (See "The Elite View.")

Criticisms of the Elite View

Critics have been quick to join in the battle with the elite view. Although they may agree that only a few people participate in politics, they argue that this minority of activists is much less unified than elite theory asserts. They point to political conflicts over taxes or the environment or overseas wars or any presidential election as examples of how elites check and balance each other. These elites compete, and democracy consists of people choosing between them through the

The Elite View

"Of all the powers the superclass possesses, one of the clearest and most important is the ability to set agendas for the rest of us." (p. 303)

"Today, the most powerful elites are global citizens tied more to international finance than national politics." (p. 320)

"Conspiracy theory is the comfort food of politics ... it fills a fundamental desire to balance perceived causes with perceived consequences and thus satisfies our sense that big outcomes are not the product of happenstance." (p. 254)

Source: David, Rothkopf. *Superclass.* New York: Farrar Straus and Giroux, 2008.

vote. Besides, some critics argue, the political ideals of democracy are probably in better, if fewer, hands than they would be under the control of an uninformed majority. Public surveys have shown intolerance for dissent among the less educated and lower classes. Hence, greater participation might, curiously enough, mean fewer liberties and less democracy, not more.

Another criticism aimed at some careless power elite supporters is that they are *conspiracy theorists*. Ideologues on both the right and left may veer close to blaming certain racial, religious, or economic groups for betraying democracy. The reasoning often becomes circular: American politics is governed by a secret conspiracy "covered up" by certain groups or people, which of course makes "proof" impossible. Such conspiracies are responsible for everything from President Kennedy's assassination to the World Trade Center bombings, the AIDS epidemic, and President Obama's birth records. These conspiracies remove politics from rational debate, polarize public opinion, and allow demagogues to manipulate naïve followers, usually to raise money.

The Debate

The debate between supporters of the pluralist and elite theories does not boil down to *whether* a small number of people dominate the political game. Even in the pluralist model, the bargaining among the groups is carried on by relatively few leaders on behalf of their groups. Clearly only a minority of people directly participate in politics, and this small group has more influence than the majority of people. The central questions are how *competitive* and *representative* these elites are.

To what degree do elites compete rather than cooperate with one another over who gets what, when, and how? How much conflict is there between, say, heads of government agencies and corporations over regulation and taxes? Or how much do they share views on major questions of policy and cooperate among themselves regardless of the "public good"? Certainly anyone reading the newspaper can point to numerous examples of conflicts over policy among groups in the political arena. Are these conflicts to be dismissed as mere bickering among a small bunch of buddies on the top? Or are vital issues being resolved in fairly open free-for-all contests?

Next is the question of how representative these elites are of the broader public. Do powerful groups reflect, however imperfectly, the wishes of the majority? In recent years, elite circles in America have opened their doors, not always voluntarily, to minorities and women. Has this made these public and private organizations more representative or at least more aware of the wishes of formerly excluded groups of people? Is this just tokenism, or can the leaders of these associations, businesses, parties, or government agencies claim to represent a more diverse, more popularly based, public opinion?

Is there, in fact, a "public opinion," or has that been distorted beyond recognition? Take the question of what we watch from the Hollywood entertainment industry. After America witnessed horrible shootings in its public schools, critics charged that popular movies, television programs, and video games were undermining traditional family values. Leaving aside whether these media deserve to be blamed for gun violence in America, do we know why media content seems so outrageous? Some say it is because an elite seeking its own profits controls what we see. Others argue that abundant violence, casual sex, and silly commercials reflect what the majority wants, as shown by opinion polls. But do these polls reflect what people actually want or what they are conditioned to want? Do elites, including elected officials, follow public opinion? Or do they use polls to manipulate the public to follow their own preferences?

A glance back at the case studies following our chapters reminds us how difficult it is to put the political game under a single umbrella of ideas. The use of the Internet in Obama's 2012 presidential campaign seems to be an encouraging sign of using modern technology to encourage grassroots participation, despite its polarizing impact. The case of the decline and fall of racial segregation is even more clear-cut—a widespread popular movement resolving a difficult political conflict, but requiring years of struggle by citizens and leaders.

The other cases are not as clear. President Bush's response to 9/11 was both timely and popular, but it hardly reflected policies produced by a broad debate among a diversity of voices. His administration's reaction to Hurricane Katrina was neither timely nor adequate, and the input of political voices unfortunately dissolved into a confusion of noise. Even in calmer times, the courts had difficulty restraining the executive's security agencies to follow the Constitution's protections of civil liberties in the war on terrorism. The study of Congress unwilling or unable to pass climate change legislation shows political leaders failing to respond to a national problem and a public concern because of the power of wealthy economic interests. And one of these interests, Google, saw no way around "playing the Washington game" through lobbyists and fundraising. Both in process and results, the pluralist and elite frameworks highlight certain parts of America's politics but ignore others.

Newer Views

The pluralist and elite approaches are two ends of a range of ideas about American politics. Recent modifications have attempted to bridge the gap between the two. One has discussed a *plural elitism*. This stresses that politics is divided into separate policy arenas where narrow elites dominate, usually at the expense of the public interest. So, for example, when it comes to deciding on government spending levels for the army, a triangle of military leaders, defense industry corporations, and key congressional committees dominate the decisions, making sure this trio of interests benefit, usually at the public expense. The general public is confused by ideology and patriotic symbols from clearly seeing the elite dominance that is occurring in these issue arenas.

Underlying this approach is the view that whether pluralists or the power elite school are right depends on which political conflicts we are talking about. Sometimes, as in town hall meetings held in many New England towns, we can see a number of views being expressed and a democratic decision being reached by the community. In other areas, such as the making of antiterrorism policies, a small number of unelected national security officials meeting behind closed doors decide issues that will affect the lives of millions. The issue being decided is likely to affect how decisions will be made and who participates. Pluralism may be most appropriate in describing a small community's politics, but the elite approach may help us understand the executive branch's making of foreign policy.

Other students of American politics have emphasized how the *government* itself acts. In both pluralism and elitism, government actions are basically viewed as the result of outside forces: in one case, compromises between different groups; in the other, the wishes and interests of a unified elite. But clearly government—its major branches and agencies—is more than a passive mirror reflecting dominant outside groups. Government has goals of its own and may even, at times, act to represent a broad national interest.

The concept of power may need to be more broadly defined to understand who is influential in politics and how. "Power" may not be just the ability to influence political decisions; it may also involve preventing issues from even reaching the agenda of decision makers. Having power may explain what does not happen, not just how behavior is changed. People may not voice grievances that, looking back, historians conclude they may have felt. Just because air pollution is poisoning children doesn't make it a political issue; women in other countries may be more oppressed than in America, and yet without leadership and awareness they may not see a political solution for their condition. Power is not just changing behavior but, in this case, preventing that change. The openness of pluralism does not guarantee needed reforms or real democracy.

The concepts we adopt as most accurately reflecting political reality are bound also to reflect our own ideals. The pluralists and elitists (and those in between) are asking not only what *is* but what *should be*. The pluralists state that politics in America is democratic, with widespread participation in decisions to which most people agree. The elitists say that politics is dominated by an elite that controls the rest of us in its own interest. The elitists contend that basic changes in the American system are needed to create a pluralist democracy, while the pluralists argue that we have one and that the means for change are available within it.

What do you think? The position you take will reflect not only your understanding and study of politics but also your political ideals, interests, and experiences. Further, the position you take will guide your future political choices.

WRAP-UP

This book has presented American politics as a game. We have discussed the nature of the game and how the competition takes place. We talked about the rules of the conflict, many of them in the Constitution, and how they have changed. Most of the book has introduced the major governmental and nongovernmental players, their history, organization, and influence. This last chapter has looked at two schools of thought that try to analyze how the game is really played and sum up who wins and loses. But we are not quite finished.

What we have called this "game" of politics is more than that. It is a contest that defines who we are as a people: whether we are selfish or generous, arrogant or compassionate, brave or fearful. Like any country, America is a mix of conflicting values and interests, amplified by great wealth and power. Which America will win out? Will it reflect an America of pioneers who expanded on the democratic principles they inherited, offering them to those who had once been excluded while defending them at great cost in blood and treasure? Or will it be a self-righteous America so lulled by material comfort that it can refuse to listen to voices seeking justice at home and abroad? The answers lie in the political game.

We did say that most of us are spectators of the game—nonparticipants. But just as politics is a special kind of game, so too are we a special kind of audience. We *can* participate in the game and, by participating, change the way the game is played and even its outcome. A respected scholar of politics wrote:

> Political conflict is not like a football game, played on a measured field by a fixed number of players in the presence of an audience scrupulously excluded from the playing field. Politics is much more like the original primitive game of football in which everybody was free to join, a game in which the whole population of one town might play the entire population of another town moving freely back and forth across the countryside.
>
> Many conflicts are narrowly confined by a variety of devices, but the distinctive quality of political conflicts is that the relations between the players and the audience have not been well defined and there is usually nothing to keep the audience from getting into the game.

Someone said that war is too important to be left to generals. In a similar spirit, American politics may be too important to be left to politicians. In whatever way you think best, get in the game.

THOUGHT QUESTIONS

1. Give examples from throughout the book that support the pluralist approach. Give other examples that lean toward the power elite.
2. Pluralism has been described as essentially "liberal," whereas elitism can be either "radical" or "conservative." Do you agree?
3. Which approach, pluralism or elitism, do you feel best describes the political game in your own community? Give examples.
4. Do you think interest in politics is growing among students? Why or why not? Is political participation by students encouraged or discouraged? How?

SUGGESTED READINGS

Dahl, Robert A. *Who Governs?* New Haven, CT: Yale University Press, 1961. Pb.
A classic study showing pluralism operating in New Haven's city government.
———. *On Democracy*. New Haven, CT: Yale University Press, 1998.
Intelligently reviews and argues the merits of democracy.
D'Souza, Dinesh. *What's So Great about America?* New York: Regnery Publishing, 2002.
An articulate conservative immigrant fires away at critics of the United States of America.
Greider, William. *Who Will Tell the People*. New York: Simon & Schuster, 1992.
This *Rolling Stone* editor gives a muckraking view of how issues are wheeled and dealed in Washington with little regard for the American people.
Lukes, Steven. *Power: A Radical View*, 2nd ed. New York: Palgrave Macmillan, 2005. Pb.
An English theorist examines the "least observable" aspects of power.
Mills, C. Wright. *The Power Elite*. New York: Oxford University Press, 1959. Pb.
A well-known sociologist's attempt to show that an elite governs America in its own interest.
Packer, George. *The Unwinding*. New York: Farrar, Straus and Giroux, 2013, Pb.
Compelling stories of how Americans' lives have broken down over the last 30 years under the battering of a dissolving economy.
Rothkopf, David. *Superclass: The Global Power Elite and the World They Are Making*. New York: Farra Straus and Giroux, 2008.
A former member of the global elite dissects it and urges it to reform the unequal, unstable world it is creating.
Schattschneider, E. E. *The Semisovereign People*. New York: Holt, Rinehart & Winston, 1961. Pb.
This landmark work presents a basic explanation of how and why some people get into politics and some stay out.

APPENDIX

The Declaration of Independence

In Congress, July 4, 1776

The Unanimous Declaration of the Thirteen United States of America

When in the Course of human events, it becomes necessary for one people to dissolve the political bands, which have connected them with another, and to assume among the powers of the earth, the separate and equal station to which the Laws of Nature and of Nature's God entitle them, a decent respect to the opinions of mankind requires that they should declare the causes which impel them to the separation.—We hold these truths to be self-evident, that all men are created equal, that they are endowed by their Creator with certain unalienable Rights, that among these are Life, Liberty and the pursuit of Happiness.—That to secure these rights, Governments are instituted among Men, deriving their just powers from the consent of the governed,—That whenever any Form of Government becomes destructive of these ends, it is the Right of the People to alter or to abolish it, and to institute new Government, laying its foundation on such principles and organizing its powers in such form, as to them shall seem most likely to effect their Safety and Happiness. Prudence, indeed, will dictate that Governments long established should not be changed for light and transient causes; and accordingly all experience hath shown, that mankind are more disposed to suffer, while evils are sufferable, than to right themselves by abolishing the forms to which they are accustomed. But when a long train of abuses and usurpations, pursuing invariably the same Object evinces a design to reduce them under absolute Despotism, it is their right, it is their duty, to throw off such Government, and to provide new Guards for their future security.—Such has been the patient sufferance of these Colonies; and such is now the necessity which constrains them to alter their former Systems of Government. The history of the present King of Great Britain is a history of repeated injuries and usurpations, all having in direct object the establishment of an absolute Tyranny over these States. To prove this, let Facts be submitted to a candid world.—He has refused his Assent to Laws, the most wholesome and necessary for the public good.—He has forbidden his Governors to pass Laws of immediate and pressing importance, unless suspended in their operation till his Assent should be obtained; and when so suspended, he has utterly neglected to attend to them.—He has refused to pass other Laws for the accommodation of large districts of people, unless those people would relinquish the right of Representation in the Legislature, a right inestimable to them and formidable to tyrants only.—He has called together legislative bodies at places unusual, uncomfortable, and distant from the depository of their public Records, for the sole purpose of fatiguing them into compliance with his measures.—He has dissolved Representative Houses repeatedly, for opposing with manly firmness his invasions on the rights of the people.—He has refused for a long time, after such dissolutions, to cause others to be elected; whereby the Legislative powers, incapable of Annihilation, have returned to the People at large for their exercise; the State remaining in the meantime exposed to all the dangers of invasion from without, and convulsions within.—He has endeavored to prevent the population of these States; for that purpose obstructing the Laws for Naturalization of Foreigners; refusing to pass others to encourage their migrations hither, and raising the conditions of new Appropriations of Lands.—He has obstructed the Administration of Justice, by refusing his Assent to Laws for establishing Judiciary powers.—He has made Judges dependent on his Will alone, for the tenure of their offices, and the amount and payment of their salaries.—He has erected a multitude of New Offices, and sent hither swarms of Officers to harass our people, and eat out their substance.—He has kept among us, in times of peace, Standing Armies without the Consent of our legislatures.—He has affected to render the Military independent of and superior to the Civil power.—He has combined with others to subject us to a jurisdiction foreign to our constitution, and unacknowledged by our laws; giving his Assent to their Acts of pretended Legislation.—For quartering large bodies of armed troops among us:—For protecting them, by a mock Trial, from punishment for any Murders which they should commit on the Inhabitants of these States:—For cutting off our Trade with all parts of the world:—For imposing Taxes on us without our Consent:—For depriving us in many cases, of the benefits of Trial by Jury:—For transporting us beyond Seas to be tried for pretended offenses:—For abolishing the free System of English Laws in a neighboring Province, establishing therein an Arbitrary government, and enlarging its Boundaries so as to render it at once an example and fit instrument for introducing the same absolute rule into these Colonies:—For taking away our Charters, abolishing our most valuable Laws, and altering fundamentally the Forms of our Governments:—For suspending our own Legislatures, and declaring themselves invested with power to legislate for us in all cases whatsoever.—He has abdicated Government here, by declaring us out of his Protection and waging War against us.—He has plundered our seas, ravaged our Coasts, burnt our towns, and destroyed the lives of our people.—He is at this time transporting large armies of foreign Mercenaries to complete the works of death, desolation and tyranny, already begun with circumstances of Cruelty & perfidy, scarcely paralleled in the most barbarous ages, and totally unworthy the Head of a civilized nation.—He has constrained our fellow Citizens taken Captive on the High Seas to bear Arms against their Country, to become the executioners of their friends and Brethren, or to fall themselves by their hands.—He has excited domestic insurrections amongst us, and has endeavored to bring on the inhabitants of our frontiers, the merciless Indian Savages, whose known rule of warfare, is an undistinguished destruction of all ages, sexes and conditions. In every stage of these Oppressions We have Petitioned for Redress in the most humble terms: Our repeated Petitions have been answered only by repeated injury. A Prince whose character is thus marked by every act which may define a Tyrant, is unfit to be the ruler of a free people. Nor have We been wanting in attentions to our British brethren. We have warned them from time to time of attempts by their legislature to extend an unwarrantable jurisdiction over us. We have reminded them of the circumstances of our emigration and settlement here. We have appealed to their native justice and magnanimity, and we have conjured them by the ties of our common kindred to disavow these usurpations, which would inevitably interrupt our connections and correspondence. They too have been deaf to the voice of justice and of consanguinity. We must, therefore, acquiesce in the necessity, which denounces our Separation, and hold them, as we hold the rest of mankind, Enemies in War, in Peace Friends.—

We, therefore, the Representatives of the United States of America, in General Congress, Assembled, appealing to the Supreme Judge of the world for the rectitude of our intentions do, in the Name, and by the Authority of the good People of these Colonies, solemnly publish and declare, That these United Colonies are, and of Right ought to be Free and Independent States, that they are Absolved from all Allegiance to the British Crown, and that all political connection between them and the State of Great Britain, is and ought to be totally dissolved; and that as Free and Independent States, they have full Power to levy War, conclude Peace, contract Alliances, establish Commerce, and to do all other Acts and Things which Independent States may of right do.—And for the support of this Declaration, with a firm reliance on the protection of divine Providence, we mutually pledge to each other our Lives, our Fortunes and our sacred Honor.

The Constitution of the United States

Submitted on September 17, 1787 by the Constitutional Convention, and became effective on March 4, 1789.

We the People of the United States, in Order to form a more perfect Union, establish Justice, insure domestic Tranquility, provide for the common defense, promote the general Welfare, and secure the Blessings of Liberty to ourselves and our Posterity, do ordain and establish this CONSTITUTION for the United States of America.

Article I

Section 1. All legislative Powers herein granted shall be vested in a Congress of the United States, which shall consist of a Senate and House of Representatives.

Section 2. (1) The House of Representatives shall be composed of Members chosen every second Year by the People of the several States, and the Electors in each State shall have the Qualifications requisite for Electors of the most numerous Branch of the State Legislature.

(2) No Person shall be a Representative who shall not have attained to the Age of twenty-five Years, and been seven Years a Citizen of the United States, and who shall not, when elected, be an Inhabitant of that State in which he shall be chosen.

(3) [Representatives and direct Taxes[1] shall be apportioned among the several States which may be included within this Union, according to their respective Numbers, which shall be determined by adding to the whole Number of free Persons, including those bound to Service for a Term of Years, and excluding Indians not taxed, three fifths of all other Persons.][2] The actual Enumeration shall be made within three Years after the first Meeting of the Congress of the United States, and within every subsequent Term of ten Years, in such Manner as they shall by Law direct. The Number of Representatives shall not exceed one for every thirty Thousand, but each State shall have at Least one Representative; and until such enumeration shall be made, the State of New Hampshire shall be entitled to choose three, Massachusetts eight, Rhode-Island and Providence Plantations one, Connecticut five, New York six, New Jersey four, Pennsylvania eight, Delaware one, Maryland six, Virginia ten, North Carolina five, South Carolina five, and Georgia three.

(4) When vacancies happen in the Representation from any State, the Executive Authority thereof shall issue Writs of Election to fill such Vacancies.

(5) The House of Representatives shall choose their Speaker and other Officers; and shall have the sole Power of Impeachment.

Section 3. (1) The Senate of the United States shall be composed of two Senators from each State, [chosen by the Legislature][3] thereof, for six Years; and each Senator shall have one Vote.

(2) Immediately after they shall be assembled in Consequence of the first Election, they shall be divided as equally as may be into three Classes. The Seats of the Senators of the first Class shall be vacated at the Expiration of the second Year, of the second Class at the Expiration of the fourth Year, and of the third Class at the Expiration of the sixth Year, so that one-third may be chosen every second year; [and if Vacancies happen by Resignation, or otherwise, during the Recess of the Legislature

---

[1] The Sixteenth Amendment replaced this with respect to income taxes.

[2] Repealed by the Fourteenth Amendment.

[3] Repealed by the Seventeenth Amendment.

of any State, the Executive thereof may make temporary Appointments until the next Meeting of the Legislature, which shall then fill such Vacancies].[4]

(3) No person shall be a Senator who shall not have attained to the Age of thirty Years, and been nine Years a Citizen of the United States, and who shall not, when elected, be an Inhabitant of that State for which he shall be chosen.

(4) The Vice President of the United States shall be President of the Senate, but shall have no Vote, unless they be equally divided.

(5) The Senate shall choose their other Officers, and also a President *pro tempore,* in the Absence of the Vice President, or when he shall exercise the Office of President of the United States.

(6) The Senate shall have the sole Power to try all Impeachments. When sitting for that Purpose, they shall be on Oath or Affirmation. When the President of the United States is tried, the Chief Justice shall preside: And no Person shall be convicted without the Concurrence of two thirds of the Members present.

(7) Judgment in Cases of Impeachment shall not extend further than to removal from Office, and disqualification to hold and enjoy any Office of honor, Trust or Profit under the United States; but the Party convicted shall nevertheless be liable and subject to Indictment, Trial, Judgment and Punishment according to Law.

Section 4. (1) The Times, Places and Manner of holding Elections for Senators and Representatives, shall be prescribed in each State by the Legislature thereof, but the Congress may at any time by Law make or alter such Regulations, except as to the Places of choosing Senators.

(2) The Congress shall assemble at least once in every Year, and such Meeting shall [be on the first Monday in December,][5] unless they shall by Law appoint a different Day.

Section 5. (1) Each House shall be the Judge of the Elections, Returns and Qualifications of its own Members, and a Majority of each shall constitute a Quorum to do Business; but a smaller Number may adjourn from day to day, and may be authorized to compel the Attendance of absent Members, in such Manner, and under such Penalties as each House may provide.

(2) Each House may determine the Rules of its Proceedings, punish its Members for disorderly Behavior, and, with the Concurrence of two thirds, expel a Member.

(3) Each House shall keep a Journal of its Proceedings, and from time to time publish the same, excepting such Parts as may in their Judgment require Secrecy; and the Yeas and Nays of the Members of either House on any question shall, at the Desire of one fifth of those Present, be entered on the Journal.

(4) Neither House, during the Session of Congress, shall, without the Consent of the other, adjourn for more than three days, nor to any other Place than that in which the two Houses shall be sitting.

Section 6. (1) The Senators and Representatives shall receive a Compensation for their Services, to be ascertained by Law, and paid out of the Treasury of the United States. They shall in all Cases, except Treason, Felony and Breach of the Peace, be privileged from Arrest during their Attendance at the Session of their respective Houses, and in going to and returning from the same; and for any Speech or Debate in either House, they shall not be questioned in any other Place.

(2) No Senator or Representative shall, during the Time for which he was elected, be appointed to any civil Office under the Authority of the United States, which shall have been created, or the Emoluments whereof have been increased during such

---

[4]Changed by the Seventeenth Amendment.

[5]Changed by the Twentieth Amendment, Section 2.

time; and no Person holding any Office under the United States, shall be a Member of either House during his Continuance in Office.

Section 7. (1) All Bills for raising Revenue shall originate in the House of Representatives; but the Senate may propose or concur with Amendments as on other Bills.

(2) Every Bill which shall have passed the House of Representatives and the Senate, shall, before it becomes a Law, be presented to the President of the United States; If he approves he shall sign it, but if not he shall return it, with his Objections to that House in which it shall have originated, who shall enter the Objections at large on their Journal, and proceed to reconsider it. If after such Reconsideration two-thirds of that House shall agree to pass the Bill, it shall be sent, together with the Objections, to the other House, by which it shall likewise be reconsidered, and if approved by two thirds of that House, it shall become a Law. But in all such Cases the Votes of both Houses shall be determined by Yeas and Nays, and the Names of the Persons voting for and against the Bill shall be entered on the Journal of each House respectively. If any Bill shall not be returned by the President within ten Days (Sundays excepted) after it shall have been presented to him, the Same shall be a Law, in like Manner as if he had signed it, unless the Congress by their Adjournment prevent its Return, in which Case it shall not be a Law.

(3) Every Order, Resolution, or Vote to which the Concurrence of the Senate and House of Representatives may be necessary (except on a question of Adjournment) shall be presented to the President of the United States; and before the Same shall take Effect, shall be approved by him, or being disapproved by him, shall be repassed by two-thirds of the Senate and House of Representatives, according to the Rules and Limitations prescribed in the Case of a Bill.

Section 8. (1) The Congress shall have Power To lay and collect Taxes, Duties, Imposts and Excises, to pay the Debts and provide for the common Defense and general Welfare of the United States; but all Duties, Imposts and Excises shall be uniform throughout the United States;

(2) To borrow money on the credit of the United States;

(3) To regulate Commerce with foreign Nations, and among the several States, and with the Indian Tribes;

(4) To establish a uniform Rule of Naturalization, and uniform Laws on the subject of Bankruptcies throughout the United States;

(5) To coin Money, regulate the Value thereof, and of foreign Coin, and fix the Standard of Weights and Measures;

(6) To provide for the Punishment of counterfeiting the Securities and current Coin of the United States;

(7) To establish Post Offices and post Roads;

(8) To promote the Progress of Science and useful Arts, by securing for limited Times to Authors and Inventors the exclusive Right to their respective Writings and Discoveries;

(9) To constitute Tribunals inferior to the supreme Court;

(10) To define and punish Piracies and Felonies committed on the high Seas, and Offenses against the Law of Nations;

(11) To declare War, grant Letters of Marque and Reprisal, and make Rules concerning Captures on Land and Water;

(12) To raise and support Armies, but no Appropriation of Money to that Use shall be for a longer Term than two Years;

(13) To provide and maintain a Navy;

(14) To make Rules for the Government and Regulation of the land and naval Forces;

(15) To provide for calling forth the Militia to execute the Laws of the Union, suppress Insurrections and repel Invasions;

(16) To provide for organizing, arming, and disciplining the Militia, and for governing such Part of them as may be employed in the Service of the United States,

reserving to the States respectively, the Appointment of the Officers, and the Authority of training the Militia according to the discipline prescribed by Congress;

(17) To exercise exclusive Legislation in all Cases whatsoever, over such District (not exceeding ten Miles square) as may, by Cession of particular States, and the Acceptance of Congress, become the Seat of the Government of the United States, and to exercise like Authority over all Places purchased by the Consent of the Legislature of the State in which the Same shall be, for the Erection of Forts, Magazines, Arsenals, dock-Yards, and other needful Buildings;—And

(18) To make all Laws which shall be necessary and proper for carrying into Execution the foregoing Powers, and all other Powers vested by this Constitution in the Government of the United States, or in any Department or Officer thereof.

Section 9. (1) The Migration or Importation of such Persons as any of the States now existing shall think proper to admit, shall not be prohibited by the Congress prior to the Year one thousand eight hundred and eight, but a tax or duty may be imposed on such Importation, not exceeding ten dollars for each Person.

(2) The Privilege of the Writ of Habeas Corpus shall not be suspended, unless when in Cases of Rebellion or Invasion the public Safety may require it.

(3) No Bill of Attainder or ex post facto Law shall be passed.

(4) No Capitation, or other direct, Tax shall be laid, unless in Proportion to the Census or Enumeration herein before directed to be taken.[6]

(5) No Tax or Duty shall be laid on Articles exported from any State.

(6) No Preference shall be given by any Regulation of Commerce or Revenue to the Ports of one State over those of another; nor shall Vessels bound to, or from, one State, be obliged to enter, clear, or pay Duties in another.

(7) No Money shall be drawn from the Treasury, but in Consequence of Appropriations made by Law; and a regular Statement and Account of the Receipts and Expenditures of all public Money shall be published from time to time.

(8) No Title of Nobility shall be granted by the United States. And no Person holding any Office of Profit or Trust under them, shall, without the Consent of the Congress, accept of any present, Emolument, Office, or Title, of any kind whatever, from any King, Prince, or foreign State.

Section 10. (1) No State shall enter into any Treaty, Alliance, or Confederation; grant Letters of Marque and Reprisal; coin Money; emit Bills of Credit; make any Thing but gold and silver Coin a Tender in Payment of Debts; pass any Bill of Attainder, ex post facto Law, or Law impairing the Obligation of Contracts, or grant any Title of Nobility.

(2) No State shall, without the Consent of the Congress, lay any Imposts or Duties on Imports or Exports, except what may be absolutely necessary for executing its inspection Laws: and the net Produce of all Duties and Imposts, laid by any State on Imports or Exports, shall be for the Use of the Treasury of the United States; and all such laws shall be subject to the Revision and Control of the Congress.

(3) No State shall, without the Consent of Congress, lay any duty of Tonnage, keep Troops, or Ships of War in time of Peace, enter into any Agreement or Compact with another State, or with a foreign Power, or engage in War, unless actually invaded, or in such imminent Danger as will not admit of delay.

Article II

Section 1. (1) The executive Power shall be vested in a President of the United States of America. He shall hold his Office during the Term of four Years, and, together with the Vice-President, chosen for the same Term, be elected, as follows:

---

[6]Changed by the Sixteenth Amendment.

(2) Each State shall appoint, in such Manner as the Legislature thereof may direct, a Number of Electors, equal to the whole Number of Senators and Representatives to which the State may be entitled in the Congress; but no Senator or Representative, or Person holding an Office of Trust or Profit under the United States, shall be appointed an Elector.

[The Electors shall meet in their respective States, and vote by Ballot for two persons, of whom one at least shall not be an Inhabitant of the same State with themselves. And they shall make a List of all the Persons voted for, and of the Number of Votes for each; which List they shall sign and certify, and transmit sealed to the Seat of the Government of the United States, directed to the President of the Senate. The President of the Senate shall, in the Presence of the Senate and House of Representatives, open all the Certificates, and the Votes shall then be counted. The Person having the greatest Number of Votes shall be the President, if such Number be a Majority of the whole Number of Electors appointed; and if there be more than one who have such Majority, and have an equal Number of Votes, then the House of Representatives shall immediately choose by Ballot one of them for President; and if no Person have a Majority, then from the five highest on the List the said House shall in like Manner choose the President. But in choosing the President, the Votes shall be taken by States, the Representation from each State having one Vote; A quorum for this purpose shall consist of a Member or Members from two-thirds of the States, and a Majority of all the States shall be necessary to a Choice. In every Case, after the Choice of the President, the Person having the greatest Number of Votes of the Electors shall be the Vice-President. But if there should remain two or more who have equal Votes, the Senate shall choose from them by Ballot the Vice-President.][7]

(3) The Congress may determine the Time of choosing the Electors, and the Day on which they shall give their Votes; which Day shall be the same throughout the United States.

(4) No person except a natural born Citizen, or a Citizen of the United States, at the time of the Adoption of this Constitution, shall be eligible to the Office of President; neither shall any Person be eligible to that Office who shall not have attained to the Age of thirty-five Years, and been fourteen Years a Resident within the United States.

(5) In case of the Removal of the President from Office, or of his Death, Resignation, or Inability to discharge the Powers and Duties of the said Office, the same shall devolve on the Vice-President, and the Congress may by Law provide for the Case of Removal, Death, Resignation or Inability, both of the President and Vice-President, declaring what Officer shall then act as President, and such Officer shall act accordingly, until the Disability be removed, or a President shall be elected.[8]

(6) The President shall, at stated Times, receive for his Services, a Compensation, which shall neither be increased nor diminished during the Period for which he shall have been elected, and he shall not receive within that Period any other Emolument from the United States, or any of them.

(7) Before he enter on the Execution of his Office, he shall take the following Oath or Affirmation:—"I do solemnly swear (or affirm) that I will faithfully execute the Office of President of the United States, and will to the best of my Ability, preserve, protect and defend the Constitution of the United States."

Section 2. (1) The President shall be Commander in Chief of the Army and Navy of the United States, and of the Militia of the several States, when called into the actual Service of the United States; he may require the Opinion in writing, of the

---

[7]This paragraph was superseded in 1804 by the Twelfth Amendment.

[8]Changed by the Twenty-fifth Amendment.

principal Officer in each of the executive Departments, upon any subject relating to the Duties of their respective Offices, and he shall have Power to Grant Reprieves and Pardons for Offenses against the United States, except in Cases of Impeachment.

(2) He shall have Power, by and with the Advice and Consent of the Senate, to make Treaties, provided two-thirds of the Senators present concur; and he shall nominate, and by and with the Advice and Consent of the Senate, shall appoint Ambassadors, other public Ministers and Consuls, Judges of the supreme Court, and all other Officers of the United States, whose Appointments are not herein otherwise provided for, and which shall be established by Law: but the Congress may by Law vest the Appointment of such inferior Officers, as they think proper, in the President alone, in the Court of Law, or in the Heads of Departments.

(3) The President shall have Power to fill up all Vacancies that may happen during the Recess of the Senate, by granting Commissions which shall expire at the End of their next Session.

Section 3. He shall from time to time give to the Congress Information of the State of the Union, and recommend to their Consideration such Measures as he shall judge necessary and expedient; he may, on extraordinary Occasions, convene both Houses, or either of them, and in Case of Disagreement between them, with Respect to the Time of Adjournment, he may adjourn them to such Time as he shall think proper; he shall receive Ambassadors and other public Ministers; he shall take Care that the Laws be faithfully executed, and shall Commission all the Officers of the United States.

Section 4. The President, Vice President and all civil Officers of the United States, shall be removed from Office on Impeachment for, and Conviction of, Treason, Bribery, or other high Crimes and Misdemeanors.

Article III

Section 1. The judicial Power of the United States, shall be vested in one supreme Court, and in such inferior Courts as the Congress may from time to time ordain and establish. The Judges, both of the supreme and inferior Courts, shall hold their Offices during good Behavior, and shall, at stated Times, receive for their Services a Compensation which shall not be diminished during their Continuance in Office.

Section 2. (1) The judicial Power shall extend to all Cases, in Law and Equity, arising under this Constitution, the Laws of the United States, and Treaties made, or which shall be made, under their Authority;—to all Cases affecting Ambassadors, other public Ministers and Consuls;—to all Cases of admiralty and maritime Jurisdiction;—to Controversies to which the United States shall be a Party;—to Controversies between two or more states;—[between a State and Citizens of another State];[9]—between Citizens of different States;—between Citizens of the same State claiming Lands under Grants of different States, and [between a State, or the Citizens thereof, and foreign States, Citizens or Subjects].[10]

(2) In all Cases affecting Ambassadors, other public Ministers and Consuls, and those in which a State shall be Party, the supreme Court shall have original Jurisdiction. In all the other Cases before mentioned, the supreme Court shall have appellate Jurisdiction, both as to Law and Fact, with such Exceptions, and under such Regulations as the Congress shall make.

(3) The trial of all Crimes, except in Cases of Impeachment, shall be by Jury; and such Trial shall be held in the State where the said Crimes shall have been committed:

---

[9]Restricted by the Eleventh Amendment.

[10]Restricted by the Eleventh Amendment.

but when not committed within any State, the Trial shall be at such Place or Places as the Congress may by Law have directed.

Section 3. (1) Treason against the United States, shall consist only in levying War against them, or in adhering to their Enemies, giving them Aid and Comfort. No Person shall be convicted of Treason unless on the Testimony of two Witnesses to the same overt Act, or on Confession in open Court.

(2) The Congress shall have Power to declare the Punishment of Treason, but no Attainder of Treason shall work Corruption of Blood, or Forfeiture except during the Life of the Person attained.

Article IV

Section 1. Full Faith and Credit shall be given in each State to the public Acts, Records, and judicial Proceedings of every other State. And the Congress may by general Laws prescribe the Manner in which such Acts, Records and Proceedings shall be proved, and the Effect thereof.

Section 2. (1) The Citizens of each State shall be entitled to all Privileges and Immunities of Citizens in the several States.

(2) A Person charged in any State with Treason, Felony, or other Crime, who shall flee from Justice, and be found in another State, shall on demand of the executive Authority of the State from which he fled, be delivered up, to be removed to the State having Jurisdiction of the Crime.

(3) [No Person held to Service or Labor in one State, under the Laws thereof, escaping into another, shall, in Consequence of any Law or Regulation therein, be discharged from such Service or Labor, but shall be delivered up on Claim of the Party to whom such Service or Labor may be due.][11]

Section 3. (1) New States may be admitted by the Congress into this Union; but no new State shall be formed or erected within the Jurisdiction of any other State; nor any State be formed by the Junction of two or more States, or Parts of States, without the Consent of the Legislatures of the States concerned as well as of the Congress.

(2) The Congress shall have Power to dispose of and make all needful Rules and Regulations respecting the Territory or other Property belonging to the United States; and nothing in this Constitution shall be so construed as to Prejudice any Claims of the United States, or of any particular State.

Section 4. The United States shall guarantee to every State in this Union a Republican Form of Government, and shall protect each of them against Invasion; and on Application of the Legislature, or of the Executive (when the Legislature cannot be convened) against domestic Violence.

Article V

The Congress, whenever two-thirds of both Houses shall deem it necessary, shall propose Amendments to this Constitution, or, on the Application of the Legislatures of two-thirds of the several States, shall call a Convention for proposing Amendments, which, in either Case, shall be valid to all Intents and Purposes, as part of this Constitution, when ratified by the Legislature of three-fourths of the several States, or by Conventions in three-fourths thereof, as the one or the other Mode of Ratification may be proposed by the Congress; Provided that no Amendment which may be made prior to the Year One thousand eight hundred and eight shall in any Manner affect

---

[11]This paragraph was superseded by the Thirteenth Amendment.

the first and fourth Clauses in the Ninth Section of the first Article; and that no State, without its Consent, shall be deprived of its equal Suffrage in the Senate.

Article VI

(1) All Debts contracted and Engagements entered into, before the Adoption of this Constitution, shall be as valid against the United States under this Constitution, as under the Confederation.

(2) This Constitution, and the Laws of the United States which shall be made in Pursuance thereof; and all Treaties made, or which shall be made, under the Authority of the United States, shall be the supreme Law of the Land; and the Judges in every State shall be bound thereby, any Thing in the Constitution or Laws of any State to the Contrary notwithstanding.

(3) The Senators and Representatives before mentioned, and the Members of the several State Legislatures, and all executive and judicial Officers, both of the United States and of the several States, shall be bound by Oath or Affirmation, to support this Constitution; but no religious Test shall ever be required as a Qualification to any Office or public Trust under the United States.

Article VII

The Ratification of the Conventions of nine States, shall be sufficient for the Establishment of this Constitution between the States so ratifying the Same.

DONE in Convention by the Unanimous Consent of the States present the Seventeenth Day of September in the Year of our Lord one thousand seven hundred and Eighty seven and the Independence of the United States of America the Twelfth. In Witness whereof We have hereunto subscribed our Names.

Go. Washington
President and deputy from Virginia

Articles in Addition to, and Amendment of, the Constitution of the United States of America, Proposed by Congress, and Ratified by the Legislatures of the Several States, Pursuant to the Fifth Article of the Original Constitution.

Amendment I[12]

Congress shall make no law respecting an establishment of religion, or prohibiting the free exercise thereof; or abridging the freedom of speech, or of the press; or the right of the people peaceably to assemble, and to petition the Government for a redress of grievances.

Amendment II

A well regulated Militia, being necessary to the security of a free State, the right of the people to keep and bear Arms, shall not be infringed.

Amendment III

No Soldier shall, in time of peace be quartered in any house, without the consent of the Owner, nor in time of war, but in a manner to be prescribed by law.

---

[12]The first ten amendments were adopted in 1791.

Amendment IV

The right of the people to be secure in their persons, houses, papers, and effects, against unreasonable searches and seizures, shall not be violated, and no Warrants shall issue, but upon probable cause, supported by Oath or affirmation, and particularly describing the place to be searched, and the persons or things to be seized.

Amendment V

No person shall be held to answer for a capital, or otherwise infamous crime, unless on a presentment or indictment of a Grand Jury, except in cases arising in the land or naval forces, or in the Militia, when in actual service in time of War or public danger; nor shall any person be subject for the same offense to be twice put in jeopardy of life or limb; nor shall be compelled in any criminal case to be witness against himself, nor be deprived of life, liberty, or property, without due process of law; nor shall private property be taken for public use without just compensation.

Amendment VI

In all criminal prosecutions, the accused shall enjoy the right to a speedy and public trial, by an impartial jury of the State and district wherein the crime shall have been committed, which district shall have been previously ascertained by law, and to be informed of the nature and cause of the accusation, to be confronted with the witnesses against him; to have compulsory process for obtaining witnesses in his favor, and to have the Assistance of Counsel for his defense.

Amendment VII

In Suits at common law, where the value in controversy shall exceed twenty dollars, the right of trial by jury shall be preserved, and no fact tried by a jury, shall be otherwise reexamined in any Court of the United States, than according to the rules of the common law.

Amendment VIII

Excessive bail shall not be required, nor excessive fines imposed, nor cruel and unusual punishments inflicted.

Amendment IX

The enumeration in the Constitution, of certain rights, shall not be construed to deny or disparage others retained by the people.

Amendment X

The powers not delegated to the United States by the Constitution, nor prohibited by it to the States, are reserved to the States respectively, or to the people.

Amendment XI[13]

The Judicial power of the United States shall not be construed to extend to any suit in law or equity, commenced or prosecuted against one of the United States by Citizens of another State, or by Citizens or Subjects of any Foreign State.

Amendment XII[14]

The Electors shall meet in their respective states and vote by ballot for President and Vice-President, one of whom, at least, shall not be an inhabitant of the same state with themselves; they shall name in their ballots the person voted for as President, and in distinct ballots the person voted for as Vice-President, and they shall make distinct lists of all persons voted for as President, and of all persons voted for as Vice-President, and of the number of votes for each, which lists they shall sign and certify, and transmit sealed to the seat of the government of the United States, directed to the President of the Senate;—The President of the Senate shall, in presence of the Senate and House of Representatives, open all the certificates and the votes shall then be counted;—The person having the greatest number of votes for President, shall be the President, if such number be a majority of the whole number of Electors appointed; and if no person have such majority, then from the persons having the highest numbers not exceeding three on the list of those voted for as President, the House of Representatives shall choose immediately, by ballot, the President. But in choosing the President, the votes shall be taken by states, the representation from each state having one vote; a quorum for this purpose shall consist of a member or members from two-thirds of the states, and a majority of all the states shall be necessary to a choice. [And if the House of Representatives shall not choose a President whenever the right of choice shall devolve upon them, before the fourth day of March next following, then the Vice-President shall act as President, as in the case of the death or other constitutional disability of the President.][15]—The person having the greatest number of votes as Vice-President, shall be the Vice-President, if such number be a majority of the whole number of Electors appointed, and if no person have a majority, then from the two highest numbers on the list, the Senate shall choose the Vice-President; a quorum for the purpose shall consist of two-thirds of the whole number of Senators, and a majority of the whole number shall be necessary to a choice. But no person constitutionally ineligible to the office of President shall be eligible to that of Vice-President of the United States.

Amendment XIII[16]

Section 1. Neither slavery nor involuntary servitude, except as a punishment for crime whereof the party shall have been duly convicted, shall exist within the United States, or any place subject to their jurisdiction.

 Section 2. Congress shall have power to enforce this article by appropriate legislation.

---

[13]Adopted in 1798.

[14]Adopted in 1804.

[15]Superseded by the Twentieth Amendment, Section 3.

[16]Adopted in 1865.

Amendment XIV[17]

Section 1. All persons born or naturalized in the United States, and subject to the jurisdiction thereof, are citizens of the United States and of the State wherein they reside. No state shall make or enforce any law which shall abridge the privileges or immunities of citizens of the United States; nor shall any State deprive any person of life, liberty, or property, without due process of law; nor deny to any person within its jurisdiction the equal protection of the laws.

Section 2. Representatives shall be apportioned among the several States according to their respective numbers, counting the whole number of persons in each State, excluding Indians not taxed. But when the right to vote at any election for the choice of electors for President and Vice-President of the United States, Representatives in Congress, the Executive and Judicial officers of a State, or the members of the Legislature thereof, is denied to any of the male inhabitants of such State, being twenty-one years of age, and citizens of the United States, or in any way abridged, except for participation in rebellion, or other crime, the basis of representation therein shall be reduced in the proportion which the number of such male citizens shall bear to the whole number of male citizens twenty-one years of age in such State.

Section 3. No person shall be a Senator or Representative in Congress, or elector of President and Vice-President, or hold any office, civil or military, under the United States, or under any State, who, having previously taken an oath, as a member of Congress, or as an officer of the United States, or as a member of any State legislature, or as an executive or judicial officer of any State, to support the Constitution of the United States, shall have engaged in insurrection or rebellion against the same, or given aid or comfort to the enemies thereof. But Congress may by a vote of two-thirds of each House, remove such disability.

Section 4. The validity of the public debt of the United States, authorized by law, including debts incurred for payment of pensions and bounties for services in suppressing insurrection or rebellion, shall not be questioned. But neither the United States nor any State shall assume or pay any debt or obligation incurred in aid of insurrection or rebellion against the United States, or any claim for the loss or emancipation of any slave; but all such debts, obligations and claims shall be held illegal and void.

Section 5. The Congress shall have power to enforce, by appropriate legislation, the provisions of this article.

Amendment XV[18]

Section 1. The right of citizens of the United States to vote shall not be denied or abridged by the United States or by any State on account of race, color, or previous condition of servitude.

Section 2. The Congress shall have power to enforce this article by appropriate legislation.

Amendment XVI[19]

The Congress shall have power to lay and collect taxes on incomes, from whatever source derived, without apportionment among the several States, and without regard to any census or enumeration.

---

[17]Adopted in 1868.
[18]Adopted in 1870.
[19]Adopted in 1913.

Amendment XVII[20]

The Senate of the United States shall be composed of two Senators from each State, elected by the people thereof, for six years; and each Senator shall have one vote. The electors in each State shall have the qualifications requisite for electors of the most numerous branch of the State legislatures.

When vacancies happen in the representation of any State in the Senate, the executive authority of such State shall issue writs of election to fill such vacancies: *Provided,* That the legislature of any State may empower the executive thereof to make temporary appointments until the people fill the vacancies by election as the legislature may direct.

This amendment shall not be so construed as to affect the election or term of any Senator chosen before it becomes valid as part of the Constitution.

Amendment XVIII[21]

Section 1. After one year from the ratification of this article the manufacture, sale, or transportation of intoxicating liquors within, the importation thereof into, or the exportation thereof from the United States and all territory subject to the jurisdiction thereof for beverage purposes is hereby prohibited.

Section 2. The Congress and the several States shall have concurrent power to enforce this article by appropriate legislation.

Section 3. This article shall be inoperative unless it shall have been ratified as an amendment to the Constitution by the legislatures of the several States, as provided in the Constitution, within seven years from the date of the submission hereof to the States by the Congress.

Amendment XIX[22]

The right of citizens of the United States to vote shall not be denied or abridged by the United States or by any State on account of sex.

Congress shall have power to enforce this article by appropriate legislation.

Amendment XX[23]

Section 1. The terms of the President and Vice-President shall end at noon on the 20th day of January, and the terms of Senators and Representatives at noon on the 3rd day of January, of the years in which such terms would have ended if this article had not been ratified; and the terms of their successors shall then begin.

Section 2. The Congress shall assemble at least once in every year, and such meeting shall begin at noon on the 3rd day of January, unless they shall by law appoint a different day.

Section 3. If, at the time fixed for the beginning of the term of the President, the President elect shall have died, the Vice-President elect shall become President. If a President shall not have been chosen before the time fixed for the beginning of his term, or if the President elect shall have failed to qualify, then the Vice-President elect shall act as President until a President shall have qualified; and the Congress may by

---

[20]Adopted in 1913.

[21]Adopted in 1919. Repealed by Section 1 of the Twenty-first Amendment.

[22]Adopted in 1920.

[23]Adopted in 1933.

law provide for the case wherein neither a President elect nor a Vice-President elect shall have qualified, declaring who shall then act as President, or the manner in which one who is to act shall be selected, and such person shall act accordingly until a President or Vice-President shall have qualified.

Section 4. The Congress may by law provide for the case of the death of any of the persons from whom the House of Representatives may choose a President whenever the right of choice shall have devolved upon them, and for the case of the death of any of the persons from whom the Senate may choose a Vice-President whenever the right of choice shall have devolved upon them.

Section 5. Sections 1 and 2 shall take effect on the 15th day of October following the ratification of this article.

Section 6. This article shall be inoperative unless it shall have been ratified as an amendment to the Constitution by the legislatures of three-fourths of the several States within seven years from the date of its submission.

Amendment XXI[24]

Section 1. The eighteenth article of amendment to the Constitution of the United States is hereby repealed.

Section 2. The transportation or importation into any State, Territory, or possession of the United States for delivery or use therein of intoxicating liquors, in violation of the laws thereof, is hereby prohibited.

Section 3. This article shall be inoperative unless it shall have been ratified as an amendment to the Constitution by conventions in the several States, as provided in the Constitution, within seven years from the date of the submission hereof to the States by the Congress.

Amendment XXII[25]

Section 1. No person shall be elected to the office of the President more than twice, and no person who has held the office of President, or acted as President, for more than two years of a term to which some other person was elected President shall be elected to the office of the President more than once. But this Article shall not apply to any person holding the office of President when this Article was proposed by the Congress, and shall not prevent any person who may be holding the office of President, or acting as President, during the term within which this Article becomes operative from holding the office of President or acting as President during the remainder of such term.

Section 2. This article shall be inoperative unless it shall have been ratified as an amendment to the Constitution by the legislatures of three-fourths of the several States within seven years from the date of its submission to the States by the Congress.

Amendment XXIII[26]

Section 1. The District constituting the seat of Government of the United States shall appoint in such manner as the Congress may direct:

A number of electors of President and Vice-President equal to the whole number of Senators and Representatives in Congress to which the District would be entitled if it were a State, but in no event more than the least populous State; they shall be in

---

[24]Adopted in 1933.

[25]Adopted in 1951.

[26]Adopted in 1961.

addition to those appointed by the States, but they shall be considered, for the purposes of the election of President and Vice-President, to be electors appointed by a State, and they shall meet in the District and perform such duties as provided by the twelfth article of amendment.

Section 2. The Congress shall have power to enforce this article by appropriate legislation.

Amendment XXIV[27]

Section 1. The right of citizens of the United States to vote in any primary or other election for President or Vice-President, for electors for President or Vice-President, or for Senator or Representative in Congress, shall not be denied or abridged by the United States or any state by reasons of failure to pay any poll tax or other tax.

Section 2. The Congress shall have power to enforce this article by appropriate legislation.

Amendment XXV[28]

Section 1. In case of the removal of the President from office or of his death or resignation, the Vice-President shall become President.

Section 2. Whenever there is a vacancy in the office of the Vice-President, the President shall nominate a Vice-President who shall take office upon confirmation by a majority vote of both Houses of Congress.

Section 3. Whenever the President transmits to the President pro tempore of the Senate and the Speaker of the House of Representatives his written declaration that he is unable to discharge the powers and duties of his office, and until he transmits to them a written declaration to the contrary, such powers and duties shall be discharged by the Vice-President as Acting President.

Section 4. Whenever the Vice-President and a majority of either the principal officers of the Executive departments or of such other body as Congress may by law provide, transmit to the President pro tempore of the Senate and the Speaker of the House of Representatives their written declaration that the President is unable to discharge the powers and duties of his office, The Vice-President shall immediately assume the powers and duties of the office as Acting President.

Thereafter, when the President transmits to the President pro tempore of the Senate and the Speaker of the House of Representatives his written declaration that no inability exists, he shall resume the powers and duties of his office unless the Vice-President and a majority of either the principal officers of the executive departments or of such other body as Congress may by law provide, transmit within four days to the President pro tempore of the Senate and the Speaker of the House of Representatives their written declaration that the President is unable to discharge the powers and duties of his office. Thereupon Congress shall decide the issue, assembling within forty-eight hours for that purpose if not in session. If the Congress, within twenty-one days after receipt of the latter written declaration, or, if Congress is not in session, within twenty-one days after Congress is required to assemble, determines by two-thirds vote of both houses that the President is unable to discharge the powers and duties of his office, the Vice-President shall continue to discharge the same as Acting President; otherwise, the President shall resume the powers and duties of his office.

---

[27]Adopted in 1964.

[28]Adopted in 1967.

Amendment XXVI[29]

Section 1. The right of citizens of the United States, who are 18 years of age or older, to vote shall not be denied or abridged by the United States or any state on account of age.

   Section 2. The Congress shall have power to enforce this article by appropriate legislation.

Amendment XXVII

Article the Second . . . No law, varying the compensation for the services of the Senators and Representatives, shall take effect, until an election of Representatives shall have intervened.

---

[29]Adopted in 1971.

GLOSSARY

104th Congress—The Congress elected in 1994 with the first Republican majority in both houses since the 1950s.

113th Congress—The Congress elected in 2012 with a Democratic majority in the Senate and a Republican majority in the House.

527 groups—Private groups usually organized to support a presidential candidate by raising unregulated money; they are a way to get around the ban on parties raising unlimited soft money; named after the part of the tax code under which they are registered.

advocacy ads—Used by interest groups to indirectly promote or defeat candidates for election; also called issue ads, they are a way of avoiding campaign spending limits.

affirmative action—An effort to give advantages to minorities by requiring and expanding job, admission, and promotion opportunities.

agenda setting—A listing of national priorities of public issues; a major media function.

anarchy—A society without government.

Anti-Federalists—Group opposing adoption of Constitution; they preferred stronger state governments and more popular participation.

appellate jurisdiction—The authority of superior courts to hear appeals from lower courts.

Articles of Confederation—A document that from 1781 to 1789 loosely unified the newly independent American states; its shortcomings led to the U.S. Constitution.

authority—Legitimate power.

"balance the ticket"—The effort by parties to represent different population groups and regions in their candidates for elected office.

bicameral—A legislature with two houses, such as the U.S. Congress with the House of Representatives and Senate.

Bill of Rights—The first 10 amendments to the Constitution, including freedoms of speech, press, religion, due process, and jury trial.

blogs—Internet websites used to form networks of people to support a political candidate or to share views on a common issue.

bureaucrat—An administrator in a large organization, often government; may refer to someone who slows things down by enforcing too many rules and red tape.

cabinet departments—The major departments of the federal government such as State and Defense, of which there are 15 now.

calendars—The agendas or schedules for legislation in Congress.

casework—The efforts by members of Congress to solve voters' individual problems with the government; an important part of their constituency service.

caucus—A gathering of all the members of a political party serving in either house of Congress.

chain—Companies that combine media, including newspapers and TV stations, in different cities under one ownership.

checks and balances—The constitutional principle that mixes together separate powers to give each branch some powers of the others; protects the functions of different branches of government.

chief executive—The president's role as head of the executive branch and its federal bureaucracy.

chief of state—The role of the president as symbolic head of the nation as well as of the government.

civil liberties—Legal protections against government restrictions on freedoms of speech, press, and religion.

civil rights—Legal protections against discrimination because of race, religion, ethnicity, sexual preference, or gender.

class action suits—Cases representing a whole class of people whose rights may have been violated.

client agency—Government departments representing and promoting the economic interests for whom they were established, such as the Labor Department for unions and Commerce for business.

coalition—A political grouping representing diverse interests organized to represent popular opinion on a particular issue.

commander in chief—The president's authority over the military; the principle behind civilian control of the armed forces.

complete incorporationists—A judicial position that the entire Bill of Rights was extended beyond the federal government by the Fourteenth Amendment and thus applies to the individual states.

concurrent powers—Those powers shared by the states and federal government, such as the power to tax.

conference committee—A temporary body of members from the two houses of Congress set up to resolve different versions of similar legislation passed by both houses.

consensus—A general agreement among the population on basic political values and "rules of the game."

conspiracy theory—An unprovable argument that the United States government as well as specific events (i.e., wars and assassinations) are controlled by a unified, secret elite.

czars—An informal term for President Obama's special advisors appointed to resolve an immediate issue, for example, the climate czar.

dealignment—A recent phase that refers to the growing lack of popular support for either major party.

democracy—A form of government in which most of the people can effectively participate.

deviating elections—Elections that show a temporary decline in popular support for the majority party.

drones—Remote-controlled pilotless aircraft increasingly used by the Obama administration to kill accused terrorists in remote overseas regions.

due process—A phrase in the Fourteenth Amendment used to incorporate freedoms of the Bill of Rights to cover states' actions, including the rights to procedural fairness and impartiality by government officials.

electoral barriers—Legal obstacles to voting, such as residency and registration requirements.

electoral college—An antiquated constitutional provision whereby voters on Election Day select electors to reflect their state's choice for president.

elites—Those who get most of society's values, especially wealth and power.

embeds—Reporters who traveled with American frontline troops in the fighting in Iraq and the earlier Gulf War.

equal protection—A clause in the Fourteenth Amendment used to prevent state officials and others from engaging in racial or sex discrimination.

equity—A flexible judicial doctrine that allows judges to resolve a case based on a sense of fairness.

exclusionary rule—A judicial rule that excludes any evidence obtained by illegal means.

exclusive and concurrent jurisdiction—Refers to whether federal courts have sole authority over a case (exclusive) or whether they share that authority with state courts (concurrent).

exclusive powers—Those powers only exercised by the federal government under the Constitution, such as the right to coin money.

executive agencies—Major departments of the government that are not in the Cabinet—for example, the National Aeronautics and Space Administration.

executive agreements—International agreements signed by the president and not needing approval by the senate because they are usually less important than treaties.

federalism—The distribution of political authority between the federal government and the governments of the states.

Federalists—Supporters of the Constitution in the campaign to adopt it; they favored a strong conservative central government.

filibuster—The right under Senate rules to delay action by speaking for an unlimited amount of time, only stopped by a cloture vote; increasingly used in recent congresses by Republicans to block the Democratic majority in the Senate.

First Amendment freedoms—Freedoms of religion, speech, press, and assembly.

Fourteenth Amendment—The post–Civil War amendment that has been used to extend the protections in the Bill of Rights to actions by state and local governments and by private individuals and groups.

fragmentation of power—A key pluralist perspective that no one group dominates American politics.

gerrymandering—Political tactic of designing legislative districts to favor one party's candidates over another's.

GOP—Grand Old Party; the traditional nickname of the Republican Party.

government—A political association that makes rules determining the distribution of values of a society and is the ultimate regulator of legitimate force.

grassroots campaigns—The effort to bring pressure on elected officials by mobilizing voters in their own districts and states using mail, phones, the Internet, or visits.

gridlock—Slang term describing the inability of the federal government, especially Congress, to act because of partisan conflicts.

hyperpluralism—The view that participation by too many groups demanding too many resources from the government leads to political paralysis.

identity politics—Groups that organize on the basis of their religious, ethnic, or sexual identity to pursue political objectives.

impeachment—The power of Congress to remove high officials of the executive or judicial branches from office for misconduct.

incumbent—An elected official currently in office with all the advantages that confers.

independents—Voters who publicly identify with neither major political party.

injunction—A court order preventing someone from violating someone else's rights.

interest group—An association organized to pursue a common objective by bringing pressure on the political process.

Internet—A global computer network allowing near-instant communication.

iron triangle—A model describing how public policy in a specific area is inflexibly decided by a trio of lobbyists, bureaucrats, and congressional committees.

joint committees—Permanent congressional bodies including both senators and representatives covering certain subjects, for example, the Joint Economic Committee.

judicial activism—The concept that the courts should be an active partner with the other branches of government in shaping policy.

judicial restraint—The opposing concept that the courts should not impose their views on other branches of the government except in extreme instances; a passive role for the courts.

judicial review—The federal courts' authority to decide on the constitutionality of the acts of state, local, and federal governments.

lame duck—The negative description of a president weakened because he is in the last months of his final term.

landmark decision—A judicial ruling that establishes a precedent that causes major changes in the law; for example, *Brown v. Board of Education* ending legal racial segregation in public schools.

leadership PACs—Modern political machines established by congressional leaders to further their ambitions by raising funds for party colleagues. See *PACs*.

legitimacy—A publicly recognized quality of a leader or institution that makes their power correct and widely accepted.

limited government—The constitutional principle by which the powers of government are limited by the rights and liberties of the people.

lobbying—The process by which interest groups and individuals influence government officials to act in their favor.

maintaining elections—Elections that continue the popular support for the majority and minority parties at the same level.

marblecake federalism—The modern mix of overlapping relations between the states and the federal government.

Mayflower Compact—An early example (1620) of American settlers' (Pilgrims) desire to be governed by a publicly accepted rule of law.

media—Those means of communications, such as television, Internet, radio, and newspapers, that permit messages to be made public.

memorandum orders—The method by which the Supreme Court decides most cases without the need for oral arguments.

national agenda—The important political issues that are the current focus of public attention; gaining control of this agenda is a major goal of national politics.

national convention—An assembly of party delegates usually selected by primaries who meet every four years to nominate their party's candidates for president and vice president; it is the party's highest governing body.

news management—Techniques used by public officials to control information going to the media.

Obamacare—The Affordable Care Act of 2010; controversial law designed to bring uninsured patients into the health care insurance system and restrain the prices people pay for medical treatment.

order—When the Court requires someone to take a specified action to ensure someone else's rights.

original jurisdiction—The authority of the Court to initially try cases.

oversight—A nonlegislative power of Congress to investigate and examine the activities of executive branch agencies.

PACs (political action committees)—Legally sanctioned organizations set up by private groups to raise campaign funds.

partial incorporationists—Judicial position that believes only preferred rights, such as the First Amendment freedoms, should be included in the Fourteenth Amendment and applied to the states.

party platform—A document stating the party's positions on issues.

plural elitism—A view of American politics as being divided into different policy arenas where various special interest elites dominate.

pluralism—A group theory of democracy that positively views the competition between many different groups as resulting in compromises that produce public policies.

political efficacy—The sense of political effectiveness, for example that efforts like voting will result in a change of government policies.

political machine—A traditional locally based party organization led by a boss who controlled government jobs and services through loyalty and corruption.

political party—An organization that runs candidates for public office under the party's name.

political questions—Controversial issues that the courts refuse to deal with because they feel they lack the capacity and that other branches are most suited to resolve.

political science—The study of social relations involving power and authority, especially those including government actions.

political socialization—The process of learning political attitudes and behavior.

politics—The process of who gets what, when, and how; actions among a number of groups and individuals competing for influence.

populism—American protest movements that periodically arise to protest dominance by an elite of the government or economy; present-day cultural populists represent religious conservatives opposing what they see as liberal control of the government and media.

pork-barrel bills—Laws designed to produce targeted local benefits from federal government spending.

power elite—A theory that American politics is dominated by a unified nonrepresentative elite.

power—The ability to influence another's behavior.

precedent, or *stare decisis*—The judicial practice by which the courts generally follow previous court decisions involving the same issue.

presidential primaries—Elections held by states to determine which nominee's delegates will be sent to the national convention.

Race to the Top—President Obama's educational reform requiring states to compete for federal funds through proposals to improve their schools.

realigning elections—Elections that show a long-term shift in the popular base of support of the majority and minority parties.

reciprocity—The congressional practice of members looking for guidance on legislation to members of their party on committees specializing in that area.

regulatory commissions—Agencies semi-independent from the rest of government charged with regulating parts of the economy—for example, the Federal Communications Commission (FCC).

Rehnquist Court—The U.S. Supreme Court, from 1986 to 2005, named after late chief justice William Rehnquist.

Roberts Court—The present Supreme Court from 2005, named after the current chief justice, John Roberts.

representative democracy—Government in which the people rule indirectly through elected representatives.

reserved powers—Those powers not delegated to the federal government that are reserved to the states or people by the Tenth Amendment.

residual powers—Those powers not spelled out in the Constitution but necessary for the president to carry out his other responsibilities; used to expand the duties of the president.

ruling class—According to the power elite view this is the privileged group that controls the major institutions of society and government.

select or special committees—Temporary congressional panels established to do specific tasks, usually investigations; an example was the Select Bipartisan Committee to Investigate Hurricane Katrina.

Senate majority leader—Leader of the Senate majority party and the Senate equivalent to the House Speaker, currently Democrat Harry Reid of Nevada.

senatorial courtesy—The practice of the Senate to only approve judicial nominees who are acceptable to the senator from that state.

seniority—An informal congressional rule by which the chairman of a committee is automatically the member from the majority party who has served the longest on the committee.

separation of powers—A constitutional principle that the powers of government should be separated into three branches of government—legislative, executive, and judicial.

Sequester—These government-wide spending cuts went into effect in 2013 (because of previous legislation) when Congress could not agree on specific budget reductions. They ended in early 2014 with a budget agreement.

single-member district—An electoral system of electing one member of Congress from each district; considered an obstacle to the rise of minor parties.

social class—A major social division based on occupation and income and the awareness this produces of relations toward other classes.

social sciences—The academic disciplines, such as history, economics, or political science, that study relationships among people.

soft money—Unregulated funds that in the past were used for state and local parties because they could be contributed in large amounts and used as a loophole to raise money for federal candidates; under the McCain–Feingold campaign reform parties were no longer allowed to raise soft money.

soft news—Entertaining lifestyle stories about celebrities, including politicians; as opposed to hard news on public affairs.

sound bite—A brief video clip of a candidate or political official speaking, often with a memorable phrase.

speaker of the House—The head of the House of Representatives and the leader of the majority party, currently Republican John Boehner of Ohio.

specialization—A congressional custom that members will remain on the same committee and become experts in its issues.

spin—Slang for putting a self-serving, favorable interpretation or slant on the news given to the media and public by government officials.

spoils system—Process of filling government positions with supporters of the winning politicians; largely replaced by the civil service.

standing committees—The permanent specialized units of both houses that draft legislation in subject areas like taxes and agriculture.

State of the Union address—A presidential speech before Congress at the beginning of the year outlining his legislative program.

strict constructionism—A judicial philosophy used by modern conservatives to restrict the power of the government to the original intentions of the framers of the U.S. Constitution.

Supreme Court of the United States—The head of the federal court system, composed of a chief justice and eight associate justices.

suspect classifications—A judicial doctrine that laws involving race, religion, or ethnicity will be subject to close scrutiny by the courts because they are presumed invalid.

Tea Party—Current conservative grassroots movement focused on reducing government spending; influential within the Republican Party.

term limits—Populist effort to limit the number of times that state legislators or members of Congress can run for reelection.

test case—Brought by interested groups seeking a favorable precedent by the courts concerning a major violation of civil rights or liberties affecting a large number of people.

TV networks—National media corporations owning numerous local television outlets to whom they produce and sell programs.

U.S. courts of appeals—Thirteen federal courts above the district courts, which mainly hear appeals from those courts.

U.S. district courts—The federal courts where most cases involving federal law are first tried.

veto—A president's constitutional power to refuse to sign legislation, thus preventing it from becoming law unless overridden by a two-thirds vote of both houses of Congress.

whips—Floor leaders in Congress who work to coordinate votes and assist the heads of the parties in both houses.

writ of certiorari—Order of a higher court to a lower court to send the record of a case for review.

INDEX

9/11/2001. *See* September 11, 2001
1992 elections, 213
1994 elections, 213
1998 elections, 100
2000 elections, 51–52, 136, 146, 149, 151, 152, 166
2004 elections, 196, 204
2006 elections, 116, 196, 214
2008 elections, 128
  fundraising, 221–223
  interest in, 201–202, 251
  Iraq war and, 119
  realignment, 214
  voter moderation, 216
  voter turnout, 196
2010 elections, 92, 127, 196, 198
2012 elections, 96, 100, 196, 201, 214, 221
  fundraising, 221
  reelection, 229–232
2012 Reelection, 229–232

A

ABA. *See* American Bar Association (ABA)
Abortion rulings, 143, 144, 149, 151, 155, 174, 188
Abramoff, Jack, 239
Access to power, 244–245
ACLU. *See* American Civil Liberties Union (ACLU)
ACLU v. Ashcroft, 171
Activism, 11–12
Activist judges. *See* Judicial activism
Adamowski, Benjamin, 218
Adams, John, 139
AdMob, 267
Advertisements, 257
Affirmative action, 159, 176, 178–182
Afghanistan war, 60, 62, 65, 87
Agenda setting, 67, 256
Agricultural interests, 238
Alien and Sedition Acts, 187

Alito, Samuel A. Jr., 135–136, 138, 145
Al Qaeda, 85, 87, 207
Amendments, 20, 37–39. *See also* Bill of Rights; individual amendments, *e.g.* Fourteenth
American Association of Retired Persons (AARP), 238
American Bar Association (ABA), 159, 238
American Civil Liberties Union (ACLU), 183
The American Farm Bureau Federation, 238
American Federation of Labor, 238
American Federation of Labor and the Congress of Industrial Organizations (the AFL-CIO), 238
American Israel Public Affairs Committee (AIPAC), 238
American Medical Association, 238
The American President, 59
Anarchy, 6
Apathy, political, 11–12, 201–208
Appellate jurisdiction, 133, 137
Appropriations Committees, 110, 111, 118
Arthur, Chester, 82
Articles of Confederation, 19, 20–21
Associated Milk Producers, Inc. (AMP), 238
Authority, 4–6, 10–11. *See also* Power

B

Baby Bells, 266
Baker v. Carr, 97, 143, 149

Baldwin, Tammy, 96
Bargaining process, 272, 273
Beard, Charles, 23–24
Bennett, Bob, 103
Bentsen, Lloyd, 225
Bernanke, Ben, 79
Biden, Joe, 52–53, 102, 225, 231, 251
Bierce, Ambrose, 247
Bill of Rights, 26–27, 166–167
Bills. *See* Legislative branch
Bipartisan Campaign Reform Act (BCRA), 246
Birth of a Nation (Griffith), 59
Blair, Tony, 210
Blanco, Kathleen, 42, 43–44
Block grants, 33–34
Boehner, John A., 101, 111
Bork, Robert, 136
Bradwell, Myra, 180
Brandeis, Louis, 167, 173
Brennan, William, 180
Breyer, Stephen G., 136, 138
Brin, Sergey, 265, 266
Brown v. Board of Education, 158, 178
Bryce, James, 40
Buchanan, James, 56–57
Buchanan-style presidents, 56–57
Budget, 117–129
Budget Act (1974), 118
Budget Control Act of 2011, 119
Budget deadlocks, 119–120
Bully pulpit, 69
Bureaucracy. *See* Executive branch; Federal bureaucracy
Bureaucrats, 71, 80–83. *See also* Federal bureaucracy
Burger, Warren, 135, 136, 143
Burger Court, 143, 155
Bush, George, Sr., 48, 58, 66, 134

Bush, George W., 49, 59–60, 135
2000 election of, 51
affirmative action and, 179–180
cabinet of, 77
as chief diplomat, 64–65
civil rights issues and, 183
as commander-in-chief, 65–66
Dick Cheney and, 52
executive orders, 64
federalism and, 34
growth of government under, 81
Hollywood and, 59
Hurricane Katrina and, 41–44, 65, 280
Iraq war and, 60, 206–207
judicial appointments of, 135–136, 145
No Child Left Behind and, 32
as party leader, 68
public opinion and, 68–69
September 11 and, 62, 69, 85–87, 121, 280
use of surveillance, 173–174
use of veto power, 116
Bush, Laura, 74
Bush Sr., 149
Bush v. Gore, 144, 145, 146, 149
Business groups, 237
Byrd, Robert C., 110

C
Cabinet departments, 76–78, 166–167
Cable Network News (CNN), 252, 254, 259, 260
Camp, Dave, 110
Campaign contributions by interest groups, 243–245. *See also* Fundraising
Campaign finance reforms, 245
Campaign spending, 251
Cantor, Eric, 101
Cap-and-trade system, 122
Careerism in Congress, 96
Carter, Jimmy, 48, 58
Caucus, political party, 101–103, 224
CBO. *See* Congressional Budget Office (CBO)

Central Intelligence Agency (CIA), 78, 80, 87, 192
The Chamber of Commerce, 237
Checks and balances, 26, 28–30
Cheney, Dick, 52, 86, 225
Child Online Protection Act, 171
CIA. *See* Central Intelligence Agency (CIA)
Circuit courts of appeals. *See* Courts of appeals
Citizens United, and aftermath, 245–247
Citizens United v. Federal Election Commission, 146
Civil libertarians, 182
Civil liberties, 36, 181–193. *See also* War on Terror
Congressional investigations and, 121
national security and, 173–174
Civil rights, 164–167, 176–186, 192–193
Supreme Court and, 156
Civil Rights Acts, 156, 159
Civil Rights Restoration Act, 138
Civil Service, 82
Civil Service Commission, 82
Civil Service Reform Act, 82
Civil War, 31, 56
Claims court, 133
Clark, Kenneth, 177
Class, voting and, 199–201
Class action suits, 182
Clean Air Act, 273–274
Clean Air Coalition, 273
Client agency, 78
Clinton, Bill
affirmative action and, 179
Al Gore and, 225
cabinet and, 77
China trade bill and, 117
Defense of Marriage Act and, 174
deficit reduction bill and, 119
election of, 213
Hollywood and, 59
impeachment of, 122
judicial appointments of, 134, 135
mistrust of, 206

National Economic Council and, 75
presidency of, 48, 58–59
welfare reform and, 33–34
Clinton, Hillary Rodham, 74, 94, 229
Clinton v. City of New York, 67
Clooney, George, 231
Cloture, 115
CNN. *See* Cable Network News (CNN)
Coalition building, 209
Colbert, Stephen, 256
Colonial government, 19–20
Commerce Clause, 144
Committee on Committees, 103
Committee system, 105–112
Communications Decency Act of 1996, 171
Communist Manifesto, 187
Community Schools v. Seattle School District, 145
Complete incorporationists, 167
Compromise
in the Constitution, 21–22, 25
pluralist theory and, 272–273
Concurrent jurisdiction, 137
Confederation Congress, 20–21
Conference committees, 105, 113
Congress. *See also* Confederation Congress; House of Representatives; Legislative branch; Senate
111th, 97, 108
113th, 96
careerism in, 96
committee system, 105–112
driver safety and, 35
funding for Department of Energy, 29
government framework and, 39
image of, 95
impeachment powers of, 121
investigative powers of, 121
lobbyists and, 238–243
makeup of, 93–102

oversight powers of, 102
presidents and, 67, 92
size of, 93
specialization in, 108–109
staff of, 112
Supreme Court and,
138–139, 150
term limits in, 96
terms of, 94–95
war powers and, 65–66
Congressional Budget and
Impoundment Control
Act, 118
Congressional Budget Office
(CBO), 118
Consenus, 273
Conservative bake sales, 176
Conservatives, 215–217
Conspiracy theorists, 278
Constitution, 18–46. *See also*
Bill of Rights; Framers,
of the Constitution;
individual amendments,
e.g. Fourteenth
Amendment
ambiguity of, 41, 45–46
antidemocracy of, 24
changing of, 37–40, 45
legal heritage of, 19–20
limited government and, 36
motives behind, 23–25
principles of, 27–40, 45–46
Supreme Court and,
138–139, 149
survival of, 18, 40–41, 45
Constitutional amendments.
See Amendments
Constitutional Convention,
21–23, 51–53
Convention. *See* National
convention
Coolidge, Calvin, 57, 60
Council of Economic
Advisers, 76
Council on American-Islamic
Relations (CAIR), 184
Council on Foreign
Relations, 276–277
Court injunctions, 185
Court of Military Appeals.
See GI Supreme Court
Court-packing bill, 142
Courts, obedience to,
184–186. *See also* District
courts; Judicial branch
Courts of appeals, 133

Cramer, Robert, 117
Crick, Bernard, 7
Crisis leadership, 53, 56
Crony capitalism, 249
C-SPAN, 260
Culture wars, 213–214
Cuomo, Mario, 173
Czars, 76

D

Dahl, Robert, 274
The Daily Show, 256
Daley, Richard, Sr., 217, 218
Danish cartoons and free
speech, 165
Dashboard, Facebook, 231
The Day after Tomorrow
(movie), 59
Declaration of
Independence, 19, 20, 23
Defense of Marriage Act
(DOMA), 147, 174
Definition of alternatives,
263–264
Democracy, defined, 7
Democracy in America
(Tocqueville), 236
Democratic Conference, 102
Democratic National
Committee (DNC), 221
Democratic Party, 210–217.
See also Political parties
changes in, 110, 222
in Chicago, 217, 218
China trade bill and, 117
fundraising, 221–223
ideology of, 227–228
judicial appointments and,
136
labor unions and, 238
national committee, 221
organization in Senate,
102–103
seniority system, 107–108
Democratic realignment,
214
Democratic-Republican
Party, 211
Detainee Bill, 191
Deviating elections, 212
Dickerson v. United States
(2000), 186
Dingell, John, 96
Discrimination. *See* Civil
rights
District courts, 132

Dodd-Frank Act, 113
DOMA. *See* Defense of
Marriage Act (DOMA)
"Don't Ask, Don't Tell"
program, 174
DoubleClick, 266
Dred Scott v. Sandford, 141,
148
Dr. Strangelove (Kubrick),
59
Drudge, Matt, 255
Due process rights, 166–167,
174–175, 189–190
Dukakis, Michael, 225
Durbin, Richard J., 102,
148

E

*An Economic Interpretation
of the Constitution of the
United States* (Beard),
23–24
Economic meltdown. *See*
Recession of 2008-2009
Economy, 8–9
Education, 31
Edwards, George, 62
Eighth Amendment, 39,
167
Eisenhower, Dwight, 57, 60,
135, 185
Eisenhower-style presidents,
57
Election Day, 238
Elections, 207, 209, 211–215.
See also Voters
Electoral barriers, 204
Electoral college, 51–52
Elitism, 4, 272–281
Emanuel, Rahm, 246
Entertainment programs,
257
Environmental Protection
Agency (EPA), 9, 117,
125, 126, 274
EPA. *See* Environmental
Protection Agency (EPA)
Equal protection clause,
166
Equity, 182
Exclusive jurisdiction, 137
Executive branch, 28–30,
48–89. *See also* Federal
bureaucracy; President(s)
and Presidency
Exxon, 237

F

FAA. *See* Federal Aviation Administration (FAA)

Facebook, 230, 255

Fathers of presidents, 60

Faubus, Orval, 185

FBI. *See* Federal Bureau of Investigation (FBI)

FCC. *See* Federal Communications Commission (FCC)

Federal Aviation Administration (FAA), 12

Federal bureaucracy, 63, 71–84

Federal Bureau of Investigation (FBI), 77, 192

Federal Communications Commission (FCC), 78, 262

Federal court system, 132–137

Supreme Court, 137–160

Federal Emergency Management Agency (FEMA), 42–43, 77

Federalism, 30–35. *See also* State and local government

electoral college and, 51–52

Hurricane Katrina and, 41–44

The Federalist Papers, 8, 24, 26, 237

Federalists and Anti-Federalists, 25–27, 210, 211, 226

Federal Reserve Board, 79

Federal Trade Commission (FTC), 267

FEMA. *See* Federal Emergency Management Agency (FEMA)

Fifteenth Amendment, 156

Fifth Amendment, 164, 174

Filibuster, 115–116

FIRE. *See* Foundation for Individual Rights in Education (FIRE)

Fireside chats, 262

First Amendment, 142, 164–172, 175, 183, 193, 250

First Continental Congress, 20

First ladies, 74

FISA Amendments Act, 173

Ford, Gerald, 58

Foreign Affairs, 277

Foreign Intelligence Surveillance Court (FISC), 173

Foreign Relations Committee, 111

Foundation for Individual Rights in Education (FIRE), 184

Fourteenth Amendment

Bill of Rights and, 166–167

due process and, 164, 174

freedom of speech and, 169

as new constitution, 24

separate but equal and, 156–158

suspect classifications and, 177, 178

Fox News, 252, 253, 259, 260

Framers, of the Constitution, 18–19, 22–25, 37, 44, 92. *See also* Federalists and Anti-Federalists

Framing, 256

Frankfurter, Felix, 153–154

Franking privilege, 99

Franklin, Benjamin, 22, 188

Freedom of religion, 171–173

Freedom of speech, 169–171, 176, 183, 184

Frost, Martin, 117

Fundraising, 221–223, 231. *See also* Campaign contributions

G

Gag Rule, 187

GAO. *See* General Accountability Office (GAO)

Garfield, James A., 82, 140

Garner, John Nance, 52

Gates, Bill, 10, 266

Gay and lesbian, 174, 181, 209

Gender. *See* Sex as suspect classification

General Accountability Office (GAO), 120

General Electric, 237

Gerry, Elbridge, 97

Gerrymandering, 97

Gingrich, Newt, 100, 218

Ginsburg, Ruth Bader, 136, 138

GI Supreme Court, 133–134

Giuliani, Rudolph, 86

Gladstone, William, 41

Global warming, 122–126

Goodwin, Doris Kearns, 74

Google, 264–268

GOP. *See* Republican Party

GOPAC, 218

Gore, Al, 51, 52, 59, 225

Government, 6–9, 11–13. *See also* Federal bureaucracy; Politics; State and local government

branches of, 28

colonial, 19–20

federalism, 30–35

interest groups and, 249

Internet and, 171

limited, 36

media and, 261–263

mistrust of, 206

pluralism and elitism in, 281

response to threatening events, 84

same-sex marriages, 174

Government corporations, 78

Gramm, Phil, 239

Grassroots lobbying, 242

Great Compromise, 22

Greider, William, 277

Grutter v. Bollinger, 179

Guantanamo, 191

Guantanamo detainees, 29, 192

Guardian (newspaper), 173

Gulf War (1991), 66

H

Hacker, Jacob, 200

Hamdan, Yaser, 189–191

Hamdan v. Rumsfeld, 189–191

Hamilton, Alexander, 22, 25, 26, 139, 147, 210

Hand, Learned, 193, 259

Hanna, Mark, 221

Hannity, Sean, 260

Harding, Warren, 57

Hastert, Dennis, 100

Hastings, Alcee, 134

Hayes, Rutherford, 51

Head of State (Rock), 59

Health care reform, 94, 97, 118, 124, 125
lobbyists and, 239
negotiations over, 227–228
Henry, Patrick, 23, 25, 139
Hentoff, Nat, 165
Hill, Anita, 136
Hirono, Mazie, 96
Hofstadter, Richard, 30
Holder, Eric, 183
Hollings, Ernest, 13
Holmes, Oliver Wendell, 37, 135, 154, 155, 165, 168
Homeland Security Agency, 76
Hoover, Herbert, 57
House of Cards, 59
House of Representatives.
See also Congress; Senate
committees of, 109–111
foreign affairs and, 65
incumbency and, 99
malapportionment, 97
organization of, 100–102
reapportionment, 99
Speaker of, 100, 102, 113
Hoyer, Steny, 101
Hoyllwood and Presidents, 59
Hughes, Charles Evans, 153
Humphrey, Hubert, 196
Hurricane Katrina, 41–44, 280
Hyperpluralism, 249, 274

I
Identity politics, 199
Impeachment, 121–122
Imperial presidency, 63
Implied powers, 141
Incumbency, 96
Independence Day, 59
Influence. *See* Interest groups
Inherent power of president, 53
Interest groups, 236–250, 268–269
campaign contributions of, 243–245
lobbyists, 238–243, 247–250
types of, 237–238
International Brotherhood of Teamsters, 238
Internet

free speech and, 171
fundraising, 231
lobbyists and, 241
as news source, 253–255
Obama and, 229–232
traditional media and, 250
Iraq war
British withdrawal, 60
congressional resolution on, 66
George W. Bush and, 60, 206–207
leaks regarding, 81
public disillusionment and, 207
Republicans and, 105
Supreme Court and, 149
Iron triangle, 241

J
Jackson, Andrew, 57, 82, 150, 211
Jackson, Robert, 170
Jamieson, Kathleen Hall, 257
Jay, John, 26
Jefferson, Thomas
checks and balances and, 53
civility in Congress and, 114
Constitutional Convention and, 23
political parties and, 210, 211
Supreme Court and, 140
two terms custom and, 40
"Jefferson-Jackson Day" dinners, 220
Jim Crow laws, 157
Johnson, Andrew, 121
Johnson, Lyndon B., 49, 57, 58, 60, 69, 225
Joint committees, 107
Judges, 133–137, 151, 182.
See also Federal court system; Supreme Court
Judicial activism, 154–155, 182
Judicial avoidance, 150
Judicial branch, 132–160
federal court system, 132–137
judicial function, 28–30
Supreme Court, 137–160
Judicial injunction, 185
Judicial interpretation, 39

Judicial order, 185
Judicial restraint, 153–155, 182
Judicial review, 36–37, 139–141 148, 150
Judiciary Act of 1789, 140
Judiciary Committee, Senate, 111
Judis, John, 214
Jurisdiction, 132, 133, 137
Justice Department, 171, 179, 182–183, 192, 237

K
Kagan, Elena, 136, 138
Kaplan, Robert D., 8
Katrina. *See* Hurricane Katrina
Keating, Charles H., Jr., 223
Kennedy, Anthony, 136, 138, 171
Kennedy, John F., 212, 225, 228, 230, 262
Hollywood and, 59
limits of President, 49
Kerry, John, 60, 227

L
Labor unions, 238, 245
Lakoff, George, 257
Lame duck, 50
Landmark decisions, 184–185
Lasswell, Harold, 3, 11
Lawyers, Supreme Court and, 150–153
LDF. *See* Legal Defense and Educational Fund, Inc. (LDF)
Leadership PACs, 218
Leahy, Patrick, 102, 111, 113
Legal Defense and Educational Fund, Inc. (LDF), 183
Legislative branch, 91–128.
See also Congress; House of Representatives; Senate
committee system, 105–112
legislation, 39
legislative function, 28–30
legislative process, 102–103, 112–116
legislators, 93, 94–99
Lesbian, gay, bisexual, and transgender (LGBT), 181

Lewinsky, Monica, 122, 206, 254, 263
Liberals, 215, 216
Lincoln, Abraham, 211
  cabinet and, 77
  crisis leadership of, 56, 57
  hollywood and, 59
  limits of President, 49
  spoils system under, 82
"Lincoln Day" dinners, 220
Lincoln-style presidents, 57
Line-item veto, 67
Lobbying, 238–243
Lobbying competitors, 267–268
Lobbyists. *See* Grassroots lobbying; Interest groups
Locke, John, 19
Loomis, Burdett, 114
Louisiana Purchase, 53
Luce, Henry, 70
Lugar, Dick, 103

M

Machine politics, 217–219
Madison, Dolly, 74
Madison, James, 8, 22, 23, 29, 140, 211, 237
  Federalist Papers and, 24, 26
Magna Carta, 19
Maintaining elections, 211–212
Majority leader, 101, 102
Majority of votes, 226
Majority party, 100–102, 107–108
Majority whips, 101
Malapportionment, 97
Marbury, William, 140
Marbury v. Madison, 37, 139
Markey, Edward J., 124
Mars Attack (Nicholson), 59
Marshall, John, 139–141, 150, 154
Marshall, Thurgood, 24, 154, 183
Mason, George, 25
Matching funds, 223
Mavericks, 229
Mayflower Compact, 19–20
McCain, John, 216, 225, 230
McCarthy, Joseph, 121
McConnell, Mitch, 103
McCulloch v. Maryland, 140–141

McCutcheon vs. FEC (2014), 246
McDonald's, 223
McDonnell Douglas, 12
Media, 250–264, 268–269
  Franklin Roosevelt and, 70
  leaks to, 81, 262
  public and, 206, 263–264
Messina, Jim, 231
Microsoft, 10–11, 266
Middle class, 199–200
Mills, C. Wright, 277
Minority leader, 101
Miranda v. Arizona, 143, 185
Miranda warning, 185, 186
Missouri Compromise, 141, 148
Missouri ex. rel. Gaines v. Canada, 158
Mobile phones, as news source, 255
Modern federalism, 32–35
Mohammed, Khalid Sheik, 191
Montesquieu, Baron de, 28
Morse v. Frederick, 170
Mothers of presidents, 60
Motor voter registration, 204
Multiparty system, 225, 226
Murdoch, Rupert, 260

N

NAACP. *See* National Association for the Advancement of Colored People (NAACP)
Nader, Ralph, 227
Nagin, Ray, 42–44
National Association for the Advancement of Colored People (NAACP), 183, 238
The National Association of Manufacturers, 237
The National Association of Realtors, 238
National convention, 223–225
National Economic Council (NEC), 75
National Farmers Union, 238
National Federation of Independent Business, 238
National Grange, 238
National Guard, 43, 185

National Organization for Women (NOW), 184
National Security Agency (NSA), 173
  phone/Internet data, collection of, 65
National Security Council (NSC), 75
National Small Business Association, 237
National Transportation Safety Board (NTSB), 12
NEC. *See* National Economic Council (NEC)
Neustadt, Richard, 62, 84
New Deal, 142, 154
New Deal Coalition, 212
New Federalism, 33
News media. *See* Media
Newspapers, 253–257, 259–262, 264
Nixon, Richard, 75, 262
  election of, 196
  parents of, 60
  public opinion and, 69
  resignation of, 48, 57–58, 122
  Supreme Court appointments of, 135
  War Powers Act and, 66
No Child Left Behind, 32
Non-voters, 201–208
Northwest Ordinance, 21
NOW. *See* National Organization for Women (NOW)
NSA. *See* National Security Agency (NSA)
NSC. *See* National Security Council (NSC)
NTSB. *See* National Transportation Safety Board (NTSB)

O

Obama, Barack, 49, 63–64, 66–67, 228. *See also* 2008 elections
  527 groups and, 246
  2012 elections, 201
  acceptance speech, 225
  affirmative action and, 180
  antiterrorist measures, 173–174
  background of, 60, 61

budget deadlocks, 119–120
budget deficit and, 110, 118
cabinet and, 77
campaign fundraising and, 222
campaign speeches of, 216, 228
challenges facing, 228–229
civil rights and, 183
communication skills of, 263
Congress and, 62
czars of, 76
donors to, 243–244
"Don't Ask, Don't Tell" program, 174
executive orders, 64
Facebook app, 230
federalism and, 34
funding for Department of Energy, 29
on gay and lesbian, 209
Guantanamo, 191
Internet campaign, 229–232
legislative process and, 93
liberal pragmatic leader, 50
limits of President, 49
lobbyists and, 240, 249
major-party candidate, 223
management style and, 75
No Child Left Behind and, 32
online operation of, 229–232
partisanship and, 114
as party leader, 68
phone/Internet data, collection of, 65
presidency of, 48, 50, 61–62
public opinion of, 70
Race to the Top program, 34
reelection, 229–232
Robert's nomination and, 148
same-sex marriage and, 209
September 11 and, 188–189
sequesters, 119–120
Sotomayor appointment, 135, 136
supporters of, 214

transparency in government and, 63–64
use of technology, 229–232
voter moderation, 216
War Powers Act and, 66
Waxman-Markey Bill and, 124
whistleblowers and, 81
White House staff and, 74–75
young voters and, 207
Obama, Michelle, 74
Obamacare, 147, 237, 251
O'Connor, Sandra Day, 136, 145, 191
OFA. *See* Organizing for America (OFA)
Office of Management and Budget (OMB), 75–76
On Democracy (Dahl), 274
One-party system, 225
Online ads, 231
O'Reilly, Bill, 253
Organizing for America (OFA), 219
Original jurisdiction, 132, 137

P

PACs. *See* Political action committees (PACs)
Page, Larry, 205
Palin, Sarah, 225, 251
Panel on Climate Change, 122
Parents of presidents, 60
Partial incorporationists, 166–167
Parties. *See* Political parties
Partisanship. *See* Polarization of political parties
Party machines, 217
Party platform, 224
Patel, Amit, 265
Patriot Act, 192
Patronage, 82, 217, 220
Patterson, Bradley, 77
Pelosi, Nancy, 101, 108
Pendleton Act, 82
People for the Ethical Treatment of Animals (PETA), 238
Perot, Ross, 213
Pierson, Paul, 200
Planks, 224
Platform, party, 224

Plessy v. Ferguson, 157–158, 178
Plural elitism, 280–281
Pluralist theory, 272–275
v. elitism, 276–281
Plurality of votes, 211, 225–226
Pocket veto, 67, 116
Polarization of political parties, 128, 215–217
Policy changes, adopt, 209
Political action committees (PACs), 243, 245–247
Political compact, 36
Political conflict, 7
Political efficacy, 206
Political elites. *See* Elitism
Political machines, 217–218
Political parties, 208–229. *See also* Democratic Party; Republican Party
around the world, 210
caucus, 101–102
polarization of, 128, 215–217
Political science, 10–11
Political socialization, 198–199, 204
Politics, 2–14. *See also* Government
of identity, 199
involvement in, 11–12, 13–14, 207, 281
Powell, Colin, 86
Power, 3–7, 10–11. *See also* Separation of powers
access to, 244–245
centralization of, 208
checks and balances, 26, 28–30
decentralization of, 208
federal bureaucracy and, 83
fragmentation of, 272
implied, 141
media and, 261–264
pluralism and elitism and, 281
presidential, 53, 56
state *v.* federal, 30–35
of Supreme Court, 147–150
The Power Elite (Mills), 277
Precedence, Supreme Court and, 149
Preferred freedoms, 167, 168

Presidential daily brief (PDB), 75
Presidential Politis (Neustadt), 62
Presidential primaries, 224
Presidential veto, 66–67, 116–117
President *pro tem,* 102
President(s) and presidency.
  See also Executive branch
  bureaucracy and, 83–84
  Congress and, 92–93
  Constitution and, 50–53, 64–66
  executive orders, 64
  expansion of powers of, 56
  history of, 53–56
  imperial presidency, 63
  office of the president, 71, 73–76
  power hats of a, 62–63
  public nature of, 68–71
  public opinion and, 68–71
  residual power of, 53
  roles of, 48, 62–68
  styles of, 48–50, 53, 56–62
  succession to, 52
  Supreme Court and, 135–136
  views of, 48, 50
  White House staff and, 71, 72–73
Press conferences, 262, 263
Presumptive legislative rationality, 177
Primary Colors, 59
Prism, 173
Privacy, right of, 173–174
Private attorneys general, 183–184
Professional groups, 238
Professional staff, 221
Progressives. *See* Liberals
Proportional representation, 226
Protective legislation, 180
Pseudoevents, 262
Public affairs offices, 262
Public education. *See* Education
Public opinion
  affirmative action and, 180, 182
  civil liberties and, 186–188
  federal bureaucracy and, 80–81
  global warming and, 122–126
  government and, 32–35, 228
  lobbyists and, 247–248
  media and, 263–264
  organizing by political parties, 209
  presidents and, 68–71
  of Supreme Court, 138, 151–152

Q
"Quick Donate" app, 231

R
Race as suspect classification, 178–180
Ratification of Constitution, 26–27
Rauch, Jonathan, 249
Reagan, Ronald, 258, 262, 263
  as activist president, 57
  affirmative action and, 159
  block grants and, 33–34
  growth of government under, 84
  Lesley Stahl and, 258
  New Federalism and, 33
  parents of, 60
  presidency of, 48, 58
  public opinion of, 70
  Supreme Court nominations of, 136
Realigning elections, 211–215
Reapportionment, 99
Recession of 2008-2009, 8–9, 78–79
Reciprocity, in Congress, 108–109
Reconstruction, 156
Regulations, 8–9
Regulatory commissions, 78–79
Rehnquist, William, 136, 143, 155, 186
Rehnquist Court, 143–145
Reid, Harry, 68, 102, 125
Religion. *See* Freedom of religion
Reno, Janet, 183
Representative democracy, 7
Republican Conference, 103
Republican National Committee (RNC), 220–221
Republican Party, 211–217.
  See also Political parties
  2010 elections, 198
  after George W. Bush, 228–229
  changes in, 119, 213–214, 222
  fundraising, 221–223
  judicial appointments and, 135–136
  national committee, 220–221
  organization of in Senate, 102–103
  same-sex marriage and, 209
  seniority system and, 107–108
  Waxman-Markey Bill and, 124
Residual power of president, 53
Reverse discrimination, 165, 177
Ricci v. DeStefano, 145
Rice, Condoleezza, 75
Rice, Susan, 75
Riders, 116
Right of privacy, 173–174
Roberts, John G. Jr., 135, 136, 138, 145, 148, 170, 171, 179
Roberts Court, 145–147
Roe v. Wade, 149, 155
Romney, Mitt, 201, 216, 222, 225, 230, 246
Roosevelt, Eleanor, 74
Roosevelt, Franklin D., 212
  during Depression, 61
  fireside chats, 262
  growth of government under, 80–81
  leadership of, 56, 57
  media treatment of, 70
  mother of, 60
  racial discrimination and, 158
  Supreme Court and, 142, 154
  two term tradition and, 40
  vice president under, 52
Roosevelt, Sara, 60
Roosevelt, Theodore, 56, 57, 69, 135

Rothkopf, David, 277
Rove, Karl, 246
Royko, Mike, 218
Rule 22, Senate, 115
Rule of law, 36
Rules Committee, 109, 111
Ryan, Paul, 225

S

Same-sex marriage, 174
Scalia, Antonin, 136, 138
Schattschneider, E.E., 263
Schmidt, Eric, 265, 267
Schudson, Michael, 208
Schultz, Debbie Wasserman, 221
Screw Google, 237
SEC. *See* Security and Exchange Commission (SEC)
Second Amendment, 167
Second Continental Congress, 20
Security and Exchange Commission (SEC), 79, 80
Segregation, 156–159, 166
Select committees, 107
Senate. *See also* Congress; House of Representatives; Legislative branch
committees, 111–112
judicial appointments, 134
majority leader, 101, 102
organization of, 102–103
presidential appointments and, 121
president of, 102
role in foreign affairs, 64–65
size of, 93
Seniority system, 107–108
Separate but equal, 155–160
Separation of powers, 20, 26, 28–30, 36
September 11, 2001, 85, 121, 173, 188–189, 191. *See also* Bush, George W.
Sequesters, 119–120
Seventeenth Amendment, 29, 95
Sex as suspect classification, 180–181
Sexual harassment, 180–181
Shays's Rebellion, 21

Sherman, Roge, 24
Sierra Club, 238
Sixteenth Amendment, 138
Slavery, 211
Three-Fifths Formula and, 22
Smith Act, 187
Snowden, Edward, 173
Snyder v. Phelps, 171
Socialist party, 227
Social Security Administration (SSA), 80
Soft money, 246
Sotomayor, Sonia, 135, 136, 138
Souter, David, 136
Speaker of the House, 100, 102, 113, 127
Special committees, 102, 107
Special federal courts, 133–134
Special interests. *See* Interest groups
Speech. *See* Freedom of speech
Speech plus, 170
Spoils system, 82
SSA. *See* Social Security Administration (SSA)
Stahl, Lesley, 258
Standing committees, 105–107
Stare decisis, 149
Starr, Kenneth, 122
State and local government, 30–35
State of the Union, 66
States' rights, 30–31
Stevens, John Paul, 136, 146
Stewart, Jon, 256
Strict constructionism. *See* Judicial restraint
Stuart, Gilbert, 97
Superclass: The Global Power Elite and the World They are Making (Rothkopf), 277
Super PACs, 246–247
Supreme Court, 137–160. *See also* Judges
Burger Court, 143
judicial interpretation and, 39
judicial review and, 36–37, 139–141 148, 150
reapportionment, 142

Rehnquist Court, 143–145
Roberts Court, 145–147
ruling on line-item veto, 67
Warren Court, 142–143, 154, 158–159
Suspect classifications, 177–181
Sweatt v. Painter, 158

T

Taft, William Howard, 57
Taliban, 87
Talk radio, 264
Taxes and growth of government, 79–80
Team of Rivals (Goodwin), 74
Tea Party, 229, 238, 349
Tea Party, 238
Teixeira, Ruy, 214
Television, 251, 254, 255–259, 262, 264
Tenth Amendment, 31
Term limits in Congress, 96
Test cases, 184
Texas 10 percent plan, 183
Third parties, 227
Thirteenth Amendment, 156
Thomas, Clarence, 136, 138
Three-Fifths Formula, 22
Thurmond, Strom, 115
Tilden, Samuel, 51
Tocqueville, Alexis de, 236
Toobin, Jeffrey, 147
Truman, Harry, 49, 60, 158
Turner, Ted, 260
Twenty-fifth Amendment, 50
Twenty-first Amendment, 38
Twenty-second Amendment, 40, 50
Twitter, 255
Two-party system, 225–226

U

University of California Regents v. Bakke, 178
Upper class, 199–200. *See also* Elitism
U.S. Term Limits v. Thornton, 96
U.S. v. Lopez, 144
U.S. v. Nixon, 135
U.S. v. Windsor, 174

V

Van Buren, Martin, 49
Ventura, Jesse, 226
Veto power, 67, 116–117
Vice president, 52–53, 224
Voters, 196–208. *See also*
    Elections
moderate views of, 216, 226
Voting rights, 205
Voting Rights Act of 1965,
    145–146

W

Wallace, George, 212, 227
Wal-Mart, 237
War on Terror. *See also*
    Afghanistan war; Iraq war
and civil liberties, 65, 66,
    173–174, 187–189, 280

War Powers Act, 65–66
Warren, Earl, 135, 142, 154,
    159
Warren Court, 142–143, 154,
    158–159
Washington, George, 22, 23,
    24, 40, 53, 208
Washington shakedown,
    267–268
Waxman, Henry, 124
Ways and Means Committee,
    110
Wealth distribution, 4, 8
Welfare reform, 33–34
West Virginia, pork spending
    in, 110
West Wing, 59
Whigs, 211
Whips, 101

Whiskey Rebellion, 53
White House office, 71,
    72–73
Who Governs? (Dahl),
    274
Who Will Tell the People?,
    277
Wilcox, Wayne, 12
Wilson, Woodrow, 35, 56, 76,
    92, 105, 189, 212
Winner-Take-All Politics
    (2010), 200
Wonder, Stevie, 225
Working class, 199–200
Writ of certiorari, 138

Y

Young voters, 207
YouTube, 253, 256